THE
ADMINISTRATION
OF THE
COLLEGE LIBRARY

THE
ADMINISTRATION
OF THE
COLLEGE LIBRARY

BY GUY R. LYLE

Director of Libraries, Emory University

WITH THE COLLABORATION OF
PAUL H. BIXLER, MARJORIE HOOD
AND ARNOLD H. TROTIER

THIRD EDITION

THE H. W. WILSON COMPANY
NEW YORK   1961

TO
MY WIFE
THE MOST HELPFUL CRITIC I KNOW

Preface to the Third Edition

The first edition of this work was published in 1944; the second in 1949. In this edition I have entirely reshaped the chapters for which I am responsible, and added to them. A grant from the Council on Library Resources, Inc., enabled Emory University to release me from my duties at the library from June 1 to August 1, 1960, to prepare this revision. Although limited for time, I submitted the text of each revised chapter to a librarian or professor who read it with care and commented on it freely and helpfully. These readers and the chapters they read are: Ruth Walling (II, VII); William Porter Kellam (IV); Garland Taylor (VIII); Anne Corbitt and Kevin Guinagh (IX); Robert M. Trent and Elliott Hardaway (X); I. T. Littleton (XI); William R. Pullen (XIV); Johnnie Givens (XV); Edna H. Byers (XVI); and Paul Cousins (XVII). I state these facts in order that the reader may know that while I cannot invoke their authority or impute to them any share of the blame for what is in this book, I spared no effort to obtain the views of others in advance of publication. My collaborators, Arnold Trotier and Marjorie Hood, have revised their respective chapters (V and VI). In the absence of Paul Bixler on extended leave from his Antioch position for library service in the Far East, two librarian-bookmen were asked to revise his two chapters. I am grateful to Thomas E. Crowder, Chief of the Special Collections Department, Emory University Library, for revising Chapter XII, Book Selection and Acquisition, and to Evan I. Farber, Chief, Serials and Binding Department, Emory University Library, for revising Chapter XIII, Selection and Acquisition of Special Types of Materials.

Like the earlier editions, this volume aims at giving the student a simple, logical, and self-contained introduction to all aspects of library administration as they apply to college libraries and at doing this in a manner that will help him to get a clear picture of college library work in its entirety and as an integral part of the college educational program. I have not tried to pour college and university libraries into the same mould. Aside from the fact that Louis R. Wilson and Maurice F. Tauber have already written the definitive work on *The University Library; the Organization, Administration and Functions of Academic Libraries* (2d ed. Columbia University press, 1956), there is a significant difference between college and university library service which must be clearly drawn if the student is to emerge from his course with a clear conception of the functions and practices of college libraries. I believe the separate treatment of college and university libraries in these two books will enable the student to view each type of library from different points of view and to ask intelligent questions about each of them. While this book is planned as a text in the teaching of college library administration, I hope that it will also be found useful for independent professional reading. While attempting the broad view, I have endeavored to be as thoroughly practical as possible.

Quite obviously a book of this kind is not original. I am under so many obligations that it is impossible to specify them all. I may not omit to thank by name the President of the Council on Library Resources, Inc., Verner W. Clapp, Dr. Judson C. Ward, Jr. of Emory University, Ruth Walling, who generously assumed my library responsibilities for the summer, and my wife for her untiring interest and for typing the manuscript. To John Jamieson, Editor of General Publications of The H. W. Wilson Company, I am indebted for a critical reading of the manuscript and a thorough job of editing. He corrected errors, suggested new interpretations, and helped to unify and condense the style and expression. The pleasure of working with him and his encouraging letters and valuable criticism will long be remembered.

G. R. L.

Decatur, Georgia
August 16, 1960

Contents

CONTENTS

List of Tables

List of Tables

List of Figures

List of Forms

List of Figures

List of Forms

I

The American College Library in the Twentieth Century

In the perspective of the last half-century, the college library in America has undergone enormous change. The process by which this change takes place appears to be continuous and inevitable so long as there are vitality and change in the college and in the society which it serves. Each of the major steps by which the library has grown deserves some consideration.

Until the last quarter of the nineteenth century the pattern of college library service was relatively simple. The library was recognized in the abstract as an important symbol in the establishment of colleges but was honored more frequently in words than in performance. Research on the history of the American college library indicates that the inadequacy of most college libraries was felt so keenly by students that the literary societies, which began to appear after the middle of the nineteenth century, undertook to establish student libraries as one of their major purposes.[1] The office of the librarian was one of the first to be differentiated after that of the presidency, but the duties of the librarian, usually a member of the teaching faculty upon whom was laid the added responsibility of caring for the library, were largely custodial. He carried the key to the room where the books were kept and saw to it that the room was tightly locked except during the few periods of the week when students were permitted to use the books. Not until the twentieth century, and for many colleges not until the twenties and thirties of this century, was there any pronounced change in the traditional role of the library as a storehouse of books and of the librarian as guardian of these books.

THE FIRST BREAKTHROUGH FOR LIBRARIES

In the first three decades of the twentieth century the use of the college library for reading and study increased greatly. In the words of Paul Bixler, Librarian of Antioch College, this was due not merely to the fact that "unprecedented numbers of books were coming off the presses or that the college population was doubling and redoubling. The base of the growth was the college Library's relationship to the curriculum and newer teaching methods." [2] World War I had a profound effect upon the college curriculum, particularly in the fields of history, the social sciences, and the humanities. New ideas, events, and discoveries could no longer be analyzed within the confines of a single textbook. At first the impact on the library was marked by an enormous increase in the use of duplicate copies of books for required reading. Later, honors courses, general reading courses, tutorial plans, and curricular innovations at Harvard, Smith, Swarthmore, and other institutions contributed to a different kind of library use which resulted in bringing more of the total resources of the library into place in aiding teaching. These two curricular developments—the substitution of assigned library readings for the textbook in many history and social studies courses and the introduction of the so-called honors courses and the like—brought about the first real breakthrough in the recognition of the library as an important aid in teaching. The adoption of the reserve reading program was widespread and it brought out of the stacks for extensive use many titles which had formerly gathered dust on the shelves. The impact on the library of honors courses was less noticeable because few institutions fully exploited library use in connection with their programs. Nevertheless the elastic and intensive library use which resulted from these programs encouraged teachers and librarians in a variety of efforts to bring the library into the general scheme of college education.

About the same time these changes were taking place, the first graduates of the newer professional library schools which were associated with universities (heretofore there had been training institutes connected chiefly with large public libraries) were finding their first jobs in colleges throughout the country. Although these librarians grew up in the shadow of the great scholar librarians, William Warner Bishop, Andrew Keogh, Theodore Koch, and others, they were a different class. In some ways they were further removed from the traditional faculty role of their predecessors. They had less educational dignity and were perhaps less dominical; they were a more empirical breed. If they had any special virtue, it was a missionary zeal to make libraries useful, and they appeared on the scene just at the moment college libraries were beginning to expand in volume and variety of service. There was much spade work to do. By striving mightily to standardize the procedures of cataloging, to develop efficient systems for handling the lending of books, and to improve and systematize the methods of ordering, exchanging, and shelving books, they improved the efficiency of library techniques and set a high standard of service. What they lacked in scholarship, they made up for in personality, missionary zeal, and management skill. By improving library technology, making more books accessible on open shelves, breaking down the traditional barriers of library aloofness and dignity, extending and improving reference services, centralizing library services, and encouraging general reading through browsing rooms, dormitory libraries, weekly book talks, and student library prize awards, they helped to dispel the museum concept of librarianship as well as its practices.

The first factors, then, in the emergence of the college library in the twentieth century were the expansion of the curriculum, the transformation of the use of the library as reflected in reserve book use and independent honors work, and the management skill and enthusiasm of a new breed of librarians. During the period of the thirties and forties librarians' efforts along the lines already mentioned were greatly enhanced by certain forces outside the college. To these outside influences are properly assigned the chief credit for the rapid advancement of college libraries in this second major period of growth.

FORCES OUTSIDE THE COLLEGE

The forces outside the college which figured prominently in the development of college libraries during the thirties and forties were the philanthropic foundations, the accrediting associations, Friends of the library organizations, and the great public libraries in America. Their contributions were paralleled by notable achievements from within the ranks of librarianship in such areas as library cooperation; microcopy; administrative organization; surveys of resources; and the planning of ever more flexible, adjustable, and attractive buildings. But these internal developments will be left for discussion in later chapters.

During the period 1929 to 1940, several foundations and notably the Carnegie Corporation of New York initiated studies of college libraries of various types with a view toward making grants to selected institutions. The foundations' representatives examined more than a thousand libraries and conferred with college presidents, faculty, and librarians on such problems as the library budget, book and periodical holdings, and staff. Writing of the benefits resulting from this program, Dr. Louis R. Wilson has this to say:

> This detailed, illuminating study and the addresses and articles by the chairman and members of the foundation's advisory committees revealed the actual status of the college library as a teaching instrument in a light in which it had never been seen before. And, more important still, revealed it to the college president, who, in the final analysis, is the person most responsible in any college community for the adequacy or inadequacy of the college library as an instrument of instruction.[3]

Quite apart from the direct benefits of the grants in building book collections and strengthening staffs, there is no doubt that in focusing attention on libraries the foundations helped considerably to raise the prestige of the library in the eyes of college administrators and faculty.[4] An important by-product of the foundation awards, growing out of the investigations made by the library committees advising the foundations, was the research and publication in book form of reports on and analyses of the college library and its collections. These publications about the college library and its building, the list of recommended books for the college library, and the standards established for adequate library service proved stimulating and useful to a great many more libraries than the selected few which received the grants.[5] Second in importance only to the Carnegie Corporation grants was the financial assistance given by the General Education Board to library schools for the training of librarians, to various metropolitan areas for establishing union catalogs and bibliographical centers, and to individual colleges and universities for book purchases, surveys of libraries, buildings and equipment, and special library projects.[6] The grants of the General Education Board were most influential in stimulating the development of library facilities as a part of the general college program and especially in assisting library development, then greatly undernourished, in the South.

College libraries also benefited indirectly from the gifts of the Rockefeller Foundation for underwriting scholarly publication, bibliographic tools, and contributions to college endowment. The contributions of all three major foundations helped to set a pattern of library giving for smaller foundations and local foundations.[7] Two recent developments in support of library interests have already had highly beneficial results. In 1956 a major gift from the Ford Foundation established the Council on Library Resources, Inc. whose "purpose is to assist in the solution of the problems of libraries generally, but more especially of the problems of research libraries, by conducting or supporting research, demonstrating new techniques and methods, and disseminating the results. . . ."[8] In conformity with its major objectives the Council has made grants for testing and development projects in library technology, book withdrawal as a means of controlling space problems of large libraries, conferences on college library book selection methods and problems, library cooperation, and research and publication.[9] The second recent grant in support of college libraries generally as distinguished from foundation grants to individual colleges was the United States Steel Foundation grant of $30,000 in 1955 for small private liberal arts college libraries. This grant has been renewed each year since 1955 and, more important, has set the pace for other corporate foundation gifts to college libraries under the administration of the Association of College and Research Libraries. The grants of corporate foundations have been most helpful in strengthening book collections.[10]

The accrediting associations of colleges and schools have also had a favorable influence on the development of the college library. Much of the progress in college educational programs is due to voluntary cooperation by colleges in associations established by the colleges themselves, and especially to the standards set by the regional accrediting and professional agencies. The library has always been included as one of the aspects of the college to be considered in accreditation. Prior to 1934, the standards of the six regional associations were rigid and quantitative in nature. Although they did a great deal of good in putting pressure on college administrators for more adequate support of impoverished libraries, they were widely criticized by educators and librarians for emphasizing minimum levels which failed to help the majority of libraries to improve beyond their current level of achievement. In 1934 the North Central Association took a step forward in studying the application to the college library of its newly adopted principle of measuring a college in terms of its program. This undertaking was intrusted to a committee under the direction of Professor Douglas Waples of the University of Chicago Graduate Library School; and the results of its study appeared in Waples' book *The Library*, one of a series of the North Central Association monographs on the evaluation of higher institutions. The Waples study analyzed and established certain basic qualitative and quantitative criteria for measuring the relative educational value of college libraries. They were adopted by all regional associations at that time and in modified form have been considered the basis of evaluation since then. Criteria of any kind, however, must be continuously revised if they are not to become static, mechanical, and standardizing in their effects. They must be kept close to the changing needs of college library service. Toward this end, the regional associations have approved frequent revisions of standards, encouraged experimentation in evaluation techniques, and enlisted librarians as participants on institutional evaluating teams and as members of their standing library committees. In general, it may be said that the accreditation programs of regional and of other voluntary college and university associations have benefited libraries in four ways: (1) by focusing the attention of college administrators and faculties on the importance of the library in the educational program, (2) by helping college libraries to see and define their objectives more clearly, (3) by establishing helpful criteria for evaluating the educational services of the library and by continuously revising these standards, and (4) by stimulating the library in all aspects of its work.[11] Despite the obvious weaknesses of accrediting methods, and they are many, it is certain that college libraries would be operating on a decidedly lower level without their stimulus.

A third factor, often originating within the college but looking outside for actual accomplishment, has been the work of the so-called Friends of the Library organizations. The development of a strong liberal arts college library, rich in book material and equipped for modern teaching, must necessarily depend to some extent upon individual gifts, donations, bequests, and memorials. From such sources have come the finest special collections in college libraries today. Even more important than the giving of books and money are the extension and development of friendly attitudes which accompany donations and endowments to perpetuate gifts. To foster this spirit of fellowship, a number of colleges established Friends organizations in the thirties whose chief purpose was to preach the gospel of good books and more books. Not all were successful by any means, but those that were generally drew their leadership from the ranks of alumni and members of the faculty. These Friends organizations served their college libraries both directly and indirectly. Directly they bestowed gifts, such as $5,000 for equipping a historical seminar, a $500 endowment for books in a special field, a bequest for a new library building, a book memorial to a deceased faculty member, and smaller gifts. Indirectly they influenced others to give, placed their libraries in contact with donors, and advised them of exceptional bargains in book purchases. Whether formally organized or not, such groups continue to be of great assistance to college libraries today.

Another factor that contributed to the development of the college library during this period was the example of the great public libraries of America. Nowhere else then or now could one get a more vivid impression of the educational and social significance of libraries in society. During the thirties and forties the great public libraries developed an enormous clientele which borrowed and read an increasing proportion of substantial books and demanded a greater volume and more intensive form of reference service. As seen by the public, these libraries provided thousands of books on open shelves, reading and study rooms for specialists in science, history, and other subject fields, special services to school children, exhibition galleries for prints and drawings, leadership for adult education and civic group discussions, film and record loans, readers' advisory service, and the

like. It is not too much to suppose that parents, teachers, and
school students—accustomed to such services—would expect the
college library to provide no less for its faculty and student body.
The intangible benefits of such an example defy exact statement
but there can be no doubt of the practical contribution of the large
public libraries to college library administration and techniques.
The public library led the way in the divisional organization plan,
in the introduction of audio-visual services as an accepted part
of librarianship, in library building planning and arrangement,
and in the use of labor-saving devices in the library field.

The Situation in the College Library Today

The development represented in the two periods of college
library history just described was an extraordinary achievement.
As late as the mid-thirties there were only thirty-two thousand
books in the Antioch College Library. A library building erected
on the foundation of Horace Mann's old home sufficed to take
care of the college library's needs. Today the College is justly
proud of its new modern Kettering Library, dedicated in 1955,
and its collections, numbering more than one hundred thousand
volumes. This is not large as good college libraries go today;
moreover, more than 75 per cent of the books have been added
since 1930. Today the Antioch College Library is more than
triple the size it was when college libraries first responded to the
challenge of a changing and expanding curriculum, and its physical facilities have more than tripled in capacity and convenience.
The new Kettering Library makes room for general education by
providing open shelves and a core collection of books of a variety
and purpose well within the comprehension of the new student.
Individual studies for students and faculty encourage independent
investigation and research. Seminars and consultation rooms
afford opportunity for students and faculty to consult reading
materials together. Microfilm readers and microcopy of all sorts
provide research materials to extend the library's inter-library
and cooperative loan arrangements. More than the book is represented in the Kettering Library. Maps, films, filmstrips, recordings, projection rooms, and other such aids to learning are provided, with facilities for their use. This is not the only accom-

plishment of the Kettering Library and it is not unique among college libraries. Rather the achievement of the Kettering Library has been repeated throughout the country in college library facilities large enough, varied enough, and rich enough to give real and genuine meaning to the favorite presidential phrase that the library is the indispensable heart of a center of learning. The college library still means a museum or storage house to some people—probably always will—but by and large this older concept of the library is on the way out.

This brings one, then, to the cardinal question: What is the college library today—its purpose, function, and role in the college? The answer to this question is not simple. The college library today generates a sense of purpose through its multiple activities, but the process of defining these activities in terms of a modern philosophy of librarianship is hampered by the absence of any national identity of purpose in the college itself and in the fact that one must use the plural form, for college library activities are not confined to anything which may be described as a single pattern.

The primary purpose of the college library is not only to provide books, journals, and other instructional materials in support of the academic program of the college, but also to encourage the formation of a lifelong habit of reading much and reading well. The carrying out of this purpose may entail such functions as these:

1. The selection and acquisition of library materials, including books, journals, pamphlets, maps, microtexts, films, records, and other materials which have become accepted tools of instruction.

2. The preparation and care of these materials, through such processes as cataloging, classification, and binding, in support of the work of instruction.

3. The provision of individual and group assistance to readers in the use of library materials, placing the proper tools in the student's hands, showing him how to proceed, and standing by to help when help is needed.

4. The encouragement of reading on the part of students in connection with their courses as well as for its own sake.

These functions do not complete the list, but they are primary and they serve to illustrate that most, if not all, functions of the college library are closely related to the major purposes of the college and to the detailed problems of the teaching process. To the extent that the college makes use of its library as an integral part of its curricular program, the library becomes a teaching instrument in itself. When Branscomb hurled his challenge to educators in the 1940's, saying in effect that "the library is not functioning in close and vital connection with the teaching program," librarians were the first to respond. Sensitive as generalists usually are in a world of specialists, they felt that somehow or other they were probably most at fault and they tried in every possible way to sell the idea of the library as an integral part of college teaching. They devised many ways for linking library service more closely with classroom teaching; if they were not entirely successful in their efforts it was due less to their lack of initiative than to the failure of the administrators and faculty members to attach the same importance to the idea of shifting the curriculum toward more reliance upon the library and less on textbooks. Nevertheless, by mid-century the college library was beginning to achieve a position of strength in the educational program and commanded greater respect than ever before from the faculty. The cumulative effect of individual library efforts, the success of library integration in the smaller progressive colleges, and the support of accrediting associations and foundations all helped to make clear the significance of the library's role in college teaching.

What lies ahead? How can college libraries maintain and improve the variety of services they now offer? The best libraries can and should be still better; the worst are a disgrace. In between, the majority can manage to provide the basic facilities, but to go beyond this requires a concert of purpose which the college administrator and faculty member share jointly with the librarian. The surest way ahead for libraries is to strengthen and develop the interest in the library of those who are responsible for its financial resources and those who have the primary responsibility for its use. The challenge to the college librarian is to define clearly and unequivocally to the administrator what constitute the essential requirements for good library service. The encouragement of the faculty to place more reliance upon total library use requires more tact, perhaps, but it also places upon the librarian the heavy responsibility of keeping informed about curricular matters and of having a sharp concept of the specific ways in which library support is desirable and possible. If the character of collegiate education is to move more and more in the direction of engaging students actively in learning for themselves, as some seem to think it should,[12] then the faculty will need to have a clearer understanding of the implications for library service. Again the college librarian will be called upon to explain and to provide for the facilities and services needed.

ESSENTIALS IN THE COLLEGE LIBRARY PROGRAM

If the college library is to function effectively in support of teaching and as an instrument of teaching in itself, there are certain requirements which must be met. Five of these are especially important. They are the maintenance of a live, growing collection; a modern physical plant; a well-qualified staff; leadership in promoting library use; and adequate financial support.

A Live, Growing Collection

Accrediting agencies, even some of the learned societies such as Phi Beta Kappa, have long been concerned too much with numbers. Libraries need to be concerned with titles and quality. There is a world of difference between the mere accumulation of a miscellaneous book stock and a well-chosen, selective library. Most college libraries would benefit from a shelf-by-shelf examination of the book shelves by the librarian and faculty in order to weed out unused duplicates, obsolete material, fragmentary files of journals, works which have no relation to the curriculum, and gift volumes which never should have been put into the collection in the first place. But simply weeding the collection is not enough, of course. In order to maintain its vitality, there must be a sufficient annual appropriation for the purchase of new books and journals and systematic procedures for making sound selections. As provider for the college, the president has the responsibility for finding the money. There are two kinds of college presidents, those who read and those who don't have time to read. If the president has a deep and genuine interest in education, he will probably be a reader and his influence will be reflected in his support of a strong book collection. As chief spokesman for the college, he is also frequently consulted about gifts for the library. If he or members of the faculty insist on encouraging potential donors to believe almost any kind of gift is acceptable—from multi-volume histories to second and third sets of standard literary writers—there is real danger that useless gifts will clutter up the shelves of the library and that collections will be accepted with restrictions that limit their usefulness and add greatly to the cost of library administration. No college can afford to be so bold as to state publicly that it will not accept gifts with strings attached any more than it can state publicly the circumstances under which it will not offer an honorary degree. But it is possible to take the more positive approach, to state persuasively the library's need for gifts, to tell what kinds of gifts will prove most valuable, to explain the principle that it is not possible to keep individual gifts intact, to show what constructively may be done about disposing of duplicates, and to make clear the college's gratitude for gifts.

The building of the collection requires a close working combination of faculty members and librarians. It rests upon the librarian to give over-all direction to the book building program, but the faculty is primarily responsible for the selection of material in the several subject fields in the college curriculum. Sound book selection requires more than specialized knowledge; it demands time, energy, and above all a genuine interest in the selection process. It is often surprising how little time and thought some faculty members devote to building their library collections. If they are overburdened with teaching, committee work, and other activities, they are likely to neglect their library responsibilities. If there are important gaps in the collection or if the books on the shelves do not serve the purpose of scholarship well, then the responsibility rests largely on the shoulders of the faculty—assuming the president has found sufficient means to maintain a respectable selective collection. The librarian also has an important part in selection because he is directly responsible for the reference collection, for checking bibliographies to reveal deficiencies in present holdings, for acquiring books of wide general interest, books which cut across the lines of departmental interest, and recreational reading of a high order. Further, he generally presents the book budget to the president, apportions the funds to be used by departments with assistance from the library committee, and sets up procedures for keeping the faculty informed about the offerings of publishers and second-hand dealers, the state of their book funds throughout the year, and the new books which are received.

A Modern Physical Plant

The physical facilities of the library have a great deal to do with its usefulness. Students in the sciences usually have adequate laboratory facilities in college. But it has been one of the chief defects of the college that it has not had comparable facilities in the so-called "reading departments" where students can work carefully and systematically. The library must cease to be the low man on the totem pole. Indeed its physical plant should be above the norm for the campus as a whole in lighting, ventilation, quietness, comfort, and variety of furnishings. Not only must the building provide the maximum in physical attractiveness and adequate space for readers and books, it must also provide for a variety of uses—consulting general reference tools or working alone at a private desk or carrel, typing without disturbing others, talking over one's library problems with fellow students or faculty members, smoking, listening to records, browsing among new books, reading a current magazine in a comfortable lounge-type chair, or examining exhibits designed to stimulate the curious or to exploit library resources. The college seeks to develop maturity. Developing maturity was never better defined than by the editor who said it is "expecting people to do their best and giving them the facilities to do it."

A Well-Qualified Staff

A third essential for the effective college library is a competent and well-educated library staff. One of the president's most important library tasks is to secure a first-rate head librarian. Too often he feels "he has it made" if he is able to accomplish this. But that is not enough. So great are the pressures of housekeeping duties imposed by the librarian's job that unless he has adequate assistance he is seldom able to plan the work properly, to keep in touch with faculty members, or to carry through adequately on changes which need to be made. If he does not go elsewhere but remains to waste his energies struggling with the hundred and one jobs that must be done, he will become immersed in the mechanics of librarianship and magnify their importance. He tends to become impatient with those who do not appreciate his effort. He runs to grievances and feels them sharply. Acceptance of limitations tends to form a hard crust on his mind which results in inflexibility, in assumptions becoming deeply imbedded, in imagination being dulled, in simple questions concerning procedures rarely being asked.

The librarian needs full-time professional assistants, clerical assistants, and part-time student help to operate a good library. At the very minimum, the librarian of the small college library needs a professional cataloger, a reference librarian, an intelligent college graduate who is capable of supervising the circulation services with student help, and an equal number of full-time clerical assistants to free the librarian and reference librarian from most of the routine duties connected with book ordering, the maintenance of vertical files, and similar duties. These librarians must know what materials are important in a college library and what are inessential, they must be capable of giving the students the kind of assistance they need in order to use the library intelligently and efficiently, and they must have a clear idea of what the library is trying to do. This sense of guiding purpose, stemming from the conception which the president and faculty have given to the college, translates itself into the daily operations of the library and determines what activities shall be undertaken and how they shall be carried out.

Leadership in Promoting Library Use

The college library may have a growing stock of well-selected books, excellent and varied physical facilities, and an able and enthusiastic library staff, and yet be insufficiently used. The ingredient that is needed is leadership in building a tradition among students of working with books and in endeavoring to engage students actively in learning how to think for themselves, which is, after all, the main purpose of a liberal education. Assuming that the first three essential requirements in the library program have been met, the responsibility for leadership in library use rests with the faculty and library staff, especially the former.

In this connection, the college librarian has certain major responsibilities. He must make books and journals freely accessible on open shelves, furnish the reference books and bibliographical tools essential to independent study, afford the opportunity for individual students to bring together at one place all the materials needed for a research paper, and provide the duplicate copies necessary for required reading. He must also keep the staff responsive to classroom needs, encouraging extra-curricular reading, and, in so far as it is possible, provide the faculty periodically with objective data to illustrate how the students are presently using the library in order to show how they are meeting the requirements and expectations of the faculty.

The faculty must play the major role in encouraging student use of the library. They must see to it that the library is used by students in an intelligent and responsible way. They must stimulate student curiosity and use the library as the investigation center for satisfying an aroused curiosity. They must make the student feel that in the last analysis he alone is responsible for his education and that the library is the principal facility for self-education. They must see to it that provision is made in the curriculum for adequate instruction in library use which is related *to real library problems* in order that the beginning undergraduate may not become discouraged and frustrated in his use of the library at the outset. These are a few of the things the faculty must do as general faculty policy and not as isolated individual faculty action. There are many other methods to promote the use of the library in a way that is educationally profitable and these are discussed in some detail in Chapters VIII and IX. However, leadership in library use does not necessarily follow any system or pattern. Much depends upon the circumstance at the moment and upon the attitude of the individual instructor.

Adequate Financial Support

Each of the preceding requirements of first-rate library service —a live, growing collection, a modern physical plant, a well-qualified staff, and leadership in library use—costs money and a great deal more money today than in the past because of inflation. The capital investment in buildings and equipment has increased tremendously. Salaries are taking a larger bite out of the library budget than ever before. Almost without exception college libraries are invariably pinched for money. The problem is accentuated by the inflationary spiral of recent years and by the fact that libraries have been so poorly financed in the past. As a practical matter, the finances of the college library are linked with the financial position of the college. The library should have a fair share of the operating budget. While the percentage allocated to the library will vary depending upon the character of the college and its educational program, the probability is that nothing less than 5 per cent of the general and educational expenditure of the college will be required to maintain first-rate library services. If there are arrearages in cataloging, serious deficiencies in book resources, special programs of independent study, or other special factors affecting library use, the percentage needed will be higher. While the allocation of library funds for specific purposes will depend on the needs of the individual institution, experience shows that a good college library usually spends twice as much, or more, for salaries as it does for books.[13]

NOTES

1. Shores, Louis. *Origins of the American college library 1638-1800.* Nashville, Tenn., George Peabody College, 1934, p. 232

2. Bixler, Paul. "Heart of the college." *Antioch notes* 30:no. 4, December 1, 1952

3. Wilson, Louis R. "The use of the library in instruction." *In: Proceedings of the institute for administrative officers of higher institutions, 1941,* ed. by John D. Russell. Chicago, University of Chicago press, 1942, p. 115-27

4. Barcus, Thomas R. *Carnegie corporation and college libraries 1938-1943.* New York, Carnegie corporation of New York, 1943; Bishop, William Warner. *Carnegie corporation and college libraries 1929-1938.* New York, Carnegie corporation of New York, 1938

5. Carnegie corporation of New York. Advisory group on college libraries. *College library standards.* New York, Carnegie corporation of New York, 1932; Gerould, J. T. *The college library building, its planning and equipment.* New York, Scribner, 1932; Mohrhardt, Foster E., comp. *A list of books for junior college libraries.* Chicago, A.L.A., 1937; Randall, William M. *The college library.* Chicago, A.L.A. and the University of Chicago press, 1932; Shaw, Charles B., comp. *A list of books for college libraries.* 2d preliminary ed. Chicago, A.L.A., 1931; supplement, 1931-38, Chicago, A.L.A., 1940

6. A.L.A. College and university postwar planning committee. *College and university libraries and librarianship.* Chicago, A.L.A., 1946, p. 69-72

7. *Ibid.,* p. 71

8. "Council on library resources, inc." *Col. and research lib.* 17:470, November, 1956

9. Council on library resources, inc. *Annual report,* 1957-date

10. Jackson, William V. "The ACRL grants program: a report of its first four years." *Col. and research lib.* 20:401, September, 1959

11. ACRL. Committee on standards. *College and university library accreditation standards, 1957.* Chicago, ACRL, 1958 (ACRL monographs, no. 20)

12. U.S. Office of education. *Independent study,* ed. by Winslow R. Hatch and Ann Bennet. Washington, Government printing office, 1960 (OE-50005)

13. "Standards for college libraries." *Col. and research lib.* 20:274-80, July, 1959; *also in: American library and booktrade annual, 1960.* New York, Bowker, 1959, p. 89-95

II

Institutional Backgrounds

College libraries do not operate in a vacuum; hence in speaking about the objectives and functions of the college library it is necessary to say something about the nature and aims of the college. The one cannot be understood without the other. College librarians are intimately concerned with professors, students, their library assignments, and, in a broader and deeper sense, the aims and objectives of the college. Within the limits of this chapter it is possible to relate only a few facts about the various types of colleges and the major characteristics of their libraries. A careful reading of the books cited at the end of the chapter on various types of colleges should provide a general view of the status of the college in American higher education.

The term "college" has been used rather indiscriminately in this country. As defined by the National Conference Committee on Standards of Colleges and Secondary Schools in 1918, a "college is an institution requiring for admission graduation from a standard secondary school, or the equivalent, and offering a four-year curriculum leading to the first degree in arts or science, of such character as to qualify for admission to a graduate school of recognized standing." But many institutions of learning using the name of college do not meet the terms of the definition given above, and many others would qualify as universities. Within the meaning of the definition itself there are colleges of many different types. Some of the more important of these are described below.

Four-Year Liberal Arts Colleges

The four-year liberal arts college is the traditionally strong college type in America. For 1955-56, the Office of Education listed 732 separate liberal arts colleges out of a total of 1,858 institutions of higher education in the United States. The heaviest concentration fell in the South with 258 colleges, followed by the Northeast (182), North Central (112), and the West (76).[1] About seven eighths of these colleges are private (most of them church-related) and about one eigth are public although the latter account for approximately half of the total enrolment.[2]

The central purpose of the liberal arts college is to foster the capacity for independent thought and to widen the student's horizon beyond his own limited experience and parochial ways of thinking. Traditionally it has emphasized cultural training and has tended to resist the insistent demands of technical or vocational training. The trend today would appear to lie in the direction of recognizing a dual need and providing the liberal education part of the program through a common core of courses required of all students. Studies such as the Harvard report on *General Education in a Free Society* and the joint committee report of the faculties of three preparatory schools and three colleges and universities, entitled *General Education in School and College,* seek in various ways to insure that the student takes courses which will not leave blind spots in his education.[3] With the expansion of curricula, with increasing specialization, and with the resulting proliferation and fragmentation of courses, there is a continuing effort to identify what should be included in this common core of courses. The problem is to secure the advantage of breadth without the disadvantage of relative superficiality.

In 1932 Professor William M. Randall made a detailed study of the library in the liberal arts college in which for the first time definite data on a wide range of institutions were carefully analyzed and tested at every point. The results of his study, presented in *The College Library*, which was published by the American Library Association in 1932,[4] revealed many interesting things about the finances, buildings, personnel, and collections of the college libraries studied. The points emphasized over and over again by the author were the wide range of resources and services available and the general inadequacy of existing standards. The most recent nation-wide survey of four-year college libraries, covering the decade 1940-41 to 1950-51, shows all libraries needing more funds for books and personnel, and serious inadequacies in physical facilities in spite of substantial increases during this period.[5] A study in 1959 of the libraries of small, privately controlled colleges receiving aid through the United

States Steel sponsored grants found virtually the same conditions —serious inadequacies in staffing and deficiencies in book collections which in quality left "a great deal to be desired." While each of the libraries was receiving more financial support than formerly, the increases were in all probability canceled out by inflation.[6] Despite these weaknesses, it appears likely that the liberal arts colleges count among their number the strongest and most important college libraries in the country.

Junior Colleges

The junior college is an outgrowth of the publicly controlled high school in most parts of the country. Its rise has been extremely rapid. In 1915 there were 74 junior colleges with an enrolment numbering 2,363; in 1959 the number had reached 677 and the enrolment had climbed to 905,062. Although the number of private junior colleges comprises 40.1 per cent of the total number, 89.1 per cent of the student enrolment is in the publicly controlled junior colleges. California, which has always been regarded as a model for junior college programs, enrolled 92,000 full-time students in junior colleges in 1959. Florida is systematically providing public junior colleges in each of its counties. Last year, in the twenty-six counties in which junior colleges were available, 75 per cent of the students enrolling in college in the state for the first time chose the junior college.[7]

Another interesting recent development is the close identification of the junior college with the community. The term "community college" is gaining favor. In New York State the first locally sponsored community junior college was established in 1950. Now there are sixteen community colleges operating under the State University of New York. The trend seems to be toward a college tied very closely to the local public school system and serving broadly the educational needs of the community, not only for college-credit courses but for advanced vocational training as well as non-credit courses for adults.

The library of the junior college is growing in importance. In 1930 the standards adopted by the American Association of Junior Colleges at its Berkeley meeting recommended a library of at least 4,000 volumes;[8] some thirty years later the Association of College and Research Libraries regarded a collection five times larger as the minimum needed to meet curricular demands and urged building up to two or three times its basic figure of 20,000 volumes for junior colleges with broader curricular offerings.[9] The library is prominently mentioned in the standards of the major regional accrediting associations. Leaders in the junior college library field as well as administrators stress the fact that the library's role can be exploited by linking library practice more closely to the classroom and vice versa and by making the library a center for instructional materials of all kinds, including visual and auditory materials. As enrolments and courses multiply, the principal problems facing the junior college library will be staffing and adequate quarters for readers and books. A recent survey of 79 junior college libraries revealed that less than half had staff help, other than student assistants, in addition to the head librarian.[10] At present there are far too many junior college libraries housed in overcrowded and inadequate library quarters and too few full-time staff workers for the librarian to do a first-rate professional job.

Teachers Colleges

Traditionally the liberal arts college had nothing to do with vocational or professional training. But as society grew in technological complexity, the liberal arts college either yielded in some measure to vocational and professional pressures or else new institutions sprang up. Normal schools came into existence in the late nineteenth century for the training of teachers. Originally the normal school was not recognized as being of college grade; even as late as 1920 only about one sixth had achieved degree-granting status. Gradually the entrance requirements were raised. A four-year college program specializing in teacher preparation leading to a bachelor's degree was developed. At this stage the name normal school was dropped and most such institutions were called teachers colleges. Richard W. Burkhardt writes that in 1951 "there were 229 institutions in the American Association of Colleges for Teacher Education that once had the name 'normal' in their title. Only five of these were left in 1954." [11] The name "teachers college" seems destined to be short-lived. Writing in

1957, Bigelow showed that the word "teachers" had dropped from large numbers of these colleges.[12] Many were called state colleges and others simply colleges or universities.

The teachers college of today is characterized by a major physical plant, enrolment running into the thousands, multi-purpose offerings, and, frequently, graduate work, in addition to the traditional practice teaching, demonstrations, and curriculum laboratories. The changes incident to the transformation from normal to teachers to state college reveal the increasing importance attached to subject field study, general education, and specialized teacher education courses. Burkhardt writes, "The real change in our teachers colleges is the program offered. The preparation of teachers is no longer regarded as training, but as professional education. Rather little of the courses taught can be classified as 'methods.' More and more of the curriculum is of a general education nature and what has been called 'subject matter.' "[13] Whether or not this has been generally achieved, most such colleges, built on the foundations of the old normal schools, now offer degree programs in music, fine arts, industrial arts, business administration, and other fields in addition to education. The growth of the schools and the raising of teacher requirements have also led many colleges to offer graduate work, particularly during the summer sessions.

In 1928 a study of the libraries of teachers colleges revealed uniformly small collections of about 16,000 volumes, a considerable duplication of titles within each library, inadequacy in the number and quality of staff, lack of uniformity in budget practice, and an apparent ignorance and indifference on the part of the college library administrator regarding the library function.[14] Ten years later some improvement had been made because of the stimulus of new accrediting standards,[15] but by 1952 library progress was dragging its feet so badly that a nation-wide survey concluded with the remark that "while the instructional program [of teachers colleges] has made great strides. . . , the libraries have tended to remain at the old normal school level."[16] Progress has been rapid during the past decade. Today it is difficult to recognize the parent normal school library in the very modern teachers college library; indeed, it is difficult to differentiate the best of teachers college libraries from the best of liberal arts college libraries with respect to book funds, salaries, and total financial support. In addition to the basic functions usually associated with an undergraduate library, the teachers college library may have special functions such as the maintenance of a curriculum materials center for textbooks and course outlines, demonstration school libraries, the provision of audio-visual aids, and the offering of courses in library science for prospective teachers as well as prospective librarians.[17]

Land-Grant Colleges

The term "land-grant college" originated from the wording of the First Morrill Act, adopted by the Congress of the United States in 1862, which provided for a grant to the states of 30,000 acres for each representative and senator in Congress, to be used for "the endowment, support, and maintenance of at least one college . . . in each state." [18] From small, struggling beginnings these colleges have developed into major institutions supporting a threefold program of resident instruction, research, and extension. Almost 20 per cent of the degrees granted in recent years have been for advanced work which suggests that a majority of the 68 land-grant colleges are universities in effect if not in name.[19] The increase in volume of activity appears to have been accompanied by an increase in specialization not only in agriculture, engineering, and home economics—the traditional fields of the land-grant college—but also in such basic subjects as chemistry, botany, and zoology.

The first extended treatment of the libraries of land-grant colleges and universities appears in the survey of land-grant institutions conducted by the U.S. Office of Education in the 1930's.[20] The most important, as it is the most obvious, observation about them is their rapid development from small college libraries to large and complex university libraries and their rapid increase in activities and support in recent years. In 1948 a study of 19 land-grant college and university libraries showed an increase in average expenditures per student from $16 in 1928 to $22.28 in 1945-46.[21] By 1958-59, these same libraries were receiving $60.79 per student. The libraries were also receiving a larger share of institutional funds. In 1928 the proportion of library to institutional expenditures was 2.52, in 1945-46 it had increased to 2.77 per cent, and in 1958-59 to 2.95 per cent.[22]

Other Types

In addition to the groups of colleges mentioned above, there are a considerable number of institutions of higher education which do not fall into any single group. There are schools and colleges attached to a particular university whose libraries are of a specialized collegiate character, such as law, medicine, engineering, architecture, and commerce and business. There are independent technological institutions supported by private, state, or federal funds, exclusive of the engineering schools of land-grant universities and state universities. Forty-four of these, about evenly divided between private and public, were listed in 1956.[23] Separate colleges for men and women form another large group numbering more than 300. Two thirds or more of the women's colleges are located in the New England and Southern states.[24] Their libraries have been surveyed and found superior for the most part.[25] Finally, and particularly in the South, there are more than 100 colleges for Negroes. The latest figures of the Office of Education show that 38 Negro colleges were under public control and 66 under private control, while the former enrolled the larger number of students. Differences in library facilities between white and Negro colleges are still marked although great progress has been made in recent years in improving the staff and physical facilities of Negro college libraries.[26]

These are some of the more important types of colleges in America. In every college there is a library whose chief function is to serve the educational objectives of the college. One may wonder at this point how it is possible to write a book about *the* college library when there are so many different types of colleges. The simple truth of the matter is that library functions are similar even though the colleges themselves show marked differences. The librarian of each public or private college, land-grant or liberal arts college, and men's or women's college will discover that his institution has its own distinctive pattern but that institutional differences affect the details rather than the principles of library administration. It is not differences among colleges that form the subject of talk whenever librarians congregate together. On the contrary it is the similarity of their problems which impresses them. Methods may differ in particular libraries; but the major functions are basically alike, and techniques of successful operation do not vary greatly from one library to another. The discussion of the administration of the college library in the following chapters, therefore, suggests—and is intended to suggest—how those who administer four-year liberal arts college libraries as well as others may think about and discharge their duties.

NOTES

1. U.S. Office of education. *Statistics of higher education, 1955-56.* Washington, D.C., Government printing office, 1958 (Biennial survey of education in the United States, 1954-56, Chapter 4, Section 1), p. 2

2. *Ibid.,* p. 54

3. Harvard University. *General education in a free society.* Cambridge, Mass., Harvard University press, 1945; Schmidt, George P. *Liberal arts college.* New Brunswick, N.J., Rutgers University press, 1957, p. 228-42; *General education in school and college, a committee report by members of the faculties of Andover, Exeter, Lawrenceville, Harvard, Princeton, and Yale.* Cambridge, Mass., Harvard University press, 1952; and others.

4. Randall, W. M. *The college library.* Chicago, A.L.A. and the University of Chicago press, 1932

5. Moran, Virginia L. and Tolman, Mason. "College library study." *Lib. jour.* 76:1906-10, November 15, 1951

6. Jackson, W. V. "The ACRL grants program: a report of its first four years." *Col. and research lib.* 20:401-11, September, 1959

7. Gleazer, Edmund J. "Analysis of junior college growth." *Junior college jour.* 30:351-60, February, 1960

8. The standards of the Association were reported by the Committee in the *Junior college jour.* 1:332-35, February, 1931, but were no longer in effect in 1940 (*Junior college jour.* 10:648, May, 1940)

9. ACRL Committee on standards. "Standards for junior college libraries." *Col. and research lib.* 21:203, May, 1960

10. Johnston, W. T. "A glance at junior college libraries." *Junior college jour.* 29:195-202, December, 1958

11. Burkhardt, Richard W. "Increasing responsibilities of teachers college libraries." *Col. and research lib.* 17:305, July, 1956

12. Bigelow, Karl W. "The passing of the teachers college." *Teachers college record* 58:409-17, May, 1957

13. Burkhardt, *op. cit.,* p. 305

14. Rosenlof, George W. *Library facilities of teacher-training institutions.* New York, Teachers College, Columbia, 1929, p. 150-1

15. Hunt, C. W. "From normal school to teachers college." *Col. and research lib.* 1:246-50, June, 1940

16. Moran, Virginia L. and Tolman, Mason. "Basic library needs of teachers colleges." *Lib. jour.* 77:1146, September 15, 1952

17. Harvey, John F. "The American teachers college library today." *Col. and research lib.* 17:308-11, July, 1956

18. Farr, Maude and Foster, E. M. *Statistics of land-grant colleges and universities, year ended June 30, 1946.* Washington, D.C., Government printing office, 1947, p. 9-10

19. U.S. Office of education. *Statistics of land-grant colleges and universities, year ended June 30, 1958.* Washington, D.C., Government printing office, 1960 (Circular no. 612), p. 7

20. U.S. Office of education. *Survey of land-grant colleges and universities.* Washington, D.C., Government printing office, 1930 (Bull. 1930, no. 9) 2 vols.

21. McCarthy, Stephen A. "Administrative organization and financial support of land-grant college and university libraries." *Col. and research lib.* 9:330, October, 1948

22. "College and university library statistics, 1958/59." *Col. and research lib.* 21:[4-6], January, 1960 (reprint)

23. U.S. Office of education. *Statistics of higher education, 1955-56.* Washington, D.C., Government printing office, 1958 (Biennial survey of education in the United States, 1954-56, Chapter 4, Section 1), p. 2

24. U.S. Office of education. *Education directory, 1958-1959.* Pt. 3, Higher education. Washington, D.C., Government printing office, 1959, p. 12

25. Bishop, William Warner. *The American college library and its librarian.* Claremont lib. series. 1:24-5, June, 1932

26. U.S. Office of education. *Statistics of Negro colleges and universities: 1951-52 and fall of 1954.* Washington, D.C., Government printing office, 1955 (Circular no. 448), p. 1

ADDITIONAL REFERENCES

American junior colleges. 8th ed. Washington, D.C., American Council on Education, 1960 (Part I, p. 3-47, discusses history and present status of junior college education)

American universities and colleges. 5th ed. Edmund J. Gleazer, Jr., editor. Washington, D.C., American Council on Education, 1960 (Part I, p. 3-73, consists of a review of American higher education)

Brubacher, John S. and Rudy, Willis. *Higher education in transition.* New York, Harper, 1958

Eddy, Edward D. *Colleges for our land and time: the land-grant idea in American education.* New York, Harper, 1957

Encyclopedia of educational research, ed. by Chester W. Harris. New York, Macmillan, 1960, p. 1454-60

Medsker, Leland L. *The junior college; progress and prospect.* New York, McGraw-Hill, 1960

Schmidt, George P. *Liberal arts college.* New Brunswick, N.J., Rutgers University press, 1957

Stoke, Harold W. *The American college president.* New York, Harper, 1959

Wriston, Henry M. *Academic procession.* New York, Columbia University press, 1959

III

The Government of the College Library

A consideration of the government of the college library involves three elements: the legal status of the college, the legal status of the library, and the librarian's formal relations with the college administration.

THE LEGAL STATUS OF THE COLLEGE

Most if not all colleges, whether liberal arts or land-grant, junior or teachers colleges, are invested by society with a corporate character. In considering any corporate form of organization, one of the first questions which arises is its legal status. Under our American system, individual state governments have more direct control than the Federal Government does over matters pertaining to the public welfare. Most colleges, as a result, owe their existence either to charters granted by special acts of state legislatures or to the educational or corporation laws of the state under which provision is made for the establishment of colleges. The charter has been defined as "a specific enactment by the legislature of the state authorizing the establishment of the institution and defining its powers and privileges," whereas establishment by articles of incorporation "consists of an agreement by the founders of the institution, drawn up under the provisions of a general statute." [1] Reeves states that the essential difference between the two methods of establishment "lies in the fact, that in the case of the former [charter] the action of the state legislature is specific, applying to one institution only, while in the latter case [articles of incorporation] the legislative action is general, the institution merely taking advantage of the provisions which were made for the incorporation of similar institutions." [2] The early college charter had the force of a contract and enabled the college to manage its own affairs. Since 1850, when the United States Supreme Court guaranteed the inviolability of the Dartmouth College charter against legislative nullification, states have usually reserved the right to amend or repeal the charter of articles of incorporation of colleges established under general laws of incorporation.

From the point of view of legal control, the most prominent distinction to be observed is that between publicly and privately controlled institutions of higher education. Public colleges are controlled by some sort of government agency, such as the state or municipal government, and the degree of control in each institution depends on the nature of the articles of incorporation. Private colleges are generally incorporated as nonprofit charitable organizations and are controlled by a private corporation whose composition and authority are laid down in the college charter. Both types of colleges are exempt from property taxes and exercise certain other powers and rights. These powers are usually vested, under the legislative act or charter which created the college, in a board of trustees which owns property, enters into contracts, accepts responsibility for the acts of its officers and employees, and provides the institution with its continuity. In private colleges the number of trustees, their mode of selection, and terms of office are usually laid down in the college charter. Ordinarily the board is self-perpetuating; that is, the trustees themselves select new members as vacancies occur. Church-related colleges usually have representation from the church, and alumni representation is frequently provided on the boards of both public and private institutions. A few boards of public colleges are elected by the people but more often they are selected by the governor and confirmed by the state legislature. State teachers colleges are frequently governed by the state board of education. By and large, the members of the boards which control public and private colleges are drawn from the ranks of prominent businessmen, lawyers, and professional people.

In operating colleges, trustees have the authority to draft and put into effect regulations to govern themselves and to define their relations with the college. Generally such rules are called by-laws and are looked upon as implementing the more general grants of authority found in the charter or articles of incorporation. In the by-laws is found such information as: the official title and address of the college, aims, officers and members of the board and their powers and duties, meetings, committees, public relations, etc. Frequently the by-laws and the charter are printed in one booklet and distributed among board members, college officers, and other interested persons.[3] In the absence of by-laws, or occasionally in addition to by-laws, some colleges have institutional documents setting forth the rules established to guide the college authorities in the internal government of the institution in much the same way as the by-laws aid the board of trustees. These are secondary documents because they depend upon the authority of the charter and by-laws, but they are useful in the effective administration of the college because they set forth the major policies governing its internal operation in greater detail than is customary in other documents. Best known of the institutional documents is the faculty handbook. Antioch, Madison, Birmingham-Southern, Ripon, Carleton, Goucher, and the Woman's College of the University of North Carolina publish faculty handbooks which define the responsibilities, duties, and relationships of the administrative staff, the faculty administrative officers, and the teaching faculty. Some of the more important topics treated include college organization, policies, teaching, student relations, the library, non-academic personnel, specialist facilities and services for faculty, and the like.

THE LEGAL STATUS OF THE COLLEGE LIBRARY

The legal status of the college library is determined, if it is determined formally at all, by the charter or articles of incorporation, the by-laws, and the institutional handbook by whatever name it is known. The charter, as the basic governing document of the college, is the source of authority although beyond an occasional reference to the authority of the board of trustees to purchase books, most charters and articles of incorporation have little or nothing to say specifically about the library.

Statements of varying length and inclusiveness about the library appear in the by-laws of some colleges but by no means in all. The by-laws of Vassar and Williams define what constitutes the resources of the library; the authority for administering these resources; the terms of the librarian's appointment and his principal duties; and the nature of the library committee's function and its relationship to the faculty and librarian. Coe and Winthrop provide in their by-laws that the professional library staff shall have appropriate faculty ranking. Williams provides faculty ranking for the librarian, whereas Vassar, whose by-laws are now being revised, provides academic status for the librarian and department heads. Where there are no by-laws, or where the library does not appear in the by-laws, there is sometimes a mention of the library in the institutional handbook. Although none of the faculty handbooks cover all the essential elements of a sound code of library government, it would appear that librarians have sometimes been consulted in the formulation of such documents. Instruction in the use of the library and the representation of librarians on faculty committees are recurring problems which few colleges seem to have solved adequately. In the Madison College *Handbook for Administrative Staff and Faculty* (1954), the librarian is assigned the responsibility for giving both formal and informal instruction in the use of the library and for "service with other members of the faculty and library staff on committees to which they are assigned by the President." The Woman's College of the University of North Carolina's *Instrument of Government* (rev. 1959) provides for the inclusion of members of the professional staff within the Faculty Council, which is the legislative body of the College.[4]

In addition to the by-laws and institutional handbooks, there are publications of an administrative and informational nature which are important in the government of the college library because they are often the only sources of information available. The library handbook, particularly the faculty library handbook, sometimes reveals administratively approved policies on such matters as the relationship of the librarian to the president, the function of the library committee, the organization of the library (including an organization chart), the regulations regarding purchasing and accounting, and the relationship of the librarian to the library committee and the faculty. Annual reports, particularly summary reports covering a number of years, not infrequently include sections particularly related to the control, organizational growth, and future planning and development of the library.

It would seem self-evident that the library—involving as it does a considerable measure of administrative responsibility, the handling of substantial funds, and relationships with all college officers and faculty—should have a clearly expressed code of library policy or government, preferably set forth in the college by-laws or some other official institutional document. Since the by-laws and institutional documents so frequently fail to mention the library, it is more than likely that in most institutions the control and government of the library are largely determined by tradition, precedent, and personalities. Unfortunately the tradition of the library in college history is not an exalted one and librarians are seldom regarded as influential policy-making personalities. Even where conflict is reduced to the minimum, there are nevertheless many sources of strain about which something can be done. One such source of trouble is the lack of a clear definition of authority. This is evident in the conflicts which take place between library committees and librarians and in difficulties concerning departmental collections. One of the chief problems in the latter case is the department head who practices the art of the *fait accompli*: the collection has already been set up— what is the librarian going to do about it? If there is no provision in library government for the establishment and administration of departmental libraries, it is exceedingly difficult to deal with this problem without repudiating what few would regard as an unauthorized act. The consequences of repudiation are usually more serious than the acceptance of the act, and so the librarian accepts the *fait accompli* without regard to the merits of the case and without making adequate provision for the care of the collections. To take another example, it may be understood by custom and tradition that the professional staff are members of the academic group, but in specific situations (e.g., the grant of a foundation for increasing faculty salaries) the librarian may well be reluctant to risk the president's impatience or his own embarrassment by seeking approval of things which he knows raise awkward problems that the president would like to avoid. When staff status depends on custom and custom alone, there is bound to be confusion. Informal agreements on library policies, moreover, do not necessarily remain effective when a new president or a new college librarian is appointed.

The code of library government, whether incorporated in the by-laws or the faculty handbook, or issued as a separate document, should cover four major areas: (1) the relationship of the librarian to higher authority, (2) the control of resources, (3) the library committee, and (4) the library staff. The important points to consider under each of these areas are summarized below:

1. Relationship of Librarian to Higher Authority
    a. The basis of appointment and the officer to whom the librarian is directly responsible
    b. The major duties of the librarian and his relationship to administrative and educational committees
2. Control of Library Resources
    a. The nature of library materials (books, periodicals, microfilms, film, etc.)
    b. The control and administration of these materials wherever they may be located
3. Library Committee: The method of appointment, composition, term of office, and advisory duties
4. Library Staff: The status of the professional staff with regard to such matters as rank, tenure, leaves of absence, and retirement

THE LIBRARIAN'S RELATIONS WITH THE COLLEGE ADMINISTRATION

The process of administering the college library involves the librarian in relationships with the president, dean, business officers, department heads, and committees. How closely do such relationships approximate what they should be, or could be, in most colleges? In many cases the answer is not closely enough. There is often neither the machinery, nor the tradition, nor perhaps even the desire to have the librarian in frequent conferences with administrative officials and committees. Yet unless there is a special effort to consult with the librarian and to keep him informed, there is real danger that the library will become isolated from constructive educational movements initiated from "above."

In the administrative area, it is most important that the librarian be consulted in budget-making and the appointment of personnel. In order to keep in touch with the faculty point of view, it is highly desirable that there be a faculty library committee to serve in an advisory capacity to the librarian. These relationships are discussed next.

Budget-Making

Aside from formal action on major policies of the college, much of the authority of the trustees is delegated to the college president. Among his principal responsibilities are the preparation and preliminary approval of the budget. Good practice makes budget-making a cooperative experience. Sometime during the middle of the fiscal year or earlier, each administrative official is normally called on to present, on forms provided by the business office, the estimated expenditures for his department for the next fiscal year. The business office may also assist in the process by making available expenditures of previous years. After the budgets have been reviewed by the president and his chief administrative officers, there may be further conferences with the officials and department heads submitting the budgets. As soon as possible thereafter, the department requests are brought together into a tentative budget which is presented to the budget committee of the board of trustees. With such modifications as develop at this meeting, the budget may then be presented to the board as a whole for consideration and adoption.

The authority to approve and modify the library budget is delegated to various officers as set forth in Table I. In most colleges the librarian is given the opportunity to prepare and submit a tentative budget. It is likewise general practice for the president to approve or modify the library request although he may exercise this authority with the assistance of one of his chief administrative officers or delegate the responsibility to the chief business officer, the dean, a president's advisory committee, or an administrative council. In colleges where the librarian is disregarded in the preparation of the budget because of a policy of extreme centralization or autocratic abuse of authority from above, there is little hope of developing an effective library service.

For comparative as well as control purposes, it is customary to classify the budget by object. Thus separate amounts are estimated for such categories as books, personnel, supplies, equipment, and travel. Each type of budget differs from the others not only in the extent to which items are classified but also in the degree of flexibility permitted in making transfers

TABLE I

ADMINISTRATIVE OFFICERS AND COMMITTEES
THAT EXERCISE CONTROL OVER THE
COLLEGE LIBRARY BUDGET*

Authority Delegated to	Librarian	President	President and Dean	Chief Business Officer	Library Committee	Librarian and Library Committee	Other
Prepare and Submit Initial Library Budget	25	1					
Approve or Modify Estimates in Library Budget		14	3	1	6	7	
Approve Allocation of Book Funds to Departments	5				6	6	
Approve Budget Transfers During the Fiscal Year	4	3		11	1		5

* Source: Information obtained from questionnaire sent to 28 college libraries

from one category in the budget to another during the fiscal year. In most instances the authority to make such transfers lies with the business manager (Table I), although it may be delegated by the president to the librarian or some other official or committee, or be exercised by the president himself. Where the book fund is allocated to departments, the librarian may delegate authority to the library committee to make the allocations, in which case the committee is empowered to make such transfers as may be necessary during the year.

Personnel

One of the most important phases of the librarian's administrative work has to do with the selection and appointment of library personnel. The lines of authority and responsibility should be clearly set forth in the code of library government but this is seldom the case. A sampling of current practice is presented in Table II. It would appear to be common procedure for the librarian to nominate the professional and clerical staff although it may be necessary to select the latter from a municipal or state civil service eligible list in certain public institutions. The president normally passes on the librarian's nominations of professional staff members but he may delegate the responsibility to the dean or share it with him. There is much wider variation in approving the employment of clerical staff members. Most frequently the authority is exercised by the president or delegated to the librarian, but in some colleges it comes under the direction of the chief business officer or a personnel director. The librarian is generally assigned the responsibility for recommending staff salary increases. In two instances in Table II, the librarian is advised in the matter of personnel appointments by the library committee. This practice is not recommended. In order to insure good appointments, it is necessary to know not only where to find first-rate candidates but also to be able to judge a librarian's special qualifications for a particular position in comparison with others. The practice of permitting the librarian to make all recommendations of personnel, supporting such nominations with full data and references, has been in effect in good colleges for a sufficiently long time to demonstrate its value as sound academic personnel procedure.

TABLE II

ADMINISTRATIVE OFFICERS THAT EXERCISE CONTROL OVER MATTERS RELATING TO LIBRARY STAFF APPOINTMENTS AND SALARIES *

Authority Delegated to	Librarian	President	Dean	President and Dean	Chief Business Officer	Librarian and Library Committee	Other
Recommend Appointment of Professional Staff	27	16	3	3		1	
Approve Appointment of Professional Staff	1		3	3		1	4
Recommend Appointment of Clerical Staff	28	8	1				
Approve Appointment of Clerical Staff	8	8		4	6		1
Recommend Salary Increases for Library Staff	19	1		1		2	5

* Source: See note Table I

The Library Committee

A third important area involving relations between the librarian and the college administration is the library committee. This committee has a long and honorable faculty tradition and is one of the major standing committees provided for in the by-laws. It may be significant to note that among four out of twenty-eight college libraries which function without a library committee, one is preparing to establish a committee as a result of a faculty self-survey, and another, after a lapse of some seven years, is re-establishing the library committee.[5] A few librarians are frankly skeptical regarding the value of a library committee; another small group is equally emphatic in its praise. The majority, however, withhold praise and criticism alike, but one may infer from what is left unsaid that the committee has not been regarded by librarians as a strong factor in library development.

There is considerable variety in the size and composition of library committees. The committee may be small (Birmingham-Southern has only five members) or it may be large (Madison College has twelve). To speak of an average would be meaningless. A large committee is favored by some college administrators who feel that this is the only way to secure adequate departmental representation. Most librarians, however, favor a small committee because with relatively few persons involved it is less difficult to arrange meetings. They also feel that personal qualifications and general interest in the library are more important considerations than departmental representation in the selection of the committee. There are in general three methods by which members of the committee are selected: (1) appointment by the president, (2) appointment by the dean, and (3) election or appointment by the faculty either directly or through a faculty committee on committees. Combinations of these methods are found in some colleges. Members serve from one to five years though there are occasional instances in which the term of office appears to be indefinite. A wise provision which insures continuity without sterility is the plan of rotating membership on the committee, with one or two new professors replacing old members each year.

In all colleges having library committees, the librarian is a member and most frequently serves as chairman or secretary of the committee. Since the committee discusses matters of policy, it would seem unwise for the librarian to serve as chairman. The committee that gets the reputation among the faculty of being a rubber stamp for the librarian is not likely to be effective either as adviser or interpreter of library matters. It is exceedingly difficult, moreover, for one who is actively engaged in administering a library to refrain from dominating the discussion of topics and consequently discouraging the less articulate members of the committee from taking part in the discussion. There is more to be said in favor of the librarian serving as secretary. In this capacity he can make sure that the official minutes are faithfully recorded, transmitted to the members of the committee and others concerned, and that a file of the minutes is preserved. Since these minutes contain decisions affecting library services and since they frequently contain recommendations or resolutions directed to the chief college administrative officers, they should be transmitted regularly to the president, dean, and chief business officer for information as well as for action on measures recommended therein. It would be helpful if the committee in all instances could be sure of having an earnest and sincere hearing from the higher authority on anything it chooses to discuss or recommend, and if—when its recommendations seem workable—there could be brisk positive action taken on them.

The nature of the library committee's activities is determined by its function rather than by the size and type of college, and consequently the committee is about the same in one place as in another. This function is prescribed in the by-laws, faculty handbook, or library handbook in terms in which the word "liaison" is frequently used. Goucher explains in its library handbook that the committee is "to advise the librarian on problems brought to it by the library staff and to serve as liaison between the library and the faculty and students." The by-laws of Williams College state that "a committee of the Faculty to be known as the Library Committee shall advise the Librarian with respect to the administration of the College Library, its rules and policy, and together with the Librarian, shall represent the interests of the College Library with the Faculty." Madison College states succinctly in its *Handbook for Administrative Staff and Faculty* that the library committee is "to advise and work with the Librarian in the development and use of library services." Coe College probably expresses the hopes of many librarians in the statement in its by-laws which reads:

The Library Committee studies library needs in view of the academic program and advises the Librarian on matters of general library policy, the development of library resources, and upon means which may best integrate the library program with other academic activities of the College. The Committee serves as a liaison group between the Faculty and the Librarian.

It is in this relationship that the committee best serves its role in promoting library usefulness. On the one hand, the library is an agency whose functions and services are college-wide and affect everyone in the college community; on the other hand, it is a tight, complex agency whose inner workings are largely unknown to those it serves except for certain obvious lending functions performed at the charging desk. It follows that the library needs information which a faculty committee can supply about new educational policies, new courses, new instructors, and new plans for campus development, because almost inevitably such matters have a direct bearing on its needs and services; at the same time the library also needs an adviser and interpreter to explain its inner workings because without being aware of it the library may separate itself from the faculty by decisions, reached at the level of day-to-day operations, which are not understood or which are frequently misunderstood. For it is on this level that the decisions reached by librarians become in time the foundation for much of the policy of the library. The library committee, with its Janus-like relationship to the faculty and the library, can help to prevent such misunderstandings and keep the library from being isolated. If historians, mathematicians, and professors of English take their turn on the library committee, they will after a reasonable period of time familiarize themselves with many of the operations of the library, understand better why librarians make the decisions they do, and inform their colleagues about the reasons for library rules and regulations when they are questioned.

In its relationship to the college and the discharge of its responsibilities, the library committee is *advisory* to the librarian. Nothing will undermine more quickly the effectiveness of the role of the library in the college than a committee which acts or tries to act in an administrative capacity. The library committee's function must always be understood as advisory and never as administrative; but it is important to use the committee in policy determination as well as in the discussion of administrative matters even if it does not have the authority or power to enforce its recommendations. If the committee is to be an effective advisory body instead of a mere shadow, there are a number of conditions which must be met in addition to those already mentioned. The committee members must be genuinely interested in the development of the library as a whole and not merely in their departmental relationships with it. The librarian must have faith in the usefulness of the library committee, must be willing to share all his information about the library with the committee, and must have the patience to let the committee gain understanding through participating in library matters of all kinds. The attitude and skill of the chairman in conducting the meetings and his willingness to stick out his chin in supporting library recommendations have much to do with the success of the committee. Faculty members are not likely to retain their interest in the committee if they are called upon to discuss inconsequential details, but neither are they likely to become enamored of a fruitless discussion of five-year plans when there is little hope of accomplishment. The distinction between what is policy determination and what are administrative matters had best be ignored. The central area of operation is that concerned with improving the library's effectiveness in teaching. Among the library matters which library committees discuss in their meetings are the following: policy on the purchase of multiple copies of books for reserve; rare and foreign books; administration and control of college archives; the library's role in handling audio-visual materials; compilation of departmental bibliographies in developing collections; surveying library resources; allocation of book funds to departments; supporting the library's request for additional book funds; planning the enlargement and remodeling of the library, or planning a new library building; library participation in regional cooperative proposals; policy on establishing a departmental collection; policy on accepting gifts; preparation of a proposal to a foundation; staff status; rules and regulations; and methods of promoting student library use.

NOTES

1. Reeves, Floyd W. and others. *The liberal arts college*. Chicago, University of Chicago press, 1932, p. 62. The basic charter or original documents of control of a large number of institutions may be examined in Edward C. Elliott and M. M. Chambers. *Charters and basic laws of selected American universities and colleges*. New York, Carnegie Foundation for the Advancement of Teaching, 1934. More recent examples are noted under 3 below.

2. Reeves, *op. cit.*, p. 62

3. Examples of by-laws: *Laws of Williams College*, 1940; *Charter and by-laws of Bowdoin College*, 1933; *By-laws of Winthrop College, the South Carolina College for Women* . . . June 28, 1957; *Charter and by-laws of Wofford College, Spartanburg, S.C.*, 1956; and *Beloit College charter and by-laws* . . . 1956.

4. Examples of the kinds of information about the library to be found in college by-laws and institutional handbooks are reproduced below from official publications of Vassar, Williams, Winthrop, Georgia State College, the Woman's College of the University of North Carolina, and Madison College. (Suggestions for revising the Georgia State by-laws are offered under the heading *Comment* after each section to illustrate further the significance of the by-laws.)

5. Information obtained by questionnaire sent to twenty-eight college libraries by the author.

BY-LAWS PERTAINING TO COLLEGE LIBRARIES

VASSAR COLLEGE. THE GOVERNANCE OF VASSAR COLLEGE. BULLETIN OF VASSAR COLLEGE 32: 23, 29-30, 33-4, 38, 45-6, 51, 61, DECEMBER 1942 (NOW IN PROCESS OF REVISION)

The *Advisory Committee* consists of three professors on indeterminate tenure, elected for three years, one member retiring each year. . . . By instruction from the trustees, the president confers with this committee which acts in an advisory capacity upon appointments, promotions, salary increases, and the dismissals of teaching members of the faculty . . . [and] upon the appointment of the librarian. . . .

The *Committee on the Library* consists of the president, chairman *ex officio*, the librarian *ex officio*, four members of the faculty, professors or associate professors, elected for two years, one from each group of studies, two retiring each year, and two members at large elected from the faculty for two years, one retiring each year. Retiring members are not eligible for re-election for the immediately succeeding term.

The committee receives the report of the librarian on expenditures for books and periodicals for the current year and recommends the method of distribution of funds for the ensuing year. It acts in an advisory capacity in the formulation of policies of the college with respect to the library and reports thereon from time to time.

Control of Library Materials: All books, periodicals, manuscripts, facsimile letters, and similar materials, purchased from college funds, belong to the college and not to departments, and are under the jurisdiction of the librarian.

The historical records of the college shall be preserved in the library. The library shall receive copies of each book, pamphlet, or program published through college funds.

The control of special departmental rooms in the library building shall be exercised by the librarian in cooperation with the departments concerned. The departments are responsible to the librarian for the safekeeping and availability of the books deposited in departmental libraries of other academic buildings.

The librarian and the members of the staff in charge of major divisions of work of the library have academic rank proper to the scale on which their salaries are established.

WILLIAMS COLLEGE. LAWS OF WILLIAMS COLLEGE. 1940, p. 14-15

VIII. *The College Library*

51. The College Library shall include all books, periodicals, documents, manuscripts, pamphlets and maps belonging to the College, other than those included in the Chapin Library, and with such exceptions as may be granted by the Librarian, they shall be deposited in Stetson Hall or in one of the several departmental collections.

52. The Librarian shall be appointed by the Trustees and shall have in the Faculty the status of a professor. The term of his appointment and conditions of his removal shall be the same as to others of that rank. The Librarian shall be charged with the responsibility for the custody and administration of the College Library.

53. The Librarian shall make an annual report to the President on the condition, operation and needs of the College Library, and shall submit a financial estimate of the expenses for the following year. He shall nominate qualified candidates for positions on the library staff. With the advice of members of the Faculty he shall expend judiciously all moneys designated for the preservation and increase of books and periodicals. He shall make all rules necessary for the operation of the College Library including specific provisions for the safe custody of books and manuscripts of unusual value and for the limitation upon their use, and shall endeavor to make the College Library as useful as possible for members of the College consistent with the protection and preservation of its contents.

54. A committee of the Faculty to be known as the Library Committee shall advise the Librarian with respect to the administration of the College Library, its rules and policy, and together with the Librarian, shall represent the interests of the College Library with the Faculty. The Library Committee shall hold at least three meetings during the college year at such times as the Committee may fix and may hold other meetings when called by the Librarian or Chairman of the Committee. The Librarian shall appoint custodians who shall be responsible for the collections not in Stetson Hall.

WINTHROP COLLEGE. BYLAWS OF WINTHROP COLLEGE . . . 1957, p. 23

XIV. *College Library*

A. Winthrop College shall operate a College Library, headed by the Librarian. The College Library shall provide a complete program of library services.

B. The Library Professional Staff shall consist of the members of the College Library staff appointed to perform professional library functions.

C. Any member of the Library Professional Staff who is employed for college-level academic purposes shall be responsible to the Librarian, and through the Librarian, to the Dean of the College and the President. Academic ranks applicable to personnel thus employed shall be professor, associate professor, and instructor.

D. Except with respect to college-level academic functions, members of the Library Professional Staff shall be responsible to the Librarian, and through the Librarian, to the President.

E. Members of the Library Professional Staff, other than the Librarian, shall have the title of Assistant Librarian.

F. Members of the Library staff shall perform their prescribed duties and shall keep such records and make such reports as the regulations of the College Library require.

G. Each member of the Library Professional Staff shall have a written contract incorporating the provision of the Tenure Plan of the College.

GEORGIA STATE COLLEGE OF BUSINESS ADMINISTRATION. OFFICIAL STATUTES AND BY LAWS . . . 1957

Article III, Section 6 The Librarian. The Librarian shall be appointed by the President with the approval of the Board of Regents.

He shall have the following duties:

(a) He shall have charge of the Library and be responsible for its proper administration. The library shall consist of all books, maps, charts, music scores, paintings, photographs, prints, manuscripts, films and similar documents and teaching aids purchased with college funds or acquired in any other manner by the college, except such as are of an administrative nature or are essential to the internal work of several departments.

(b) The Librarian shall recommend to the President the appointment of all members of the library staff and he may recommend that they be given appropriate academic rank.

(c) He shall authorize the purchase of all items listed in (a) above that are purchased with library funds, and all supplies and equipment for the library.

(d) He shall recommend to the President, the Administrative Council, and the faculty, through an appropriate committee of the college faculty as provided by the bylaws, the adoption of such measures as will promote the efficiency and increase the usefulness of the library.

[Comment: In (d) substitute for "through an appropriate committee of the college faculty" the phrase "in consultation with the faculty library committee."]

Article IV, Section 1 The Administrative Council shall consist of the President, who shall be *ex officio* the presiding officer, the Administrative Dean, the Dean of Students, the Dean of Women, the Comptroller, the Registrar, the Librarian, the Deans of the respective schools, four members of the faculty of the college, two elected annually by the faculty of each school of the college. The Registrar shall be *ex officio* secretary of the Council.

Article V, Section 1 The Faculty Council shall consist of the Administrative Dean, who shall be *ex officio* the presiding officer, the Deans of the respective schools, and six faculty members, three from each school elected annually by the faculties of their respective schools. One of the faculty members shall be elected secretary.

[*Comment*: The statutes provide for the proper library relationship to administrative officers but it is equally important that the librarian be so placed in relation to the faculty that he will be able to keep informed about the Faculty Council's discussions on educational policy, procedures, curriculum, etc.]

Article VI, The College Faculty, Section 1 The College Faculty shall consist of the President, who shall be *ex officio* the presiding officer, Administrative Dean, the Dean of Students, the Librarian, the Professor of Military Science and Tactics, the Comptroller, the Registrar, who shall be *ex officio* secretary of the faculty, the Deans of each school of the college, the professors, the associate professors, the assistant professors, and the instructors.

[*Comment*: Only the Librarian is named above. Yet Art. III, Section 6 (b), above, provides for appropriate faculty rank for the library staff. Clarification is needed.]

Bylaws, Article IV, Section 9

Library Committee:

(a) The Library Committee shall be composed of the combined membership of the library committees of the School of Business Administration and the School of Arts and Sciences, and the Librarian without voting power.

(b) The duties of the Committee, in cooperation with the Librarian, shall be as follows:

(1) To review annually the status of the library, the statistics on the number of volumes, circulation, and expenditures. It shall have the power to recommend facilities or expenditures for the improvement of the operation of the library.

(2) To consider and report to the Faculty any matter concerning the library which should receive the attention of the Faculty.

(3) To receive from the Faculty or from any school or department recommendations or suggestions which may aid in the development, promote more efficient service, or encourage greater use of the library.

[*Comment*: Committee is given both advisory and administrative powers. The Committee should be advisory. The formation of the Committee by the combination of two school library committees serves to emphasize a narrow, representative function rather than to encourage the formation of a college-wide Committee whose interests are to represent the College as a whole and not any one part or parts thereof. Since the librarian is responsible for administering policies which the Committee has a considerable part in establishing, he should be a member of the Committee, probably *ex officio*, with voting power.]

WOMAN'S COLLEGE OF THE UNIVERSITY OF NORTH CAROLINA. AN INSTRUMENT OF GOVERNMENT FOR THE FACULTY . . . GREENSBORO, N.C. REV. APRIL, 1959, p. 5

Section IV, Bylaws . . . B. Composition of the Faculty Council*
5. Members of the Library staff with the title of librarian, with the privilege of voting as designated for instructors.

*Faculty Council—the legislative body of the Faculty

MADISON COLLEGE. HANDBOOK FOR ADMINISTRATIVE STAFF AND FACULTY. 1954, p. 13-14.

Section III, The Faculty and Instruction: Library and Staff
General Statement: The Library serves the faculty, staff, and students by providing a carefully selected collection of books, periodicals, and other printed materials to implement the instructional program of the college, to provide for students' personal reading, and to assist the faculty in their study and research. All policies and regulations of the Library are established to carry out these purposes.

The Librarian: The Librarian serves under the supervision of the President and the Dean of the College and is directly responsible to the Dean. The Assistant Librarians, who are directly responsible to the Librarian, assist him in the administration, supervision, and operation of the library. Some of the Librarian's more important duties are:

1. The recommendation of the appointment, promotion, and dismissal of professional and clerical members of the library staff.

2. The selection, training, supervision, and rating of all student library assistants, subject to the policies formulated by the Director of Admissions and Student Aid.

3. The formulation of policies and regulations governing the use of library materials by students, faculty, and other users of the library.

4. The responsibility for making studies leading to the improvement of library services, resources, and facilities.

5. The selection, cataloging, binding, storing, and safeguarding of all library materials (including books, pamphlets, periodicals, films, filmstrips, microfilms, microcards, recordings, and other printed materials owned by the College) other than those materials used in laboratories.

6. The preparation and submission of requisitions for all library materials through the Business Office of the College for purchase by the State Division of Purchasing and Printing.

7. The responsibility for giving both formal and informal instruction in the use of the Library to all undergraduate students, and, as Head of the Department of Library Science, providing professional library science courses for school librarians and teacher-librarians.

8. The preparation of book lists, exhibits, bibliographies, and other aids to enable students and members of the faculty to make more effective use of library materials.

9. The provision of books from the Teachers' Reading Course of the State Department of Education for teachers of this region.

10. Service with other members of the faculty and library staff on committees to which they are assigned by the President of the College.

Additional References

Benjamin, P. M. "Relation between the librarian and the college administration." *Col. and research lib.* 16:350-2, October, 1955

Biggs, Martha. "Codifying college library policy." University of Illinois Library School *Occasional papers,* no. 14, 1950

Wilson, Eugene H. "Government and control of the college library." *In*: Fussler, H. H., ed. *Function of the library in the modern college.* Chicago, University of Chicago Graduate Library School, 1954

IV

Administrative Organization

Professor Floyd W. Reeves, of the University of Chicago, defines the nature of administrative organization as "the arrangement of the personnel for the accomplishment of the objectives for which the institution exists," and he adds that "it includes the division into groups of all those activities necessary to achieve the desired objectives and the allocation of such activities to individuals." [1]

Before attempting to understand the manner in which library activities are usually organized, the inexperienced student of librarianship should know something about the nature of these activities. The chief activities and operations common to all libraries are, therefore, briefly reviewed at the outset. From this picture, it is then possible for the student to consider the method by which libraries commonly departmentalize their activities for carrying out their objectives. The determination of departmental groupings is based on the functions to be performed. Organization is not an end in itself, but if it promotes efficiency and coordinates the various activities of library management, it contributes directly to the part the library can play in instruction and research.

An incomplete list of the activities carried on by college libraries follows. It should be borne in mind that it is a catalog of activities and does not profess to set forth the organization for their performance even though the activities are grouped under certain descriptive headings.

Administrative

    Formulating and administering policies, rules and regulations

    Planning the development of the book collection

    Maintaining close relationships with administrators, faculty, students, committees, and others

Preparing reports, surveys, studies, and analyses of library services

Preparing and administering the budget when approved

Recommending for appointment, instructing, and supervising the library staff

Guiding plans for a remodeled, enlarged, or new library building

Seeing that library quarters and equipment are kept in good condition

Purchasing supplies and equipment

Handling general library correspondence

Making library resources and services well known to its users

Cooperation with other libraries in the area

Participation in local, state, and national library activities

Selection and Acquisition of Library Materials

Collaboration with the faculty in the selection of library materials

Bibliographic verification of all orders and searching before ordering to avoid duplication

Ordering all books, periodicals, and other library materials

Systematically checking bibliographies to evaluate the collection, and preparing lists of needed items

Administering the book funds and maintaining proper accounting

Establishing and maintaining efficient acquisition records

Preparation of Materials

Cataloging and classifying books and other library materials

Searching for catalog information, preparing master cards, and adapting Library of Congress cards

Assigning subject headings

Typing, revising, and filing cards

Supervising the mechanical preparation of books and other library materials

Maintaining essential records and statistics

Assistance to Readers

    Providing for the efficient lending and return of books and other library materials

    Explaining the arrangement and facilities of the library

    Answering reference questions

    Compiling bibliographies and indexes

    Borrowing and lending material on inter-library loan

    Giving bibliographic instruction in the use of the library

All such activities as are listed above are applicable to almost any good college library because the essential functions are similar.[2] The grouping of these activities into departments and the manner in which lines of responsibility descend from the librarian to the staff vary in different libraries although the general pattern of departmentalization and assignment of duties is much the same.

The President and the Librarian

Until recently the librarian was, as a rule, directly responsible to the president.[3] In an increasing number of colleges and universities today, the librarian is made responsible to the president through an academic vice-president or dean. This change has come about as a result of recent efforts at reorganization in colleges and universities and is in line with the span of control principle that there should be only a small number of major administrative officers reporting directly to the president.[4] These top executives usually include the academic vice-president and the officers in charge of student affairs, financial matters, and public relations. Although this change in administrative organization occurs most frequently in universities, it has also manifested itself in the colleges (Fig. 1). It places the librarian at a disadvantage in presenting the needs of a developing library program unless the academic vice-president or dean is exceptionally well informed about library matters and has the educational vision to give the library strong support.

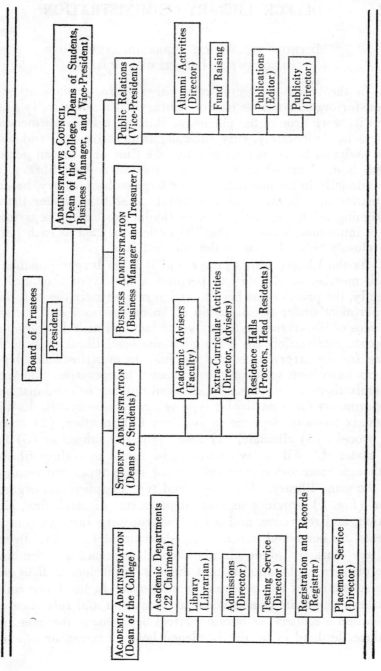

FIGURE 1

CARLETON COLLEGE: FUNCTIONAL ORGANIZATION OF COLLEGE ADMINISTRATION

Organization chart showing librarian responsible to the Dean of the College with only four major administrative officers directly responsible to the President.

Methods by Which Libraries Are Most Frequently Departmentalized

In the small college library either there appears to be no need for organization or else the library has automatically organized its work around the particular skills of a few staff members. There is, deliberately, very little departmentalization, and duties are assigned to the person who has the time or who can perform them best. Thus organization in the small college library, and occasionally in the medium-sized or large college library, becomes a matter of adaptation to individual capabilities rather than of assigning related activities to a particular position or department. It is important, however, that the duties assigned to each person be closely related even in the smallest library.

As the library grows larger and it is no longer possible for each member of the staff to perform a variety of functions efficiently, the practice has been to assign related activities to a single department under the direction of an experienced staff member. Dozens of librarians can testify to the fact that such delegation and departmentalization are essential if the head librarian is to find time for the larger aspects of the job. In most instances departments have been set up for convenience in operation, and consequently there is no generally accepted number or combination of departments for a particular type or size of library. E. A. Wight lists six bases of departmentalization: (1) function, (2) activity or process, (3) clientele, (4) geography, (5) subject or (6) form of material.[5] All six types are to be found in college libraries although more often than not one or more types are combined in the same library. The traditional type of functional organization (Fig. 2) provides separate departments of cataloging, circulation, and reference, and not infrequently the last two compartments are combined into a single department (Fig. 3). In most college libraries where circulation and reference are combined, the obvious explanation is that there is insufficient staff to cover the schedules of two separate departments. In the large college library, where the combination of circulation and reference may be called a readers' or public services department, the intent is to reduce the load of an overburdened head librarian or to enable

FIGURE 2

EXAMPLE OF TYPICAL FUNCTIONAL ORGANIZATION

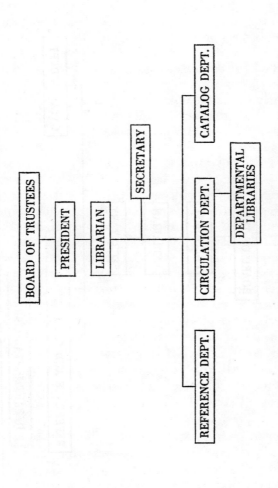

Example of typical functional organization. Order work, not so extensive as to require a separate staff, is taken care of by the Librarian and secretary. Departmental libraries are usually not large and are attended by a departmental secretary although under the general supervision of the Librarian.

FIGURE 3

FUNCTIONAL ORGANIZATION COMBINING REFERENCE AND CIRCULATION SERVICES

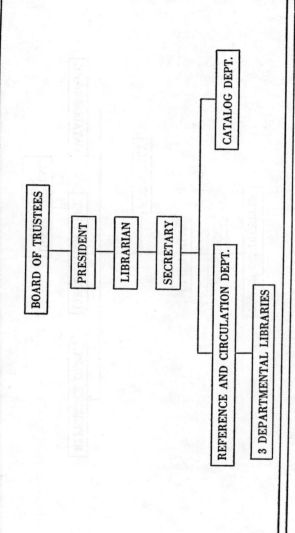

Example of functional organization plan in which reference and circulation services are combined in one department. The combined unit is common, and is known sometimes by the dual name and sometimes as a Readers or Public Services Department. Acquisitions may be set up as a separate department if the quantity of work justifies it. There may be other separate departments such as Serials and Audio-Visual Aids.

him to devote more time to the acquisition and preparation of materials. While a majority of the colleges have a separate catalog department, there are college libraries where the readers' department finds its counterpart in a technical services department combining the duties of acquisition, cataloging, preparation, and binding under one head. Beloit and Wellesley follow this pattern, a practice found much more widely in university than in college libraries. McAnally suggests a third variation of functional arrangement which he describes as a "bifurcated functional organization" in which all library activities are considered either readers' services or technical processes.[6] The libraries of Goucher College (Fig. 4) and Northwestern State College of Louisiana follow this organizational form.

Activity or process as a basis of organization is illustrated by photoduplication and book repair while departments organized by form of material are most commonly found in separate divisions for serials, documents, and special collections, the last named embracing rare books, maps, and manuscripts which require special methods of preparation and preservation. Geography and subject bases of departmentalization are often closely related or combined and are most frequently represented in the college by departmental libraries about which more will be said later. McAnally suggests that "subject- or reader-centered departments" have come about as a result of faculty pressure upon librarians to give more attention to their clientele,[7] and certainly in the university field the reorientation of the library toward the educational program as evidenced in the subject division plan is the most revolutionary change in library organization in the past two decades. The subject divisional arrangement rests on several assumptions: (1) that an open shelf system is preferable to closed stacks; (2) that the books on open shelves should consist of a selection of the most frequently used volumes; (3) that the various types of material on a subject—books, reference sets, periodicals, pamphlets, etc.—should be kept together instead of being separated by form, and (4) that the curricular needs of faculty and students can best be served by reading rooms organized around groups of related subject fields under the direction of librarians with advanced training in subject fields. A few college

Figure 4

GOUCHER COLLEGE: FUNCTIONAL ORGANIZATION OF LIBRARY ACTIVITIES

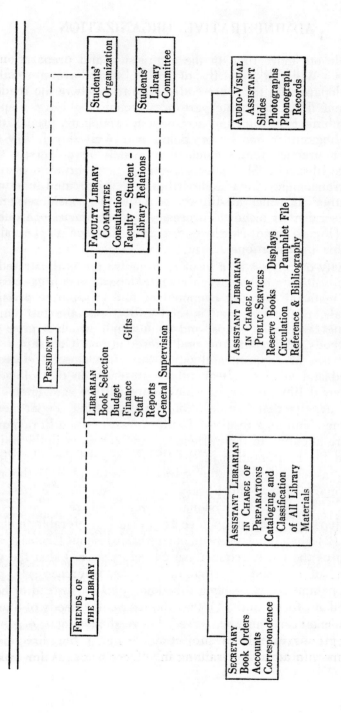

Functional organization in which all library activities (audio-visual aids excepted in this case) are considered either technical services or readers' services.

libraries have adopted this plan in the arrangement of their materials but it is obviously impossible for the average college library to provide the personnel for staffing separate reading rooms.[8]

From this review of the methods by which college libraries organize their work, four generalizations may be drawn. The first is that the college library is usually organized by function (departments of circulation, cataloging, etc.) and that this arrangement has generally proved satisfactory. Certain fringe or auxiliary functions such as budgeting, personnel, and accounting which do not fit into the departmental system are normally considered the responsibility of the librarian. A second generalization is that as the college library grows larger its activities grow more complex. This sets in motion pressures for greater specialization in library work and special skills in handling library operations. New activities, new ideas for handling operations, faculty pressures, and inventions all exert an influence on the library organization pattern, and as a result of these pressures the basic departments subdivide or new departments are established based on geography and clientele (department library), curricular subjects (art library), or form of material (serials, documents, microfilm). With increasing specialization and the resulting fractionation of library activities, some of the newer departments may be poorly coordinated or supervised and the librarian may be overburdened with administrative detail. A third generalization is that neither the assignment of activities to departments nor the nomenclature used for the titles of positions is standardized in college libraries. Lack of uniformity may be less important, as Keyes Metcalf has pointed out, than "making clear to everybody concerned that there is a definite assignment." [9] On the other hand writers in the field of administrative theory emphasize the importance of grouping related activities together. If there is little uniformity in the assignment of activities, there is even less in the titles of library positions. The importance of a standardized terminology is brought out in the A.L.A. *Classification and Pay Plans* which demonstrates the use of titles to distinguish between professional and clerical work, designates the nature of the work to be performed (catalog librarian, order clerk), and indicates the relative rank of positions (senior catalog

librarian).[10] The fourth generalization is that while there are
excellent articles on the principles of administrative organization
in university libraries and numerous organization charts of individual libraries, the writers have been less successful in suggesting practical directives for improving college library organization. In lieu of these guides Dr. Andrew Horn has suggested
that the library self-survey its library operations, define its activities and duties, draw an organization chart to represent the existing organization, and assemble into a staff manual all the codes,
policies, and rules which constitute the administrative regulation
of the library. The point is that the study and definition of
activities will lead to simplification and clarification and that
proper attention to a streamlined flow of work is more important
than the formal structure of organization.[11]

DEPARTMENTAL LIBRARIES

If one wants an impression of "systematic lack of system"
in college library administration, one gets it from an inspection
of departmental libraries more quickly than by any other means.
In this discussion the term "departmental library" is used to include all such collections as are variously known as departmental
libraries, branch libraries, division libraries, laboratory, and office
collections.

The most important, as it is the most obvious, observation to
be made is that most college libraries, large or small, strong or
decentralized, have departmental libraries of all sizes and in all
fields of instruction (Table III). The collections range in size
from less than a hundred volumes to several thousand volumes
and cover such subject fields as art, science, education, chemistry,
biology, physics, music, geology, mathematics, psychology, journalism, and astronomy. The largest collections are in science or
some combination of the physical or natural sciences. Most frequently one finds departmental collections in chemistry, biology,
and physics, in that order. There are a few departmental libraries
which operate independently of the main library. At the other
end of the scale, there are a few large departmental libraries
such as science and art which are wholly integrated with the

TABLE III

ADMINISTRATION OF DEPARTMENTAL LIBRARIES

Library	No. of Dept. Libs.	Range in No. of Volumes	Books Purchased by Lib.	Books Purchased by Dept.	Books Cataloged in Main Lib. Catalog	Books Cataloged in Dept. Lib. Catalog	Staffed by Library	Staffed by Dept.
Beloit	3	500–2500	x		x	x		x
Bowdoin	5	189–1000	x	x Art Lib.	x		x Part-time library staff, 2-3 hours each library daily	
Bryn Mawr	8	1000–10,000	x		x			
Carleton	5	120–1200	x		x	x Author	Unsupervised	
Coe	1	1500	x		x	x		x Manual of procedures prepared by Library
Earlham	2	1000–20,000	x	x Coate Lib.	x	x		x
Hamilton	4	1325–8885	x		x	x		x
Lawrence	5	131–1086	x		x			x Not officially staffed; under supervision of faculties involved
North Texas State	5	1000–2900	x		x	x		x
Randolph-Macon	4	116–2067	x		x	x		x Library inventories
Reed	3	3000–5000	x		x	x	x Student help only	x
Washington and Lee	7	60–3500	x	x	x	x	Unsupervised Non-circulating Library inventories	
Wellesley	8	3100–25,000	x		x	x :	x Art, Music, Science	x Other five
Williams	5	5000–10,000	x		x	x	x	x

administration of the college library. In most instances, however, the departmental libraries are only under the nominal control of the college librarian. The books are generally purchased and cataloged by the college library but the budget scarcely ever makes it possible to pay for adequate staffing. Consequently the collections remain unsupervised or are given perfunctory attention by a departmental secretary, or at best are given an occasional kind of custodial service and inventory.

The principal argument for the departmental library is the matter of *convenience* to the users of the particular library. This advantage is real when the information sought from the departmental library is brief, is needed at once, and does not require reference to the holdings of the college library. As against this advantage, there are serious disadvantages created by the short hours of opening, the frequent necessity of hunting up some member of the faculty in order to get access to the collection, the natural unwillingness to lend freely to students and faculty in other departments, the cost of duplicating materials and services, the time consumed in making special trips for the borrowing and return of volumes, and the frequent failure to find books because the departmental shelves are disarranged or the charging records are incomplete and inadequate. The headache of administering and using a poorly run departmental library is not the only drawback. The departmental system tends to disjoin the disciplines and to make the identification of what constitutes general education still more difficult. A Catholic scholar and librarian states that the departmental library works against the purpose of true education:

> In an age when specialization threatens to warp men's minds by giving exaggerated importance to select and sometimes insignificant branches of knowledge, the librarian has the paramount duty to do all in his power to vitiate the evil. Every departmental library in a college or university deprives the students of those departments of the opportunity of a general education. Their existence implies to the students that these branches of knowledge are the only fields that have real significance. The policy tends to turn out college graduates who are only half-educated.[12]

Even so faculty-oriented and sympathetic a critic as Dr. Harvie Branscomb presents three major disadvantages to offset the convenience which the departmental library affords its particular users: (1) it is less efficient and more expensive, (2) the boundaries of a number of departmental fields are highly artificial and a partition of the book collection along these lines obstructs a great deal of the most fruitful sort of study, and (3) it deprives some readers of the general reference and special services of a strong central library.[13]

It is evident from the foregoing that sharp criticism can be leveled against the departmental library, but it should not be sweeping. The librarian must be broad-minded enough to see the faculty member's point of view.[14] In the scientific field there may be justification, under certain conditions, for a departmental collection outside the main library. This view is voiced by Dr. Henry M. Wriston, a leader in the educational field whose views on librarianship are held in high respect:

> The student of science, whether faculty or undergraduate, works primarily in the laboratory. He is the only student in the college whose first concern is not with books. I do not believe he is adequately concerned with books or the literary expression of his work and thought, but those are personal opinions of no great importance. The fact is that the laboratory, its techniques and procedures, is his first concern. But in connection with the laboratory there is need to consult the literature. It is in the nature of reference work, usually, rather than sustained reading. The books used in this connection are seldom or never outside the field of science, and, broadly speaking, are not the kind of science books that would appeal to a general reader. If the science books are housed together, there is much to be said for a divisional library right at hand.[15]

Implicit in Dr. Wriston's statement is the idea of a departmental library embracing a working collection of reference materials in all fields of science. Such multiple collections or divisional libraries, as they are sometimes called, are found in science at Beloit, Earlham, and Wellesley. The collections are centrally administered and staffed by the main library. Whether the same argument justifies the establishment of separate departmental collections in each of the scientific disciplines is open to question. Either much duplication of fringe material will have to be provided at the cost of the richness of a more extensive collection, or else the individual scientist will have to seek his material in several libraries.

If one assumes that the growth of departmental libraries should be controlled, the question naturally arises as to how such control can be established. There are three principal sources of control. The first of these is limitation of money. If the college library is not adequately financed for doing the major job of library service on the campus, then the extension of departmental libraries will drain away funds which might otherwise be used to strengthen the whole library service and will consequently weaken the educational effectiveness of the college. While it is true that most colleges are constantly faced with serious financial problems, the limitation which money places upon the proliferation of departmental libraries is unfortunately not effective for too long. To ask a college president to turn down the request of a powerful chemistry department for a branch library is to ask him to govern himself by a different philosophy from that which prevails in most colleges. The second control is a statement of policy on departmental collections. This statement should set forth the authority, requirements, staffing, and financing necessary before a departmental library can be established. Such a statement, prepared with the advice of the library committee and with the unequivocal endorsement of the president, should prove a strong deterrent to the establishment of department libraries except in instances where there is real need and the conditions can be met. The third control is the librarian himself and his ability to present clearly the case against the proliferation of departmental libraries whenever the need arises.

NOTES

1. Reeves, Floyd W. "Some general principles of administrative organization." *In*: Joeckel, Carleton B., ed. *Current issues in library administration.* Chicago, University of Chicago press, 1939, p. 1-21

2. For a more detailed listing see A.L.A. Board on personnel administration. *Descriptive list of professional and non-professional duties in libraries.* Chicago, A.L.A., 1948

3. Wilson, E. H. "Government and control of the college library." *In*: Fussler, H. H. *The function of the library in the modern college.* Chicago, University of Chicago Graduate Library School, 1954, p. 30-1

4. Russell, John D. "Changing patterns of administrative organization in higher education." *Annals of the American academy of political and social science* 301:26, September, 1955

5. Wight, E. A. "Research in organization and administration." *Lib. trends* 6:141-46, October, 1957

6. McAnally, Arthur M. "Organization of college and university libraries." *Lib. trends* 1:23, July, 1952

7. McAnally, Arthur M. "Departments in a university library." *Lib. trends* 7:458, January, 1959

8. Swearingen, Bethany C. "Divisional plan at Millsaps evaluated." *Mississippi lib. news* 22:21, March, 1958; Watson, E. P. "Divisional reading rooms in college libraries." *In*: Southwestern library association. Conference 12th, 1948, New Orleans, *Proceedings*, p. 87-90; Sharpe, Jean M. "Rockford college library." *Lib. jour.* 65:1064-5, December 15, 1940. The subject division arrangement has been abandoned at Rockford since the appearance of the above article. Northwestern State College, Natchitoches, La., has a subject division arrangement.

9. Metcalf, Keyes. "Departmental organization in libraries." *In*: Joeckel, Carleton B. ed. *Current issues in library administration.* Chicago, University of Chicago press, 1939, p. 100-01

10. A.L.A. Board on salaries, staff and tenure. Subcommittee on budgets, compensation and schemes of service. . . . *Classification and pay plans for libraries in institutions of higher education.* Vol. II, Degree-conferring four-year institutions. 2d ed. Chicago, A.L.A., 1947

11. Horn, Andrew H. "Organization and staffing." *Lib. jour.* 82: 3147-52, December 15, 1957

12. Martin, Brother David. "Departmentalitis." *Catholic lib. world* 20:179, March, 1949

13. Branscomb, Harvie. *Teaching with books.* Chicago, Association of American colleges and A.L.A., 1940, p. 133-4

14. Broberg, J. W. and Dunbar, R. E. "Current status of departmental libraries in chemistry." *Jour. chemical education* 28:435-6, August, 1951

15. Wriston, Henry M. "The place of the library in the modern college." *In*: Wilson, Louis R. ed. *Library trends.* Chicago, University of Chicago press, 1937, p. 176

V

Cataloging and Classification

Since the library staff of the typical degree-granting college or junior college is relatively small,[1] the problem of organization in the average college library is more one of functions than of personnel. This being true of the library as a whole, it obviously applies to particular library operations, such as cataloging and classification.

ORGANIZATION

In some libraries, the acquisition and cataloging work have been brought together in a single department, and, occasionally, binding has been combined with these processes. In the very large organization, operating in a spacious building, this scheme whereby all the technical processes are placed under a single head proves advantageous by promoting more effective coordination and integration of these operations, by helping to hold to a minimum the duplication of certain library records, and by limiting the span of administrative control. In the average college library, however, where the relatively small staff makes it feasible for the librarian to keep in close touch with the work of all departments, it is quite possible to attain these benefits without adopting this particular plan of organization.

The Librarian and the Catalog Department

The processes carried on in the catalog department have as their general purpose the incorporation of books and other library materials into the classified and cataloged collections of the college library. If the library organization is large enough to make possible a separate cataloging staff, it becomes the duty of the college librarian to decide which operations relating to this general purpose are to be carried on by this staff. He must select a catalog librarian and, with the latter's advice, set up the rest of the cataloging staff. For this staff, he must provide suitable working quarters and appropriate equipment. In addition, he must establish certain broad policies relating to the work and personnel of the department.

To the catalog librarian he should delegate definite authority and responsibility for such matters as the following: formulating and recommending policies which are the concern of the catalog department but which also affect the work of other divisions of the library; giving advice on policies affecting the catalog department; planning the departmental budget; selecting the departmental personnel; making decisions about departmental transfers, working schedules, work assignments, and other personnel matters, in accordance with general library policies regarding such things; formulating and directing departmental routines and practices; and, within the limits of general library policy, deciding upon the purchase of departmental equipment and supplies.

As has already been pointed out, the college librarian must decide which of the several technical operations are to be performed in the catalog department. The production and maintenance of the library catalog obviously belong there, and few will question the logic of associating the classification and shelf-listing of books with the work of the catalog department. It is also a common practice to assign to this department the mechanical preparation of books for the shelves. Accessioning, however, is in some libraries regarded as being properly a function of the order department. Similarly, the taking of inventories of the book stock is in most libraries thought to belong within the province of the circulation department. Circumstances peculiar to the individual library may indicate which way these questions should be decided. The important thing is that the librarian, having given due consideration to the several factors, should make a practical decision and then definitely place the responsibility for carrying on each activity.

In a college library system which includes one or more divisional or departmental libraries with adequate provision for administration and service, the librarian must make the decision whether the cataloging of books for these libraries is to be done by the staff of each departmental library or by the cataloging staff of the general library. The principal point made by those favoring decentralized cataloging is that it makes possible better adaptation of classification and cataloging, particularly subject headings, to the special needs of the users of the departmental library. The weight of opinion, however, is on the side of centralized cataloging. Dean Works, for instance, points out that "cataloging is an excellent illustration of a type of library work in which there is a distinct advantage in centralization. It makes for economy and a good quality of work to have all persons doing cataloging organized in one group so as to give the largest opportunity for differentiation and specialization." [2] The advantage claimed for decentralization can be secured to a high degree under the centralized plan by proper coordination between the general catalog department and the departmental library. But, whichever scheme is adopted, provision should be made for centralized catalog records so that the full resources of the entire library system may be discovered in one central catalog. This is important not only to students and faculty, but also to the staff of the general library, and especially to the order and reference departments.

Interdepartmental Relations

The catalog department shares with the other departments the library's responsibilities in the college program. Consequently, it must coordinate its efforts effectively with these departments. Like reference work and circulation work, cataloging is essentially a service function. The better the service rendered by the catalog department to the reference and circulation departments, the better can be the service rendered by these departments to the college community. These public service departments can help catalogers keep informed as to the specific needs of library users. Catalogers should be eager to receive such helpful information. By making wise use of such knowledge, yet without yielding either its authority or responsibility, the catalog department can develop a catalog and a classified collection which will serve most effectively the needs of faculty and students.

The relations between the catalog department and the order department must be particularly close if each is to do its work efficiently. Speed, accuracy, and economy in ordering library materials depend to a large degree upon the records made by the catalog department. Likewise, the effectiveness of cataloging services depends in part upon the cooperative efforts of the order department. The library material which the catalog department is to catalog and prepare for use is received from the order department. To avoid unnecessary handling and other wasteful duplication of effort, only those items which it has been established are to be incorporated into the library collections should be routed to the catalog department. Any information relating to these materials which the order department has obtained should be passed on to the catalogers if it is likely to prove helpful to them. The records maintained by each of these departments are important to the other and to the rest of the library as well. They all should be closely integrated to the end that unnecessary duplication be avoided.

Division of Work

The division of work in a catalog department employing several persons is likely to proceed along various lines. The principle of work division which takes into account the differences in training and experience of the personnel is too well recognized to require elaboration. There may also be division on the basis of departmental functions, and, in the case of the professional staff, on the basis of subject, language, or type of material.

Division along functional lines will separate the clerical from the technical processes. Following out this process, accessioning, arranging and filing cards, typing and reproducing cards from master copies, the processes involved in the mechanical preparation of books, and other clerical activities, may be divided among the clerical staff in some logical way which will take due cognizance of the special skills and other qualifications of these staff members. Similarly, such technical operations as classifying, assigning of subject headings, descriptive cataloging, and revising may be divided among individuals or groups making up the cataloging staff.

Organization on the basis of subject and language qualifications is quite common in the larger libraries. The ability to work with books in foreign languages is important, of course; and in the case of books in languages not understood by other catalogers, it is only common sense to assign them to the catalogers who can handle those languages. Because of the special techniques involved in the processing of serial publications, it is not unusual to assign this kind of library material to a special cataloger. The cataloging of manuscripts, rare books, maps, music scores, microfilms, and other special materials all require a degree of specialized knowledge for which work division on the basis of types of material is indicated.

The extent to which the work of the catalog department can be divided depends chiefly on the size of the staff. Obviously, the problem is simple enough when the cataloging is done by one cataloger with the assistance of a part-time student clerk. As the number of staff members increases, problems of organization and work division inevitably become more complex. The head of the catalog department is quite likely to find the solution to these problems by using a combination of two or more schemes of division, that is, by function, subject, language, and type of material. By so doing, he is likely to employ most successfully the special skills, knowledge, and interests of the individuals comprising the staff.

In studying the problem of work along functional lines, the question of separating descriptive cataloging from classification and subject heading work is bound to come up. Although the separation of descriptive cataloging from the other two processes may prove advantageous, the person doing the classifying should also establish the subject headings, because the mental processes involved in these operations are essentially the same. It should not be overlooked, however, that the advantage gained by this kind of specialization will be canceled, in part, by decreasing specialization along other lines—subject, language, and type of material. It must also be kept in mind that specialization may go too far; with some catalogers, excessive specialization will result in loss of interest, with others, in a narrowing perspective. But this is a risk rarely encountered in the average college library where the duties of the catalogers are of necessity varied. In any case, both administrators and catalogers would do well to bear in mind that although the work of the department may be reported in the form of statistical data, a truer picture of accomplishment is given by the measure of satisfaction realized by the users of the catalogs and the books.

PERSONNEL

As has already been pointed out, division of work in the catalog department along functional lines will separate the technical from the clerical processes. It follows, then, that the personnel will fall logically into two main divisions: the professional staff to carry on the technical operations of cataloging, classification, and revision, and the clerical staff to perform the duties involved in the mechanical preparation of material for the shelves, the typing and arranging of catalog cards, and other work not requiring professional library training.

Professional Staff

In its *Classification and Pay Plans,* the American Library Association outlines the specifications for eleven professional positions in the catalog department of the college library.[3] These range from the position of junior catalog librarian to that of chief catalog librarian of the largest college library. To indicate the character of these professional positions, it is feasible to summarize here the description of the one that seems most typical of the cataloging situation in the college library. Here the "catalog librarian," under the supervision of the chief librarian, has charge of the cataloging and classification of books in a library where this work is not departmentalized, and may be required to do other library work. A list of the typical tasks to be performed by the cataloger includes the following: cataloging, classifying, and assigning subject headings; making master cards and adapting Library of Congress or other cards; keeping the shelf list; revising and filing cards; supervising or handling processing details; developing the catalogs and cataloging procedures to meet the needs of the college; searching for catalog information; making recommendations and decisions in matters of cataloging policy; maintaining a manual of cataloging routines; keeping essential records and statistics; preparing reports and memoranda; and handling correspondence.

To qualify for this kind of position, one should be a college graduate and, in addition, should have completed one year's work in an accredited library school. Furthermore, he should have a working knowledge of classification and cataloging procedures and of the uses of catalogs, bibliographies, and book lists; a knowledge of modern library organization, procedure, policy, aims, and service, particularly as they relate to cataloging; a knowledge of books; a reading knowledge of one or more foreign languages; skill in the performance of cataloging; and an appreciation of the objectives and procedures of higher education. The personal qualities desired for one holding this position include: accuracy, good judgment, orderliness; resourcefulness; ability to organize work; ability to follow instructions; ability to get along well with superiors, co-workers, and subordinates.

The American Library Association specifications do not include experience in the list of minimum professional qualifications for this position. However, since this staff member will be the sole cataloger in the library organization, previous experience is of particular importance; hence, a year or more of actual cataloging experience under the direction of a competent cataloger in a larger college library is especially recommended.

Clerical Staff

The American Library Association *Classification and Pay Plans* provides for three grades of clerical positions in college library cataloging service: [4] the "junior catalog library clerk," "senior catalog library clerk," and "head catalog library clerk." Only in libraries of the largest colleges will the size of the staff make it possible to employ a cataloging clerk in each of the grades described. The majority of college libraries do well to have one full-time clerk in the catalog department. In actual practice these libraries depend chiefly upon part-time student help to perform most of the clerical tasks described in the American Library Association *Plans*. These tasks include typing and adapting Library of Congress cards from copy supplied; withdrawing cards from the catalog and shelf list; filing cards; distributing catalog cards received on order; shelf-listing; changing records for items added or withdrawn; operating mimeograph and other duplicating machines; marking books; bookplating; and other related processes. The minimum qualifications for this work are graduation from high school, typing ability, and accuracy. If the clerical assistant has one or more years of college training and a knowledge of foreign languages, he will prove invaluable in the cataloging service. It is important in any case for the catalog librarian to make the fullest possible use of clerical and student assistants before any additional professional staff help is added to the department.

Working Quarters and Equipment

When he faces the problem of finding appropriate working quarters for the cataloging staff, the library administrator must first settle two questions: (1) How much space is needed? (2) Where should it be provided?

Library plans have too often erred in allowing insufficient space for catalogers and in making inadequate provision for future expansion. Those who have studied the problem recommend that a hundred square feet of floor space be allowed for each cataloger.[5] Since this estimate, in addition to space allowed for desk, chair, and book truck, includes the space needed for shelving, records, and aisles for unhampered movement of people and trucks, it ought to be regarded as a minimum standard. Actually, in a new building an allowance of a hundred and twenty-five square feet of floor space for each staff member may prove none too high when it is considered that additional office space can rarely be provided to keep pace with a growing staff.

The question as to the best location for the catalog department is somewhat complex. The processes which are carried on in the department form a continuous chain with those performed in the order department. The workers in each department depend on the records of the other; and, to an important degree, the bibliographical and biographical collection of reference tools maintained for the use of catalogers serves simultaneously the needs of order assistants. In view of these facts, it is evident that the catalog and order departments should be close neighbors.

The catalogers' work requires them to consult the general catalog constantly, and it frequently sends them to the reference room in search of particular facts. They also need to make many trips to the book stacks, either to examine material there or to fetch it to their desks. These are facts which must be considered by the librarian; but in many libraries it is difficult to locate the catalog department ideally with respect to all these factors or without going against the best interests of the library in general. So far as circumstances permit, however, the department should be located conveniently at least with respect to the public catalog, the order department, and the reference room.

The principal items of furniture in the department are desks, work tables, chairs, and book trucks. Card cases will need to be provided to hold one or more of the following official records: (1) the shelf list, (2) the official catalog, (3) the name authority file, (4) the subject heading authority file, and (5) the record file of material "in process." Sufficient shelving should be installed to facilitate efficient routing and handling of books. All equipment should meet the standards of material and workmanship maintained by the established manufacturers of library furniture.

Unless they are required to make typewritten process or copy slips, catalogers do not need typewriters themselves, but the clerical assistants responsible for typing catalog cards, or for adding call numbers and headings to unit cards, will require typewriters, preferably electric, equipped with the special library keyboard and a card holding device. For duplicating unit catalog cards, the special equipment necessary for carrying on whatever method of duplication has been adopted must be supplied.

Books are the professional tools of those who catalog and classify library materials. Some of these tools—classification tables, cataloging rules, subject heading lists, special departmental rules and routines—are so constantly referred to that copies must be either on each cataloger's desk or within convenient reach. Others, less frequently consulted, or too costly to duplicate, need to be kept in the department on special shelves, or, preferably, on a counter equipped with shelves. Here catalogers should find, for example, an English language dictionary, copies of the most needed bilingual dictionaries, essential biographical dictionaries, style manuals, filing codes, and classification schemes.

Types of Catalogs

The library catalog in book form, found commonly in European libraries, has a number of points in its favor. It is convenient to use; it can be carried easily from place to place; copies may be placed for use in every room in the library as well as in other college buildings; it occupies but a fraction of the space needed for even a small card catalog. On the other hand, it is inflexible in that entries can neither be added nor withdrawn. Hence it is out-of-date as soon as it is compiled. If you add to this the fact that the cost of printing such a catalog is considerable, it is understandable why the interest of the library administrator in this form of library catalog is largely academic.

Despite the fact that it lacks some of the advantages of the book catalog, the card catalog is widely established in American college libraries. It is flexible; entries may be rearranged, added, withdrawn, revised, and replaced. Hence it can always be up-to-date.

In most college libraries, the card catalog is arranged as a dictionary catalog; that is, entries for authors, subjects, titles, and forms of literature have been combined in a single alphabetical file. Since the arranging of a large number of cards comprising all types of entries presents many problems, it is necessary to adopt a set of filing rules, such as the A.L.A. *Rules for Filing Catalog Cards.*[6] These rules are based on a comparative study of filing rules which had appeared in print and of the filing practices followed in selected public and university libraries. Under certain types of headings, rules for both a grouped and an alphabetic order of arrangement are given. It is necessary for each library to adopt and follow whichever alternative in each instance will best serve its needs.

Even a tyro ordinarily experiences little difficulty in using a dictionary catalog if it is small. As it grows in size, however, the arrangement of the many entries becomes increasingly complex so that the average user finds it more and more difficult to discover readily the information he wants. The divided catalog, which has received much attention in recent years, is one of several methods devised to lessen this difficulty.[7] Though several schemes of division are possible, libraries experimenting with the divided catalog show a preference for this plan whereby author and title cards are kept together in one file and the subject cards are arranged in a separate file.[8]

The arrangement in separate alphabets of the different catalog entries is not altogether a new idea; but their separation for the purpose of avoiding the complexities inherent in a dictionary catalog is a relatively recent development. The principal advantages claimed for the divided catalog are: (1) it is easier to consult; (2) it simplifies filing; and (3) it makes more obvious the subject approach to books.[9] The library which for one or more of these reasons decides to divide its catalog should not expect also to reduce its cataloging costs by this change. On the contrary, since it makes necessary some additional cards, direct costs would increase somewhat. Moreover, at times the divided catalog causes inconvenience to the user because it requires him to consult two files to find information which a dictionary catalog would enable him to find in one place.

Since the divided catalog has been tried out in only a small number of libraries, it will be safer for college libraries not to adopt it until its superiority over the standard dictionary catalog is clearly established. Instead, they should study every method which will help to make the dictionary catalog a satisfactory tool. Important among these are: a system of arrangement based on a good filing code; proper labeling of cases and trays; adequate use of guide cards; generous use of information and reference cards which will tie together related entries; inserting explanatory cards at the beginning of any file in which the arrangement is not easily understood by the user; prominent posting of principal filing rules; instruction in the use of the dictionary catalog to all who need it; and ready assistance at the catalog by a professional librarian.

The classified, or systematic, catalog, which is preferred in many European libraries over the dictionary catalog, has found little acceptance in America, especially in college libraries. This type of catalog is arranged according to whatever system of classification is used for the book collection. In this respect it is like the shelf list; but in its best form it is composed of three parts, namely, (1) an author-title file, (2) a subject file arranged by the library classification, and (3) an alphabetical index to the subject file.

The shelf list provides a separate entry for every title in the library which has a distinctive call number and it records all copies of each book belonging to the library. Since the cards in this file are arranged by call number, it is feasible to make the shelf list serve some of the purposes of a classified catalog. For instance, since in a functioning library the books are not all on the shelves at any time, the shelf list may best answer the question as to what books the library has in a particular subject division of the library classification.

The cataloging staff uses the shelf list chiefly to avoid duplication of call numbers, to promote uniformity and consistency in assigning classification and book numbers, and as a check list in taking inventory of the book stock. In some libraries, it serves as a substitute for the standard accession record. Since it constitutes a complete record of the book collection, the shelf list, like the accession record, may be used for purposes of insurance. Finally, by showing the growth of each classification division as compared with the others, the shelf list enables the library administrator to control his acquisition program so as to achieve a balanced book collection.

A number of the larger libraries maintain in the catalog department an official catalog which is intended primarily for the use of catalogers and classifiers. The character of this catalog varies considerably in different libraries, but it generally includes author entries, added entries, and cross references. Authority cards and subject entries may also be made a part of this file.

In the college library where the collection is not large and the general card catalog not too distant from the catalog department, an official catalog is not needed. Inasmuch as most of the information supplied by this file is found also in the public catalog, the official catalog represents the kind of duplication of records which libraries generally cannot afford and which they should seek to avoid.

In the following description of the nature, organization, and administration of the work of the catalog department, it is assumed that the library employs a sufficient number of people to make possible the separation of professional and clerical duties and, further, some division of professional work in the catalog department. It should be understood that in a smaller department, although the organization and administration of functions become less complex, essentially all the operations discussed below are also carried on, even though they may be concentrated in the hands of one or two staff members.

Routing of Books

The catalog department will receive from the order department all library materials which are to be processed. The catalog librarian will need to establish a routine which will regulate the distribution and routing of material through his department. In developing this routine, he will have to take into consideration the following points: (1) books to be accessioned will have to be separated from material not to be accessioned; (2) books urgently needed must be given precedence in every operation over others not in immediate demand; (3) division of the material according to the kind of cataloging treatment it is to receive is necessary; and (4) routing must be planned with respect to the logical sequence of operations and the personnel responsible for them.

A good routine will accomplish the proper grouping and routing of materials with a minimum of handling of books and crossing of lines of traffic. A graphic representation of the routine in the form of a flow-chart will help attain these ends. For the most part, the application of the routine will become largely automatic except, perhaps, for that part which relates to the segregation of material which is to receive "selective" cataloging treatment. As this process involves the exercise of considerable judgment based on a good knowledge of published materials and library policies, it is likely to be performed by the catalog librarian himself.

Accessioning

Earlier in this chapter it was pointed out that accessioning of books may properly be made a function of the order department. In a library where this arrangement exists, accessioning logically should be done promptly after it is definitely established that a book is to be added to the library. The accessioning of unbound parts of sets and serials, of course, is generally delayed until the parts are bound. Since the accession record is to serve as a register of volumes added to the library in the order in which they are received, it is important to make this record before the volumes are distributed for cataloging. Hence, if the accessioning is done in the catalog department, it normally precedes any of the other operations carried on in this department.

The accession record has long been established as one of the essential library records. The principle of having in the library a complete record of acquisitions still finds wide acceptance; but more and more libraries have reached the conclusion that maintaining it in the traditional form is more costly than the uses of the record will justify. Consequently, some libraries have adopted an abridged accession record in which each entry is limited to the most essential items of information. Other libraries have discontinued the keeping of a special register of accessions because, with some additions, e.g., cost, source, and date of acquisition, the shelf list could be made to serve all the important purposes for which the standard accession record had been kept.

Cataloging and Classification

Most of the processes covered by the terms cataloging and classification need to be done by trained catalogers, but some of the simpler and routine operations may be done by clerical assistants working under the supervision of a cataloger. Clerks, for example, may do the preliminary searching in the catalog to identify added copies or different editions as well as the form of entry for new books by authors already represented in the catalog. They may also do all except the more difficult shelf-listing. The extent to which work of this type can be assigned to clerical workers will depend on the amount of such help which is available and the ability and experience individual clerks bring to the job.

The end purpose of the functions of the catalog department is to make the total material resources of the library fully and efficiently accessible to the college community. This concept will help to give due emphasis to the importance of the classification system and the cataloging methods whereby this purpose is to be accomplished.

Classification. Although many library classification systems have been devised, a realistic approach to the problem as to which system to adopt in a particular college library requires a choice between only two—the decimal classification of Melvil Dewey and the Library of Congress classification. By far the largest number of college libraries use the Dewey decimal classification, but this fact, by itself, should not lead one to infer that the decimal system is superior to the Library of Congress scheme. More significant, no doubt, is the fact that the first edition of Dewey's classification came out in 1876, whereas the first Library of Congress schedules were still in preparation at the turn of the century. By the time this newer scheme was far enough along to be considered for use in libraries other than the one for which it was invented, its older rival was widely established in American libraries of all types and had become virtually the only classification system familiar to the general library user. These historical circumstances must be given a prominent place in any attempt to explain the present disproportion in the number of libraries using these two classification systems.

The literature devoted to the relative advantages and disadvantages of the two systems is extensive. The librarian confronted with the problem of having to make a choice will need to review this literature critically, and, after objectively balancing the strengths and weaknesses of the one against those of the other, decide in favor of that system which promises to satisfy best the needs of the users of his library.[10]

Once a classification system has been adopted, it is necessary to establish the special policies which are to govern its application and interpretation in the particular library.[11] In the case of the decimal classification, it will be necessary to determine how close the classification needs to be in its many divisions. The decision must be based chiefly on the size of the book collection and the probable future expansion of its principal divisions, but it will be influenced also by the question whether or not users are to have direct access to the shelves.

Failure to adhere to the code of rules defining the library's classification policies is almost certain to result in reduced user satisfaction and may ultimately necessitate costly reclassification. Locally developed special classification schedules, even if well planned, often prove less a help than a hindrance either because they conflict with the standard system or because they grow obsolete with the passage of years. Even minor modifications should be adopted only if the need for them is carefully established.

In this connection, a word of caution with respect to the substitution of letters for classification numbers may be in order. The Dewey classification suggests the use of F for all fiction in English and B for all individual biographies. Although the adoption of these shorter notations may be warranted in popular libraries, their use has certain drawbacks which, especially in academic libraries, need to be carefully weighed against the evident advantages. Not only do these deviations defeat to a degree the essential purpose of bibliographic classification, namely, the organization of the library's collections in such a way as to serve effectively the instructional program of the institution, but the use of these letters in a classification based on a numerical scheme tends to confuse the uninitiated library user, both when he tries to locate books so marked on the shelves and when he attempts to discover such works in the shelf list.

Subject Headings. It has already been pointed out that a close relationship exists between classification and subject heading work and that both, if separated from the other cataloging processes, should be done by the same person. The official record of the subject headings used in the library and the standard published lists are the essential tools for assigning subject headings and making subject reference cards. The official list may be in the form of a card file containing subject headings and subject subdivisions which have already been established, and also all subject references which have been made. A simpler method for maintaining such a record is to mark a copy of the standard

printed list used as a basis for subject heading work in the library
with a check for every subject heading when first used and to
indicate similarly every subject reference as it is made.

There are two current lists of subject headings which form
the foundation for subject heading work in American libraries,
namely, the Sears list [12] and the Library of Congress list.[13] Although the Sears list is well suited to the needs of small and
medium-sized libraries, particularly public and school libraries,
college libraries generally will find it advantageous to base their
subject heading work on the Library of Congress list. The arguments favoring the use of this list are reinforced by the following
considerations: (1) separately issued auxiliary lists may be used
effectively with the general list; (2) the tracings of the subject
headings on Library of Congress printed cards simplify subject
heading work; (3) the cumulative supplements to the list contribute greatly toward keeping subject heading work up-to-date.
It must be borne in mind, of course, that the Library of Congress
list was designed for a library of several million volumes and
that any smaller library will need to apply the headings in that
list with discretion. Good judgment, based on a knowledge of the
needs of the library, will have to be exercised particularly with
respect to the use of indicated subject subdivisions.

Descriptive Cataloging. That part of the cataloging process
which relates to the identification and bibliographic description
of books, as distinguished from the processes of classification and
assigning of subject headings, is called descriptive cataloging. It
involves the making of a copy or process slip which, after the call
number and subject headings are added, contains all the information needed for cataloging a title fully. If, as is the general
practice, this master copy slip is to be used by the typist for
making the complete set of catalog entries, any additional information needed by the typist is noted on the slip.

The catalog is the chief means whereby the contents of a
library may be discovered and approached. To accomplish this
function satisfactorily, the catalog must be constructed on a scientific basis, "on rules and regulations that insure uniformity and
accuracy so that it will be a dependable tool. . . ." [14]

In American libraries, the standard authorities for making such a catalog are the *A.L.A. Cataloging Rules for Author and Title Entries* [15] and the *Rules for Descriptive Cataloging in the Library of Congress.* [16] To secure the full benefits of standardization made possible by these codes, the college library would do well to adhere to them, deviating from individual rules only when the exceptions clearly meet better the special needs of the users of the catalog. Since the aforementioned codes form the basis for the printed Library of Congress cards, the college library accepting the same rules of entry can, by purchasing these cards, not only avail itself of the high standard of bibliographic work achieved at our national library, but can also profit by the economies made possible by the use of these cards.

If Library of Congress cards are available for a publication, the cataloging process is greatly simplified. The procedure to be followed for securing these cards should be based on a careful study of the *Handbook of Card Distribution.* [17] This will make possible the fullest use of the Library of Congress card service at minimum cost to the library. The practice of placing card orders, either by number or by author-title order, at the time the book order is prepared is followed in many libraries and is to be recommended at least for all titles for which printed cards are likely to be available. This procedure makes for increased efficiency in cataloging and reduces to a minimum the interval of time between the arrival of the book in the library and the filing of the cards in the catalog.

When printed cards are used, the cataloger does not have to prepare a full copy slip; a brief entry, with the call number and indication of whatever adaptations of the printed card the typist is to make, is sufficient. The preparation of the card order may be left to a clerical assistant who also sees to the distribution of the cards when they are received.

Although college libraries are encouraged to use Library of Congress cards as much as possible, they are cautioned against following these cards blindly. The Library of Congress and decimal classification numbers on these cards are a real help in classifying, but they must be used with discrimination and not

in conflict with special library policies. Judgment must also be
exercised in the use of the secondary entries, particularly as to
number, which are traced on the Library of Congress cards.

It should also be pointed out in this place that, in the preparation in the college library of local unit cards for the ordinary
current publication, the standards of detailed bibliographic description set by the Library of Congress are not necessarily recommended. Certain simplifications and omissions in the transcription
of the title page, collation, and notes may very well effect economies without reducing the usefulness of the catalog. In deciding
these matters, the actual needs of the users of the catalog should
be the primary consideration.

Revising. Consistency and accuracy in a catalog are so important that final revision of the cataloger's and classifier's work,
before the catalog cards themselves are made, is an accepted part
of the routine in most libraries. The work of revision requires
competence in all phases of cataloging work and familiarity with
the cataloging and classification policies of the particular library;
hence it is commonly regarded as one of the principal duties of
the head of the department.

Considerable judgment and discretion on the part of the reviser are needed to keep in check a tendency toward devoting a
disproportionate amount of time to revision. To do his work well,
he needs to take into account both the character and importance
of the cataloged material and the competence of the cataloger.
With the average book, the correctness of the main and added
entries, the classification, and the subject headings should receive
most of his attention, close examination of the transcription of the
title page and the bibliographic description being required only
with books involving special problems. Careful and detailed revision of a cataloger's work should not be continued after he has
demonstrated his accuracy, ability, and knowledge of library
policies, and, for titles for which Library of Congress cards are
used, only the classification may need to be checked.

Shelf-listing. This process involves assigning to a newly cataloged title a distinctive call number and making and filing a
temporary or permanent shelf card. For the permanent shelf card,
either a copy of the unit card or a brief typed card may be used.

In assigning a call number to a book, the shelf-lister adds to the class number the author or Cutter number, the work mark, and any other symbol needed to make the call number distinctive and to place the book in its correct place on the shelves.

Shelf-listing is done in some libraries by the cataloger as a step in the preparation of the copy slip. However, since the author number is normally based on the main entry, many libraries think it more logical to have this process come after the copy slip has received the approval of the reviser. When this is the established routine, efficient practice will concentrate the work of shelf-listing in the hands of one person, generally a clerical assistant working under the supervision of a cataloger.

Reclassification and Recataloging

A certain amount of reclassifying and recataloging is a part of the normal routine in every library where a serious effort is made to maintain a classified and cataloged collection according to standards which promise to serve adequately the needs of the library users and, at the same time, produce reasonable administrative efficiency in the technical processes. Only a relatively small part of this work involves the correction of errors. More of it has to do with the reclassifying made necessary by the unforeseen growth of particular divisions of the book collection and by the revisions and expansions in the schedules of the classification system. In most libraries, routine recataloging is made necessary in part by old entries which are inadequate for present needs, but most of it occurs in the application of cataloging rules governing changes in the names of personal or corporate authors and the various changes peculiar to serial publications.

Necessary as this work may be, the problems created by it are minor compared with those which must be solved when extensive recataloging and the complete reclassification of the book collection from one system to another are contemplated. A classification which has proved inadequate to the needs of a growing collection, or a catalog which is so inaccurate, incomplete, and inconsistent as to handicap seriously the service to users and the efficiency of the library staff, may make radical reorganization necessary. But the cost in money and labor is so great, and the probable dislocations in records and service while the project is under way so considerable, that the library administrator must give careful consideration to the following questions: (1) Are the deficiencies of the old classification system so great and the faults of the catalog so serious as to hamper materially service to students, faculty, and staff? (2) Will no measures short of complete reclassification and wholesale recataloging suffice? (3) Will complete reorganization effect important improvements in the library's service to the college? (4) Will the results justify the costs?

After completing the most intensive investigation made to date into the problems of reclassification and recataloging, Tauber concluded that such an undertaking could be justified only if it seemed likely that the results would warrant the very heavy costs involved.[18] If, after a thorough study of its own situation, a college library comes to the conclusion that reclassification and recataloging are necessary, it must develop a practical plan for carrying out the project. Such a plan, Tauber points out,

. . . would include a definite program of organization and administration based upon a careful study of the library's conditions; the choice of a classification which the experience of a representative sample of academic libraries and the attitudes of a sample of faculty members indicate might satisfactorily be the Library of Congress system; the authorization of a definite appropriation for the work based upon the maximum length of time to be devoted to the work and the character of the work to be done, and both of these items emerging from the type of service the library renders; the use of a special staff, unless the library has an unusually large staff and acquisitions are so small that the staff members have nothing else to do; the limitation of the extensive modification of the Library of Congress system if it is adopted for use; and the institution of routines and procedures which provide for continuous and even service to the users as well as for efficiency in the technical processes.[19]

With respect to operating procedures, the plan should make definite provision for the necessary staff, working quarters, and equipment. It should outline the general policies as to (1) the extent and kind of recataloging, (2) the use of subject headings, and (3) the application of the new classification system. It should include decisions regarding the essential library records involved in the project. It should determine the order of work by classes and establish the policy which is to govern the treatment of current acquisitions. And, finally, it should provide routines covering the mechanical processes.

Card Reproduction and Typing

Since the number of cards needed for each title cataloged in college libraries is relatively small, the use of Library of Congress printed cards is recommended whenever they are available. Even in libraries where a depository set of Library of Congress cards, proof-sheets of these cards, or a copy of the *Catalog of Books Represented by Library of Congress Printed Cards* and its successor, *The National Union Catalog*, make it possible to use the bibliographic work done by the Library of Congress without purchasing its cards, it is doubtful that reproducing unit cards locally will effect enough of a saving to be worth the extra trouble.

Every library acquires some books or other library materials for which no Library of Congress cards have been printed, in which case the library must make its own cards. When the number of cards needed is small, that is to say less than four or five, typing each card is likely to prove most economical. Each typed card, however, must be examined by the cataloger for possible errors, and this factor must not be overlooked in the analyzing of costs. When a larger number of cards is required, it is necessary to know something about the methods and costs of reproducing the unit card.

Some libraries have employed the hectograph, or a similar device making use of the same principle, for card reproduction. Although low in cost, the resulting cards are not very satisfactory, principally because the special ink required for this process tends to fade.

More libraries have adopted a process involving the use of a stencil duplicator, such as the Dick mimeograph which is especially adapted to the reproduction of catalog cards. Most stencils can be cut with a standard typewriter equipped with the special characters most frequently needed in catalog entries.

Card duplication by an offset process, for example by Multilith or Xerox-Multilith, involves the purchase or rental of expensive equipment which cannot be justified for the reproduction of the small number of cards per title required by most college libraries. Of course, if such equipment is already available to a library, its use for this purpose should be considered.[20]

If local unit cards are to be made, the cataloger's copy slip is followed first for making the necessary number of duplicated cards. The cards and the copy slip are then turned over to the typist who makes the correct entries by typing at the head of the unit cards the headings indicated on the copy slip. The preparation by the typist of sets of cards from Library of Congress cards is essentially the same as in the case of local unit cards, except that call numbers must also be typed on and, in some cases, minor adaptations of the printed cards may be necessary. If no printed cards are available and the number of cards needed is too small to justify the making of unit cards, the typist types the entire set, but generally uses the shortened form except for the main entry card.

When the typist has completed the necessary entries, the cards and the copy slip are sent to the cataloger who, after proofreading the typed parts, passes the cards on to be filed.

The card stock for catalog cards to be used in any of the permanent records of the library should be selected to meet specific requirements with respect to wearing qualities. The cards should bend without breaking, should not fray too easily, should take erasures well, and be resistant to soiling. They should be accurately cut and punched so as to permit easy handling in the card trays. Specifications for card stock should approximate the standards established for card stock used for Library of Congress cards.

Filing

The filing of cards into the library catalog, shelf list, and other card records is essentially a clerical function, but it demands the closest supervision until the filer is thoroughly familiar with the filing rules and has attained such a degree of accuracy as to make further supervision unnecessary.

The filing process is generally accomplished in two steps. First, all the cards to be filed into the catalog are arranged according to the official filing rules; then they are filed into the catalog. If revision is to follow, the filer leaves the newly filed cards on top of the tray rods.

Staff Manual

A departmental staff manual, supplementing the general staff manual of the library, is a useful device for facilitating the management of the catalog department. By promoting uniform understanding and practice, it will contribute to staff efficiency and improve the quality of work. A useful guide to the older staff members, the manual can be particularly valuable as an aid in orienting new assistants.

Departmental manuals will vary in scope according to the needs of different departments, but the following parts should be considered as basic: (1) a description of the departmental organization, (2) a statement and interpretation of the functions of the department, and (3) a relatively complete compilation of departmental policies and routines. The third part mentioned should include policies and routines relating to such matters as cataloging, classification, card orders, handling of special categories of materials, flow of material through the department, mechanical preparation of books, preparation of cards, filing, compilation of statistics, etc.

A manual of this sort needs to be kept strictly up-to-date; to facilitate revision, a loose-leaf record is recommended.

MECHANICAL PREPARATION OF BOOKS

The processes involved in the preparation of the books for the shelves are commonly performed by clerical assistants. A list of these processes includes the following: (1) cutting pages of books with uncut edges; (2) adding marks of ownership by means of bookplates and by ink, embossing, or perforating stamps; (3) labeling; (4) pasting book pockets on the inside of front or back covers; (5) making and inserting book cards; (6) tipping in date slips; (7) lettering call number on the backs of books.

In general, all these operations may be performed after the cataloger has penciled the call number in the book and has completed those steps in cataloging in which examination of the book is necessary, but the first four steps are often completed before the books are distributed to the catalogers. Labeling is, of course, not necessary if the call number is lettered directly on the binding, which, in many libraries, is accomplished by means of an electric stylus and special transfer tape. In libraries not using a circulation record requiring a book card, the making of these cards and the pasting in of book pockets will be omitted.

Marks identifying books as the property of a particular library are generally necessary. That the use of such marks in several places in each book discourages theft is not clearly demonstrated. Since they do not add to the appearance of the book, it is suggested that these marks be used sparingly and that they be made no larger than necessary to acccomplish their primary purpose.

INVENTORY

The taking of inventory involves the checking, with the shelf list, of the book collection and of records which account for the whereabouts of books not located on the shelves. Its chief purpose is to discover what books are missing from the library and unaccounted for so that those which are not found may be either replaced or withdrawn from the catalog records. The detection of discrepancies in library records and the discovery of books in need of repair are incidental but useful by-products of the process.

The general procedure for taking inventory includes the following steps: (1) arranging the books in correct order on the shelves, (2) comparing the shelf-list cards in their order with the corresponding books on the shelves and noting any books not found there, (3) checking the record of books not located with the circulation records and other records which might account for these books, (4) making a periodic search for missing books, (5) replacing lost books which are needed by the library, and (6) canceling or withdrawing catalog records of books not found or replaced.

Since inventory work is done most efficiently when practically all the books are in their places on the shelves and when demand for library service is at a minimum, college libraries generally take inventory during a vacation period. In libraries where there is departmentalization of functions, the responsibility for this work is commonly given to either the circulation or the catalog department. In case the inventory is taken by the circulation department, its staff customarily completes the first four of the steps listed above, whereupon it lets the order department know what books are to be replaced and passes on to the catalog department information involving the canceling or withdrawing of catalog records and the correcting of discrepancies in these records.

REPORTS AND STATISTICS

The making of an annual report to the librarian covering the year's work of the department is one of the responsibilities of the catalog librarian. The general purpose of this report is to transmit to the librarian those facts respecting the department and the classified and cataloged collections of the library which he needs in connection with the performance of his general administrative duties and in the preparation of his annual report. The catalog librarian can make good use of the information contained in the report in planning and improving the work of the department. Moreover, an up-to-date file of annual reports provides a valuable historical record.

The report commonly consists of a written survey accompanied by an appendix of essential statistical tables. The narrative report should be concise but, aside from the survey of work accomplished, may well call attention to problems and suggestions regarding personnel, methods, equipment, etc.

The keeping and compiling of statistics is costly. It is important, therefore, to discover what statistical data are really needed, so that no time will be wasted on those that have no practical value. Because of their importance to the library, it is advisable that the librarian and catalog librarian decide together what statistics are to be kept. In most libraries statistics relating to the following are likely to prove useful: (1) accessions, (2) book records (by number of titles, by number of volumes, and by classes), (3) card records, and (4) records of kinds of material (books, serials, pamphlets, maps, etc.)

Generally, catalogers keep their own daily statistics which at the end of each week, or month, are turned over to the catalog librarian, or to the person to whom the duty has been assigned to compile the weekly or monthly statistical records. These records form the basis for the statistical tables presented in the annual report of the catalog librarian.

Costs and Economies

The considerable number of articles on cataloging costs which have appeared in library journals over the years and the amount of attention this subject receives at library conferences are indicative of its importance in the minds of librarians. Although no one has yet devised a way of determining how much cataloging should cost, there is a growing conviction that it consumes too large a portion of the library's budget.

As a first step toward a solution of this problem, libraries have attempted to find out what it costs them to catalog a book. But unless such figures are secured by means of scientific cost analyses, they cannot be accepted as a basis for comparison. Recognizing this, some librarians have attempted to apply to cataloging processes the methods of cost analysis used in industry, in the hope that eventually standard unit costs might be established for different types of libraries. Miller made an important contribution toward this goal in his analysis of acquisition and cataloging costs in a university library.[21]

Despite the progress that has been made, we do not have at present standard unit costs even for one type of library. Yet these must be established before we can compare cataloging costs with a standard of quality of cataloging. As Miller states it: "Unless an operation or service has been measured in terms of cost, the cost of the operation or service cannot be measured against a criterion of quality or other standard. Libraries are generally lacking in both kinds of measurements." [22] Reichmann, in a more recent discussion of the problem, concludes: "No evaluation of operational costs is realistic and meaningful unless the final product is taken into account. The question whether cataloging costs are too high depends lastly on an evaluation of the dictionary catalog and of close classification." [23]

Cataloging costs are influenced by many factors, such as the needs of the library users, the standards of service, the size and character of the book collection, the physical arrangement of the library, the administration and organization of cataloging, and the efficiency of the staff. These factors contribute to the difficulty of interpreting cost figures correctly. Nevertheless, college librarians should continue their efforts to solve the problems of cost analysis. Even with the procedures developed thus far, imperfect as they are, it is possible to obtain worthwhile results.

In possession of the data secured by the cost analysis, and the job analysis which is part of it, a librarian is better informed about the time and money spent on each process and will therefore not be entirely in the dark when he studies ways whereby the processes may be performed more efficiently. The data may disclose, for example, that certain processes for which professional training is not absolutely necessary are consuming too large a share of the time of the professional staff and that some reorganization will enable the librarian to use his clerical help to better advantage.

No matter what may be the actual figures of cataloging costs in a library, it is safe to say that they are too high if ways can be found to do the work more economically without lowering standards of adequate service. Both administrators and catalogers have a real responsibility to study the cataloging services in relation to the needs of students, faculty, and staff, and to analyze all phases of the work of the department with a view to satisfying those needs efficiently and economically.

It is well for those who are searching for means to make cataloging less costly to keep in mind that the gains should be real, not imaginary—that reducing expenditures is not in itself the solution. They should make certain that suggested changes will effect savings in the general library budget, not merely a transfer of costs from one department to another or a postponement of payment till some later date. They should avoid as much as possible changes which, while resulting in economies for the library, cause excessive inconvenience to the users of the library. Particular care should be taken not to sacrifice reasonable standards of accuracy for economy.

Economies should logically start with the larger things and proceed down to the smaller details. Accordingly, the librarian should first make sure that the administration, organization, and working conditions in the department are conducive to efficiency.

The catalog librarian must see to it that he has an adequate and competent staff, that clerical and professional processes have been carefully defined and separated as far as practicable, that full advantage is taken of mechanical equipment and aids, that departmental routines are made thoroughly efficient, and that information from other departments needed in cataloging is fully utilized. In consultation with other departments, the librarian and catalog librarian should decide what library records are actually needed with a view to eliminating all unnecessary duplication.

In the actual processing of library materials, many economical practices may be employed. When funds are limited, self-cataloging methods may be applied to certain categories, e.g., documents, maps, pamphlets, educational tests, school catalogs, and serials. The principles of selective cataloging may be applied to material to be recorded in the catalog. As a result (1) detailed cataloging would be limited to rare books; (2) standard cataloging methods adopted by the library would be used for ordinary acquisitions; (3) simplified cataloging methods would be applied to less important material; and (4) no cataloging would be done in the case of ephemera that can be organized in vertical files.

The kind and amount of detailed information to be given on catalog cards is not a matter to be settled by the catalog department alone; the general policy should be established by the librarian acting with the advice of all library departments. With respect to the problem of effecting economies in descriptive cataloging, Mumford suggests: (1) reducing as much as possible the information requiring lengthy research on the part of the cataloger; (2) shortening or omitting entirely certain details in transcribing title pages; and (3) eliminating as far as possible rules and practices which result in time-consuming and debatable points for the cataloger, such as collation and notes.[24]

Economies may be effected in various other ways. The number of entries per title may be reduced; this applies to subject entries as well as other added entries. The analyzing of books and series may be curtailed or, in the case of sets analyzed in reliable bibliographies or library indexes, dispensed with entirely. The use of form cards in the catalog can be greatly extended to reduce the amount of descriptive cataloging.

Cooperative cataloging and centralized cataloging have proved the most effective means for reducing costs in this area. The kind of joint effort represented by the cooperative cataloging projects initiated by the American Library Association and carried forward by the Library of Congress with the help of many other libraries could be greatly extended. Centralized cataloging on a national scale, whereby a single agency prepares and distributes catalog cards to all libraries that care to avail themselves of this service, would produce catalog cards of high standard at relatively low cost. The card service provided by the Library of Congress since the turn of the century is the best demonstration of what centralized cataloging might accomplish if that library could supply cards for all books acquired by American libraries.[25]

Most recently, a plan for "cataloging-in-source" raised high hopes that the ultimate answer to the problem of economical and expeditious cataloging was virtually at hand. According to this scheme, publishers would print in their current publications facsimiles of catalog cards based on copy provided by a central cataloging office which libraries would then transfer by means of a "cataloger's camera" from the books themselves to cards and which, following the addition of call numbers and indicated headings, they would then file directly into their card catalogs.

These hopes received a severe jolt, however, when the Library of Congress upon the completion of its "cataloging-in-source" experiment concluded that "a permanent, full-scale Cataloging-in-Source program could not be justified from the viewpoint of financing, technical considerations, or utility."[26]

NOTES

1. "College and university library statistics, 1958/59." *Col. and research lib.* 21:25-88, January, 1960. See statistics showing total number of employees in terms of full-time equivalents.

2. Works, George A. *College and university library problems.* Chicago, A.L.A., 1927, p. 114

3. A.L.A. Board on salaries, staff and tenure. Subcommittee on budgets, compensation and schemes of service. . . . *Classification and pay plans for libraries in institutions of higher education.* Vol. II, Degree-conferring four-year institutions. 2d ed. Chicago, A.L.A., 1947, p. 23-33

4. *Ibid.,* p. 88-90

5. Bishop, William W. *Practical handbook of modern library cataloging.* 2d ed. Baltimore, Williams & Wilkins, 1924, p. 22-23. See also discussion of offices and working quarters in Chapter XVI.

6. A.L.A. *A.L.A. rules for filing catalog cards.* Chicago, A.L.A., 1942

7. Thom, Ian W. "The divided catalog in college and university libraries." *Col. and research lib.* 10:236-41, July, 1949

8. Adams, Winona. "The divided catalog in practice." *PNLA quar.* 7:48-50, October, 1942

9. Grosser, Dorothy. "The divided catalog: a summary of the literature." *Lib. resources and technical services* 2:238-52, Fall, 1958

10. Clemons, Harry. "D.C. versus L.C." *Libraries* 35:1-4, January, 1930; Fellows, Dorkas. "Library of Congress classification vs. Decimal classification." *Lib. jour.* 50:291-5, April 1, 1925; Gulledge, James R. "L.C. vs. D.C. for college library." *Lib. jour.* 49:1026-7, December 1, 1924; Hanson, James C. M. "Library of Congress classification for college libraries." *Lib. jour.* 46:151-4, February 15, 1921

11. Merrill, William S. *Code for classifiers.* 3d ed. Chicago, A.L.A., 1954

12. Sears, Minnie E. *Sears list of subject headings.* 8th ed. New York, H. W. Wilson Co., 1959

13. U.S. Library of Congress. Subject cataloging division. *Subject headings used in the dictionary catalogs of the Library of Congress.* 6th ed. Washington, Government printing office, 1957. Kept current by monthly and cumulative supplements.

14. Mann, Margaret. *Introduction to cataloging and the classification of books.* 2d ed. Chicago, A.L.A., 1943, p. 107

15. A.L.A. Division of cataloging and classification. *A.L.A. cataloging rules for author and title entries.* 2d ed. Chicago, A.L.A., 1949

16. U.S. Library of Congress. Descriptive cataloging division. *Rules for descriptive cataloging in the Library of Congress.* Washington, Government printing office, 1949

17. U.S. Library of Congress. Card division. *Handbook of card distribution.* 8th ed. Washington, Government printing office, 1954

18. Tauber, Maurice F. "Reclassification and recataloging in college and university libraries: reasons and evaluation." *Lib. quar.* 12:845, October, 1942

19. Tauber, Maurice F. "Reclassification and recataloging of materials in college and university libraries." *In*: Randall, W. M. ed. *The acquisition and cataloging of books.* Chicago, University of Chicago press, [1940], p. 218-19

20. Dawson, John M. "Duplicating machines." *Lib. trends* 5:256-64, October, 1956. Description includes those for card reproduction. A.L.A. Division of cataloging and classification. Committee on administration. *Methods of catalog card reproduction in American libraries.* Chicago, Microphotographic laboratories of the University of Chicago libraries, 1949. (Microfilm)

21. Miller, Robert A. "Cost accounting for libraries: acquisition and cataloging." *Lib. quar.* 7:511-36, October, 1937

22. *Ibid.*, p. 513

23. Reichmann, Felix. "Cost of cataloging." *Lib. trends* 2:290-317, October, 1953

24. Mumford, L. Quincy. "Cataloging problems and research libraries, part II." *Col. and research lib.* 3:172-5, March, 1942

25. Haykin, David J. "Way to the future: cooperative and centralized cataloging." *Col. and research lib.* 3:156-62, March, 1942

26. U.S. Library of Congress. Processing department. *The cataloging-in-source experiment; a report to the Librarian of Congress by the Director of the Processing department.* Washington, Government printing office, 1960, p. 47

ADDITIONAL REFERENCES

Dean, Hazel. "Size of cataloging staffs in academic libraries." *Col. and research lib.* 7:52-7, January, 1946

Dickson, Janet S. "Centralized cataloging in college and university libraries." *Col. and research lib.* 8:225-31, July, 1947

Eaton, Thelma. "Classification in college and university libraries." *Col. and research lib.* 16:168-76, April, 1955

Haykin, David J. *Subject headings; a practical guide.* Washington, Government printing office, 1951

Headings, Bernice E. "The service load of a cataloger in a small college library." *Lib. resources and technical services* 3:117-19, Spring, 1959

Jackson, Sidney L. *Catalog use study: director's report.* Chicago, A.L.A., 1958

Morsch, Lucile M. "Scientific management in cataloging." *Lib. trends* 2:470-83, January, 1954

Ruffin, Mary Beverly. "The catalog librarian as an administrative officer in the college or university library." *Lib. jour.* 63:908-10, December 1, 1938

Shera, Jesse H. and Egan, Margaret E. *The classified catalog; basic principles and practices.* Chicago, A.L.A., 1956

Swank, Raynard C. "The catalog department in the library organization." *Lib. quar.* 18:24-32, January, 1948

Swank, Raynard C. "Cataloging cost factors." *Lib. quar.* 26:303-17, October, 1956

"Symposium on the division of professional activities in the catalog department." *Catalogers' and classifiers' yearbook* 5:36-44, 1936

Tauber, Maurice F. "Classification of books in college and university libraries." *Lib. quar.* 12:706-24, July, 1942

Tauber, Maurice F., ed. "Current trends in cataloging and classification." *Lib. trends* 2:171-355, October, 1953

Tauber, Maurice F. and others. *Technical services in libraries.* New York, Columbia University press, 1954. See especially chapter XIV, "The cataloging department: administrative problems."

VI

Circulation Work

Circulation work is that phase of library activity which is most exposed to observation by the library's patrons. If the only duties performed at a loan desk are checking books, keeping records, and "collecting pennies" for overdue books, the impression is made that library work is only a matter of routine duties performed by clerks. Such an organization of functions does little to win recognition of the library as an educational force on the college campus. Under capable, vigorous, and imaginative leadership circulation work can become the nerve center of the library, the point where students are encouraged to come for help. Dealing with students is not the same kind of problem as making budgets, selecting books, and cataloging materials. It means working with human beings and implies not only large responsibilities but even greater privileges: the opportunity to help the student who has no idea of what he needs and to direct him to the material that will be useful in his studies; to develop good relations with members of the faculty; and to assist in the instructional program of the college.

Consciously or unconsciously, everyone connected with the library performs the functions of circulation work. These functions are: (1) to make books easily accessible to all readers; (2) to supply other pertinent material when the desired book is not available in the library or is charged out; (3) to give instruction in the use of the card catalog and point out its use as the key to the resources of the library; (4) to interpret the library through friendly and efficient service to all readers. Even in the larger colleges where certain of these functions may be delegated to the reference department, the reader generally receives his first introduction to the library at the loan desk. Failure at this point to provide helpful, friendly direction and guidance in reading and in the use of the library may have a damaging effect on the prestige of the library. The circulation staff provides liaison between readers and books. Success in carrying out this work will depend upon an understanding of the educational function of the college library, careful planning and organization of circulation duties, genuine interest in all types of readers, and a familiarity with books in a variety of subject fields.

ORGANIZATION

Effective circulation service requires a workable organization. Whatever administrative machinery is used, it must comprehend specific objectives and such existing conditions as the size of the library, the arrangement of the building, the number of staff members, and the nature of the curriculum. The library is vitally concerned with making available to students material that is assigned by professors. Therefore, provision should be made for taking care of assigned readings, recommended supplementary material, and the general book collection from which students draw information and materials for individual investigations. In the small college library all duties relevant to the provision of assigned material are centered at the main loan desk. In the medium-sized and large college library the assigned and supplementary reading materials are usually handled in a separate reserve room. Books housed in the reserve room are used principally in the library building because the demand for them is so great that they cannot be circulated for the two-week loan period. Access to the general collection is provided through the main loan desk, the reference department, and other divisions, depending on the size of the library and the method of handling special materials such as microfilm, pictures, and phonograph records.

The physical arrangement of the library building has an important bearing on the organization and efficiency of circulation service. If the card catalog and book collection are not quickly and easily accessible to the loan desk, the staff is handicapped in the help it can give to students in using the catalog and in selecting books from the shelves. The ability of the circulation staff to foster general reading is determined to a considerable extent by the availability of space for exhibits, book displays, and a place for comfortable reading. In short, the ability of the staff to give service as directly and with as little difficulty as possible is dependent in no small degree on adequate space and equipment conveniently arranged in areas where readers and books are brought together.

The organization of circulation work must also take into account the manner of dividing the work among members of the staff. In the small college library the service to readers centers at the loan desk and the work is done by the librarian and student assistants. As the library grows, the librarian finds that he must delegate to full-time assistants those parts of the work for which he no longer has time. At first he delegates the duties to the assistants but assumes the responsibility for their supervision; then, when the work of supervision becomes too great in volume, he sets up a circulation department with a supervisor in charge. The supervisor, usually known as the head of the circulation department, gives a great deal of time to making plans and to directing work, and is aided in the performance of the functions of circulation work by staff and student assistants. At first, perhaps, the supervisor or circulation head takes charge of all circulation and reference services. Later the work may grow large enough to have two separate departments. As the library grows still larger and more complex, some libraries create a readers' division with the heads of both the circulation and the reference departments responsible to an assistant or associate librarian. The advantages claimed for such a plan are that: (1) it provides a means of coordinating services to readers; (2) the staff is more easily trained in a thorough understanding of its contribution to education on the college level; and (3) some duplication of technical routines is eliminated.[1]

CLASSIFICATION OF DUTIES

When the volume of circulation and the use of the library reach a point where several full-time staff and student assistants are needed in circulation work, it becomes necessary to analyze the duties and consider the qualifications of the staff members who perform these tasks. It is difficult in circulation work to divide professional and non-professional duties because of the conditions under which staff and readers are brought together at the loan desk. There is evidence in library writings and from job

classifications that some library administrators distinguish duties
"which require somewhat less than professional training and somewhat more than clerical." [2] To illustrate how duties are allocated
in circulation work, an outline of the classification and assignment of duties in one college library is presented below. The staff
consists of two full-time professional staff members, one part-time
professional assistant, three full-time non-professional assistants,
and approximately twenty-five student assistants.

Professional Duties	*Staff Member Responsible*
1. Establishing policies and procedures	Professional
2. Selecting and training personnel	Professional
3. Organizing and directing work of the department	Professional
4. Compiling reading lists	Professional
5. Developing and maintaining good relations with other departments in the library and with members of the faculty	Professional and non-professional
6. Interpreting rules and regulations to students	Professional and non-professional
7. Guiding students in the selection of library materials	Professional and non-professional
8. Interpreting the card catalog to students	Professional and non-professional
9. Planning book exhibits and informal book displays	Professional and non-professional

Clerical Duties	*Staff Member Responsible*
1. Charging books to readers	Professional, non-professional, student assistants
2. Renewing books	Professional, non-professional, student assistants
3. Collecting fines	Professional, non-professional, student assistants
4. Handling reserve routines	Non-professional

5.	Supervising fines and overdue records	Non-professional
6.	Handling records for books in circulation when requested	Non-professional
7.	Keeping statistics on library use	Non-professional
8.	Preparing student assistant pay-roll	Non-professional
9.	Discharging books	Student assistants
10.	Shelving books	Student assistants
11.	Searching missing books	Student assistants
12.	Filing cards	Student assistants

From this illustration it is apparent that administrative duties involving policy, personnel, and organization are assigned to the professional staff members; that duties which bring staff readers together at the loan desk are performed by professional and non-professional staff members; and that the clerical tasks—filing, discharging, and shelving—are done chiefly by non-professional assistants and student assistants. It is equally evident that when staff members come in contact with readers at the loan desk, it is impossible to separate duties completely. If the division of duties is clearly formulated, however, and if the outline on paper is reinforced through a written manual, and discussion at staff and student assistant meetings, the quality of library service to readers will be greatly improved. The assignment of duties outlined above is of course not the only possible arrangement. In some libraries the duties at the loan desk are handled entirely by non-professional assistants and student assistants; in others by professional librarians; and in still others by professional librarians assisted by non-professional assistants and student assistants. The exact arrangement will depend to a large extent upon: (1) the college curriculum, (2) the extent to which students use the library for individual investigation, (3) the number of students in the college, (4) the size of the staff, and (5) the value which the librarian attaches to circulation work. These factors also influence the ratio of professional librarians to non-professional assistants. As the use of the library increases, the ratio of non-professional to professional staff tends to rise.[3]

QUALIFICATIONS FOR CIRCULATION WORK

Since the loan desk is the first and most frequent point of contact between readers and library personnel, the reputation of the library for good service depends on the reaction of students and faculty to the circulation staff. Sometimes the reaction is unfavorable because the staff is not academically or personally qualified. In some cases staff members at the loan desk consider the work clerical and routine and do not see the opportunity for helpful service. And in many instances the circulation department is used "as a training ground for new library personnel. While this arrangement provides good experience for new staff members, it reduces the efficiency of the department and carries unwarranted implication that circulation work in itself is not a worthy career." [4] The sad part is that when this attitude prevails in the library, students and members of the faculty will also accept it.

Since the library's reputation for excellent service is affected by all the staff in the circulation department, the selection and training of qualified personnel is of first importance. It has already been pointed out that administrative duties require an understanding of the principles of librarianship and are the responsibility of the staff member with professional library training. The non-professional assistant, however, can be taught attitudes, methods, and library procedures through systematic training and supervision. To work effectively at the loan desk the non-professional assistant should have at least the four-year liberal arts education or its equivalent. He needs to know the problems of students from first-hand experience, to be able to direct them in using the library, and to have an awareness of important works in a variety of subjects and an enthusiasm for helping readers.

Members of the circulation staff should not confine their interests to library methods and procedures. Since they work closely with students and members of the faculty, they should know something about methods of instruction and materials needed for classes. They should become acquainted with the interests of faculty and students outside the library by participating in campus activities such as lectures, concerts, and forums. It is equally important that staff members possess that very real but not easily defined quality, "approachableness," of which a principal ingredient is friendliness. Courtesy, good judgment, and self-control are important personal qualities in promoting the services of the library. Since records and routines are necessary to efficiency in getting books to readers, the qualities of accuracy and orderliness are desirable. But while techniques and routines are essential, they must be subordinated to the spirit of helpful, intelligent guidance in working with young people.

WORK AT THE LOAN DESK

The library endeavors to supply, as far as the means placed at its disposal permit, all the books that students require for class use, for information, or for general reading; and it has, besides, the important function of guiding the students in the use of its resources. The matter of guidance deserves particular consideration by members of the library staff who come in direct contact with students and members of the faculty at the loan desk. Guidance in finding material and in helping students to use the library intelligently should always be regarded as a major function of circulation work.

It takes time to help a reader find information when he has only the vaguest idea of what he wants. The chief routine duties at the loan desk, which must be carried on continually, are to charge books, to renew books, and to see that books are returned; these are time-consuming tasks. If the circulation librarian is engaged in supervising the work at the desk and in checking out books, he can spare only a few minutes to give hasty assistance to the reader. Students are reluctant to go to a desk where everyone is obviously busy and ask for help; hence they often go away without the material they need. How often one hears a reader say, "I am sorry to bother; you seem so busy." Since guidance and information services are an important function of the circulation staff, as they are in many college libraries, then more time is needed for the circulation staff, as Humphrey Bousfield admonishes, to "come from behind the loan desk and meet the student, anticipate his difficulties and help him. If he receives friendly help and suggestions the first few times he comes to the library, he will soon feel he belongs there and will have the assurance and knowledge to help himself in the future. In addition, he will have a feeling of friendship in the library and a desire to come in of his own accord, not just when he has to complete an assignment." [5]

How can the circulation staff find more time to work with students? One answer is for librarians to recognize that there is a place in circulation work for people with good educational qualifications but without professional training who, with in-service training and supervision, can assist students and members of the faculty at the loan desk. These non-professional assistants can also handle some routine duties and supervise student assistants. Another answer is the systematic organization and simplification of circulation procedures so that they can be performed quickly, kept in the background, and made secondary to the instructional aspect of circulation work. Some of the routine duties can be kept in the background if the circulation files are removed from the front of the loan desk and student assistants file cards and discharge books at a less conspicuous place.

It is true, of course, that guidance and assistance are given to students through the reference department in those libraries that have a reference librarian on duty during all the busy hours of the day. If the student body is large, it is impossible for the most efficient reference librarian to help all students who need assistance. Quick reference requests—informational and directional questions asked by many students at the loan desk— can be answered at that point if well-trained assistants are available to give such help. The amount of time and personal attention given to quick reference requests will depend on the nature of the inquiry, the ability to handle the question easily without recourse to the reference collection, and the circumstances at the time. In all such aid, the circulation assistant must follow the basic principle of helping the student to help himself.

The chief circulation librarian must spend a great deal of his time selecting and training student assistants; preparing schedules for loan desk service; charging and discharging books; keeping records; caring for the book collection; handling interlibrary loans to other libraries; and evaluating loan desk services. Philip J. McNiff has aptly pointed out that the person in charge of services to readers will find himself so involved in the supervision of routine that it will be difficult for him to preserve his sense of perspective. He writes:

> He would do well to remember that: "The only excuse for the perfection of routine processes is that they shall contribute to a fuller and better development of the library's essential services." This means not the custodianship of books nor the mere providing of books as they are wanted but also, as noted by Justin Winsor, ". . . inducing an improvement in the kind of reading." [6]

Training and Supervising Student Assistants

The head of the circulation department selects student assistants and assigns them to the place in the department where they will work. It is the responsibility of all members of the circulation staff who work with the students to direct and supervise their work. Student assistants who are not thoroughly trained and supervised are of little value. Where there are few student assistants, training can be given through individual instruction, but where there are large numbers it is desirable to provide some plan of group instruction at the time they are employed. The nature of this training, as well as procedures for selecting and evaluating student assistants, is discussed in Chapter XI.

Preparing Schedules

The circulation staff is responsible for giving continuous service to readers during the hours the library is open. In order to provide this service a regular schedule is necessary, with the hours of the professional staff and student assistants so distributed that the loan desk is adequately covered. It is in the interest of staff morale to divide the work fairly, taking into account, of course, personal qualifications, experience, and training, and to consider individual preferences for hours of work as long as this can be done in fairness to all. In making desk schedules the staff is considered as a whole, so that the persons on duty are balanced in experience as well as in number. However, there are certain hours in the day when heavy use is made of the library, and it is necessary to anticipate these periods and to schedule sufficient staff to give adequate service at such times.

Most librarians agree that a trained librarian should be on duty at the loan desk every hour the library is open. If the staff is small and if the library is open for a long period of time, it may be necessary to leave an experienced student assistant in charge of the desk during slack periods. The physical well-being of the staff member as well as the interests of service must be considered. In preparing individual schedules for the professional staff, an effort should be made to relieve the strain caused by long hours at the loan desk by assigning to each person special duties worthy of the staff member's particular interest and ability. Constant changes in schedules are not desirable, but a certain amount of flexibility is needed to meet emergencies such as illness and periods of unusually heavy demand.

If the library is kept open during vacation and holiday periods, the arrangement of schedules must be made in such a way as to insure the best service while giving the staff the full benefit of the holidays to which it is entitled. Summer vacations are usually staggered during June, July, and August. Although it is important to have a trained staff member in charge during the Christmas and spring holidays, compensation for this duty should be time off directly before or after the holiday period. The assignment of holiday work should be distributed fairly to all staff members according to a definite schedule.

Charging and Discharging Books

An efficient charging system will show: (1) what books are charged out to readers and where books are that are not in their proper place on the shelves; and (2) when books charged to readers are due for return. This information is kept by means of one or two records, the most important of which is the book file, sometimes called the class file, in which charges for all books lent are arranged by the library book classification or call numbers. Some libraries attach importance to a borrower's record which will show what books are charged out to a reader. Such a record has been found useful in making reading studies, and, in large colleges, in clearing the library records of students and faculty at the end of the year. Brown and Bousfield point out, however, that "this record is not kept in a majority of libraries partly on account of the expense of keeping three records and partly because its use is exceptional." [7] The usefulness of the borrower's record for making reading studies is also open to question. The purpose of the reading study determines the nature of the data which the investigator needs to assemble. If the intention is to furnish a complete picture of student reading, the typical borrower's record is unreliable, since it represents only free loans and reserve loans.

To show what books are charged out to readers and when these books are due, librarians usually employ either a double or a single record charging system.

Double Record Charging System. In this system, two separate records are used to show what books are charged out and when they are due. The book record, which shows where books are or to whom they are charged when they are not on the shelves, is arranged by call number or author in the book or class file. The second record, which shows when books are due, is arranged in a date file under the date the book is due, or, as is sometimes the case, the date lent. Cards for these records are provided in one of several ways, determined by the practice of the individual library. Some libraries prepare and insert two book cards in the pocket of each book. Others employ only one book card, which is used for the charge, and the call slip, used to locate a book, serves as the record for the date file.

Single Record Charging System. In an effort to reduce routines and to speed up the process of charging and discharging books, some libraries combine the two records on a single card and provide a simple, quick way to check the book or class file and withdraw charges for overdue books. Helen Geer's book, *Charging Systems*, describing a variety of systems used in college and public libraries,[8] shows that the tab and punch card system, which uses the McBee Keysort call card, is employed by college libraries more frequently than other systems. Several adaptations of the visible tab are reported in professional writing.[9] The date tab system, based on a call card especially designed for a single charging record, has been used effectively in several college libraries. The essential feature of the system is a visible date tab which extends a quarter of an inch above the top of the call card (3 x 5 inches). The tabs may be numbered 1-31 or 1-12 depending on whether overdues are pulled by the day or by the month due. Since the tabs for identical dates are in the same location on all cards, the single book or class file serves also as the date due record, and it is an easy matter to withdraw overdues by checking only the column in which a given date appears.[10] An interesting adaptation of the date tab is reported by Margaret Peebles.[11] Tabs are in three locations across the top of the call card (3 x 5 inches) representing days in the week when books are due: Monday, Wednesday, Friday. The return date is stamped on the tab.

The same principle of a single record is followed in the McBee Keysort punch card, which provides an economical way of sorting cards rapidly and accurately. Each card (3 x 5 inches) has round holes punched adjacent to the edge of the card. The holes represent days in the week on which books are due: Monday, Wednesday, and Friday. The part of the card between the hole and the edge of the card is cut away. The notch thus made establishes the desired classification of cards for sorting (e.g., by date due). Overdues are withdrawn by a process of removing the cards from the trays in groups and running a long sorting needle through the hole corresponding to the date being checked. Since the same hole for all charges due on a given day is notched, the cards fall out in order filed. Before the cards are returned to the file they are renotched to fall out one week later.[12]

Systems which require manual filing and withdrawing of records from the file are time-consuming for libraries with a large circulation. Mechanical systems used successfully in public libraries fail to meet the requirements of the college library which needs to know the location of every book when it is not in its proper place on the shelves. Some college libraries, however, have adapted mechanical systems to meet their needs. One such system employing a single card has been used in several university libraries where International Business Machines are available.[13] The Gaylord Electric Charging machine is preferred by some libraries for charging two-week loans,[14] but the filing and withdrawing of cards is done by hand. The IBM Circulation Control System has been in operation in the Brooklyn College

Library since 1958. Henry Birnbaum, Chief Circulation Librarian at Brooklyn College, has written a manual to explain how the system operates.[15] With the increase in student enrolment in all colleges and the emphasis on separation of clerical and professional duties, libraries are looking to "the day . . . when new machines will provide the perfect charging system: economical, complete, and without delay." [16]

Keeping Records

From the foregoing discussion it is apparent that college libraries must keep certain types of records as a means of providing an efficient system of charging books to readers. They also keep records to determine how nearly satisfactory the circulation service is in meeting the requests of readers, to provide an approximate measure of library use, and to record the types of material used.

Aside from the fact that books may be charged out to students and faculty, some books in the library are not always available when called for because they are: (1) temporarily located in special collections within or outside the library, such as the reserve book collection or the departmental or dormitory library; (2) "missing" from the shelves; (3) temporarily removed from the shelves for binding, repair, exhibit, or other purposes; or (4) charged to readers for use in stack carrels or in seminar rooms. It is necessary, therefore, to keep records which will show where these books may be located when they are not in their proper place on the shelves.

All records mentioned above may be most economically handled if they are combined in the single book or class file. Since it would entail a great deal of time to remove cards for "missing books" from the file each time the books are searched for on the shelves, libraries generally keep a separate duplicate file of "missing" books. A systematic procedure for searching for "missing" books is important because a haphazard method of handling this problem may seriously affect the service of the library. When a book is not available on the shelves and not recorded in the book or class file, a "search" file is established and requests for all "missing" books are held there during the time the books are searched. Searching routines are developed and an assistant is assigned to check the shelves regularly for these books. He begins by consulting the shelf list to verify call number, author and title, and continues by checking the sorting shelves, mending shelves, new book shelves, snag shelves, and book displays. Files at the loan desk are also checked from time to time. The person who does this work regularly will soon become aware of places where missing books are likely to be found. If they are not accounted for within a definite period, a card is placed in the book or class file, and the search record is transferred to a "missing" file. The length of time a card is held in the "search" file is determined by the demand for the book and the time required to make a thorough check on its location. All requests for books are held in the file regardless of the number of times requested. As soon as enough repeat calls occur, or, if for any reason there is a special need for the book, it is replaced. At the end of each semester all books remaining in the "missing" file are considered for replacement. Cards for books that are not of sufficient importance for immediate purchase are returned to the "missing" file where they are held until the books are considered for final replacement or withdrawal. The length of time these records are held in the "missing" file will be determined by conditions within the individual library. In libraries taking an annual inventory, titles in the "missing" file are generally incorporated into the list of "missing" books in inventory, and all "missing" books are considered for replacement at the same time. Records for all books missing in inventory are held in the book or class file until they are brought up for final replacement or withdrawal. Some libraries consider one year a reasonable length of time to hold these records; others hold them for at least three years. As soon as a decision is made to withdraw "missing" books, all catalog records should be changed immediately.

The circulation department has also the responsibility of keeping statistics of library use. One regional accrediting agency specifies: "Records of the use of the library by faculty and students should be kept. . . . Ready access to the books themselves, however, should not be sacrificed in order to measure this use. These records are only one indication of the use made of the library. The type and extent of use of the library by faculty and students is, of course, the most important evidence of its effectiveness." [17] The regularly recorded statistics of use include: (1) the total number of volumes lent for home use, exclusive of reserve books, broken down by (a) loans to faculty, (b) loans to students, and (c) loans to others such as alumni and community users, and (2) overnight reserve book loans.

Although these statistics are the ones usually kept by libraries, they are not entirely satisfactory as a measure of use or as an aid to library administration. By ignoring the use of books and other materials *inside* the library, they leave out what must certainly amount to a substantial part of library use. On the other hand, to keep regular detailed records of use within the library would require more staff time than the results could possibly justify. Consequently, it is highly desirable to supplement the regularly recorded statistics of use with special studies of short duration. For example, a study over a period of a few days of the ratio between home circulation and the total use of library materials may prove revealing for a report to the college administrator. If there is control at the loan desk of recent unbound periodical issues, this record may prove useful in deciding whether or not to bind a periodical, and when periodicals may be sent to the bindery with the least amount of inconvenience to readers. Should it become necessary to separate little-used material because of lack of space, circulation records may also be helpful in determining which volumes to put in storage. A study of the use of books in the reserve collection may help to reduce the number of inactive books on reserve. Information from such a study may be used to persuade faculty members who overload the reserve shelves to be more selective and to encourage the broader use of the library.[18]

Supervising the Care of the Book Collection

Since the library is concerned primarily with books, it is obvious that much attention must be given to the physical care of the book collection. Requirements for the proper care of the collection include: (1) adequate space for the storage of books, with proper control of temperature and humidity; (2) space at the end of the shelves to allow for expansion without a constant shifting of volumes; (3) liberal use of book supports to hold books in place; (4) special shelving for quarto and folio books which require careful handling; and (5) provision for housing rare and finely printed material. As far as possible, the arrangement of books in the stacks should follow the order of the classification system.

The care of the book collection involves more than provision for its physical arrangement. Books, like other material things, wear out, and it is necessary to make a continuous check on the collection to find worn volumes which need to be mended or rebound. The decision to rebind, replace, or withdraw a worn volume is based on answers to such questions as these: (1) Is the title available in a better edition? (2) Is there a later edition or more recent material in other books? (3) Is the old edition important for historical purposes, or does it contain something of value not in a more recent edition? (4) Is the title out of print and difficult to replace? (5) Are there several duplicate copies which are no longer in use lying idle on the shelves? This phase of circulation work requires a careful check of bibliographical aids, consultation with the faculty to determine the importance of the material and the best editions or translations for replacement, and close cooperation with the division of the library responsible for the preparation for binding.

The circulation department has a primary responsibility in the conservation and maintenance of the book collection. A systematic plan for "catching" books which need binding well in advance of the time they will be used is essential. The service of the library, particularly the availability of books for required reserve reading and freshman term paper topics, must be efficiently geared to the curricular schedules in order not to reduce the quality of the student's preparation. It becomes important, then, to make certain that well-worn volumes which will see much use are rebound before the beginning of the course or the assignment of term papers. This requirement can be met if books circulated for two weeks are checked by a circulation staff member before they are shelved and if the reserve librarian examines all copies of books when they are removed from reserve shelves at the end of each semester or curricular period. If some such plan is not followed, it may mean disintegration to the point where rebinding cannot be done, or may mean removing volumes from the shelves just when they are needed most.

In order to keep the book collection active and up-to-date, these types of material should be withdrawn systematically: (1) excess duplicate copies; (2) popular books no longer in demand; (3) old editions replaced by later revisions; (4) early printings of the classics which are poorly printed on inferior paper stock and poorly bound and illustrated; (5) material on questions no longer current; (6) books more than ten years old in science and economics.[19] Discarding is not a primary responsibility of the circulation department but circulation assistants are in a strategic position to check on material that should be weeded out of the collection.

If the difficulty of finding books in a large collection is to be minimized, the shelves must be arranged as conveniently as possible for self-service. There should be a liberal use of large, legible guides and shelf labels to enable students to locate books easily and quickly. Direction signs and regulations concerning the use of the stacks (e.g., where to leave books for reshelving) should be placed on bulletin boards throughout the stacks. To be effective the signs must be brief and direct, and they should be neatly printed. Pages are scheduled regularly to reshelve books left by readers at designated places; and continual shelf reading is necessary to keep books in order. This is accomplished more systematically if each page is assigned a definite section of shelves to read and is required to keep a record of his work from day to day.

Testing the Efficiency of Loan Desk Service

Records of books called for and not supplied provide a very practical means of testing loan desk service. The test requires very little additional work for the staff and may run continuously or at intervals during peak periods of library use. In most cases, it is sufficient simply to indicate by a single word, such as "out," "bindery," "reserve," or "missing," the reason why a book is not available. From this record the circulation librarian can determine what percentage of books is supplied, what percentage is not supplied, and the causes of the failure to supply books which are not available.

A careful study of the reasons why certain books were not available when requested points to weaknesses in service that should be remedied. Frequent calls for volumes at the bindery may indicate that there is a need for speeding up the delivery of bindery shipments, or that the current use of material should be considered more carefully before books are sent to the bindery. Consistent failure to locate books may indicate that they are mis-shelved or that the book or class file does not contain records for all books charged out. The study will reveal other ways of reducing the number of "unavailables," such as: (1) filing current book charges more frequently, (2) sorting and reshelving returned books at frequent intervals, and (3) making a close check on the work of student assistants responsible for shelving and shelf reading. Requests from students for books charged to the faculty on extended loan will show the extent to which this privilege interferes with the work of students. Repeated requests for the same book may disclose that duplicate copies are needed or in other instances that the book collection does not have adequate material on a particular subject. By means of such a study, recommendations for duplicates and the purchase of additional material can be based on "call-frequency" plus the judgment of the circulation staff.

RULES AND REGULATIONS

It is necessary for all concerned to have a clear understanding of the rules and regulations under which the circulation service is administered. Without such an understanding, there is liable to be a great deal of confusion and dissatisfaction among readers.

Who May Borrow Books

College libraries make loans to their own students and faculty as a matter of course. In addition, many of them furnish books and reading services to alumni, residents of the town, citizens of the state, students of neighboring colleges and schools, and visiting scholars and professors.

Alumni. An effort should be made to furnish alumni with technical and scholarly works which they may need. In a number of libraries alumni are permitted to borrow from the general collection books not required by students or faculty. Where considerable service is given, it is largely to graduates living in the community or nearby towns. Library policy in making loans to alumni is affected by library facilities in the region, by the size of the library, and by the demand for books by students and faculty.

Residents of the Town. College librarians recognize that their libraries have books and services which residents of their communities will find helpful and stimulating, and if circumstances permit they usually grant borrowing privileges to these residents.[20] A study of eighty-three private, four-year institutions within the North Central Association area showed that 90 per cent of these libraries gave borrowing privileges to alumni and persons living in the community upon proper identification.[21] Some libraries require a fee or deposit for the privilege of borrowing books.[22] Oberlin College Library has a contract with the village in which it is situated. Under the contract, the public library is housed in two rooms of the college library and the same librarian serves both libraries. In return, the public library pays the college library for salaries, supplies, ordering, and binding books. Townspeople and students borrow from both libraries.[23]

Citizens of the State. Libraries supported by state funds are sensitive to the needs of the people of the state. Their collections are freely available for reference use to those who come to the library. On the other hand, it is generally accepted as a matter of principle that residents of the state should first make use of the resources of the local and state libraries. If they are unable to secure what they need from these libraries, they are then permitted to use the collections of the college library.[24] This policy is illustrated in the following regulation of a particular library:

It is recognized that the Woman's College Library (University of North Carolina) has special resources of interest and value beyond the College community and can render many services to the people of North Carolina. The Woman's College Library offers the privilege of using its resources to non-college persons where their needs cannot otherwise be met or are not otherwise provided for. The Library offers these privileges subject to its prior commitments to the demands of the College community and subject to its responsibilities for adequate control of the building and the collections.

Students From Neighboring Colleges. If there are several colleges in a community or nearby areas, provision may be made for direct borrowing and lending of books to all students and members of the faculty. Members of the faculty are usually given full library privileges at each library. Some libraries prefer to lend material to outside students through inter-library loan. If students of one college are accepted freely as borrowers by another college the privilege is normally a result of formal agreement between the two colleges. If no such agreement exists, the student may be required to present a letter from the librarian of his college before he is allowed to take out books. This procedure enables the librarian to make sure that he has exhausted the resources of his own library before asking for library privileges elsewhere. Where the resources of one library are placed at the command of others by agreement, it is always understood that the first obligation of each library is to supply the materials commonly needed by its own students and faculty.

Students From the Public Schools. Books which are not available in the school or public library may be furnished on inter-library loan or by direct loan to teachers who assume the responsibility for the return of the books. Students who need debate and other reference material not in the school library may be given permission to use the college library, but arrangements of this kind should be made in advance by the teacher or school librarian. School libraries which meet the minimum standards are normally expected to take care of the library needs of school children.

Visiting Scholars and Professors. Some college libraries endeavor to develop special resources in some appropriate field of teaching or in printed matter related to a region or culture. Williams, Pomona, Antioch, Oberlin, Allegheny, to mention but a few, are repositories of books which one cannot find elsewhere. They consequently place themselves under a certain obligation to make such materials available to scholars everywhere. In most college libraries this privilege is accorded without question to visiting professors and scholars.

Readers' Privileges

Regulations concerning the loan of books to campus readers are made to meet the needs of three groups of users: (1) undergraduate students, (2) graduate students if the college offers graduate work, and (3) faculty. Restrictions in use are justified only when they promote the interests of the majority or if the materials are especially rare.

Number of Loans. Libraries place few restrictions on the number of books readers may borrow at a time. With an adequate book collection and a system of reserving books in demand for assigned readings, there is little need to limit the number of books which faculty and students may borrow. The lending of journals is usually restricted to faculty and graduate students.

Length of Loans. The length of the loan period should meet the needs of all students and provide for constant use of library materials. Two weeks is the customary loan period of most college libraries for books borrowed from the general collection. This traditional period of loan is being extended in a number of libraries to four weeks, with the exception of popular new books which are still lent for two weeks. This is the practice at Colby, Bryn Mawr, Bowdoin, Swarthmore, and Vassar, to mention a few. Hamilton College Library loans for the semester, with two-week recall stipulation when another reader wants the book.[25] Some consideration should be given to a three-month loan for the summer months. One library loans books at the end of the college year for use during the summer. A restriction is placed, however, on books needed for the courses taught in the summer term. The factors which determine the practicability of adopting a longer loan period are (1) the teaching methods of the college, (2) the size and quality of the book collection, (3) the size of the student enrolment, and (4) the speed with which books in circulation can be recalled when requested by another student.

An extended loan period is usually granted to graduate students for material needed in the field of their research. Some libraries permit graduates to charge out books for one semester. Other libraries find it desirable to limit the period to one month with the privilege of renewal. Still other libraries make the decision on the type of material borrowed and the purpose for which it is wanted. Material needed for the preparation of theses, for example, may be charged for a semester, whereas other books charged to the same reader are subject to the regular loan period. Special loan privileges should always be given to students in honors work and general reading courses.

Faculty members are almost always given special privileges when the requirements of teaching and research make such privileges desirable. This privilege does not apply, however, to the extended use of fiction, popular non-fiction, or to materials restricted for use within the library building. The failure of faculty members to return books within a reasonable time sometimes seriously interferes with efficient circulation service, and may, if it becomes a habit, point to a fundamental weakness in the library administration. If the librarian is not strong enough to handle matters of this sort where faculty members are involved, the administration should take steps to strengthen his hand in order that the problem may be dealt with effectively. It is considered a good policy in many libraries to request the return or renewal of books at the end of the semester, and to require that all books be brought back to the library at the end of the regular academic year. Where this plan is employed, the faculty members are given the privilege of renewing books immediately if they are needed and are not requested by other readers. When books charged to a faculty member are needed during the semester for student or reserve use, they are subject to immediate recall.

Renewals. Although few libraries have extended loan privileges for undergraduates, the majority provide for the renewal of books at the end of the regular two-week loan period and many do not restrict the number of renewals if the books are not in demand. New fiction, new non-fiction, and other books likely to be in popular demand are often designated as non-renewable. Renewal in other cases is at the discretion of the librarian in charge of the desk. The process of renewal is done in different ways in different libraries, but it simplifies matters to have the length of the renewal the same as that of the original loan.

Books Held on Request. One of the most appreciated individual services the library can offer to students and members of the faculty is the privilege of leaving at the loan desk a request for books in circulation and for new books on order. The person making the request fills out a form card which is filed at the loan desk and later sent to notify him that the book is available. When the card is filed, it is desirable to check on the number of borrowers who have requested the book. This enables the circulation assistant to give the reader an approximate idea of the time he may expect to receive the book, and also provides the information for making decisions on the duplication of titles in demand.

Restricted Loans

The brevity of most periodical references, the availability in the reference collection of expensive and comprehensive indexes to the contents of periodicals, and the expense and difficulty of replacing bound volumes if they are lost or damaged, all suggest the need for limited loans of such material and care in their handling. When loans are essential for faculty or for some special student use, it should be possible to arrange for this privilege with the approval of the head of the circulation or the periodical department. Special attention should be given to faculty and graduate students in their use of periodical materials. Normally they have the privilege of being able to borrow for a limited period any specialized journals except for the current issues.

In addition to periodicals, there are other types of material whose circulation is sometimes restricted. These materials include finely printed and illustrated books, rare books, college publications, reference books, and reserve books. Books necessarily limited in circulation because of their format, cost, or rarity are housed separately in a special room or a locked section in the stacks. The use of this material is restricted to examination in the library, except when needed for classroom use by members of the faculty. Duplicate copies of the publications most likely to be in demand in the college history collection are sometimes made available for circulation in the general collection. Under special circumstances borrowers may be allowed to charge out works of reference. The regular reference books such as encyclopedias, dictionaries, and yearbooks are naturally excepted from this privilege. Some librarians make exceptions to the usual loan privilege for expensive, scholarly sets of works of authors. This practice may be advisable if no special edition is requested by the student and if the library provides an adequate supply of less expensive editions of the titles in the author's set which are in demand.

Overdues and Fines

It is the responsibility of the borrower to return books when they are due or to request a renewal if they are needed for a longer period. As a convenience to the reader and in the interest of getting books back, the library sends overdue notices. The length of time after a book is due before an overdue notice is sent varies in libraries from one day to five weeks. Sending overdue notices within two or three days after books are due or reminder notices on the day books are due is time-consuming. It is questionable to what extent these notices influence readers to return books.[26] At least one library, following a study of this matter, has given up sending overdue notices except on the first and fifteenth of each month.

Fines are imposed not to increase the library's funds but to ensure the return of books so that they will be available for other readers. Although there are libraries that do not charge fines,[27] and although there is little to be said in defense of the fine system, no one has yet devised a more workable scheme for impressing students with the necessity of returning books on time. Fines in college libraries vary from two cents to fifteen cents a day. The common rate for overnight reserve books is twenty-five cents for the first hour and five to ten cents for each additional hour the book is kept out. There should be a maximum overdue charge for a book. This may be an arbitrary amount set by the library; some libraries stop the fine when it reaches the price of the book. It has been pointed out that fines are penalties and have no relation to the price of the book, but "no reader retains good will toward a library that charges him a ten dollar fine on a three dollar volume." [28]

The library's main concern in the administration of fines is to reduce the amount of time and effort spent in bookkeeping and correspondence. Some libraries discount fines 50 per cent if they are paid at the time a book is returned, reserve books excepted. Another plan is to allow from three to five "days of grace" before the fine is charged. This plan is an incentive to students to return books within the days allowed, and it is hoped the library will have to spend less time collecting small fines.

Reserve Book Service

Under the lecture and assigned reading system so generally followed in college teaching, libraries find it necessary to segregate on separate shelves or in a special room large numbers of books which the faculty assign to their students for reading. In most cases there are several duplicate copies of required readings because the assignment periods are short and a large number of students have to do the same reading. In addition, the faculty often place on the reserve shelves books which they hope their students will read over and beyond the required assignments.

In the small college library reserve books are kept back of the main loan desk because there is insufficient space or staff to handle them in a separate room. In the larger libraries where reserve books are kept in a room or several rooms there are three standard methods for arranging the books: [29] (1) the closed-shelf system where all reserve books are kept behind a desk and the student asks an assistant for the book he wants; (2) the open-shelf system where all books are placed on open shelves around the room, easily accessible to all students; (3) the combination system, which meets the need of most large libraries, where the heavily-used books are kept behind a desk (so that the student must sign for a book each time he uses it) and the other books are on open shelves. The usual loan period is two hours for books used in the building during the day, and overnight for books borrowed for use outside the library. The three-day and one-week loans are more convenient for books placed on reserve as suggested for collateral reading. Fines are usually heavy enough to ensure the prompt return of reserve books.

Since the reading of reserve books constitutes so large a proportion of the students' use of the library, the efficient administration of reserves is quite obviously a matter of great importance in teaching. In most large college libraries, the reserve work is supervised by a professional librarian, but there are a number of libraries in which the full responsibility is assigned to a non-professional assistant. In the small library where the staff is not large enough to have one person in charge of reserves, the work is handled at the main desk by student assistants under the supervision of the librarian.

Because the reserve book system touches the work of the professors so closely, the reserve librarian must have sufficient poise and self-confidence to meet the faculty and to discuss their reserve needs in a way that will enlist confidence and respect. The preparation of books for reserve involves many details: it requires ability to organize the work in a systematic way, energy and enthusiasm to handle the physical routine, and accuracy and orderliness to prepare and maintain the necessary records. "Competent leadership," writes Dr. A. F. Kuhlman, "is needed for large reserve collections not merely for a mastery of the infinite administrative detail but to play the role of teaching colleagues of the faculty in attempting to increase the educational value of books. All too large a portion of the operation of most reserve book collections is in the hands of clerical book checkers who put in hours, rather than in the hands of experienced mature persons who are intelligently interested in the educational problems and opportunities presented by their task." [30]

Open or Closed Shelves for Reserve Books

From an educational standpoint few librarians deny that open-shelf reserves meet the needs of students and faculty members more satisfactorily than closed reserves. Perhaps the principal educationally significant aspect of open-shelf reserves is the fact that many teachers place supplementary as well as assigned readings on the shelves, and the student has an opportunity, within limits, to select for himself. There are faculty members, however, who place far too many books on reserve for suggested readings, and the reserve shelves are filled with books that would have served their purpose better from the regular shelves. At least this is the feeling of librarians whose attitude on this problem is expressed by one librarian who writes: "I wonder often if the lengthy reading lists that fill countless shelves of the average college reserve reading rooms do not, in the end, limit the student's library adventure in discovering and exploring the library's resources for himself." [31]

The administration of open-shelf reserves becomes a problem only when the college reaches a size where it is necessary for the library to provide an extensive reserve collection for the use of a large number of students. The principal arguments used against the open-shelf arrangement are (1) that it is difficult to prevent the loss and misplacement of books in great demand; (2) that it is expensive to provide enough duplicate copies for unregulated use from open shelves; and (3) that it encourages the thoughtless student to withdraw more books than he needs, thereby depriving other students of their use. The theft of books from open reserves considered in relation to the educational value of having these books on open shelves is perhaps less serious than is generally supposed. There is no doubt that the library will lose some books and that readers will sometimes be inconvenienced by the misplacement of others, but open reserves continue to be favored even where the collections are large. In 1930, for example, the reserve book collection of Teachers College, Columbia University, consisting of 13,000 volumes, was transferred from closed to open shelves. Among the advantages claimed for this particular test were the following: (1) students no longer waited in line for their books; (2) the red tape of charging books was eliminated by giving all students free access to reserve books; (3) students found their books with ease and appreciated the opportunity of going to the shelves, where they found a well-selected group of books on a considerable range of subjects; and (4) members of the staff were able to devote more time to advisory and reference assistance. [32]

In 1950 the Lamont Library at Harvard had 22,000 books and pamphlets, representing approximately one fourth of the book collection, on reserve. Most of the collection was on open shelves in the stacks, arranged alphabetically by author in broad subject classifications such as English, history, philosophy.[33]

Effective Use of Reserve Book Collection

If the system of handling reserves is to function smoothly and serve the needs of students and faculty, the following conditions are desirable:

1. Instructors should be asked to make sure that materials for required readings are in the library well in advance of the time classes begin. A form should be given to the instructor on which to list his readings for individual courses.[34] The form should request information on such matters as: (1) the name of the course, (2) the number of students likely to be in the class, (3) the author (surname and initials) and complete title of each book, (4) the date when the books should be ready for use, and (5) the date when the books may be removed from reserve.

2. Instructors should be required to send in their lists in ample time for the reserve librarian to assemble and prepare the books for reserve before assignments are made.[35] Out of every list which goes on reserve a certain number of books are likely to be in circulation, in the bindery, or where they cannot be readily found on short notice. Instructors turning in a list the day an assignment is made encourage a few aggressive students to hurry to the library to charge out the books before they are placed on reserve. These books have to be recalled and it is natural that the students who were so prompt in getting them out will be reluctant and somewhat slow about returning them. The result is that the remainder of the class is often compelled to miss the reading assignment because of the instructor's tardiness.

3. Instructors should be encouraged to distinguish on their reserve lists between the books they require their students to read and those they suggest for supplementary reading. The reserve librarian then knows what books are likely to be in greatest demand and can make every reasonable effort to see that sufficient copies are available to meet student needs. At the same time, he can arrange for a more liberal loan period for supplementary readings, if the instructor so desires, as an incentive to students to do more than the required readings.

4. The number of duplicate copies of books in demand should be sufficient to enable the students to do their required reading in the time allowed. Although formulas have been worked out for estimating the number of copies needed in relation to such factors as the number of students taking the course and the length of the assignment,[36] no solution to the problem of duplication has proved entirely satisfactory. Some libraries have adopted an arbitrary ratio of one book to every ten students taking a course. A number of librarians, reluctant to spend funds for duplicating books which they regard as impermanent at best, have set a maximum limit to the number of copies of a title the library will purchase. In other colleges the instructor has taxed the student for all or part of the cost of purchasing class duplicates. No single ruling will satisfy all needs, but it should be kept in mind in laying down a policy that reserve books are part of the instructional equipment of courses and that libraries have a primary responsibility in supplying instructional reading materials. The problem should not be avoided or evaded by dismissing reserve book service as a subordinate phase of library service to be supported on a starvation budget. If the library exists to serve the primary needs of courses of instruction and if the method of teaching requires the use of reserve books, then the library cannot escape its responsibility for making a liberal provision of duplicate copies to meet these needs.

5. The reserve book collection should be kept as free as possible of inactive reading material. Frequent studies of the use of books on reserve will help to reduce the number of books which are not read and which may more usefully be made available for two-week circulation in the general collection.[37] Where instructors have a habit of putting on reserve an unreasonably large number of books which are seldom used, the reserve librarian can do a great deal toward reducing the number by pointing out other methods by which these books can be brought more conveniently to the attention of students.

The arrangement of books on the reserve shelves should facilitate their use by students and promote the educational effectiveness of particular courses. Most instructors prefer to have their books for a particular course or group of courses shelved together. A common arrangement in open-shelf reserve rooms is (1) to group books by teaching departments, (2) to arrange them by course under each department, and (3) to alphabetize them by author under each course.

Beyond these major requirements for effective reserve book service it is somewhat difficult to generalize without entering upon a discussion of techniques which may not apply to more than a few libraries. One fact, however, stands out clearly as fundamental to the successful operation of the reserve book room —that no college library can provide effective reserve book service without the full cooperation of the faculty. Dr. Henry M. Wriston has clearly pointed out in his excellent appraisal of college library service that "reform of the reserve" book service lies as much with the faculty as with the librarian because "the entire institutional policy regarding courses, credits, and methods of instruction is reflected in the reserve shelves, their extent, and the rules governing their use." [38] The difficulties consequent to the provision of required readings for large numbers of students can be solved if the faculty understand what the library problems are and can be persuaded to give careful attention to the suggestions made above.

NOTES

1. Jesse, William H. and Towne, J. E. "The readers' division chief." *Col. and research lib.* 6:317-21, September, 1945

2. McCoy, Ralph E. "Personnel in circulation service." *Lib. trends* 6:43, July, 1957; McNeal, Archie L. "Ratio of professional to clerical staff." *Col. and research lib.* 17:221-2, May, 1956

3. "Standards for college libraries." *Col. and research lib.* 20:275-6, July, 1959

4. McCoy, *op. cit.*, p. 45-6

5. Bousfield, Humphrey G. "Circulation department: organization and personnel." *Col. and research lib.* 6:49, December, 1944

6. McNiff, Philip J. "Administration of circulation services." *Lib. trends* 6:18, July, 1957

7. Brown, Charles H. and Bousfield, H. G. *Circulation work in college and university libraries.* Chicago, A.L.A., 1933, p. 134

8. Geer, Helen T. *Charging systems.* Chicago, American Library Association, 1955. For each system, Miss Geer gives information on equipment used, charging and discharging, renewals, etc.

9. Helen, Sister. "Simplified circulation records for a college library." *Lib. jour.* 66:201-3, March 1, 1941; Tollefson, Horace A. "Reid scotch-tape tabs serve any size of circulation." *Lib. jour.* 73:181-2, February 1, 1948

10. Hood, Marjorie J. and Lyle, G. R. "A new system of book charging for college libraries." *Lib. jour.* 65:18-20, January 1, 1940

11. Peebles, Margarete. "Charge it, please." *Southeastern librarian* 3:65-6, Summer, 1953

12. Kilgour, Frederick G. "New punched card for circulation records." *Lib. jour.* 64:131-3, February 15, 1939; Hocker, Margaret L. "Punched-card charging system for a small college library." *Col. and research lib.* 18:119-22, March, 1957

13. Pratt, E. Carl. "International business machines' use in circulation department, University of Florida Library." *Lib. jour.* 67:302-3, April 1, 1942

14. Daniels, Marietta. "How it is done at Washington University." *Lib. jour.* 64:397-9, May 15, 1939

15. Birnbaum, Henry. *IBM circulation control at Brooklyn College Library: general information manual.* New York, International Business Machines Corporation, 1960

16. Parker, Ralph H. "Adaptation of machines to book charging." *Lib. trends* 6:40, July, 1957. The Council on Library Resources has announced plans for a study of circulation methods in all types of libraries in four areas: book preparation for circulation, registration, charging and discharging books, and processing overdue books—Library of Congress. *Information Bulletin* 19:369, July 5, 1960

17. Southern association of colleges and secondary schools. "Standards for colleges of arts and sciences and teacher training colleges." *Proceedings of the sixty-fourth annual meeting.* Louisville, Kentucky, December, 1959, p. 198

18. Wriston, H. M. *Academic procession.* New York, Columbia University press, 1959, p. 136-8

19. Woods, Donald A. "Weeding the library should be continuous." *Lib. jour.* 76:1196, August, 1951

20. Shaw, Charles B. "The college library and the individual reader in the community." *In:* Goucher College. *The college library in a changing world; a conference celebrating the opening of the Julia Rogers Library, Goucher College,* April 9-10, 1953, p. 34

21. Stickle, Nellie R. *Community service programs of selected liberal arts college libraries.* (Unpublished Masters thesis, Columbia University, 1951) p. 16

22. Miller, Marvin A. "Loan clientele of state university and land-grant college libraries." *Col. and research lib.* 6:38-44, December, 1944; Littleton, I. T. "Off-campus library services of universities." *Col. and research lib.* 20:301, July, 1959

23. Thornton, Eileen, Librarian, Oberlin College. Letter, June 29, 1960

24. Littleton, *op. cit.*, p. 301

25. Pilkington, Walter. "Liberal arts laboratory." *Lib. jour.* 85:51, January 1, 1960

26. Kozumplik, William A. "Why collect overdues?" *Lib. jour.* 76: 100, January 15, 1951

27. Pilkington, *op. cit.*, p. 51

28. Bauer, Harry C. "Circulation service and public relations." *Lib. trends* 6:58-9, July, 1957

29. Lansberg, William R. "Current trends in college reserve room." *Col. and research lib.* 11:121-2, April, 1950

30. Kuhlman, Augustus F. "How reserve book collections can be made effective." *In*: A.L.A. *College and university library service*, ed. by A. F. Kuhlman. Chicago, A.L.A., 1938, p. 104-5

31. Faison, Georgia H. "Teaching with books in a reference department." *Southeastern librarian* 7:19, Spring, 1957

32. Hill, Aubrey L. "Reserve books on open shelves." *Wil. lib. bull.* 5:621-5, June, 1931

33. Lansberg, *op. cit.*, p. 123-4

34. Ciolli, Antoinette. "Teachers, reserve lists, and librarians." *Wil. lib. bull.* 20:370, January, 1946

35. Gray, Gordon W. "Teachers, reserve lists, and librarians." *Wil. lib. bull.* 19:695, June, 1945

36. Helm, Margie M. "Duplicate copies of collateral references for college libraries." *Lib. quar.* 4:420-35, July, 1934

37. Beach, Robert F. "Some useful techniques in the reserve book room." *A.L.A. bull.* 33:186-7, March, 1939; Wriston, op. cit., p. 136-8

38. Wriston, Henry M. "The place of the library in the modern college." *In*: Wilson, Louis R. ed. *Library trends*. Chicago, University of Chicago press, 1937, p. 159-85

Additional References

Carter, Mary D. and Bonk, W. J. "How- and where-to weed." *Lib. jour.* 85:198-200, January 15, 1960

Dunlap, L. W. "Services to readers." *Lib. trends* 1:49-57, July, 1952

Hagerty, M. M. "Reserve book system; a positive view." *Wil. lib. bull.* 26:387-8, January, 1952

Hamlin, Arthur T. "College and research library contributions to adult education." *Lib. trends* 8:51-61, July, 1959

Jesse, William H. *Shelf work in libraries*. Chicago, American Library Association, 1952

Rift, Leo R. "An inexpensive transaction number charging system with book record." *Col. and research lib.* 18:112-18, March, 1957

VII

Reference Service

Dr. William Warner Bishop once defined reference work as the service rendered by a librarian *in aid* of some sort of study, the reference librarian as an interpreter of library resources, and reference literature as dictionaries, encyclopedias, almanacs, catalogs, compends, and other books held in the library for consultation. These definitions are practical though not exhaustive. They convey the general meaning of the terms *reference service, reference librarian,* and *reference literature* as used throughout this chapter.

OBJECTIVES

Reference work in college, university, and public libraries often seems the same; many of the books are identical, and to some extent the library patronage overlaps. But there are substantial differences; two of the most important will be mentioned here for the light they throw on the function of reference work in college libraries. First, it is important to keep in mind that reference librarians deal chiefly with undergraduates in college libraries and with graduates and research workers in university libraries. Some argue that this simplifies the problem for college libraries because, as they say, "undergraduates read under relatively strict direction," whereas "graduate students are left to their own resources—and such help as they can get from the librarians." Others feel that the reverse is true. They point out that the graduate student has the assistance of his instructor, who advises as to the literature of his special field, and that he naturally turns to his instructor for advice as he proceeds rather than to a reference librarian. The undergraduate, on the other hand, is much more likely to look to the reference librarian as a source of help in time of trouble. He comes to college a shy and self-conscious youth, often with little confidence in his own ability and greatly in awe of the machinery of academic life. Because of the size of freshman classes, his personal relationship with the instructor is reduced to a minimum. He is nearly submerged in outlines and syllabi; he is confused by oral directions; and he is afraid to ask his instructor for further explanation for fear of making himself appear foolish to his classmates. If he can overcome this timidity when he first comes to the library, it is the reference librarian who becomes his confidant. Through a few moments of individual instruction in the reference room as occasions arise, either in response to questions from the student or through perceiving that the student is having difficulties in getting what he wants, the reference librarian can win his confidence and contribute to the future success of the library in dealing with him.

In the public library the demand made upon the reference librarian is for definite information for immediate use; the patron is seldom interested in learning the process of acquiring information by and for himself. The college student may make the same demand for immediate delivery, and there are times when he should be given the precise information he wants—instantly. In general, however, it is the duty of the reference librarian to help the student learn how to find the material himself; it is part of his teaching function to cooperate in training the student to use his own talents and energies. All this is possible in the college library. The student body is relatively stable. It is possible to build each year on the work of the previous year. And the questions asked are in part, at least, a repetition.

It goes without saying that the reference service of the college library is intended to meet the needs of faculty and administrators as well as students. Beyond this, if called upon, most college libraries are willing to share their books and services with scholars outside the college family and with non-academic users in the community who have a serious purpose and whose needs cannot be met by other local library resources.[1] In working with all these groups—students, faculty, administrators, and outsiders—the reference purpose is to (1) provide answers to inquiries requiring specific information, (2) teach students to use the library, (3) provide bibliographical and other research assistance, and (4) locate and make available less commonly used materials not in the college library. These functions are considered below in relation to the groups to be served following a brief discussion of organization and personnel in reference work. The selection of reference books is discussed in the chapters on book selection and acquisition; instruction in the use of the library is dealt with in the next chapter.

ORGANIZATION

In reviewing the history of reference work in research libraries from 1875 to 1940, Dr. Samuel Rothstein shows clearly how reference service developed from the very simple efforts of helping readers, often discouraged by administrators and faculty, and how the public library, which was the initial agent in personal assistance, set the pattern for such service. By the turn of the century librarians were recommending the appointment of special assistants for "the work of answering questions" and by 1915 "reference work was ordinarily accepted as a necessary service of the individual library and in many cases invested with the prestige of departmental status." [2] Unfortunately, the college library lagged behind. Even today there is a good deal of vagueness in the minds of college administrators and faculty members about the purpose and importance of reference work. A major difficulty seems to be one of interpretation. In 1938 only thirty-five out of three hundred college libraries had a reference librarian and fewer still had a reference department. [3] The picture is better today but reference service is still not supported on a par with cataloging and circulation services in the college library.

The organization of reference service in the college library varies greatly. Among twenty-five leading college libraries, eight were found to have a separate reference department, six combined reference and circulation in a single department, and four made no special provision for reference service. Four others maintained reference service without departmental status. In small libraries the reference work devolves upon the librarian. This is not desirable because the harassed librarian can seldom devote more than a few minutes at a time to reference questions. In several of the larger college libraries the general reference service of the main library has been extended to subject fields by means of departmental libraries in art, education, and science. This extension foreshadowed the subject divisional plan in university libraries but few college libraries have the funds to employ subject specialists. The reference competency, however, that comes from long experience in working with a subject collection is well known. To retain this advantage and at the same time have a unified general reference service, some librarians have argued for staff specialization as a substitute for subject specialization. In an article which received considerable attention at the time of its appearance, the late Dr. Peyton Hurt of Williams College pointed out the requirements and advantages of staff specialization as a means of conserving the interests of the general reader and at the same time rendering service to the specialist.[4] It was his opinion that the reference librarian should become a specialist in the history and bibliography of a field, not through long experience as reference librarian in a restricted subject collection or through special subject matter training, but through systematic study of the literature of the field. In this way, he hoped, the advantage of specialization might be obtained without decentralizing the library's reference materials through the establishment of separate subject collections. There are good arguments for both points of view, but the more important consideration is whether specialization *per se* is a good thing for college libraries. There is little doubt that it has its place in university work where specialization is the rule and where the undergraduate, unfortunately, is often left largely to his own devices. In a college library, the undergraduate is all-important and help can be given far more effectively if the reference librarian has the breadth of knowledge and human understanding to feel a real interest in the inquirer's needs. Narrow concentration in a field does not necessarily contribute to this ideal. While it is proper and undoubtedly important that the reference librarian have special interests—a diversity of interest is all to the good—a concentration of study in one field may impair his understanding of undergraduate students.

The extensive use made of periodicals in college library work has a further bearing on the organization of reference service. In most colleges this material is ordered, cataloged, and made available in much the same manner as books; that is, through the facilities of the order, catalog, circulation, and reference departments. There are college libraries, however, in which all work with serials, including reference, is handled in a separate serials department or by a serials librarian. Because it is impossible to classify a reader's need in advance, the obvious advantage of segregating this special type of material is offset to some extent by the fragmentation of reference services and indexes. The student comes to the library wanting material about a certain subject; unless the instructor has unimaginatively standardized the process of getting material, the student is not particularly concerned in what form he finds it—whether the material he needs is in a book, a journal, or a government publication. If he is obliged to move from one area of the library to another because of the arrangement of materials and services, he may become frustrated and his initial enthusiasm for his subject may turn to discouragement. If it is physically possible to do so, a student working on a term paper should be able to find all his references in printed bibliographies, reference books, and periodical indexes at one place. In most college libraries the collections are not so large that it is impossible to have this arrangement, and the resulting advantages outweigh the claims of reference service from a separate serials department.

In addition to administering the conventional collection of reference books and indexes, the reference librarian is frequently called upon to organize and make available uncataloged collections of materials such as federal and state documents, newspapers, pamphlets, maps, and college catalogues. These are all important materials for reference purposes and they should be conveniently arranged so that readers can help themselves and the reference librarians can assist in the process when necessary. At the same time, if the burden of receiving, assembling, and arranging these materials is added to the reference librarian's duties, it is at least questionable whether the time involved might not be more profitably spent in assisting students and faculty. The important point to bear in mind is that the assistance given to readers in using the library's resources is a full-time job and that it should be assigned to a professionally trained librarian of superior ability. If it is most economical and convenient in the local situation to add the processing duties of special materials to the reference librarian's position, then adequate clerical assistance should be provided. Dozens of reference librarians can testify that their responsibilities are poorly defined and that the demand on their time for organizing materials and making up for deficiencies in other departments of the library curtails their work with readers. William M. Randall offered this pertinent criticism in his *The College Library*: "The task of bringing about a contact between the books and the students is left largely to the faculty of the institution and to the least mature and inexperienced members of the library staff." [5] The charge is still largely true. So long as the college is satisfied to leave the essential hookup between readers and books in the library to clerks and students at a circulating desk, the educational contribution of reference service can only be limited.

Staff: Qualifications for Reference Work

To fulfill the duties of reference service in a college library, and to rise to the level of the opportunities which this work presents, the librarian needs a somewhat formidable array of virtues. A scholarly quality of mind, broad general knowledge, and familiarity with bibliographical tools and with the methods of scholarship are essential. A good memory is helpful although one's memory can and should be fortified by a systematic recording of sources and a liberal policy of cross-referencing in the files and catalogs. Knowledge is not enough; on a par with knowledge and perhaps above it in helping undergraduates is human understanding, sympathy and patience in dealing with students, and an appreciation of the teaching function in reference work. Intellectual curiosity, imagination, and a sense of humor are desirable traits. Lacking them the reference librarian is likely to lose his sense of proportion and to emphasize the less important or unimportant details.

It is exceedingly difficult to describe the qualities of the ideal reference librarian; it is easier to point out the weaknesses of a poor one. The most obvious fault of the poor reference librarian is that he lacks intellectual curiosity and the kind of mind that would enable him to appreciate either the content or the methods of scholarship. He also lacks a certain thoroughness and persistence which go with scholarship. He has only a fair knowledge of bibliographical tools and library resources. In his hands interlibrary loan work is merely a high-grade clerical activity. While he plays up to persons who carry weight on the campus and goes to no end of trouble in their behalf, he is abrupt in dealing with students, a trait which stems from a lack of sympathy and patience. He is too quick in jumping to conclusions and often fails to get all the facts or to evaluate the ones he has. Because he holds a position where even a slight amount of personal assistance brings profuse thanks, he has no conception of his own shortcomings, no healthy uneasiness about the quality of his work.

WORK WITH STUDENTS

The task of the reference department in working with students is to (1) furnish information on all subjects, (2) give personal guidance in the use of the card catalog, bibliographies, abstracts, and indexes, (3) consult about term papers, theses, etc.—methods of finding material and bibliographic form, (4) instruct freshmen in the use of the library, and (5) supplement individual and class instruction by the preparation and publication of lists, bibliographies, and guides to collections, types of material, or ways of locating material. The reference and other books in the library's collection used in carrying out these functions are many and varied—encyclopedias, dictionaries, handbooks, almanacs, directories, atlases, biographical reference books, indexes, abstracts, national and subject bibliographies, union lists, guides to subject literature, and guides to library resources.

The kinds of questions classified as information or fact-type questions stem from class assignments, student activities, or the student's individual curiosity. A student comes to the library for the name of the man who invented the quadratic equation, another for a list of the hundred great books read as part of the curriculum of St. John's College, and a third for a map showing the boundaries of the Iron Curtain. Then there are information questions of a type which might be said to bridge the gap between reserve reading and the independent use of the library—the first groping among library catalogs and periodical indexes—questions relating to civil rights, price fixing, and the comparative population figures on trade unions in different parts of the world. Excluding inquiries concerning the location of specific reference books in the library, these fact-type and information questions constitute the majority asked by students.

The test of the library's usefulness in answering information and fact-type reference questions is the ability of the staff to see that students get the information they want or the knowledge of where to get it as quickly and precisely as possible. It is dangerous to generalize from a few instances, but it would sometimes appear that some reference librarians err in giving the reader more information than he needs or wants. These librarians suffer from an excess of zeal. In their desire to be helpful, they forget for the moment that the function of quick information service is to save the reader's time. Between making a display of one's ability to dig out information from any number of sources and referring the reader to a single source, even if it is only a newspaper clipping, it is usually better to choose the latter—if it answers the question. Too much help dampens the enthusiasm of the seeker after knowledge and wastes his time.

The assistance given to students in connection with term papers, theses, and other class assignments involving wide use of reference materials is probably the primary task of the reference librarian. The ideal student-library relationship in these circumstances is pictured by Abraham Barnett, librarian of social sciences reference service of the Purdue University libraries. He writes:

> The preparation for a library assignment ought to be characterized generally by an attempt to make the student see that in coming to the library he passes from the guidance of one benevolent intellectual authority to that of another—from the professor to the librarian—who is responsible for a distinctive part of his education. This kind of orientation gives a continuity to the experiences of the student, and his life in the library does not become a lacuna in his education.[6]

The librarian begins at the student's level, gets a clear understanding of his research problem, introduces him to the card catalog and periodical indexes, and then, as the search for sources proceeds, brings him into touch with more specialized bibliographies of the subject which he is investigating.[7]

Among instructors there is some division of opinion as to the extent of reference help that the librarian should offer to students, but this generally springs from a lack of comprehension as to the function of the reference librarian or failure to consult with the librarian.[8] The teacher works under a distinct handicap when the reference librarian is not familiar with the purpose of the class assignment; the reference librarian is limited in the help he can give students if the faculty does not require, appreciate, and use his knowledge. Faculty members can cooperate by making sure that the student clearly understands the assignments, determining whether the library has sufficient material on the topics assigned, emphasizing selection and quality instead of form and quantity, and providing the student with full and accurate bibliographical references in directing him to sources. The reference librarian, for his part, must help students to find what they want, and not find it for them himself. Often, it is true, it is much easier to find the reference for a student than to tell him how to go about finding it for himself, but if the reference librarian takes this quicker method, he is neglecting an opportunity to instruct the student, a duty which rests upon librarians no less than upon professors. There are no serious differences between reference librarians and faculty on the subject of the reference function which could not be quickly solved if the instructor came to the library to discuss with the reference librarian his student assignments, the availability of materials, and the kind of library use he expects of his students.

Individual instruction of students in the use of the card catalog is a daily task shared by the more experienced members of the circulation staff. For a large proportion of the students the classification symbols, scheme of filing, and cross-reference cards simply do not exist. Although it is expensive and frequently catch-as-catch-can, this kind of daily personal guidance is extremely valuable because it comes at a time when the student has a real need for the information. To supplement personal guidance and class instruction and to assist the student in helping himself, most college libraries prepare and publish a handbook which lists and locates the general periodical indexes, basic reference books, and special materials such as the document and pamphlet collections. The handbook may also contain brief hints regarding practical procedures in the use of these materials.

Reference work with students requires the full cooperation of all members of the library staff. The reference librarian particularly must recognize that he may sometimes have to sacrifice his own desire to be useful and the grateful thanks of an important teacher if the inquiry is one which can be more satisfactorily answered by another member of the staff. The circulation librarian must recognize that he can often save the time of the reference librarian for more serious reference questions by handling directly the simpler type of inquiry that comes up at the loan desk. The cataloger, when informed of the type of work being done in various subjects, must see to it that new books on these subjects are put through for the reference department as promptly as faculty "rush orders" for reserve. With college libraries open as many as fourteen hours a day and all too frequently greatly understaffed, the library is compelled by the logic of duty and necessity to organize its reference service as efficiently as it does the routines of its circulation department. Obviously, this implies a careful study of the periods when reference service is most needed, a policy of promoting the full use of library resources and personnel and not simply those labeled as "reference," and the assurance that students will receive some measure of expert reference help at all hours during the day and evening.

WORK WITH FACULTY AND ADMINISTRATION

In the division of the field of instruction that leaves the teacher the responsibility for initial suggestions, stimulation, and final criticism, Miss McCrum claims for librarians a special eminence in the knowledge and use of subject bibliography.[9] If it is agreed that an elementary knowledge of bibliography is essential to the expeditious and fruitful use of the library by undergraduate students, then it is the responsibility of the reference librarian to see that bibliographies are available and that the faculty know of their existence and special usefulness. For while the reference librarian can do much through personal and individual guidance to introduce students to bibliography, the faculty have the primary responsibility so to conduct their work that students will want and, if necessary, will have to use these tools in preparing term papers and bibliographies. The most useful index to bibliographies in the college library for the undergraduate and teacher is the card catalog, assuming that the user is familiar enough with its arrangement to use it intelligently. Between this simple and incomplete record and the exhaustive bibliographical guides for the researcher, the sources of knowledge of books are many and of varying kinds. If the subject is one of prime interest, the student or teacher may be fortunate enough to find in his college library a standard bibliography covering the field of his investigation. Examples of such bibliographies are to be found in every good college library reference collection, but they are not available in all subjects or even in all teaching fields; they are often difficult to discover, and they may —for the purpose of undergraduate student use—be unwieldy and insufficiently evaluative. From his first-hand knowledge of bibliography and student abilities and needs, the reference librarian can render both the teacher and the undergraduate student a real service by preparing and frequently revising critically annotated subject lists of the most useful practical bibliographies in each teaching field.

The necessity and importance of consultation between the instructor and the reference librarian about class assignments, term papers, and the like have already been mentioned. It cannot be emphasized too strongly, however, that the reference librarian is under a severe handicap without such cooperation in correlating reference service with instructional requirements. In the area of fact-finding and information questions, it might be supposed that faculty members and administrators would have less need than students for reference assistance. This is not necessarily the case. In the first place the administrator is frequently too busy to look up such information for himself, and in the second place both he and the instructor are without experience in locating all the information they require. The field of information is an immense one. Faculty members engaged in research frequently need help in answering questions on the frontiers of their fields where their subjects touch the content of other fields and where the sources of information are not clearly charted. In this category fall many of the odd, unusual, or out of the way questions which may involve the reference librarian in a long search.

There are, of course, many other reference services—many of a personal nature—which will help to promote a close working relationship between the library and the instructor. From his intimate knowledge of the materials in the library, the reference librarian may sometimes be able to assist an instructor in the preparation of syllabi and course outlines, not only in his own field but in related fields. An alert reference librarian can serve by preparing bibliographies on subjects committees are commissioned to study, such as curriculum improvement, counseling, and comprehensive examinations. A college president has emphasized the importance of the reference staff in preparing briefly annotated bibliographies of books and articles dealing with college education in general and has suggested that similar lists relating to teaching problems peculiar to specific departments would be a help. These are suggestive only. An energetic and resourceful reference librarian with imagination and a keen sense of purpose can extend the range of his services and assert himself to great advantage in regard to the needs of instruction.

WORK WITH NON-CAMPUS USERS

Many adults, libraries, business firms, and organizations in a community will have occasional need for reference assistance from the college library. The library has both defensive and positive reasons for providing such assistance. The defensive reason is that it is necessary to have good public relations, and college presidents take it for granted that the library will provide any service it can to promote favorable public relations. The positive reason is that the library recognizes its responsibility to scholarship generally even though it may not be able to draw the line between what is scholarly and what is casual among the outside pressures for assistance.

No one will dispute that the basic purpose of the college library is to supply the library needs of its institution. Therefore, the important principle in handling outside reference questions is to go as far as possible without permitting service on the campus to suffer. There will be questions for each library to ponder. Is the nature of the outside request trivial or serious? Has the user exhausted the resources of the local public library? Has he a special claim to assistance as an alumnus, a friend of the college, a visiting scholar from another college? Should teachers and professional people be given special consideration? The answers to these questions and others will not be the same in any two institutions because of differences in the local situation, but helpful suggestions may be obtained by studying the community service programs of other colleges.[10]

PROVIDING ACCESS TO MATERIALS NOT IN THE COLLEGE LIBRARY

Another quite generally recognized function of the reference service of the college library is the assistance it renders in locating and securing material which is not available in the college library. Significant alongside this and illustrative of the same type of assistance is the advice given to students and faculty about the location of special collections and the strength of subject fields in other libraries. Inter-library loan work is assigned to the reference department because the bibliographical tools which are used to verify and locate materials—bibliographies, indexes, union lists, library directories—are to be found in the reference collection.

If it is clear that no university or research library can supply all the library needs of its patrons, then obviously the college library with fewer books and smaller funds must of necessity depend upon inter-library loans for supplementing its collections. To be sure the basic book needs of most college libraries are similar but there is no way of calculating precisely what the faculty and advanced students will need to support modern scholarship. The flood of demands for research material may be controlled at the college level but it cannot be cut off entirely without risking intellectual famine. This is precisely what the framers of the 1952 *General Interlibrary Loan Code* had in mind when they stated that "interlibrary loan service *supplements* a library's resources by making available, through direct loans for a *short* period of time, materials located in other libraries and not owned by the borrowing library." [11] Excluded as types of material one library is not justified in borrowing from another are: "current fiction, *current issues of periodicals* (some libraries may be willing to lend current issues of foreign or little used periodicals) ; *inexpensive items currently purchasable* in this country; books for class use; a high percentage of books basic for a thesis. . .; current books for which there is anticipated *a recurring demand* in the borrowing library."

The 1952 *Code* represents a liberalization of inter-library loan rules of the past and, significantly from the point of view of the college library, widens the scope of lending to include not only "unusual books" intended to aid the researcher in advancing the boundaries of knowledge, but also materials "for serious study." In effect, this means that for the first time the *Code* honors loans for undergraduates where necessity and urgency indicate the need for such loans for advanced courses, honors work, or independent investigation. Further liberalization of the current *Code* has been made possible by formal or unwritten code agreements drawn locally for a group of cooperating college libraries or the colleges and universities of a metropolitan area.[12] If these more liberal policies are to prevail, it is important that the borrowing library recognize its responsibility in locating the most likely source where the material may be borrowed, scattering requests in order that one or two places will not be asked to furnish the majority of loans, verifying the title of the publication requested before borrowing, and supplying complete bibliographical information in accordance with the standard A.L.A. *Interlibrary Loan Request Form* which reduces both routine and supplies.[13] In order to carry out this obligation faithfully and well, the reference librarian needs a formidable array of bibliographical tools including trade and national bibliographies, union lists, directories, catalogs of libraries, guides to library resources, and other bibliographies. In handling inter-library loans he must be accurate and thorough, provide full information to the lending library, and make certain that borrowed materials are handled with great care. The reference librarian should also make available to the faculty a simple statement covering the purposes and main procedures in borrowing books on inter-library loan, indicating deviations from the main *Code* which local inter-library agreements permit.

In recent years the proliferation of material in photocopy form has brought a new tool to supplement and extend inter-library loan, and special provision for the borrowing of such material is provided in the *Code*. The reference librarian has the obligation to encourage the substitution of photocopy for the original publication in considering an inter-library loan, especially when the items needed are located in journals. Some of the larger libraries will no longer lend journals, a trend which is said to be increasing, and under these circumstances there is no alternative to buying or borrowing photocopy. Still another opportunity to utilize photocopy in the inter-library loan process is presented by the major microtext projects such as the *American Periodical Series, Early American Imprints, 1639-1800*, the dissertations indexed in *Dissertation Abstracts*, and others. "On a small scale, the libraries of New Hampshire, Maine, and Vermont are reporting to one another on their holdings, and the availability for interlibrary loan, of microcopy continuations and subscriptions to large-scale projects." [14] Most newspaper files are now maintained on microfilm and these, too, are available through inter-library loan.

Finally, in even a brief review of reference services in locating material not available in the local library, one may with advantage call attention to the service which the well-informed reference librarian can render in directing students and faculty to libraries whose special holdings and collections will meet an urgent and real need. Whereas the need for the *Posthumous Sermons* of George Crabbe (London, Hatchard, 1850) can be met through inter-library loan, the request for an unpublished speech by John Rutledge necessitates locating the main depositories of Rutledge material before the researcher can be advised where to go for his material. It is the business of the reference department to send the student, or more often the faculty member, to the right library.

NOTES

1. Hamlin, Arthur T. "It's up to college librarians." *Lib. jour.* 75:1458-61, September 15, 1950

2. Rothstein, Samuel. *The development of reference services through academic traditions.* . . . Chicago, A.L.A., ACRL, 1955, p. 29, 37 (ACRL monographs no. 14)

3. Fenton, D. M. "Reference librarian." *Jour. of higher education* 9:153-6, March, 1938

4. Hurt, Peyton. "Staff specialization." A.L.A. *bull.* 29:417-21, July, 1935

5. Randall, William M. *The college library*. Chicago, A.L.A. and the University of Chicago press, 1932, p. 54

6. Barnett, Abraham. "The professor and the librarian. . . ." *Liberal education* 45:243-4, May, 1959

7. Pritchard, Hugh. "Reference work at Amherst College Library." *Col. and research lib.* 14:172-3, April, 1953

8. Cheney, Frances N. "The reference librarian looks to the faculty." *Peabody jour. of education* 28:277, March, 1951; Faison, Georgia H. "Teaching with books in a reference department." *Southeastern librarian* 7:15-16, Spring, 1957

9. McCrum, Blanche P. *An estimate of standards for a college library*. Lexington, Va., Journalism laboratory press, Wash. & Lee University, 1937, rev. ed., p. 100

10. Rawley, G. R. *The public services of selected Texas college libraries in 1952* (unpublished Master's thesis, University of Texas, 1956); Stickle, Nellie R. *Community service programs of selected liberal arts college libraries* (unpublished Master's thesis, Columbia University, 1951)

11. "General interlibrary loan code 1952." *Col. and research lib.* 13:350-8, October, 1952; the 1952 code, reflecting successive revisions toward liberalizing inter-library loans since the 1917 code, was modified slightly in 1956 to include the final revision of the inter-library loan form. This latest revision appears in the *American library annual and book trade almanac, 1959*. N.Y., Bowker, 1958, p. 64-73

12. Wright, Walter W. "Interlibrary loan; smothered in tradition." *Col. and research lib.* 13:334-5, October, 1952

13. Palmer, F. M. "Interlibrary loan form; a five-year report." *Lib. jour.* 81:2167-9, October 1, 1956

14. Close, Virginia L. "Microcopy in the library." Dartmouth College *Library bull.* 1 (ns):9, October, 1957

ADDITIONAL REFERENCES

Bishop, William W. "The theory of reference work." *In*: Moody, K. T. ed. *Library within the walls*. N.Y., H. W. Wilson Co., 1929, p. 17-26

Cheney, Frances N. "Whither the general reference librarian?" *Southeastern librarian* 2:25-34, Spring, 1952

Hamlin, A. T. "College and research library contributions to adult education." *Lib. trends* 8:51-61, July, 1959

Hutchins, Margaret. *Introduction to reference work*. Chicago, A.L.A., 1944, p. 138-56

Jackson, W. V. "Specifics of interlibrary organization." *In*: Illinois University, Graduate school of library science. *Library as a community information center*. Champaign, Ill., Illini Union bookstore, 1959, p. 36-50

Knox, Margaret E. "The development of a staff for reference work." *In*: Illinois University, Graduate school of library science. *Library as a community information center*. Champaign, Ill., Illini Union bookstore, 1959, p. 137-51

Uridge, M. D. "Interlibrary lending and similar extension services." *Lib. trends* 6:66-86, July, 1957

VIII

The Educational Function of the College Library

There are three levels of college library use. All three are related to the type of curricular program, the method of teaching, and the attitude of the instructor toward the use of the library in his teaching. The first may be called the textbook level, the second the reserve book level, and the third the independent study level.

To get right down to bedrock, there is the college library that serves largely as a central study hall for students reading their own textbooks. This level of library service was characteristic of most library use during the first quarter of the present century and still flourishes today in more colleges than one cares to think about. The library is used as a central study hall mainly because the teaching program consists of lectures, textbook assignments, drills, and frequent tests. However complacently the administration and faculty view the spectacle of students crowding the reading rooms of the library, the fact remains that most of them are there studying their own textbooks and appear to have no incentive to use the library except as a refuge for quiet study.

When a required or an attractive elective course strays beyond the textbook, the library reaches the second level of service. At this level the library is called upon to put on reserve a few essential titles or a large number of titles from which students may select a few books to read. The required readings are duplicated in sufficient number to permit simultaneous reading by an entire class of a sequence of chapters from one or more books, less satisfactorily, of a single chapter from one or more books, or—least satisfactorily—of selected paragraphs from chapters of several books. Without definite data one cannot speak too firmly and finally about such matters, but it is probably fair to say that this level of use, combined with study hall use, characterizes the patronage of most college libraries today.

The third level of library use is brought about by the kind of teaching which is associated more often with the laboratory than with the library. For convenience sake it is referred to now and hereafter in this chapter as "independent library use." However it is called, independent library use is the product of the kind of teaching which goes on in the laboratory where the biology or chemistry student learns to work out his own problem, observing the processes of growth and reaction from the plants and animals and chemicals used in the experiment. Instead of listening passively to the classroom lecture, the student is lured into becoming an active participant in his own education, with the teacher simply serving as guide and counselor. In this type of teaching, the student comes to the library to select, sift, organize, and evaluate such information as he needs for the purpose of class discussion. The purpose here is not merely to give the student experience in securing information that is pertinent to his topic or problem but also to sharpen his power of discrimination and his critical faculty.

When the purpose is the cultivation of sensitivity and reflection, of analysis and judgment, rather than the inculcation of information and ready-made conclusions, the teacher and student . . . cut through the devices that protect them from thought and emotion and have recourse to books that encourage them to think and feel for themselves.[1]

The foregoing opinions are supported by the findings of two recent studies. In the spring and winter of 1954, Dartmouth College, which has one of the finest libraries in the country, made a spot survey of student reading in the library, dormitories, and fraternities and found that in the library "63 per cent of all respondents were *using their own textbooks exclusively*; 33 per cent were using library-owned books, of which two-thirds were Reserve-Desk books." [2] In the same year, Patricia Knapp was gathering data at Knox College for her dissertation on library use. Mrs. Knapp was interested in determining the association between borrowing and scholarship and between borrowing and the courses which stimulated it. In summarizing the results of her study in *Illinois Libraries*, she concluded that the library "functions in support of a minority . . . of the courses offered." [3] And with respect to independent library use, her findings indicated that only 10 per cent of the courses offered utilize the library in the fullest sense of the word. These studies support earlier findings mentioned in Branscomb's *Teaching With Books* and, in spite of their obvious limitations as single case studies, reveal a pattern of use which is not uncommon among colleges with similar curriculums.

The pattern of library use revealed by these studies makes it clear that students are neglecting the resources of the library because there is no adequate incentive for them to read beyond their textbooks and library reserve readings. One could, on the basis of the studies, experience, and the stated and implied obligations of a liberal educational program, generalize a bit further. He could predict with some assurance that any attempt to build an educational program dedicated to developing the maximum of independent student effort will require (1) faculty motivation of a kind that will inspire more students to work independently with library materials, and (2) adequate instruction in the use of the library and bibliographical tools. Each of these requirements deserves further explanation.

Faculty Motivation for Independent Library Use

As librarians know, there are a few faculty members in every college who actively engage their students in using the library as a kind of laboratory for learning "how to manage their own education." [4] These teachers know the library is an extension of the classroom and they expect their students to use it and to use it intelligently in preparation for discussions in class, seminar reports, and papers. For this kind of teaching, there must be a two-way flow of information between instructor and librarian, nothing startlingly new, but a conscious effort on the part of both parties to contribute as follows. For his part the instructor should:

1. "Know the library's resources and adapt his teaching so that the student has the chance to use them in pursuing the subject matter of the course." [5] Too often faculty members reduce library

effectiveness in instruction by being themselves uninformed regarding library resources and the means of using them.

2. Consult with and give effective direction to the student in the library. This is not the present rule by any means. No matter how intelligent the student is or what school he has come from, he needs library guidance. If faculty members will not take the trouble to come to the library, if they are not easily available for consultation, and if they are indifferent to their own potential utilization of books, then the "presence of a magnificent library on the campus is merely ironic." To use Felix Morley's striking analogy, "it is like an impressive power plant, equipped with generators that aren't hooked up to any transmission lines."

3. Make assignments for library investigation that are difficult but not too difficult—assignments which do not require an exceptional degree of ability and insight for the young student to do a creditable piece of work.

4. Avoid standardizing the method by which the student must acquire his material—"My instructor said I must use two encyclopedias, three books, and five magazine articles."

5. Make library problems vital and interesting to the student and not just a fruitless exercise in using the library as an end in itself.

6. Prevent students from selecting the same topic or topics which will result in their clamoring for the same library material.

7. Invite the librarian in an early meeting of the class to discuss general reference books and bibliographies if the students have not had instruction previously.

8. Consult the librarian on the availability of special materials (vertical file) and special collections (local history collection) that might be useful and available to students in their investigations; and

9. Urge students to seek the assistance of the reference librarian in learning more about special bibliographical aids pertinent to their studies as they proceed with their research. Many students hesitate to ask for such help; they seem to feel that the librarians are engaged in more important tasks. The faculty member knows his students in a personal way. He can make it clear to them that the reference librarian is glad to help them

when a real need arises. "It is possible to develop independent ability without wasting time and becoming profoundly discouraged." [6]

For his part, the librarian should:

1. Be personally acquainted with his teaching colleagues and know as much as possible about their characteristic methods of teaching.

2. Make himself familiar with the curriculum and keep informed about current changes so that he will have a clear conception of what needs to be done in the library in response to new curricular developments.

3. Remind faculty members on every occasion—in library committee meetings, in personal conversations, in library memoranda—of the varied opportunities for using library resources in teaching.

4. "Know what tools and materials the instructor is using so that students are not only given assistance in using them properly but encouraged to learn of other tools . . . that are not called for in the course. . . ." [7]

5. Bring new materials and library services to the attention of the faculty—through periodic acquisition lists, notices sent to instructors upon the arrival of titles they have ordered, notes on important library additions and services in the faculty or library bulletin, and personal contacts.

6. Make recommendations for improving the collections of primary and secondary sources needed for class discussion, reports, and papers; books which cut across the lines of academic disciplines; duplicates of key works used in discussion groups; new editions; gaps in journal files; etc.

7. Provide patient, studied assistance to individual students in using reference and bibliographic tools pertinent to their research.

8. Acquaint faculty with unique and unusual materials available in the library's special collections that might profitably be investigated by students in their research.

9. Provide the research student with an individual study carrel where he may bring together his own material with library books for the duration of his research.

10. Provide if possible a seminar room for advanced classes where it is necessary to use library books and bibliographies in connection with the class discussion; and

11. Bring together materials for an instructor, at least temporarily, when it will encourage him to involve students in library projects requiring the use of widely scattered resources.

A good many instructors use the library and many librarians respond to faculty needs in the ways indicated above but not in any complete sense. Their efforts are fragmentary and incomplete, and partial efforts are not enough. The independent use of the library cannot be accomplished piecemeal. "The program must be all-embracing, must include the whole of the teaching faculty and the whole of the library staff working together and informed of each other's activities." [8]

INSTRUCTION IN THE USE OF THE LIBRARY

In 1949 the writer expressed the opinion that "current practice in library instruction . . . still lags far behind what has been shown in tests to be necessary if students are to use the library effectively in their college work." Special studies, numerous plans, and many articles on individual library methods of giving such instruction have not solved the problem within the past decade, but they have contributed toward a clearer picture of what needs to be done. If students are to spend less time going to lectures and preparing for course examinations and more time learning for themselves in the library, as many administrators and college professors have recommended, then faculty members are going to have to abandon the too prevalent belief that all the student needs to know in order to use the library intelligently are a few facts about the card catalog and the *Reader's Guide*. To explode this fallacy one need only observe the library during the freshman term paper week. For the majority of students this is just a mad scamper at the last minute, a hasty and superficial examination of periodical indexes, with a harassed reference librarian devoting a few seconds to each student inquiry; it reveals a shocking uncertainty about the ways of getting at reliable information. Most of the students do not even ask for help; they are naturally reluctant to venture an inquiry when the librarian is so obviously hard pressed.

Instruction in the use of the library takes three forms: (1) introduction during Orientation Week, (2) instruction of new students in elementary library tools, and (3) instruction of upperclassmen in reference books and bibliography pertaining to their special fields. It should be kept in mind that no part of this instruction is complete in itself and that all three efforts must be supplemented by individual library assistance at the reference desk.

Orientation or Freshman Week

During Orientation or Freshman week students are given a friendly introduction to the library. Few librarians are wholly satisfied with this introduction; as one librarian has put it: "Orientation is useful, yes, but doesn't do all we hope." The usual procedure is to meet the students in small groups for a one-hour combined lecture and tour of the library. The purpose is to make the student feel at home and to give him a few simple hints on how to look up material in the catalog, how to find it on the shelves, and how to charge it out. The librarian or a member of the staff gives the lecture, which is often illustrated by slides and charts, and student library assistants or seniors experienced in library use conduct the tours. Some librarians offer more detailed instruction but this seems unrealistic during the rush of Orientation week. The time to give more detailed instruction is when the student is going to use the library. While the student is not likely to remember very much about his Orientation tour, it offers an opportunity to greet him personally and to distribute and call attention to useful information in the library handbook.

Instruction of New Students in the Use of the Library

Numerous studies have been made to determine the ability of students at various class levels to use the library, and the results show that many enter college, and not a few leave college, without having mastered the technique of using the library effectively.[9] The whole purpose of such instruction is to make the student as independent as possible in the use of the library and to develop his confidence and ability in locating information. It is intended to show him how to find quickly and easily bibliographical material, book reviews, material on a subject in periodicals (from the selection of the proper indexes and abstracting services to the location of the journal on the shelf), identify proper names (people, places, mythology, fictional characters, theories, associations), find statistics on various subjects, and locate pro and con material on a subject. Every freshman should receive instruction in the use of the library and many professors of the non-bookish type would profit greatly by sitting in on such instruction. A number of studies have been made to show how libraries are endeavoring to provide this instruction [10] and they bear out the general belief that it will not do to give a few lectures on this subject and expect that the student thereafter will know his way around the library. In connection with the instruction there must be problems which require the student to use the library intensively in connection with his course work so that he will become acquainted in actual practice with the possibilities of the library. To try to attain this aim in a few lectures is almost as ineffectual as trying to teach boy scouts how to make various kinds of knots without letting them handle the rope.

Of the numerous types of instruction now given by libraries almost all are variations of three specific methods: a lecture to all new students, sometimes combined with a tour; a required course for all new students; and instruction coordinated with one of the subject courses, usually at the time of a research paper. The required course extends from two lectures, often with laboratory problems and tests, to a full semester course. When instruction is mandatory for all new students, screening tests are sometimes given [11] to check on the students' ability to use the card catalog, periodical indexes, and basic reference books. The fact that relatively few students are exempt from courses on the basis of such tests further confirms the need for instruction. Some type of practical problem or test accompanies almost every form of required instruction.[12] The usual method of lecture and discussion in presenting material is supplemented by film, slides, and television.[13]

The most prevalent type of instruction is that which is offered in connection with existing courses in the curriculum. It is fragmentary, unorganized, and inadequate, but it is hooked up with a definite class assignment and makes sense to both the instructor and the student. Most commonly the instruction is given in the required freshman course in English and is timed to coincide with the student's need to use the library for his first research paper. The instruction usually consists of one or two lectures by the librarian or the instructor to each of the freshman English sections. Sometimes it is supplemented by displays of the principal tools and bibliographies of sources. Occasionally instruction is given in some other course such as history or speech but wherever it occurs it usually falls to the librarian to take the initiative and make the arrangements.[14] One library reports an interesting innovation in which the reference librarian works with the history professor in class sections held in the library. The professor and librarian work together in showing the students how to use the library, introducing them to bibliographies in history, general bibliography, and the preparation of the written paper. If the experiment proves successful, it will also be used in beginning English and political science courses. Probably the most far-reaching plan of instruction which places the major work of instruction upon the faculty is the one advanced by Patricia Knapp in an article entitled "A Suggested Program of College Instruction in the Use of the Library." [15] One cannot help admiring the brilliance of this idea, but the odds against the librarian's being able to persuade the faculty to adopt such a program are unfortunately overwhelming. In its favor, one must also acknowledge that it gave the stimulus to a truly imaginative and yet practical suggestion made by Georgia H. Faison, the distinguished former reference librarian of the University of North Carolina, for joint faculty-library cooperative enterprise in a plan of instruction in the use of library and bibliographic techniques. Miss Faison recommends a threefold program of library use to the faculty: first, "a relatively short list of titles required of all students; second, a longer list of suggested readings, from which selections could be made; and third, a simple statement advising the students that additional material pertinent to the course could be found under specified headings in the card catalog and through the periodical indexes." The third approach would encourage independent library use. In further explanation she writes:

The idea behind this third section might be extended to the bibliographies, required of the students as appendages to their term papers, by asking each to cite subject headings, or other library aids that had been helpful in preparing the report. . . . As the student progresses through the junior and senior years, this third section would be expanded to meet his developing bibliographic and research needs. Should he choose later to enter graduate school, this acquired familiarity with bibliographic and library techniques would stand him in good stead, and supply a firmer foundation for the subject-field centered bibliographic courses of his graduate years. If his choice should be otherwise, his college life still would have been enriched through a broader and more independent contact with library resources.[16]

Instruction of Upper-class Students

The type of elementary instruction given to freshmen and new students is not adequate preparation for a senior or honors student making extensive use of the library's collections in a special field or writing a paper utilizing primary sources, government documents, and microtexts. In actual practice, however, it would appear that most students are expected to learn about these tools by using them. There are scattered references in the professional writings identifying some types of advanced instruction at South Carolina State College, Ohio Wesleyan, Harding, and Louisville.[17] Faculty opinion favors such instruction although there are marked differences among the views of instructors and departments regarding the nature and method of giving such instruction. From a sampling of opinion among sixty instructors in liberal arts colleges, forty-four (73.3 per cent) favored individual guidance and direction of the student by the major professor or faculty advisor. Less than one fourth recommended either an advanced course in library instruction (covering general bibliographies, subject bibliography, and research methods) or a separate course in subject literature or bibliography,[18] although a few instructors desired some aid from the librarian in instruction.

In attempting to discover how advanced instruction or guidance is actually given, the writer asked the librarians of twenty-eight leading college libraries about the practice in their respective institutions. Twelve of the libraries assumed responsibility for giving instruction in subject bibliography upon the invitation of the instructor. The librarians felt that such instruction was needed but that the proffered aid in special bibliographical instruction was seldom requested. Where there were large departmental collections, the librarians in charge were likely to be called upon to give a lecture or lectures in the subject field of their collections. The libraries of two colleges offered a formal course, one in chemical literature and another in educational materials. In a few departments the faculty were said to be giving individual student guidance in bibliography and research methods; three offered a formal course of instruction in chemical literature. Sixteen of the libraries offered no instruction in library use or bibliography to upperclassmen; no library instruction of any kind was given by the faculty in twenty of the colleges. What seems obvious from these surveys is that present efforts at advanced library instruction are incomplete and fragmentary. Judging by expressions of faculty opinion, librarians are likely to secure a larger measure of faculty cooperation if they emphasize individual student guidance rather than a formal course in advanced library instruction or subject bibliography.

In concluding this summary of the faculty-library relationships and library instruction that are necessary in college teaching, attention should be called to the need for graduate schools to make better provision for the training of future teachers in library uses and potentialities. This need was voiced by Dr. Louis R. Wilson in 1940 and he and his colleagues subsequently published a syllabus which could be used as the basis of a graduate course on the college teacher and the library. In this syllabus, entitled *The Library in College Instruction* (1951), Dr. Wilson points out that the graduate instruction which students get in methods of research and in the preparation of their dissertations is not an adequate substitute for training in the use of instructional materials at the college level. This observation strikes close to the heart of the problem and deserves more serious attention by individual librarians, library associations, and graduate deans than it has received. Few of the young teachers who have graduated and entered college teaching since the publication of Dr. Wilson's syllabus have had a really skillful command of the basic facts and techniques of library use. Without this background for understanding library problems and methods, the future college instructor is handicapped not only in his ability to instruct students in the use of the library but also with respect to his own potential utilization of books.

From a discussion of the problems and probabilities of relating the library to the classroom, of instructing students in library use, and of inducing students to make more intensive and more independent use of the library, one may with advantage turn to some of the interesting developments of the past two decades which have strengthened the library's effectiveness in accomplishing institutional objectives. No attempt will be made to discuss basic services, which are treated in separate chapters in this book. Nor is it possible to cover all the subjects that might be discussed appropriately in this connection. The topics selected, chosen by the test of their contribution to educational objectives, include open stacks, improvements in library planning, a broader conception of library materials, library surveys, and library cooperation.

OPEN STACKS

Most statements of objectives in college catalogues focus upon general education, which, although interpreted variously, implies the attainment of some measure of organized knowledge of each of the major groupings of subjects—humanities, social sciences, and sciences. The library's basic relation to general education is well pointed out by Paul Bixler. "General education," he writes, "cannot take root unless the student is given the intellectual freedom to participate in choosing his own reading. The college library contributes to that freedom by providing open shelves— free access to books in their common, intellectual association." [19]

Free access or open shelves means simply that students get their own books from the shelves—that there is an absence of barriers between readers and books. The term is used to distinguish between two methods: the old, under which students selected books from the card catalog and made application for them at the circulation desk; and the new, that of requiring students to get their own books from the book shelves. Free access means more than simply letting students know they *may* use the stacks directly if they wish; it implies that the student must go to the shelves himself, and, by comparing books dealing with the same subject on the shelves, select from them according to his needs and interests.

In spite of this appreciative note on free access or open stacks, it would be a disservice to education if, as Dr. Garland Taylor warns, librarians were to encourage "the too naive belief that merely opening the stacks will induce the lazy and the incurious to make resourceful use of books." [20] Open stacks make possible the intelligent use of library resources. Whether these resources are used, however, depends on how well the faculty face up to their responsibility for encouraging library use.

IMPROVEMENTS IN LIBRARY PLANNING

Perhaps as much as anything else, changes in library building design and arrangement have enabled librarians to shape their services to meet teaching needs. These changes have come about largely as a result of the mutual conferring of librarians, architects, college administrators, and faculty at library conferences and special meetings,[21] the strong emphasis given in library discussions and publications to the idea of the library as a teaching instrument,[22] and the example of flexible, open planning in many notable new buildings.[23] The library in the modern college merges reading space and book stacks. Students are permitted to move about freely and are provided with carrels, typing rooms, talking and smoking rooms, and other conveniences in addition to reading and study areas. Faculty are accommodated with private studies, conference rooms, and facilities for seminars. The whole program from floor planning to equipment is designed to improve the opportunity for bringing faculty, students, and books together in stimulating and pleasant surroundings.

BROADER CONCEPTION OF LIBRARY MATERIALS

There can be little question where the college library has a smoothly functioning audio-visual aid program, it has extended its contribution to instruction beyond what is possible with traditional library materials. Since World War II the role of audio-visual media in classroom teaching has greatly expanded. The use of these newer non-book materials has been encouraged by college administrators, and librarians have been urged to apply their techniques of acquisition, classification, and organization to non-book materials and to look toward centralizing audio-visual services in the library.[24] A survey of 575 colleges and universities in 1952 showed that "84 per cent of the reporting institutions had an AV service of some kind. Eighty-nine institutions (15 per cent) reported a centralized AV service in the library. . . . Decentralized services were reported in 302 (53 per cent) of the institutions. In 22 (5 per cent) of the reporting institutions, the library operated the largest AV service on the campus." [25] In this same study a majority of the librarians in all institutions generally believed that "the library should incorporate audio-visual materials into their service patterns."

Audio-visual materials are centralized in the libraries at Antioch, Carleton, Earlham, Goucher (slides, photographs, records), DePauw, Mount St. Scholastica (Kansas), and Southwestern at Memphis, to mention but a half dozen. In its program, Antioch offers such aids as film, recordings, tape, slides, filmstrips, and other graphic materials, but its principal classroom service is obtaining motion pictures. Its audio-visual librarian provides the teacher with informational resources for selecting film, and arranges a time and place for showing it. The equipment used includes various types of film, filmstrip, and slide projectors, record players, and television.

LIBRARY SURVEYS

College librarians have led the way in studying through self-survey the strengths and weaknesses of their libraries' collections and services.[26] They have not done this alone, of course, but have wisely called on all the specialized knowledge of the faculty for help in appraising collections. As a result of this initiative there has been considerable stirring in college circles about the role of the library in the college and more than a few deans and presidents have become concerned about the needs of the library and the means of improving its usefulness. Within the past decade certain of the regional accrediting associations have adopted a new program of evaluation in which the individual college makes a self-survey before the association sends out a visiting team to inspect the college. The library has figured prominently in this self-survey as well as in the investigation and report on the college and its self-survey by the accrediting association's visiting committee.[27] Librarians have been invited to participate with increasing frequency as members of the visiting committee. All of this has produced results which defy exact measurement but which have set dozens of college administrators and professors to thinking hard about the educational effectiveness of the college library.

Within recent years, many colleges have authorized outside library consultants to conduct intensive studies of their libraries. These studies have been made either as separate investigations or in connection with broader institutional surveys.[28] A number of these have been initiated by the board of higher education of the church in church-related colleges; others have come about as a result of grants for self-surveys by the Fund for the Advancement of Education and the other foundations interested in libraries. All of these have had as a primary goal the discovery of the steps that can be taken to bring about a greater use of the library in the instructional program.

LIBRARY COOPERATION

Every college library has demands for books and journals which go beyond the minimum required for effective teaching in the liberal arts range of subjects. The exceptionally strong college library can meet most of the needs of its faculty and students; the small college library may have difficulty in supplying even the legitimate demands of its users. In all cases it is plain that, in greater or less degree, the college library must be able to command resources beyond its own holdings.

The epitome of library cooperation among college libraries is to be found in the Hampshire Inter-library Center.[29] The Center includes among its cooperating members Amherst, Mount Holyoke, Smith, and other libraries within a radius of five miles and provides for direct faculty borrowing, generous inter-library loan privileges for students, cooperative purchasing of specialized journals, transfer of little-used materials, sale of unnecessary duplicates, and central storage.[30] It is the natural complement of all other types of library cooperation. Between this and the customary exchange of books through inter-library loan, there are many gradations of cooperation. It is not possible to establish a pattern because many factors such as geography, institutional restrictions, and the size and development of the libraries concerned control what can be done. But cooperation is a traditional characteristic of libraries and even among the smallest libraries it can take various forms. Cooperation in lending and borrowing books on inter-library loan can be extended within a region by group agreement to permit a more liberal policy of exchange than is provided in the *General Interlibrary Loan Code*. When there is more than one college library within a restricted geographical area, it will plainly be to the advantage of their respective institutions if all faculty and students are accepted as borrowers, with the understanding, of course, that each library will supply its own commonly needed materials. The extension of library facilities to visiting scholars wherever they may reside is a desirable activity. Frequently libraries within a region, state, or local area desire to facilitate inter-library loans through the publication of a union list of journals. The importance of this tool for locating files is so generally recognized that few college librarians would hesitate to contribute the record of their library holdings in joint bibliographical undertakings of this sort. Informal cooperation in buying can help to solve the problem of acquiring publications which are necessary but infrequently used, and can be rewarding when expensive sets of journals or large microfilm projects are involved. If cooperative purchasing of this kind is to be successful, the colleges must be located fairly close together. The procedure may involve simply a telephone call when major isolated purchases are involved or it can be a more formal arrangement, as when there are agreements regarding the purchase and holding of specific materials in various fields of knowledge. In a few cases college libraries have served temporarily as public libraries for the local community until such time as the public library service could become a reality. When both exist in a community, cooperation is possible in building collections and in direct service for specific purposes or groups. Quite properly there may be a division of the field or abstention on the part of the college library in developing collections in the field of local history, genealogy, or technical publications of use in community industries. While this is only a fragmentary treatment of cooperative projects, it should convey to the individual small college librarian some vision of specific ways, however limited, in which he might become part of the larger cooperative movement. Cooperation should not be thought of as a means of saving money. Like most good things, it costs a lot of hard cash. Its *raison d'être* is to extend the usefulness of total library resources to faculty and students.

NOTES

1. Arragon, R. F. "The relationship between the library and collegiate objectives." *In*: Fussler, H. H. ed. *The function of the library in the modern college.* Chicago, University of Chicago Graduate Library School, 1954, p. 10

2. "What is a library?" Dartmouth College *Library bull.* 1(ns):46, April, 1958

3. Knapp, Patricia. "College teaching and the library." *Illinois libraries* 40:832, December, 1958

4. "What is a library?", *op. cit.*, p. 47-8; for an example of the type of professorial technique needed to inspire students to make extensive and intelligent use of the library, *see* Clark, Edward M. "How motivate student use of the library?" American association of university professors *bull.* 39:413-20, Autumn, 1953

5. McDiarmid, E. W. "Library in the improvement of instruction." Missouri library association *quar.* 16:34, June, 1955

6. Antioch College. Kettering library. *Faculty handbook.* p. 6

7. McDiarmid, *op. cit.*, p. 38

8. Devlin, Eleanor. "Thoughts on freshman orientation." *Catholic lib. world* 29:27, October, 1957

9. Hurt, Peyton. "The need of college and university instruction in the use of the library." *Lib. quar.* 4:436-48, July, 1934; Feagley, Ethel M. "Teachers." *In*: National society for the study of education. *Forty-second yearbook.* Part II. *The library in general education,* ed. by N. B. Henry. Chicago, University of Chicago press, 1943, p. 303-6; Reed, Lulu R. "Do colleges need reference service?" *Lib. quar.* 13:232-40, July, 1943

10. Smith, Johanna B. *Library instruction in liberal arts colleges* (unpublished Master's thesis, Western Reserve University, 1949); Hughes, Mrs. Adrian. "Instruction in the use of the library in Alabama colleges." *Alabama librarian* 2:7-8, January, 1951; Copeland, L. Griffin and others. "Library instruction at the college level." *Florida libraries* 3:6, 29-31, March, 1953

11. Feagley, E. M. and others. *Library orientation test for college freshmen.* N.Y., Columbia University, Teachers College. Bureau of publications, 1955

12. See, for example, Ranstead, D. D. and Spencer, S. H. "Freshman library orientation program." *Lib. jour.* 84:152-4, January 15, 1959

13. Hale, Mary Y. "Instruction in the use of the library." *Tennessee librarian* 5:49, April, 1953; Bolander, L. H. "TV classroom on library techniques." *Lib. jour.* 80:2471-2, November 1, 1955; Williams, George L. *An automatic and continuous program of education in the use of library materials* (unpublished Master's thesis, Kent State University, 1951)

14. Sellers, Rose Z. and Ciolli, A. "A college library reports on its freshman lecture program." *Col. and research lib.* 20:474-6, November, 1959; Block, H. M. and Mattis, Sidney. "Research paper; a cooperative approach." *College English* 13:212-15, January, 1952; librarian and instructor cooperate in giving actual instruction at Beloit, Kalamazoo, DePauw, Vassar, Wellesley.

15. Knapp, Patricia B. "A suggested program of college instruction in the use of the library." *Lib. quar.* 26:224-31, July, 1956

16. Faison, Georgia H. "Teaching with books in a reference department." *Southeastern librarian* 7:19, Spring, 1957

17. Brice, E. W. and Copeland, E. A. "Elements of research and library instruction." *Journal of educational research* 45:293-8, December, 1951; Smith, Yvonne E. *Instruction in the use of the library at Ohio Wesleyan University* (unpublished Master's thesis, Western Reserve University, 1952); Hale, *op. cit.,* p. 48; Lewis, K. W. *A plan for instruction in the use of library materials to be given at the University of Louisville* (unpublished Master's thesis, Western Reserve University, 1955)

18. Withrow, Elizabeth A. *Library instruction for advanced students in the liberal arts colleges* (unpublished Master's paper, Division of Librarianship, Emory University, 1960), p. 28-30

19. Bixler, Paul. "Heart of the college." *Antioch notes* 30:no. 4. December 1, 1952

20. Letter from Dr. Garland Taylor, Dean, William Jewel College, Liberty, Mo.

21. Cooperative committee on library building plans, established at Princeton in 1944; continued by ACRL Buildings Committee institutes whose proceedings appear in the ACRL Monograph series. The Cooperative committee's work culminated in publication of John Burchard's *Planning the university library building.* Princeton, Princeton University press, 1949

22. Adams, C. M. "The college-library building." *In*: Fussler, H. H. ed. *The function of the library in the modern college.* Chicago, University of Chicago Graduate Library School, 1954, p. 62-73; Branscomb, Harvie. *Teaching with books.* Chicago, Association of American colleges and A.L.A., 1940; *A laboratory-workshop library for Princeton.* Princeton, The committee on the new library, Princeton, 1944; *The library as a*

teaching instrument. Iowa City, The University library planning committee, State University of Iowa, 1945; Wilson, Louis R. and others. *The
library in college instruction.* N.Y., H. W. Wilson co., 1951

23. Ellsworth, R. E. "Colorado University's divisional reading room
plan." *Col. and research lib.* 2:103-9, March, 1941; Metcalf, Keyes D.
"Lamont library; function." *Harvard library bull.* 3:12-30, Winter, 1949

24. Shores, Louis. "Audio-visual dimensions for an academic li-
brary." *Col. and research lib.* 15:393-7, October, 1954; Stone, C. W.
"The place of newer media in the undergraduate program." *In*: Fussler,
H. H., ed. *The function of the library in the modern college.* Chicago,
University of Chicago Graduate Library School, 1954, p. 94-9

25. Bennett, Fleming. "Audio-visual services in colleges and universities in the United States. . . ." *Col. and research lib.* 16:11-19, January,
1955

26. McCrum, B. P. "A college library makes its own survey plan."
A.L.A. *bull.* 31:947-52, December, 1937; Weber, D. C. "Criteria for
evaluating a college library." Association of American colleges *bull.* 43:
629-33, December, 1957; Lang, J. "Evaluating a college library." *Catholic lib. world* 31:91-5, November, 1959

27. Gelfand, M. A. "Techniques of library evaluators in the Middle
States association." *Col. and research lib.* 19:305-20, July, 1958

28. Jesse, W. H. *Survey of the library of Northwestern State College.
La.* Natchitoches, La., Northwestern State College, 1947 (mimeo.); Orr,
R. W. and Carlson, W. H. *Report of a survey of the library of the Texas
A & M college.* The College, 1950 (mimeo.); Tauber, M. F. and Jesse,
W. H. *Survey of the libraries of the Virginia Polytechnic institute.* The
Institute, 1949; Tauber, M. F. *Barnard College library; a report on
facilities and services.* Barnard College, 1954; Harwell, R. B. and Tal-
madge, R. L. *Alma College library: a survey.* Chicago, A.L.A., 1958

29. Thornton, Eileen. "Cooperation among colleges." *Lib. trends*
6:309-25, January, 1958

30. McKeon, Newton F. "College libraries working together." *In*:
The college library in a changing world. . . . Goucher College library,
April 9-10, 1953, p. 38-45

ADDITIONAL REFERENCES

Branscomb, Harvie. *Teaching with books.* Chicago, Association of American colleges and A.L.A., 1940

Conference of Eastern college librarians. *Library-instructional integration
on the college level.* . . . Chicago, ACRL, 1955 (ACRL monographs
no. 13)

Higher education in the South. . . . With a preface by O. C. Carmichael.
Chapel Hill, University of North Carolina press, 1947, p. 130-43

Johnson, B. L. *Vitalizing a college library.* Chicago, A.L.A., 1939

Johnson, B. L. and Lindstrom, Eloise, eds. *The librarian and the teacher in general education.* Chicago, A.L.A., 1948

Mattis, Sidney. "College library and the teaching process." *Journal of higher education* 23:313-18, June, 1952

Mayhew, Lewis B. *General education: an account and appraisal. . . .* N.Y., Harper, 1960

Wilson, Louis R. and others. *The library in college instruction.* N.Y., H. W. Wilson co., 1951

IX

The Encouragement of Extra-Curricular Reading

Before World War II a discussion on the topic suggested by the title of this chapter would have brought an immediate and enthusiastic response and released a flood of convention talk about the new browsing room, dormitory libraries, and prize awards for the best student private library. The inevitable complement in library objectives to supporting formal classroom instruction was the promotion of voluntary reading by students. Of course this activity took a little staff time and promotion, but most librarians considered it time well spent. Then at the beginning of the forties came a terse little volume entitled *Teaching With Books* in which Harvie Branscomb leveled a shooting iron at the extra-curricular reading efforts of college librarians and, as a consequence, won many of them away from the browsing room and its pretty cousins. The efforts of these librarians were henceforth directed wholly toward shaping the library program to meet the needs of courses. Rather recently, however, there has been something of a reversal of this trend of the forties. National Library Week, begun in 1958 and held annually since then, recognizes as one of its college objectives the encouragement of the student's use of the library and reading beyond the formal requirements of the curriculum. The American Book Publishers Council, through its Committee on Reading Development, has devoted increasing attention to projects of mutual interest to publishers and librarians in promoting the reading of college students. In 1955 the Council, in cooperation with Queens College, presented a panel of distinguished speakers on the subject of stimulating lifetime reading habits in college.[1] And in 1958, in an even more elaborate program sponsored by the Council on Library Resources and the University of Michigan, librarians, faculty members, and college administrators came together seeking ways and means to kindle in the undergraduate a lifelong enthusiasm for reading books.[2]

If these conferences signal a genuine concern on the part of educators with the problem of general reading—of students who are able to read but don't—it is difficult to see how college librarians can remain indifferent. The problem is not new, of course, and neither are the remedies, but if the renewal of interest helps to publicize the low estate of reading in this country and to clarify the basic reasons for this situation, then it will have accomplished its purpose. From the Michigan conference, librarians learn that only seventeen out of one hundred American adults were reading a book at the time of a sampling in 1957. At the same time in England, the figure was 55 per cent. Much of the weakness in American education stems from the lack of good reading habits at all educational levels. More encouraging, education is shown to have a definite relationship to reading and "the lifetime reading habit would certainly seem to be influenced by the college reading experience." [3]

What can the library do to promote lifetime reading habits in college? The solutions are no newer than the problem although one of the most recent proposals goes further than anything suggested heretofore in recommending a required course in extra-curricular reading for credit. The student would be expected to do all the reading he could on a subject that interested him, meet with his instructor or librarian supervisor once a week, and submit a list of his readings at the end of each semester. Grades would not be given but credit would. The program would be completely informal, but the student would be obliged to read extensively before he could graduate.[4]

One learns from the Michigan conference that, collectively and individually, the faculty have a great deal to do with extra-curricular reading. Colleges must create an atmosphere wherein student sentiment is increasingly brought to favor intellectual and cultural rather than physical and social activities. Courses must be shaped toward the stimulation of interest in outside, independent reading. The instructor is in large part the key to the success or failure of the library's effort. If he has what

William Dix of Princeton calls "a sort of world-almanac approach to books," the library is defeated at the outset. If, on the other hand, he is himself a reader and actively encourages the reading habit in students, then the librarian can do a great deal to assist in this effort. Some of the methods and plans libraries have developed to encourage the reading habit are discussed in the remainder of this chapter. The very fact that one talks about the reading habit implies that the student naturally and automatically turns to books and that he has a source of reading material from which he draws naturally and habitually—it may be his private collection, the college bookstore, or the library. For most of the students it is the library.

FREE ACCESS

If students are to turn naturally and habitually to books, they must be freely and conveniently accessible. Free access to books has been largely adopted, and delay in introducing a change so obviously helpful in encouraging reading has been due in most cases to the unsuitability of older buildings. But recent buildings, with few exceptions, have been planned to give a full measure of free access to books, with stacks and reading facilities adjoining so that students may move about the building freely and without any barrier between them and the books. Good lighting and plenty of comfortable chairs make browsing convenient and easy.

THE BOOK SERVICE

Finding the right titles to promote extra-curricular reading is important. Newton F. McKeon wants no pandering to popular taste. The general reader should be supplied with books that have meat in them. He writes:

In providing for the natural reader there must be no debasement or lowering of standards. Fastidious selectivity for this purpose is essential. But granted this, there must be attained, in so far as possible, a fine excess, a generous supply, various and full of possible surprises, discoveries, and delights, allowing full play for serendipity to operate, a plentiful show of the wealth and splendor of books.[5]

Intellectual austerity in selection, yes, but not too much of it for the beginning freshman or he won't become a reader. It does no good to make a student stretch his mind too much; a distaste for reading is sure to follow. Books should be chosen for their intelligibility to the general reader. Fortunately most librarians realize this position and agree with William Dix that "the college librarian . . . should go about cultivating the members of the faculty insidiously, even subversively, trying to convert them, if necessary, to the idea that one of their objectives is to make people want to read—want to read anything. The first thing is wanting to read."[6] Here one comes close to the heart of the matter. The student must first feel that the instructor wants him to read outside the specific requirements of the course and that it will be profitable to do so, profitable even for his academic record. And second, in the beginning he must be led to books he will enjoy; later he will learn to discriminate. A student of English with no concept of scientific method and thought can enlighten his darkness by reading Rachel Carson's *The Sea Around Us* or Heinz Haber's *Man in Space,* whereas the student of science can learn much about the history and achievements of artistic thought by reading E. H. Gombrich's *The Story of Art.* By their own interest in coming to the library to look over the books and current magazines, by their own example of broad general reading, and by their references to books in their class lectures, the faculty can demonstrate the value and importance of general reading.

The obligation in book selection to suggest the probable value of new titles of wide general interest rests primarily upon the library staff, but the faculty members should be encouraged to make recommendations. One library makes a regular practice of inviting two faculty members and two librarians to select the so-called "recreational" reading and rotates the membership of the committee each year. In this way professors of English, philosophy, and physics take their turn in selecting books of a general nature and later, in personal contacts and in class, share their enthusiasm with students. For many faculty members such a committee assignment is their first introduction to the general reading program of the library.

READING CENTERS IN THE LIBRARY

The efforts of librarians to encourage general and recreational reading are many and varied. One can see the process by examining the files of *Library Literature*, whose many references under books and readers suggest new solutions to old questions and unexpected solutions to new questions. The browsing room was a *sine qua non* in promoting general reading in the late twenties and thirties. Browsing rooms brought books out of closed stacks and placed them on open shelves where they might be examined in comfortable surroundings or be taken out for home use. At first the collections emphasized the standard works but later concessions were made and the selections included many works of travel, biography, literature, art, music, and fiction. After the first period of enthusiastic interest, the praise grew more restrained. By 1949 there were distinct rumblings of discontent, led by faculty members who felt that the overburdened syllabus did not provide enough time for their assignments, which were based on a different set of books from those displayed so attractively in the browsing room. Browsing rooms still exist in many college libraries,[7] but their most worth-while characteristics have been incorporated into the planning of new buildings or have been modified to meet new reading situations. Books and readers are brought closely together in the newer library buildings; as Dr. Warner G. Rice, English scholar at the University of Michigan, has observed: "Not least like our supermarkets are our libraries, spacious, inviting, fully stocked, and with everything neatly and accessibly arranged." In place of a special room for the display of the classics and older works, there is an alcove or room where the latest books are kept together for several months for the convenience of readers before they are shelved in the stacks.

A modification of the browsing room idea is to be seen in Antioch's "Core Collection" of selected curricular readings, new books, and reserve readings. This collection consists of about 20,000 volumes, selected by the library staff and faculty, of the "currently most used and important books broadly representing every field of knowledge." To these are added the new books and reserve readings. In order to keep the collection live, books which are least used are removed at the end of the year and placed in the stacks. According to the Antioch library handbook for faculty, the "Core Collection" serves a number of purposes:

> It affords readers an opportunity for "browsing"—but without segregating this type of reading. . . . It also gives the new student a collection of important but varied reading material within his comprehension. . . . Perhaps most important of all, the Core Collection includes on its shelves reserve reading alongside books for general examination and reading. It is the belief of the Librarian that Reserve Books have a very important role in teaching, but that they should not dominate student experience to the exclusion of other types of reading.

A similar attempt to combine "the virtues of the browsing function, which has been too little exercised, with those of the reserve-book system, which perhaps has been used too much" is described by the Educational Services Advisor to the library at Dartmouth. Describing the program as purely experimental, Alexander Laing hopes to encourage reading in connection with course work by providing, in the library's browsing room, a restricted collection of all the books on the general reading program of the first two years "so that each student can make an intelligent choice of the book which he will then secure, either by purchase at the bookstore or from multiple copies shelved in the main stack." [8] A similar service is to be offered in connection with the reading requirements for English 2. These books are shelved together in the browsing room instead of the reserve book room to encourage a more leisurely examination of titles and to enable the student to make choices better suited to his interest and taste.

The function of browsing is not confined in libraries to a browsing room or to a special tie-up between assigned readings and browsing facilities. It may be fostered by placing a shelf of new books next to the circulation desk, by book displays with appropriate posters related to matters of topical interest on the campus, by exhibits, by talks (by faculty members or others) which show students the value and the necessity of reading independently, by the influence and example of well-read professors and librarians, and most of all by the cooperation of these two "natural allies" in creating an atmosphere favorable to reading.

In this connection, there is the stimulating example of a professor of English who works with the librarian in the preparation of poetry exhibits and readings:

> For each exhibit which I prepare, the librarian and her staff schedule a coffee hour for students and faculty members. I generally speak briefly about the exhibit and then present a program of readings with the assistance of colleagues from the English department. A question period and informal discussion follow the readings. As an example, at the coffee hour for the exhibit called "Their First Books," Professor Conrad Schuck read a passage from *A Farewell to Arms,* a brief scene from *Our Town,* and a group of poems by Stephen Vincent Benet, William Vincent Sieller, Louise Townsend Nicholl, John Masefield, Langston Hughes, e. e. cummings, and Oscar Wilde. We have found that the question periods are as popular as the readings themselves and that students repeatedly request information about the writers. . . . I feel strongly that the library exhibits and the coffee hours have been largely instrumental in increasing the demand for the modern poetry course. I hope that the course has been partly responsible for the increased poetry circulation of the library. The professor of poetry and the college librarian are natural allies and collaborators in an important work.[9]

BOOKS IN RESIDENCE HALLS

Librarians are well aware of the fact that the provision of reading, whether required or voluntary, must take into account the conditions of student life. Time is ever at a premium on the college campus. The dormitory library is thought to be one answer. It is small, comfortable and informal, and immediately at hand whether the student has fifteen minutes to wait before dinner or needs relaxation before going to bed. "These are our 'browsing rooms,'" says Amherst's librarian. They are indeed, because they contribute to what the president of the Viking Press considers one of the essential requirements to developing the reading habit, "an atmosphere in which books—other than texts—are made as much a part of the student's life as they possibly can be."[10]

There are two kinds of residence hall libraries, the curricular type represented by the House libraries at Harvard and Yale, and the recreational reading type represented by most dormitory collections in colleges. Since the former are large self-contained collections found only in a few of the major universities, they

are not discussed here. While there is no up-to-date census of
recreational collections in college residence halls, such collections
are found at Allegheny, Amherst, Albion, Cottey, Washington and
Lee, Ripon, Williams, Vassar, Goucher, and Carleton, to name
but a few. When managed by the library, the operation of the
collections follows closely the arrangements described at Cottey
College:

> Each of the dormitories designed to house 100 girls is arranged
> in ten suites, each with a living room furnished with davenports, com-
> fortable chairs, tables, lamps, pictures, and a book case. . . . The library
> sends collections of books from the general library to the book cases in
> the various suites. The collections vary from fifteen to thirty books a
> suite. . . . Before the opening of school a member of the staff . . .
> selected the books with a few suggestions on the part of the librarian.
> When the second year students arrived, they were asked to come in and
> look over the books for their suites and make any additions or subtrac-
> tions they wished. Collections are changed twice a semester . . . [and]
> include short stories, poetry, plays, humor, fiction, and some biography.
> There are unabridged dictionaries in several of the suites.[11]

At Syracuse University, the collections vary from twenty to
forty books, and exchanges may be made monthly, or less frequently, according to the wishes of the students.[12] The collections
at Amherst range from nine hundred to two thousand volumes
and are purely recreational except for a few reference books.
The selection of titles is made by the faculty or library staff
curator who has full discretion in the handling of the collections.
In a number of colleges, perhaps most, the collections are managed independently by the students although the library may
assist in the selection of titles. At Carleton and Vassar, collections of fifty to a thousand volumes are selected by the librarian
and periodically inventoried. Paperbacks form the backbone of
the twenty-four cadet dormitory libraries at West Point. The
collections, numbering two hundred titles in each library, are
chosen by the library and faculty from *Paperbound Books in
Print* and are administered jointly by the library and the Special
Activities officer. The most popular titles are fiction, historical
novels, speculative and imaginative literature (Huxley, Orwell),
and science.[13]

Dormitory libraries have not met with unqualified approval.
Some colleges have tried and abandoned them because of lack

of interest, loss of books, and the thorny problem of caring for the collections. If library funds are not available for student supervision of the collections, then alternative solutions are to work through the dormitory counselors and hostesses or a student library committee and student hall presidents. In any event, students should be given as much responsibility as possible in the operation of the libraries. Even when the dormitory or fraternity libraries are independent student activities, it is desirable to have library or faculty advisors. Otherwise there is the danger that the program will become a haphazard, half-hearted operation built on a poor assortment of textbooks, gifts, and subscription sets. Nothing is better calculated to discourage reading.

ENCOURAGING STUDENT BOOK-BUYING

Further inducements to developing a genuine interest in and enthusiasm for reading are to be seen in (1) efforts to promote the reading and sale of paperbacks, (2) prize awards for student private libraries, and (3) library cooperation with the college bookstore.

Paperbacks

Some libraries have developed a system of presenting for sale to students and faculty a wisely chosen assortment from the multitude of excellent works now being issued in paperbacks.[14] There are mechanical problems but the assets are rich. Expert faculty help in selection may be secured; publicity may result from references made in the classroom. A teacher mentioning a title will know that he can send students to a convenient place to buy it. And what is of greatest importance, students may develop the habit of buying books. The instructor can tell a student he must buy a text but he cannot extend his demand any further. Many titles a student should really have to deepen his knowledge in a field, or to show the field at the border in contact with another, or to provide an original interpretation of some aspect of it, cannot be put on the required list. The assertion in class that such volumes are available in a library alcove or at the bookstore at a quarter to a dollar and a half may lead to an exciting response. If a student with even minimal interest will start reading F. L. Allen's *Only Yesterday*, David Reisman's *The Lonely Crowd*, or R. H. Tawney's *Religion and the Rise of Capitalism*, to mention titles in the three categories above that might have value in social studies, then the student is quite likely to go right on reading. There is the further possibility, of course, that he might buy books treating areas in which he does not intend to specialize, the scientist probing the seven lively arts in their ancient and modern guises, the humanist delving into some of the popularizations of the sciences.

Other colleges and libraries have different methods of stimulating the reading habit through book buying. A plan developed at Antioch is worth mentioning because it has since been followed by a number of colleges, although it is seldom reported in library writings. At Antioch, students are given an opportunity to buy library duplicates and discards at bargain prices at an annual auction conducted by the library. Several hundred volumes, drawn from the duplicate and exchange collection, are placed on display tables in the library for a week. During this time most students have at least one opportunity to examine the books and record their "names" and "bids" on the card attached to each volume. Bidding is left open until the library closes on Saturday. At times the "bidding is spirited," according to Antioch's librarian, Paul Bixler, and "there is often stimulated an informal discussion of books and their values which occurs in no other way." [15] And another librarian writes: "Library book sales of duplicates and surplus material are worth all the trials and hazards that may accompany them. Those libraries that promote them in divers ways—Minnesota, Iowa, Stanford, among others— are performing a service to the student body that can earn affection and respect for the library." [16]

Student Prize Awards

Swarthmore College was one of the first to establish an award to encourage student book-buying. Library awards are offered by Beloit, Carleton, and Washington and Lee. In other colleges such as Smith, Wellesley, and Randolph-Macon, the annual student library award is sponsored by the local or college bookstore, or it may be jointly sponsored by the library and bookstore.[17] A very large number of libraries have at one time or another found the means to sponsor an award from their own funds, from gifts solicited from friends, or from funds raised through a sale of duplicate books. All of these have been prompted by the idea that if students begin to buy and use their own books in college, they will discover the value and pleasure of reading and will be likely to continue to buy books after graduating from college.

There are various methods of arranging for the awards and of handling the details connected with them. The usual award is twenty-five to fifty dollars in cash or the equivalent in books, and it is common practice to have students nominate their own libraries for consideration in the contest, to have a local committee including the librarian sift the number of entrants down to three or four, and then to have outside and independent judges select among these.

After the awards are made, the best student libraries, in the opinion of the judges, are placed on exhibit in the library or at some central college place where all students may see what their book-minded classmates have developed in the way of personal collections during the college years. This plan undoubtedly makes students more aware of the importance of acquiring a permanent collection of books by the time they graduate; and the opportunity afforded all students to see the libraries adjudged the best provides a natural stimulus to the development of many good collections. In talking with the students about the contest, the librarian stresses that it is not the size of the collection that is important. It is rather the exactness with which the books fit into the interests and enthusiasms of the student, the high quality and content of the collection, and the quality of paper, printing, and edition that count in judging and make the award significant.

The number of entrants for the prize awards in different colleges apparently has not been very large, but students are reported to have shown considerable interest in viewing and criticizing the respective merits of the libraries judged; and some students, at least, have entered the contest another year under the stimulus of seeing what others have done.

Library Cooperation With the College Bookstore

Close cooperation has been established in some colleges between the library and the college bookstore in developing plans to encourage student reading. It may take one or more of several forms: the joint sponsorship of the sale of paperbacks, prize awards for student private libraries, or book talks. Regardless of whether there are formal or informal ties between the two, the college bookstore can be an effective force in creating an intellectual atmosphere on the campus if its function is not limited to selling textbooks. The cooperative Hathaway House Shop in Wellesley has 2,510 members, about half of whom are Wellesley College students. In addition to text and trade books, it provides a rental library and a rental collection of reproductions of paintings. The Macon Bookshop in Lynchburg, Va., maintains a stock of about one thousand of the higher-priced paperbacks in addition to many trade titles in general literature, history, biography, science, and religion. Although the Bull's Head Bookshop of the University of North Carolina is associated with a university rather than a college, one cannot neglect it in any discussion of libraries and bookstores. It is located in the University Library, administered by the Library, and operated on a nonprofit basis. Its many services include the sale of trade books and paperbacks, the operation of a rental collection, arrangements for faculty book talks to students, and the ordering of out-of-print books for individual customers. It is comfortable, inviting, and conducive to browsing.[18]

An interesting example of library-bookstore cooperation is reported by the University of Southern Illinois Library. Next to a display of a wide assortment of some two thousand paperbacks, the Library urges students by poster to build their own libraries from good paperbacks. If the student decides he wants a title, he fills out an order blank which is then checked by the Library before it is sent to the University bookstore. As reported in 1952, the sales from the beginning averaged more than one hundred a month.[19]

In summarizing the efforts of college librarians to promote the reading habit, one cannot, on the whole, offer a very encouraging picture. The fault may lie in the scarcity of worth-while published information about these activities rather than in the activities themselves. But one thing is certain. It is not going to be easy to foster the reading habit among the new generation of students. They come to college conditioned against reading by having lived all their lives in modern streamlined homes which seldom contain libraries. They come conditioned against reading by the tempo and technology of modern living which emphasize bustle and superficiality instead of reading and unhurried reflection. They come to college shy and self-conscious about books, and they are not likely to be influenced to read beyond their assignments with the conscious purpose of self-cultivation. Someone, perhaps it was Arnold Bennett, said habits which arrest development can be replaced by habits which encourage development. And as the habit of pipe-smoking is often developed after one reaches college, so the habit of reading can be developed if students are encouraged to think that this is the thing to do. It is important, therefore, that the library be capable of attracting not necessarily every student but most students, and that it should be their natural resort when they are not in class or when their time is not otherwise claimed. If the library is to attract, it must first of all be accessible on a well-beaten track; it must be capable of accommodating those whom it attracts in surroundings that are reasonably spacious, and comfortable above the norm for the campus as a whole. It must contain book-lined rooms where students can read poetry aloud and pontificate about philosophy to their hearts' content. It must have other rooms, also furnished with a good supply of the classics and moderns, where a student may read quietly and undisturbed, with plenty of elbow room between him and the next person. It must contain as many as possible of the amenities which are necessary or desirable for cultural development. It should be possible for a student, under one roof and in a pleasant atmosphere, to read quietly, to talk with others, to listen to a record by Beethoven or Schubert, to view a fine reproduction of a masterpiece of French impressionism, to relax with a pipe and a soft drink, to type an essay, and to view a documentary film.

Ideally, the student should be continuously reminded of reading, by professors and librarians as well as by his physical surroundings. Even the college president should place a few books on his desk to impress the students during interviews. The business of reminding students of the importance of reading is primarily the faculty's responsibility, and it is wholly their responsibility to give students the time to read outside their textbooks and assigned readings.

Notes

1. "Development of lifetime reading habits." *Wilson lib. bull.* 31: 452-4, February, 1957
2. The proceedings of this conference were published in a book entitled: *Reading for life; developing the college student's lifetime reading interest,* ed. by Jacob M. Price. Ann Arbor, University of Michigan press, 1959
3. Price, *op. cit.,* p. 4
4. Cadle, Dean. "Credit for extra-curricular reading. . . ." *Wilson lib. bull.* 32:216-17, 19, November, 1957
5. McKeon, Newton. "The nature of the college-library book collection." *In:* Fussler, H. H. ed. *The function of the library in the modern college.* Chicago, the University of Chicago Graduate Library School, 1954, p. 55
6. Dix, William. "Catching fire with a book." *Wilson lib. bull.* 31: 451, February, 1957
7. Thirteen out of twenty-four college libraries queried in the summer of 1960 reported having browsing rooms with collections ranging in size from 500 to 5,000 volumes. Among the 13 are Bowdoin, Carleton, Wellesley, Woman's College of U.N.C., Washington and Lee, Albion, North Texas State College, Allegheny, and Randolph-Macon. Four of the thirteen felt the browsing room made no contribution to promoting reading habits.
8. Laing, Alexander. "Reading programs." Dartmouth College *Lib. bull.* 2 (ns):2-3, October, 1958
9. Drew, F. B. "Librarian and teacher—allies for poetry." *Lib. jour.* 84:1562, May 15, 1959
10. Guinzburg, Harold K. "Educate students so they want to read." *Wilson lib. bull.* 31:450, February, 1957
11. Homes, Nellie. "The case for dormitory libraries." *Missouri lib. quar.* 11:29, March, 1950
12. Allen, Fern. "The dormitory library." *Lib. jour.* 76:920-3, June 1, 1951
13. Forman, Sidney. "Paperbacks at West Point." *Lib. jour.* 84: 1189-90, April 15, 1959
14. Hamlin, Arthur T. "Paperbounds in college libraries." *A.L.A. bull.* 52:32, January, 1958; "Shop Talk" (Hamilton College Library Self-service Bookstore). *Publishers' weekly* 163:211, January 17, 1953; "Operation paperback." *Lib. jour.* 84:1185-7, April 15, 1959

15. Bixler, Paul. "We sell books too." *Publishers' weekly* 138:111, July 13, 1940

16. Ready, William B. "Libraries and the refreshment of reading." *Col. and research lib.* 19:146, March, 1958

17. Schulenberg, W. E. "Student library contest." *Wilson lib. bull.* 26:168, October, 1951

18. Littleton, I. T. "The Bull's Head bookshop—a unique library bookstore." *Col. and research lib.* 19:471-3, November, 1958

19. Stone, E. O. "The encouragement of reading through ownership of books and book selection." *Col. and research lib.* 13:309-13, October, 1952

ADDITIONAL REFERENCES

Bontemps, Arna. "Reading and the college student." *Tennessee librarian* 12:9-11, October, 1959

Clifford, J. L. "Reading and the college library." *Col. and research lib.* 18:369-74, September, 1957

Gray, William S., and Rogers, Bernice. *Maturity in reading; its nature and appraisal.* Chicago, University of Chicago press, 1956

Hamlin, A. T. "Role of the college library in adult reading." *In*: National society for the study of education. Committee on adult reading. *Adult reading; fifty-fifth year book, part 2.* Chicago, University of Chicago press, 1956, p. 136-56.

Josey, E. J. "Encouraging reading by incoming freshmen." *Lib. jour.* 84:2571-3, September 15, 1959

Wecter, D. "General reading in a university library." *Harvard lib. bull.* 4:5-15, Winter, 1950

X

Personnel

The effective participation of the college library in the instruction of students in the use of library tools and bibliography, in defining and carrying out the objectives of the college in collaboration with the faculty, and in extending the use of library materials in education requires a well-qualified and numerically adequate staff of trained librarians. The position of the staff in library service is pivotal. The student body, faculty, and public using the library are peculiarly sensitive to its oversight, judgment, and enterprise.

SIZE

In addition to the head of the college library, the typical library staff consists of librarians and non-professional assistants, with considerable student help. Efforts have been made to fix the number in terms of enrolment, as in the case of the *Land-Grant Survey* which recommended five full-time trained librarians for the first five hundred students, ten for one thousand students, and four additional staff members for each additional five hundred students.[1] Obviously the number of staff members needed depends upon the work to be done. If the service is stripped down to the attendants needed to buy, catalog, and hand out over the desk the relatively few books necessary for class work, then the number is very small. If the library is to meet most of the needs and expectations of the faculty and students, then the number is much larger. A more scientific approach is contained in the A.L.A. *Classification and Pay Plans*[2] in which the size of the staff is based roughly on the service demands made upon the library. This service load is derived from a formula of service units based on the size and characteristics of the college's enrolment (underclassmen, upperclassmen, honor students, graduate students) and the size of its faculty. For the purpose of illustration, it may be assumed that a particular library's service unit load totaled 3,998 units. According to the A.L.A. *Classification and Pay Plans*, this library would belong in Class Four and would have a minimum staff of three professional persons for the first 800 service units, plus one more for each additional 500 units, plus the chief librarian. The number of professional positions in the example used, therefore, would be nine or possibly nine and one-half in full-time equivalent. The number of non-professional positions recommended in the report ranges from a minimum of 40 per cent of the number of the professional positions to a maximum of 60 per cent. Student assistants are counted in the non-professional group, in terms of full-time equivalent.

In the preparation of the A.L.A. formula, tests to insure its validity were made with a large number of institutions of varying types and sizes. In using the formula as a basis for estimating staff size, however, it is important to keep two things in mind. In the first place the recommendations are minimum. It is expected that average libraries and better than average libraries will exceed the estimates and requirements. In the second place it is recognized that no computation of a library's service load can be exact. It is claimed only that the method of determination in terms of service units is more nearly accurate than the older method of estimating staff size in terms of student enrolment.

One can scarcely write about the size of the staff without making some reference to the ratio between professional and non-professional positions. The A.L.A. proposal that the non-professional staff number 40 to 60 per cent of the professional staff is below Dr. Archie L. McNeal's later recommendation that there be two non-professional for each professional staff member in university libraries.[3] College libraries have fewer librarians, of course, and therefore fewer supervisors to teach non-professional workers. The median for 140 libraries of private colleges with enrolments of one thousand or more is five professional to six and one half non-professional, including student help in full-time equivalent.[4] It may be impossible to answer the question as to what the proper ratio should be in all cases or even to suggest a range as the A.L.A. does, but this is no reason why, with any given staff in any particular situation, common sense should not apply. It would seem desirable in view of the scarcity of librarians and the large amount of routine in library work for college librarians to take a sharp look at their positions and endeavor to bring the ratio closer to Dr. McNeal's recommendation. The best value of a professional staff member is secured only when he is free as much as possible from tasks which can be performed equally well by those without professional training.

PROFESSIONAL AND NON-PROFESSIONAL STAFF

The A.L.A. *Classification and Pay Plans* sets up two types of services, omitting sub-professional employees who are included in the public library classification plans, but combining student service with the clerical. Professional positions are described as "executive, bibliographical and those requiring contact of a professional nature with the public." Clerical positions are "similar to clerical positions in the business and other offices of the institution." [5] E. W. McDiarmid believes "the distinguishing feature of non-professional duties is that they are either (1) performed according to adopted practice and methods or (2) performed under the direction of someone who exercises judgment in deciding how they should be done." [6] This definition is helpful even though, taken out of context, it implies rather less confidence than is desirable in the ideas and responsibility of the clerical staff. Professional staff members have no monopoly on initiative and judgment.

The distinction between professional and clerical duties can perhaps be clarified by a specific illustration drawn from the field of cataloging.

Cataloging is a clerical task when it consists only of checking the volume in hand with the information from a standard professional tool, such as the A.L.A. *Booklist*, or Library of Congress or Wilson cards, and copying the appropriate entries in standard form. Original cataloging of fiction, when no classification number is used and no subject headings are used, may be safely rated as "clerical." Duplicating cards, typing headings and filing cards according to established rules are further examples of non-professional work. . . . The professional level is reached in cataloging when the work involves knowledge of the content of the material being cataloged in relation to an established system of classifying knowledge. [7]

The distinction between professional and non-professional work is far from being recognized in college library practice today. It should be underlined that the importance of the distinction is no longer a matter of status or even of improved library service. It is dictated by the stringency of the labor market. There are few librarians available, and good librarians cannot be secured for positions which involve a large proportion of routine work. Librarians must not only think of non-professional staff members for these positions but they must also plan for these intelligent non-professional workers a career which is more stimulating to them than ordinary jobs in business. They must be made to feel that their work is more than routine and that those among them who are college graduates and have real ability can look forward to performing most of the operational duties outside of cataloging and reference.

QUALIFICATIONS OF THE LIBRARIAN

In discussing the role of the library in higher education, Dr. Louis R. Wilson has this to say about the librarian:

The modern college exacts higher qualifications of its librarian than formerly. It no longer considers the possession of an A.B. degree and the completion of one year of training in a library school sufficient equipment for the librarian who is to become a successful administrator, a wise counselor in the use of books, and a force in shaping college instructional policies. It insists that the librarian must be a person of imagination and initiative, that he must have a sound understanding of library administration and some subject field, and that he must know how to relate the use of the library to the educational program of the college.[8]

The emphasis in this quotation is on the training, progressiveness, and mental attainments of the college librarian. One might add that if he is to be a leader in the college community, he must be a person of character, integrity, and professional idealism. Few enter—or should enter—the library profession to make money; ideals for the most part must be the determinant. These ideals include an unshakeable belief in the importance of books, an ambition to make books easily and conveniently available to readers, and a faith in the ability of librarians to share with others the task of bringing readers to books.

Administrative Ability

It would appear a truism to declare that the college librarian should have the qualities of a good administrator; yet so important are the librarian's instructional relations to the faculty that this

requirement is not so generally or so permanently borne in mind as it should be. Dr. Harvie Branscomb correctly states that the administrative problems of the university library are more complex than those of the college library, but it must be stressed that one of the best services the college librarian can render is to be a good administrator and leader in the library. It is essential that the librarian assume a large measure of administrative responsibility, including the supervision of the staff, the proper budgeting and expenditure of library funds, and the oversight of the library building. These functions require frequent consultations and close relationships with the president, business officers, deans, and department heads; and the librarian must impress them with his sound business judgment and ability to manage the library's affairs. He must also hold the confidence of the library staff by his ability to develop a systematic organization of library work, to conduct the many types of transactions involving the administration and faculty, and to administer personnel, budgets, and services in a satisfactory manner.

The qualities of the executive have been described in many books and articles. One of the best brief summaries for the librarian is given by Randall and Goodrich,[9] who state that administrative ability consists generally of four things: (1) the power to see clearly the significance and the implications of a problem; (2) the ability to analyze a known problem in such a way as to identify the important parts of its structure; (3) the genius to see the relations between apparently isolated facts and to grasp their combined significance and thus come to a conclusion; and (4) the capacity to secure cooperation from others. To attain even to an approximation of these qualities, the librarian first must understand thoroughly the objectives of the library in the particular college program, the functional organization of library materials, and the problems and needs of those he serves. One who has not the personal ability to work with others and to secure their cooperation will have difficulty in becoming an effective administrator, but he may improve his chances for success considerably by making a serious effort to understand the psychological factors involved in personnel relations. It is possible to take college courses which can be helpful in learning to work successfully with people, and there are useful books on personnel management and personnel administration, some of which are listed in the references at the end of this chapter. In the space available here it is possible only to mention a few of these factors briefly.

Mutual confidence is an important factor in satisfactory personnel management. If the librarian is to have confidence in the staff, he must first have confidence in his own judgment. "Indecision is fatal to good administration," write Randall and Goodrich, but "self-confidence must not develop into obstinacy." [10] Staff members respond to a librarian who will take responsibility; conversely, they are likely to be wary of one who hesitates because of lack of confidence in his own judgment or who tries to "pass the buck." Mutual confidence implies also that the librarian should have full confidence in the staff. The best evidence of his trust is the degree to which he is willing and able to delegate authority in work to be done. To be given a particular job to do and to have the satisfaction of seeing its final accomplishment is a great motivator. On the other hand, always to be doing something patiently as a subordinate and under constant supervision and checking, and to see nothing of personal accomplishment in what is done, has a very demoralizing effect. The librarian is also responsible for cultivating and maintaining an *esprit de corps*. In plain language, this amounts to keeping the staff informed of college and library policies and plans, discussing plans with the staff and securing their opinion, giving everyone on the staff a square deal in matters of promotion and salary, providing for the physical comfort of workers, showing appreciation of satisfactory performance, and being fair and impartial in criticism. Sometimes grievances and friction will show up in the staff for reasons which have nothing to do with the librarian's personal administration. It is then his job to determine the cause of friction and to eliminate it firmly and openly. He cannot hope to do this unless he knows each staff member well and has the courage to deal firmly with older and experienced members of the staff as well as with new members. One other factor merits careful consideration even in a brief summary. The attitude of the librarian in administration should be democratic. The greatest danger to satisfactory personnel relations and effective library service is illustrated by the librarian who is domineering, autocratic, and inconsiderate in handling people in subordinate positions. As President Mildred H. McAfee of Wellesley College once pointed out in a talk to college librarians:

It is easy to forget how really unimportant we are in our own right. A president has less reason for existence apart from the institution than the library does, but not much less. You know the danger signals for me and my presidential colleagues. While I was a teacher, I asked my college president for some advice about my office, and he said, "Don't bother me with that. That's what I hired you for." "I hired you"—a bad symptom when the college president begins to think of himself as the boss, his colleagues as his employees." [11]

The librarian is the one to take the initiative in formulating administrative policies, but he should see to it that his policies do not constitute dictatorship. Consideration for subordinates is not only essential for maintaining an *esprit de corps*; it is also the best way to secure good work.

Scholarly Interest and Understanding of the College Program

Practically all writers stress the importance of an understanding on the part of the college librarian of scholarship in teaching and research. It is no less important that he be personally acquainted with his faculty colleagues and with their characteristic methods of operation. Likewise, it is important that he be kept minutely posted on the current curricular and administrative policies so that he may have a sharp conception of the specific areas in which library support may be helpful. If he is not consulted and kept informed about curricular matters and administrative policy, his help in these matters will, of course, be negligible.

In speaking about the librarian's scholarly qualities, Branscomb, Russell, Parker, and others do not have in mind that he should be a scholar in the sense of an eminent specialist or research man.[12] There is one very practical reason why he cannot be. His work allows him no time for the continuous application to a single subject that is essential for the specialist. His working hours are long, he is interrupted at every turn, and his administrative duties leave him little free time. As a librarian, however, he should be familiar with the methods of research, have a thorough knowledge of bibliography, and be competent to assist readers in their search for information. He should also be widely read and well enough informed about the collections to be able to assist in their development. It is the librarian's ability as a bookman, indeed, that Dr. Lawrence Clark Powell prizes most highly: "Give us librarians who have an overwhelming passion for books, who are bookmen by birth and by choice, by education, profession, and hobby. Properly channeled and directed, this passion for books is the greatest single basic asset a librarian can have." [13]

In these days of increasing enrolments, rapid technological developments, and frequent self-examination of the educational program, it is important also for the librarian to be something of a planner and to be able to convey to his colleagues and staff a sense of the direction in which the library is moving. How can the quality of library service be maintained in face of increasing enrolments and librarian shortages? Which of the new technological developments offer opportunities for improving the library's service? What new projects are contemplated in the coming year? What hope is there that the library can secure resources to move ahead? Problems of this kind confront every library, and it is the responsibility of the librarian to be aware of them and to devise plans for meeting them if the library is not to drift along accepting limitations and moving in directions never consciously considered.

Ability to Work With Students

The ability of the librarian to work with students is a requirement so widely recognized by the profession and so frequently emphasized in the several chapters of this book that it calls for no extended mention here. One word of caution may be in order, however. So sharply have librarians focused their attention on faculty-library relationships that there is danger the librarian may not fully appreciate the fact that the library is primarily intended to be of service to students. The library fails to fulfill its function if the librarian doesn't know what students need, how their needs may be met, and what students expect of the library. His greatest asset in this connection is a staff that is sympathetic, understanding, and interested in working with young people.

All that has been said above with respect to the qualifications of the head librarian is, in varying degrees, applicable to the other members of the library staff. Since for most students the staff at the public desks signifies *the Library*, it is obvious that sympathetic relations between students and the library staff are of crucial importance in making a college library a real library and not just a storage house.

RECRUITMENT AND SELECTION OF THE STAFF

College librarians have been trying, without too much success, to recruit promising young college graduates into the library field. Studies seem to show that the gap between library school placements and the demand for librarians is widening. Low salaries, it would appear, are not the only adverse factor in recruitment. The shortage is also connected with the expense of securing a professional degree under the new Master's program, the opportunity for high-paying jobs in business and industry without training beyond the A.B. degree, the time involved in a fifth year of study for a library degree, and the trend toward early marriage and large families.[14] The low prestige of librarianship—true of almost any kind of work or position outside of classroom teaching on a college campus—has something to do with the difficulty of persuading young people of first-class abilities and qualifications to enter the library field. As in the case of teaching at the secondary level, there are few nonmaterial compensations for low salaries, low prestige, and little time for serious study and writing outside of one's working hours. It is seldom that adequate provision is made in the college library budget for staff travel, visits to other libraries, and attendance at institutes. Since most college libraries are understaffed, the competition for needed professional staff is severe and the winner is the one with the most money to offer. Wyman W. Parker would take exception to this generalization. He thinks there are dedicated people who feel that the intangible benefits of working on a college campus offset the librarian's low pay and somewhat anomalous status. He suggests that the best source for new librarians is the college itself and he looks to the "good and understanding professor and the enlightened and enthusiastic librarian" to use their influence in bringing newcomers into the field. He feels that more could be done to recruit librarians from among the ranks of (1) student assistants (if they are given "varied experience" and "opportunity for initiative" in their library assignments), (2) faculty members who are "not entirely at ease in their profession of teaching," and (3) businessmen who are "unhappy enough to get out or, at least, to contemplate an escape from the system." [15] To these one might add public school teachers, from whose ranks colleges and, especially, schools have drawn heavily for recruits to the library field. In recruiting from other fields, the librarian should be wary about what he is getting. Here it is well to remember Dr. Parker's admonition: "One must guard against the maladjusted, the floater, the failure and the flashy. Library work is too important these days to offer a refuge for the incompetent or a sinecure for the lazy."

There are many and varied suggestions for attracting new recruits into the library profession. Mrs. Kathleen Stebbins calls attention in her book on personnel administration to career days sponsored by librarians for high school students, the practice in business and industrial firms of sending out teams of recruiters to college campuses, counseling service by the college librarian, work-study programs, pre-professional training, talks about librarianship as a career, and more and larger scholarships.[16] Other librarians have reported on individual programs and on the factors which influence college students to become librarians.[17] There appears to be no one answer to this problem; but it is believed that many of the recommendations in the professional writings, particularly those relating to the personal contacts of the librarian with students, the provision of student assistant positions of a varied and challenging nature, and the organization of career meetings with small groups of juniors and seniors, will help to narrow the gap between the supply and demand for good librarians in the college library field.

No administrative duty of the librarian is more important than the right selection of the staff. Time spent in organization, acquisitions, cataloging, or reference service will be only partially effective unless the staff is well educated and competent. At the moment, staff selection is more a matter of getting than choosing, but even this is only half the problem; the other half is keeping the good people one finds. The usual procedure for getting names of possible candidates is to write to the library schools. Aside from the difficulty of securing names when so few graduates are available, a weakness of the library school recommendation is the emphasis which it places on the current graduating class. Seldom does one receive the name of a graduate of two or three years back when experience would often prove helpful in filling a position. Another limitation of the library school recommendation is the increasing frequency with which institutional personnel officers are taking over the placement services of the library schools. One cannot blame the library school for unloading this task from the rounded shoulders of its faculty, but the individual recommendation of a well-known and respected library school professor is worth more than a bushel of the multiple-form dossiers which emanate from college placement offices. For recruitment in the higher grades of service, the librarian may visit library schools for personal interviews, or he may seek contacts through friends in the library field or at library meetings. Advertising in library periodicals is becoming more common and is said to be helpful in locating prospective candidates.

The main requirements sought in selecting the staff are a liberal education and professional training, at least to the extent of the Master's degree in library science, although there are libraries which accept graduates of four-year colleges who have a major in library science. In a certain limited sense, professional library training is the more indispensable of the two main qualifications because most college libraries face numerous technical problems such as the re-examination of catalog policies and procedures, a complete overhauling of circulation procedures, or the development of acquisition procedures to take care of a growing volume of work. In a wider sense, a liberal education is a more important qualification. It is the belief of many librarians that no one can successfully conduct the business of a growing college library without library training and experience; but the most complete knowledge of library technique will not qualify a staff member to take his place in academic life, to mingle easily with members of the faculty, to keep posted on the current curriculum, or to have a clear conception of the specific ways in which library service may support the teaching program. The recommendations of library school faculties, supervisors where candidates have worked, and former college teachers with whom the candidate is well acquainted can be of inestimable value in evaluating these qualifications. It helps when the librarian knows the person or persons making the recommendations.

When the applications have been sifted down to the best candidates, the librarian may suggest an interview if distance and travel expense do not make this impractical. The chief value of the interview is the opportunity it affords to make some assessment of the candidate's personality. The academic and professional qualifications are primary but it is also desirable that the prospective employee have a stimulating and agreeable personality and be able to fit in with the library staff. This quality can best be gauged in an interview which, if properly handled, also affords the prospective staff member an opportunity to size up the new library situation and its staff.

The final steps in the appointment will vary in different institutions, depending on who exercises the final authority. Generally speaking, however, the process of selection is completed when the librarian's nomination is approved and the chief executive officer of the college has notified the candidate of his appointment to the library staff. The notification may be made by wire, but it should be confirmed in a letter stating the date of the appointment, the position, the salary, and whether the appointment is temporary or permanent after a period of probation. Ordinarily all first appointments are for one year only, with the hope and expectation that if the candidate's services are satisfactory and he or she is content the contract will be renewed. In one library, the librarian informs the candidate of his appointment immediately after a decision has been made, and states that the confirmation will be sent by the president of the college. This has the advantage of making sure of the services of a candidate who might be considering other opportunities, and it enables the librarian to confirm the arrangements regarding vacations and other matters which are sometimes omitted from the president's appointment letter. When the final appointment is made, it is common courtesy to inform the other applicants that the position has been filled. The librarian should also inform the library schools that an appointment has been made whether or not one of their candidates has been chosen.

After a library staff member has been appointed and comfortably located in suitable lodgings, he should be introduced to the college administrative officers, the members of the faculty, and his associates. He should be instructed in the general policies of the library and be given specific instructions regarding his special duties by the librarian or his immediate supervisor. Not only is the adjustment of the staff member to his position necessary, but he should be given a good deal of help, encouragement, and direction during the first few months of his work.

STAFF STATUS

When librarians speak of academic status they mean that the college should regard the professional library staff as members of the instructional staff instead of the administrative or clerical staffs. This status, says the Committee on Academic Status of the Association of College and Research Libraries' University Section, "may be defined as the formal recognition, in writing, by an institution's authorities, of librarians as members of the instructional and research staffs. The recognition may take the form of assigned faculty ranks and titles, or equivalent ranks and titles" with faculty privileges of "tenure, academic freedom, sabbatical leaves, equitable salaries, holidays, insurance and retirement." [18] The Committee further states that faculty status carries with it certain definite obligations for the librarian.

The first requirement is for intellectual activity, including a keen interest in the intellectual life of the campus. The librarian must accept responsibility for independent learning and continual intellectual growth. Next, the librarian must accept responsibility for educational statesmanship; his activity touches upon all areas of academic life. Status also calls for the highest level of professionalism in performance of his duties.

The librarian must be a creative member of the academic community. He performs an educational function and should be interested in research and publication to advance the frontiers of his profession, or in administrative studies which make a contribution to this advancement. He should be interested in professional organizations, and has an obligation for faithful service to his institution.[19]

What is the actual status of college librarians today? Are they given faculty status with rank or equivalent rank, social acceptance by the majority group, and the same privileges as faculty with regard to tenure, academic freedom, and retirement? A partial answer is supplied by a comparison of three general studies (applying to many institutions rather than to a particular library's staff program): Gelfand's 1949 survey of library staffs in 50 eastern liberal arts colleges; Lundy's 1951 study of faculty status for librarians in 35 representative universities; and Downs' 1957 survey, the most recent of its kind, of the current status of library staffs in 115 major universities.[20] In 1949, Gelfand's picture of the librarian in the academic community showed that faculty rank and status were accorded to 24 per cent of this group, although 72 per cent of the head librarians held faculty rank. In 1951, Lundy's study revealed that 40 per cent of the group clearly identified the library staff with the teaching and research staff. Another 20 per cent had accepted librarians into the faculty with various reservations and limitations, and about 40 per cent either regarded librarians as a special professional group or else had come to no conclusion as to the best method of recognizing the work of librarians. Dr. Downs' 1957 survey of librarians in leading universities shows that 54 per cent of the universities grant faculty status to librarians, with or without specific faculty ranking. In 35 per cent of the universities, the librarians are regarded as a separate professional group or as part of the administrative-employee class. Significantly, Downs notes that in 11 per cent of the total, in publicly controlled universities, the librarians came under the civil service regulations, although some top-ranking staff members in this group were exempt from civil service. While progress is gradual, it is evident from these general surveys that the trend is in the direction of giving librarians full academic status with most of the rights and privileges of faculty members. Even among librarians who are accorded faculty status, few receive identically the same salary, the same vacations, or the same sabbatical privileges as faculty members. Neither do all librarians agree that staff members must have faculty rank and titles to maintain a position of dignity and importance on the campus. Nevertheless, in spite of the diversity of opinion, more and more colleges and universities are identifying their library staffs with the academic group. It is perhaps more important in the college than in the university library because the staff belongs to a small minority group and the librarian may even be the only representative of his group. In the opinion of Dr. Downs, who has given more thought and study to this matter than most, faculty status will be achieved for all college and university libraries eventually and such status will help to create the best kind of library service to students and faculty. And, of course, he is fundamentally right, although to win and deserve it librarians must remember the obligations as well as the privileges that go with it. It should be further pointed out that all regional accrediting associations but one specify faculty status for the head librarian, that the Western College Association extends faculty status to the head librarian and department heads, and that the Southern Association of Colleges and Secondary Schools states that all members of the professional staff shall have "faculty rank, comparable salaries and privileges." [21]

SALARIES

Salaries in the professional group represent a serious problem in librarianship if colleges hope to attract outstanding people to their library positions. Only in recent years have significant advances been made and these have been mostly in beginning salaries. Since 1948-49, in a selected group of private college libraries, the salaries of the head librarians have increased 65 per cent, those of department heads 82 per cent, and those of all other professional librarians 80 per cent. In spite of these substantial increases, the median salary of librarians in non-supervisory positions amounted to only $4,667, and this group included many experienced librarians as well as beginners. The distribution is shown in Table IV.

Whatever its inherent attractions, the college library field will not draw good people and particularly young men to librarianship unless the remuneration offered compares favorably with that of the faculty. Table V summarizes the information obtainable for a comparison of faculty and library salaries for 1958-59. It is clear that the librarians are not receiving salaries commensurate with the faculty. Without suggesting that the equivalent ranking shown in Table V should hold in every institution, it is felt that the college should accept the principle that the professional librarian should not be paid less than the faculty, and that the one profession should not be less attractive than the other. Just as this principle has been applied in general in schools and in government service, so it is considered it should apply in the college field. The remuneration of the staff is one of the tests of the value attached by the college to its library service.

CONDITIONS OF WORK

Staff status and salary are two of the most important factors in employee satisfaction and performance, but there are other conditions also which have an important bearing on the staff member's attitude toward his work. These conditions include physical factors, library hours, hours of work, vacation, leaves of absence, and promotion and tenure. Each of these is discussed briefly below.

Physical Conditions

As a means of isolating and ranking certain factors relevant to the librarian's satisfaction with his work, a recent study investigated approximately one hundred catalogers in academic libraries and asked them to indicate their opinions on the importance of seventeen points. These points included such varied factors as status, salary, opportunity for advancement, interdepartmental cooperation, and a number of physical factors. Ranked in order of importance, the factors listed by the catalogers as most essential were: proper lighting, interdepartmental coopera-

TABLE IV

INCREASE IN LIBRARY SALARIES IN TWENTY-THREE PRIVATE COLLEGES WITH ENROLMENTS OVER 1000 *

(Median used for Librarian's salary; median mean for others)

Position	1948-49	1958-59	Per Cent Increase
Librarian	$4,500	$7,450	65%
Department Head	2,975	5,437	82%
All Other Professional Assistants	2,593	4,667	80%

* Source: *Col. and res. lib.* 11:151-63, April, 1950; 21:54-7, January, 1960

TABLE V

COMPARISON OF MEDIAN MEAN SALARIES OF FACULTY AND LIBRARIANS IN PRIVATE COLLEGES WITH ENROLMENT OVER 1000 FOR THE YEAR 1958-59 *

	LIBRARY		FACULTY		
Title	No. of Institutions	Salary (12 months)	Salary (12 months)	No. of Institutions	Title
Librarian	92	$7,476	$8,050	26	Professor
Department Head	74	4,950	6,330	25	Associate Professor
All Other Professional Assistants	82	4,500	4,670—5,610	23—27	Range of Instructor to Assistant Professor

* Source: *Col. and res. lib.* 11:151-63, April, 1950; 21:54-7, January, 1960; U. S. Dept. of Health, Education, and Welfare, Office of Education. *Higher education planning and management data,* 1958-59, p. 52

tion, cordial intrastaff relationships, sufficient and proper equipment, adequate working space, and clear demarcation of lines of authority.[22] The emphasis placed upon purely physical factors may come as a surprise to many college librarians but it is an indication not only of the importance of these factors in good staff morale but also of the deficiency of many libraries in good working conditions and modern equipment. The physical plant and equipment needs are dealt with in a later chapter.

Hours of Service

There is considerable variation in the number of hours that college libraries are kept open. The size of the staff, the number of departments to be staffed, and the student enrolment are factors which affect library hours. The latest survey of hours based on replies from seventy-eight liberal arts colleges with enrolments between five hunded and one thousand students puts the median number of hours at seventy-six per week. More than half the libraries are open on Sunday afternoon and evening. The most common closing hour during the week is ten o'clock.[23]

There has been a tendency in the past few years to extend hours in the university library, and many college libraries have followed suit. A whole set of pressures originating in large part because of unsuitable conditions of study in the dormitories, rising enrolments, and an administrative habit of accommodation in dealing with students, has tended to blur the distinction between proper library use and study hall use. As a consequence a number of college libraries have been told to extend their open hours until eleven at night or midnight. Under such conditions the quality of library service is bound to suffer if the administration has not also provided funds to staff the public service departments with at least one trained librarian at all hours the library is open.

Hours of Work

The hours of work of individual staff members should not exceed thirty-eight a week, although the latest study of college library working hours reveals a range of thirty-five to forty-eight hours. In a recent study 64 (42 per cent) of the colleges reporting have a forty-hour week; 126 (83 per cent) report a working week of forty hours or less.[24] If a thirty-eight hour week does not meet the library's need, then the librarian should seek additional staff and not overtax the present personnel at the expense of the quality of library service. Sunday hours are normally covered on a rotation basis with staff members allowed compensatory time off during the week.

This brief summary should not be interpreted as a recommendation for a fixed schedule of working hours for each librarian. The library has to be properly staffed at all times, to be sure, but if all contacts between members of the staff and the faculty are restricted to the circulation desk because of the rigidity of working schedules, it will be difficult to get the faculty to see the importance of the librarian's work except as a mechanical chore. Schedules are necessary to smooth library operation but it should be possible to allow some desk-free time to enable staff members to attend campus affairs and cultivate faculty-library relationships during working hours outside of contacts incident to getting books.

Leaves of Absence

1. *Vacation*: As in the case of hours of service, the length of vacations and leaves of absence for illness vary greatly in different libraries. In 1958 a study was made of these matters in 150 colleges accredited by the North Central Association of Colleges and Secondary Schools having enrolments between five hundred and two thousand. In this study all holiday time other than legal holidays was counted as vacation time. Forty colleges allowed four weeks' vacation or one month, and eighty-eight gave more than a month. Only twenty-two allowed less than four weeks, and nine of these were in one state.[25] Approximately the same results were obtained from an earlier study of vacations in medium-sized colleges and universities. In 1954, twenty-nine out of forty-nine libraries responding to a questionnaire said they allowed four weeks' vacation a year. Sixteen libraries allowed between five and eight weeks and four permitted only three weeks.[26]

2. *Sick Leave*: Colleges make few regulations about sick leave but make adjustments depending upon individual cases. In the study of North Central colleges previously mentioned, eighty-three libraries made provision for sick leave but twenty-two of these stated that no particular time was specified. In the same study, sixty-four libraries replied that no special provision was made for sick leave although many of these indicated that salaries were paid during illness. When definite periods of leave were specified, the amount of leave ranged from five days to six months. "In order of rank the most common sick leave periods . . . [were]: 15 days (18 colleges), 12 days (9 colleges), 30 days (8 colleges), 14 days (6 colleges) and 40 days (6 colleges)." [27] A majority of the colleges in this study did not permit sick leave to accumulate. Clerical sick leave is more frequently specified in college personnel regulations and provision for library clerks conforms to the general college rules.

Retirement

It is particularly important that the library staff participate in some form of retirement provision because salaries are not adequate to provide for old age or disability. The average age of compulsory retirement in colleges varies between sixty-five and seventy. In state institutions the librarian is most likely to participate in the state retirement and annuity plan which provides for contributions from both the individual and the college. In case of a move to another state or to a private college, the employee forfeits the state investment but receives a refund of his contributions plus interest. A second type of retirement provision is the Teachers Insurance and Annuity Association contract to which the individual college may contribute on a matching basis with the employee. If the contribution extends to 5 per cent of the annual salary and if the librarian is also covered, as is generally the case, by Federal Social Security, now requiring 3 per cent each on the part of the individual and the institution on the first $4800 of salary, this means that about 16 per cent of the gross salary is being set aside for retirement benefits. One great advantage of the Teachers Insurance and Annuity Association plan is its transferability, which makes it a permanent pension plan that continues if a person moves to a new position.

A third type of retirement is written with insurance companies on a group basis. The American Library Association has such a plan. In both these last two plans, contributions may be made separately by the individual or they may involve both the individual and the college.

The extent of college librarian participation in retirement plans has not been studied factually on a wide basis recently. In 1958, 137 out of 150 colleges reported retirement plans which included professional members of the library staff.[28] Most of these colleges were also covered by the Federal Social Security program. A much more comprehensive study published in 1950 for the A.L.A. Committee on Annuities, Pensions and Life Insurance found that "the professional librarian is eligible to participate in the retirement plans of about three-fourths of the institutions which have them for faculty . . . [and] in about 40 per cent of the institutions with retirement plans, library clerks are eligible to participate." [29]

Promotion and Tenure

The important consideration in promotion is the quality of the staff member's accomplishment, and this must be gauged by something more substantial than an opinion based on a few recent contacts or the general impression of a supervisor who always gives his subordinates the "benefit of the doubt." At the same time there is no place for elaborate service rating forms and management fact-finding reviews in the procedures of the typical college library which simply does not have the staff or time to bother with such procedures. Philip E. Hagerty suggests a periodic review and discussion of performance between librarian and staff and the keeping of a simple record of the review for the employee and the librarian's files. The only elements of work performance which should appear on the form are suggested below—with plenty of white space between the questions to permit the librarian to write down his impressions:

1. *Amount of Employee's Contribution.* How industrious is the employee? Is he a consistent producer? Does he do all that he is capable of performing? What does he need to do to increase his contribution?

2. *Quality of the Employee's Work.* Does the employee use approved methods? Is his work accurate and acceptable? Does his work meet the quality standard of the unit? How can the employee improve the quality of his work?

3. *Amount of Supervision Needed.* Does the employee follow instructions? Can he work without excessive help from his supervisor? Does he lean on others in the group? Does he obey or disregard the appropriate rules of conduct?

4. *Relationships With Others.* Does the employee work without friction? Does he aid or hinder teamwork in the group? Is he appropriately responsive to authority? How can the employee improve his relationships? [30]

Vacancies should always be filled by promotion from within the library if possible. Candidates should be sought outside the library only if no staff members are eligible for the position. On the other hand, if an employee is to fill a higher position in another department or phase of the library work, it is desirable to have him understudy the post to be filled for at least a short period. This may not be easy to arrange but it should be done whenever possible.

If the library staff has faculty status, then the tenure provisions of the faculty will apply to the librarians. A statement of tenure for librarians, adopted by the American Library Association in 1946,[31] sets forth principles which closely conform in substance to the 1940 statement of principles of tenure of the American Association of University Professors.[32] According to the latter a period of seven years of service gives the faculty member sufficient time to show his ability and also allows the institution to make a considered judgment of the individual's potential contribution. Some colleges adopt the time period and others award tenure only with the rank of associate professor. Both methods illustrate how difficult it is to establish a precise assimilation of faculty and library procedures. The turnover in library staff is so great that few staff members would attain tenure status on the basis either of rank or of a seven-year period of probationary service. Nevertheless some trial period is desirable and the college library should reappraise its staff at regular intervals. Following such a reappraisal it should be possible to promote certain staff members to levels in which permanent tenure is desirable: not all members of the staff may attain such tenure. The final appointment with tenure should not be given until it has become clear that the best interests of the library and the individual are served by his remaining a permanent member of the staff.

Dismissal

The customary practice of allowing a probationary period of employment of at least one year should provide sufficient time to judge whether a librarian or non-professional assistant is going to make good as a permanent employee. If there is some question about the staff member's ability to handle the work he is doing but not about his general ability, he should be given an opportunity to work in some other department of the library. If the staff member has been given every reasonable chance and it is clearly in the best interests of the library to terminate the appointment, he should be given the utmost consideration when he is informed of this decision. Most librarians would not make an independent decision on the discharge of an employee. Such an important matter would be discussed with the department head and perhaps with other senior librarians or members of the college administration. It is important that the staff member be given the opportunity to resign and ample time to look for a new position. He should be given a clear explanation of the reasons why his work is unsatisfactory. The librarian should offer to help him in securing another position but in so doing he should not be given a false impression of what the librarian can say about him by way of recommendation. These are the obvious elements of dismissal procedure. The department head and librarian who shirk their responsibility in this regard are doing a disservice to the library and to the staff member involved. It is not an unkindness to refuse to reappoint an employee if the decision is made early and if the employee is given plenty of time to find another position.

The Professional Development of Librarians in Service

There are a number of administrative devices for developing the ability and usefulness of staff members in service. Some of these matters are discussed under this heading. It should be emphasized, however, that no administrative device can remedy an originally poor choice or take the place of the librarian and senior staff in setting the standard for a type of service which shows pride in the profession, stimulates an imaginative approach to one's work, and fosters a sense of dependability and responsibility to the library users and to the library. What one librarian has to say about supervisory responsibility in administering a clerical staff applies equally well to the incoming professional staff:

> The supervisor is in the most sensitive spot. . . . It is the supervisor who sets the tone of the operating unit and who is largely responsible for the attitudes of its members. It is the supervisor who stimulates the cooperation of staff members toward the common good so that the task each performs is seen in its relation to the whole of the library. In the end, it is upon the supervisor's success in developing an attitude of identification with the organization, sound performance, and pride in accomplishment, that the goal of a stable, productive, and satisfied clerical staff will be achieved.[33]

In the college, which has few staff members, the key to success in supervisory work is the example of the librarian and senior staff members. They must make each newcomer feel that he is an important part of the library team, but he must also be made to realize that the standards are high and that success has to be earned.

Orientation of the New Staff Member

In any progressive library program, an essential feature is the practice of acquainting all new staff members with the policies of the college and of the library, with the general layout and special features of the library, and with the functions in the particular division of the library in which the new staff member will work. An important part of this induction plan is the emphasis which the librarian places upon the educational function of the library. An effort is made to give each newcomer an understanding of the proper approach towards aiding students in a way that will be educationally significant. The librarian also indicates clearly what the new staff member may expect in supervision. He gives him a sense of being accepted as part of the library team and he demonstrates the courtesy which will be expected of the newcomer in his relations to others. As a rule the new assistant in the college library is chosen for a particular position. If he is unable to make a proper adjustment to this position, he may be considered for some other work in the library, but if he fails there his service should be terminated. Whenever possible, the new employee is given some opportunity for experience in all or most divisions of the library's work, even though this may not last beyond an orientation period. The knowledge of what goes on in each phase of the library program is indispensable to good service in any one branch.

Staff Manual

Policies and procedures are numerous and varied in all departments or phases of the college library's operation. When the most important of these are codified in a staff manual, they provide an invaluable guide to the new staff member, to the student help, and to the department heads of the larger college library. The compilation of the staff manual is time-consuming, but no substitute will prove quite so satisfactory or efficient provided it is kept continuously up-to-date. Ordinarily, staff manuals do not prescribe the actions of the staff member in the instructional phases of his work which entail individual judgment and responsibility; the main purpose is to insure that policies, rules, and regulations are soundly based and understood by all staff members.

Staff manuals are usually of two types, the general administrative manual and the departmental manual. The former is a kind of "bible" for all employees, covering such matters as the organization of the library, major policies, procedure memoranda, personnel regulations, and general information. The departmental manual details the procedures in a specific department and is more likely to be found in the large college or university library. Copies of the administrative manual should be kept in loose-leaf form on every department head's desk and those sections pertaining to personnel should be given to all employees. Instructions for the preparation of manuals and their use are contained in numerous articles in the professional writings. Frequent revision of the manual is essential and a thorough index greatly facilitates its use.[34]

Staff Meetings

The staff meeting provides an opportunity for the exchange of ideas on procedures, services, and problems as they arise. For this reason, it is desirable to hold regular meetings, not less often than once a month, and to arrange a time when all staff members can be present. In the medium-sized and large college library, it may be possible to use library time for the meeting, arranging the schedule so that only one or two members are absent on regular duty, and providing for a rotation of work so that all members have an opportunity to attend most of the meetings. In one library the staff meets at a monthly luncheon meeting and follows this with an hour of business or discussion.

In addition to providing an opportunity for a free exchange of ideas on current problems of library administration and routine, the staff meeting furnishes the logical means for introducing new plans and procedures before they go into effect. The good administrator is interested in the promotion of staff discussion of all aspects of the library's work from a realistic assessment of present weaknesses to discussion of future policy. Such discussions not only provide a balanced consideration of all facts before decisions are made, but promote interest and *esprit de corps*.

If the staff meeting is to be truly effective as a means of improving librarians in service, some librarians feel it must concern itself with something more than the work staff members are doing every day and how they are doing it. Kenneth Gapp stresses the importance of using the staff meeting for a critical approach to librarianship. He points out that librarians have not yet formulated clearly a philosophy of librarianship in terms of educational objectives and corresponding activities. "The discussion with the staff of the main advances in professional research, of the development of techniques, of policy, and of educational objectives keeps alive interest in the newer phases of library service." [35] Another writer suggests that instead of general meetings small staff seminars be conducted by members of the staff who are enrolled in courses in the college.[36] Some of the advantages and difficulties of holding staff seminars for discussing the literature of special subject fields are described by a third writer.[37] Under the leadership of the librarian, several meetings during the year might appropriately be held with the president's and the librarian's annual reports as textbooks. Constructive recommendations of students and faculty might be considered. In some colleges members of the faculty and administration are invited to speak to the library staff on recent developments in their fields. Properly planned and managed, such a program might be a very effective method for improving personal acquaintanceships and communications, two of the major problems in wide areas of American academic life.

Low salaries, a schedule of relatively long hours, and frequent understaffing are three obstacles to the continuing education of the library staff. There is a fourth. Even under the best of conditions, librarianship has a tendency to become routine and largely automatic. There is routine work even in duties which are predominantly professional, and a great deal more of it in work that goes on behind the scenes. There is the ever-present danger that such routines will induce a sense of complacency and an acceptance of things as they are.

In the good college, there is a continual challenge to the librarian and the staff to make the library a factor of ever-growing importance in instruction. The librarian cannot meet this challenge if he permits himself or his staff to become too preoccupied with routine work. The librarian and staff must continue to grow with the college. Unless they are constantly on the alert mentally and imaginatively, they will not be able to develop a type of library service which is effective in teaching. In small colleges with limited staffs, the responsibility for stimulating professional staff interests rests largely with the librarian. In larger libraries, the department heads are more continuously in contact with the staff and it is up to them to set the example in showing an awareness of the need for continued growth.

Informal Methods of Continuing Education

The informal self-education program of the library staff consists mainly of reading, attending every kind of cultural entertainment, such as lecture and music programs, and participating in personal and professional meetings.

The importance of wide reading in professional and educational journals and books requires no special comment. New ideas, a better understanding of present practices, and an awareness of different points of view are some of the values that come from systematic reading. Some devices such as the routing of books and journals to each staff member, the allowance of library time for professional reading, and the provision for the discussion of professional literature at staff meetings have been found useful in stimulating professional reading.[38] Staff reading should not, of course, be confined to professional and educational writings. As a member of a college community, the librarian ought to read widely enough and deeply enough in the various fields of knowledge to be as well-informed as a non-expert can be. Lucy Fay and Louise Richardson in separate articles have each voiced the views of many librarians in emphasizing the importance of reading systematically in the literature of subject fields, and the former has suggested a practical plan for a staff group study program.[39] Hurt has outlined the most fruitful way to study the basic concepts of a particular field. His suggestions, stated briefly, are these: (1) secure a topical outline of the subject content of the field; (2) give brief consideration to the principal encyclopedic works; (3) locate and examine all guides to the literature of the field; (4) prepare a basic list of textbooks and other general works devoted to the entire field and examine some of the outstanding titles; (5) make a similar study of the books and monographs devoted to special phases of the subject; (6) give attention to the sources of printed materials, i.e., the learned societies, institutions, agencies, and individuals responsible for the production of the best publications in the field; (7) become familiar with the periodical literature and serial publications; (8) consider the pamphlets and ephemeral material; (9) make a thorough study of the reference books; (10) note the related fields having publications of interest; and (11) learn the current trends of research.[40]

If a member of the staff is interested in writing and speaking, he should be encouraged even if this entails some release from his scheduled duties. When a person writes or speaks, he submits his own powers of thinking and reasoning to public scrutiny. If he encounters criticism, he learns from that; if his views are accepted, this gives him an added incentive and an invigorating pleasure in his work as a whole.

Active participation in local, state, and national library meetings and inspection visits to other libraries are encouraged as two of the best means of improving staff performance and stimulating further study. The discussion of mutual problems which takes place at these meetings enables the staff member to visualize current practice, prevents staleness, and provides that continuous knowledge of what is being done which is so vital to a broad and progressive professional viewpoint. Much can be learned about current techniques from the exhibits at these meetings. Membership in learned and educational organizations may be of equal importance, particularly to the librarian, because such bodies afford stimulating contacts and opportunities to relate librarianship to scholarship and the broader field of education. Visits to other libraries, publishing houses, and binderies provide opportunities for studying specific problems in actual practice and afford interesting and valuable contacts. Attendance at institutes affords opportunities for an exchange of ideas when individuals interested in the same subject carry on discussions stimulated by the formal lectures or panels of the institute. Financial assistance for travel is highly desirable.[41]

Formal Study on Campus

Continued formal study, in service and during leaves of absence, is an important source of refreshment and reinvigoration. Attendance at classes while in service is one of the best methods of keeping the staff intellectually competent. It enables the staff member to remedy deficiencies in his own undergraduate training, to broaden his point of view, and to deepen his knowledge. From taking courses the librarian also learns much about the assignments and the classroom technique of individual instructors. This will help him to keep the library sensitive to classroom needs. Administrative provision for the encouragement of professional staff attendance at classes should include time off for the class meetings and free tuition.

Leaves of Absence for Study

While most colleges recognize the importance of leaves of absence for scholarly study and research, the trend is away from the traditional sabbatical, which came after each seven-year period of service, in favor of leaves based on specific project requests. There is little factual information in print about the opportunity for librarians to participate in such leave. In Boughter's analysis of staff benefits in 1958 in 150 colleges "56 per cent of the colleges indicated provisions for sabbatical leave, but librarians are included in only 47 per cent. Discrimination against the library staff regarding sabbatical leave exists mainly in private colleges." [42]

While few college libraries are sufficiently well staffed to permit leaves of absence without strain, it is customary to allow such leave without pay for continued formal study or for a particular project. If the librarian has sufficient initiative and ambition, he can secure some leave in addition to his summer vacation for an institute meeting or summer school study. Where sabbatical provisions apply, the normal procedure is to allow the full salary for a quarter or a semester or half-pay for a full year. In a number of instances exchanges have been effected between employees of two libraries, either in this country or abroad.

ETHICAL RELATIONS OF LIBRARIANS

There are two conditions which distinguish a profession from a vocation or trade. The first is the mastery of a special body of subject matter as a prerequisite for admission into the profession of one's choice and the second is an attitude towards one's work which subordinates monetary rewards and personal ambition, and, in its ideals at least, seeks to serve mankind. [43] A profession has a code which defines the relationship of the individual or group to society. Although vulnerable in several places, the profession of librarianship has sought to raise the standards of training of its membership and has set forth a code which suggests the responsibilities of the librarian to the governing authorities, to the public which the library serves, to the library of which the librarian is a part, to the profession, and to society at large. [44]

It is an excellent code and reflects great credit on the American Library Association and its leaders, but like all codes it has little meaning unless its members practice and enforce it. The question of ethics in general requires a great deal more emphasis in library school than it receives. In medicine this professional morality is not left to chance. Even in his medical training the student receives instructions about his duties to mankind and to his profession. When he graduates he takes the Hippocratic Oath. If in practice he violates his oath in any way, he can be expelled from the profession.

It is quite impossible to deal adequately with the subject of library ethics within the limits of this text but it may not be amiss to say a few words about the librarian's attitude toward his profession and his fellow librarians. This may be the place to mention the fatal spell which numbers seem to cast over so many good librarians. The misdirected efforts of those who endeavor to increase the size of their library holdings by letting down the bars of selectivity or by dubious methods of counting unconsciously start a chain reaction which hurts the entire profession. When librarian A reports a record-breaking year in acquisitions which doubles the figures of his neighbors on approximately the same book budget, the word soon gets round to the faculty and administrators of the other colleges. Pressure is put upon librarian B to change his method of counting or to add more rubbish so that he too can report that the year's acquisitions extend from Baton Rouge to some mountain peak in Alaska. The pathetic thing about these inflated claims is that they seem to impress the authorities more than the quality of the library's book selection and reference service. Moreover, the infection spreads rapidly from acquisitions to circulation figures and so forth. The same infatuation with mere size can lead a profession to overemphasize growth in membership at the cost of lower standards.[45]

In personnel matters, the professional librarian who has been delegated authority and responsibility for a specific phase of the library's work should exercise independent judgment and accept the responsibility which the position requires. This means that a department head not only exercises the privilege of recommending promotions for members of the department when they

are deserved, but also assumes responsibility for not recommending promotion or salary increases when they are not merited.
The department head should strive for harmony in supervising
the work of the department but this does not excuse him for
passing the buck when it comes to making decisions on discipline,
dismissal, vacations, and the like. The attitudes and judgments
involved in these situations are not mere matters of administrative efficiency. They go much deeper and involve the character
and integrity of the library supervisor and are closely identified
with the highest ideals of a profession.

With respect to the new staff member's attitude, it may be
mentioned without too much risk that good manners are an
asset. While older librarians are more democratic these days
than their forebears, this does not give the new librarian the
license to ignore their higher status entirely. It is good to be
warm and friendly in one's relations with other staff members
but the new employee should not feel compelled to make the
round of every department to relay the latest gossip. And it
should be remembered that when it is necessary for the order
librarian or the cataloger to talk to the reference librarian or
some other staff member in a public reading room, he should
do so in reasonably quiet tones. There are librarians who expect
readers to be quiet as mice but who burst into the reading room
and talk at the top of their voice. There are also librarians who
seem to have many calls upon their time outside—from associations, bridge clubs, and other private interests. No librarian in
his right mind expects the staff member to spend all his leisure
time working for the library or reading heavy books, but it should
be unnecessary to repeat that the library job has first claim upon
his time. No librarian who is a man as well as a librarian is
aghast at discovering that he has employed a genial and gregari-
ous extrovert, but the latter should be advised that the senior
members of the staff will take more kindly to him if he exercises
a little reserve in their presence. It is fine to cultivate as many
faculty acquaintances as possible on the campus, but this does not
excuse the young librarian for continued absences from the
reference desk when he is scheduled to be there. Salaries may
not be as good in the library field as in banking, but this does not
mean that the disgruntled librarian should go about the campus

speaking of the sacrifices he is making by staying in the library field. One is tempted to tell him to offer his talents elsewhere. One last word to the youthful librarian who may read this. When a department head or the head librarian raises a question about one's attitude toward one's work or about one's discipline in working with student employees, this is not the occasion for a display of hurt feelings. If one is to get anywhere in his profession, he must learn to take constructive criticism.

NOTES

1. U.S. Office of education. *Survey of landgrant colleges and universities.* . . . Bulletin 1930, no. 9, vol. I, part VIII, "The Library." Washington, Government printing office, 1930, p. 695-6

2. A.L.A. Board on salaries, staff tenure. . . . Subcommittee on budgets, compensation and schemes of service. . . . *Classification and pay plans for libraries in institutions of higher education.* Vol. II, Degree-conferring four-year institutions. 2nd ed. Chicago, A.L.A., 1947, p. xix-xxiii

3. McNeal, A. L. "Financial problems of university libraries." *Col. and research lib.* 15:407, October, 1954; Voigt, Melvin J. "Ratio of professional to clerical staff." *Col. and research lib.* 16:76-7, January, 1955

4. "College and university library statistics, 1958/59." *Col. and research lib.* 21:57, January, 1960

5. A.L.A. Board on salaries. . . . *op. cit.*, p. xv-xvi

6. McDiarmid, E. W. "Training of clerical and subprofessional workers." *In:* Berelson, B. R., ed. *Education for librarianship.* Chicago, A.L.A., 1949, p. 235

7. Wight, E. A. "Separation of professional and non-professional work in public libraries." *California librarian* 14:31, September, 1952. A very useful article adaptable to the needs of the college library. Provides a simple outline of a method for analyzing library tasks and suggests principles for classifying related tasks.

8. Wilson, Louis R. "The role of the library in higher education." *In:* Vanderbilt University. *The inauguration of Oliver C. Carmichael as chancellor.* . . . Nashville, Vanderbilt University, 1938, p. 58-9

9. Randall, William M. and Goodrich, Francis L. D. *Principles of college library administration.* 2nd ed. Chicago, A.L.A. and the University of Chicago press, 1941, p. 113-17

10. *Ibid.*, p. 116

11. McAfee, Mildred H. "The college library as seen by a college president." *Col. and research lib.* 2:301, September, 1941

12. Branscomb, Harvie. *Teaching with books*. Chicago, Association of American colleges and A.L.A., 1940, p. 86-9; Russell, John D. "Professional education for librarianship." *Lib. quar.* 12:775-93, December, 1942; Parker, Wyman. "College-library personnel." *In:* Fussler, H. H. ed. *The function of the library in the modern college*. Chicago, University of Chicago Graduate Library School, 1954, p. 75-8

13. Powell, Lawrence C. *A passion for books*. Cleveland, World publishing co., 1958, p. 122

14. Stebbins, Kathleen B. *Personnel administration in libraries*. N.Y., Scarecrow press, 1958, p. 23

15. Parker, *op. cit.*, p. 78-9

16. Stebbins, *op. cit.*, p. 25-31

17. There is a wealth of literature on recruiting. Among many good publications, *see* Reagan, Agnes L. *A study of factors influencing college students to become librarians*. Chicago, ACRL, 1958 (ACRL monographs, no. 21); Blackburn, F. M. "Recruiting for librarianship." *Col. and research lib.* 18:461-6, November, 1957; Dalton, Jack. "Recruiting for college and university librarianship." *Virginia librarian* 2:31, October, 1955; Bupp, Reno W. "Recruitment—university librarian's point of view." *Southeastern librarian* 8:95-8, Fall, 1958; "Library scholarships and fellowships." *In: American library and booktrade annual, 1960*. N.Y., Bowker, 1959, p. 187-8

18. ACRL University libraries section. Committee on academic status. "Status of college and university librarians." *Col. and research lib.* 20:399-400, September, 1959

19. *Ibid.*, p. 400

20. Downs, Robert B. ed. *The status of American college and university librarians*. Chicago, A.L.A., 1958 (ACRL monograph no. 22), p. 13-7, 112-45, 146-55

21. ACRL. Committee on standards. *College and university library accreditation standards—1957*. Chicago, ACRL, 1958 (ACRL monographs no. 20), p. 14; Veit, Fritz. "The status of the librarian according to accrediting standards." *Col. and research lib.* 21:127-35, March, 1960

22. Herrick, M. D. "Status of worker morale among college catalogers." *Col. and research lib.* 11:35, January, 1950

23. News note from Robert Agard, librarian of Earlham College. *Lib. jour.* 85:1777, May 1, 1960

24. Boughter, Vivian R. "Salaries, work week, vacations, benefits, and privileges of college librarians." *Col. and research lib.* 19:127, March, 1958

25. *Loc. cit.*

26. Muller, R. H. "Work week, vacations, and salaries in medium-sized universities and colleges." *Col. and research lib.* 15:84, January, 1954

27. Boughton, *op. cit.*, p. 127-8

28. *Ibid.*, p. 128

29. Stieg, L. F. "Retirement plans for college and university librarians." *Col. and research lib.* 11:16, January, 1950

30. Hagerty, Philip E. "Evaluation of personnel." *In*: Yenawine, Wayne S. ed. *Library evaluation.* Syracuse, Syracuse University press, 1959, p. 21-9

31. "Tenure in libraries; a statement of principles adopted by . . . the A.L.A., June 21, 1946." A.L.A. *bull.* 40:451-3, November, 1946

32. American association of university professors. "The statement of principles, 1940, academic freedom and tenure." American association of university professors. *bull.* 28:84-90, February, 1942; a later printing with a list of organizations endorsing the statement from 1941 through 1953 appears in the American association of university professors. *bull.* 42:41-6, Spring, 1956

33. Weber, Dorothy. "The clerical staff." *Lib. trends* 3:57, July, 1954

34. Winckler, P. A. "Staff manual." *Lib. jour.* 84:1771-2, June 1, 1959; see also "Staff manuals; a selected bibliography on their preparation and use." *News notes Calif. lib.* 50:389-92, April, 1955

35. Gapp, Kenneth. "The librarian's task in improving personnel." *Col. and research lib.* 1:132, March, 1940

36. Fowler, Julian. "The staff meeting as a departmental seminar." *Col. and research lib.* 1:326-7, September, 1940

37. Messick, Ann. "Library staff seminar." *Lib. jour.* 63:171, March 1, 1938

38. Muller, Robert H. "A program for staff reading." *Col. and research lib.* 14:235-9, July, 1953; Yerke, Theodore B. "When is a librarian well-read?" *Col. and research lib.* 15:210-1, April, 1954; Burton, Howard A. "Maximum benefits from a program for staff reading." *Col. and research lib.* 15:277-80, July, 1954; Bob, Murray L. "The nature of staff reading." *Col. and research lib.* 16:135-7, April, 1955

39. Fay, Lucy E. "A program of in-service training in college and university libraries." *Col. and research lib.* 8:214-7, July, 1947; Richardson, Louise. "Developing a college library staff." *Col. and research lib.* 1:324, September, 1940

40. Hurt, Peyton. "Staff specialization." A.L.A. *bull.* 29:417-21, July, 1935

41. Pope, Mary F. and Thompson, L. S. "Travel funds for university library staffs." *Col. and research lib.* 11:22-7, January, 1950

42. Boughter, *op. cit.*, p. 128

43. Flexner, Abraham. *Universities.* N.Y., Oxford, 1930, p. 29-30

44. A.L.A. Committee on code of ethics. "Code of ethics for librarians." A.L.A. *bull.* 33:128-30, February, 1939 (also in *American library and book trade annual, 1960.* N.Y., Bowker, 1959, p. 82-4) ; reprinted at the end of this chapter.

45. Lundy, Frank A. "Philosophical concepts of professional organization." *Col. and research lib.* 20:487-95, November, 1959

ADDITIONAL REFERENCES

A.L.A. Personnel administration board. Subcommittee on personnel organization. . . . *Personnel organization and procedure: a manual suggested for use in college and university libraries.* Chicago, A.L.A., 1952

Dahl, Richard C. "Professional development programs." *Lib. jour.* 79: 2280-83, December 1, 1954

Horn, A. H. "Personnel factors in administration." *Lib. jour.* 83:803-5, March 15, 1958

McCoy, Ralph E. and others. *Personnel administration for libraries: a bibliographic essay.* Chicago, A.L.A., 1953

McDiarmid, E. W. "Training for clerical and subprofessional workers." *In*: Berelson, B. R. ed. *Education for librarianship.* Chicago, A.L.A., 1949, p. 232-48

Martin, Lowell, ed. *Personnel administration in libraries.* Chicago, University of Chicago press, 1946

Mayer, T. L. "Training the staff for professional participation." *Wilson lib. bull.* 24:601-3, April, 1950

Paton, W. B. "Staff training in libraries." *Library association record.* 60:243-8, August, 1958

Richards, Benjamin B. "In-service training." *Illinois libraries.* 40:216-19, March, 1958

Wight, E. A. "In-service training of professional librarians in college and university libraries." *Col. and research lib.* 10:103-7, April, 1949

Woodburne, Lloyd. *Principles of college and university administration.* Stanford, Cal., Stanford University press, 1958

CODE OF ETHICS FOR LIBRARIANS *

PREAMBLE

1. The library as an institution exists for the benefit of a given constituency, whether it be the citizens of a community, members of an educational institution, or some larger or more specialized group. Those who enter the library profession assume an obligation to maintain ethical standards of behavior in relation to the governing authority under which they work, to the library constituency, to the library as an institution and to fellow workers on the staff, to other members of the library profession, and to society in general.

2. The term librarian in this code applies to any person who is employed by a library to do work that is recognized to be professional in character according to standards established by the American Library Association.

* A.L.A. code. A.L.A. *bull.* 33:128-30, February, 1939

3. This code sets forth principles of ethical behavior for the professional librarian. It is not a declaration of prerogatives nor a statement of recommended practices in specific situations.

I. RELATION OF THE LIBRARIAN TO THE GOVERNING AUTHORITY

4. The librarian should perform his duties with realization of the fact that final jurisdiction over the administration of the library rests in the officially constituted governing authority. This authority may be vested in a designated individual, or in a group such as a committee or board.

5. The chief librarian should keep the governing authority informed on professional standards and progressive action. Each librarian should be responsible for carrying out the policies of the governing authority and its appointed executives with a spirit of loyalty to the library.

6. The chief librarian should interpret decisions of the governing authority to the staff, and should act as liaison officer in maintaining friendly relations between staff members and those in authority.

7. Recommendations to the governing authority for the appointment of a staff member should be made by the chief librarian solely upon the basis of the candidate's professional and personal qualifications for the position. Continuance in service and promotion should depend upon the quality of performance, following a definite and known policy. Whenever the good of the service requires a change in personnel, timely warning should be given. If desirable adjustment cannot be made, unsatisfactory service should be terminated in accordance with the policy of the library and the rules of tenure.

8. Resolutions, petitions, and requests of a staff organization or group should be submitted through a duly appointed representative to the chief librarian. If a mutually satisfactory solution cannot be reached, the chief librarian, on request of the staff, should transmit the matter to the governing authority. The staff may further request that they be allowed to send a representative to the governing authority, in order to present their opinions in person.

II. RELATION OF THE LIBRARIAN TO HIS CONSTITUENCY

9. The chief librarian, aided by staff members in touch with the constituency, should study the present and future needs of the library, and should acquire materials on the basis of those needs. Provision should be made for as wide a range of publications and as varied a representation of viewpoints as is consistent with the policies of the library and with the funds available.

10. It is the librarian's responsibility to make the resources and services of the library known to its potential users. Impartial service should be rendered to all who are entitled to use the library.

11. It is the librarian's obligation to treat as confidential any private information obtained through contact with library patrons.

12. The librarian should try to protect library property and to inculcate in users a sense of their responsibility for its preservation.

III. RELATIONS OF THE LIBRARIAN WITHIN HIS LIBRARY

13. The chief librarian should delegate authority, encourage a sense of responsibility and initiative on the part of staff members, provide for their professional development, and appreciate good work. Staff members should be informed of the duties of their positions and the policies and problems of the library.

14. Loyalty to fellow workers and a spirit of courteous cooperation, whether between individuals or between departments, are essential to effective library service.

15. Criticism of library policies, service, and personnel should be offered only to the proper authority for the sole purpose of improvement of the library.

16. Acceptance of a position in a library incurs an obligation to remain long enough to repay the library for the expense incident to adjustment. A contract signed or agreement made should be adhered to faithfully until it expires or is dissolved by mutual consent.

17. Resignations should be made long enough before they are to take effect to allow adequate time for the work to be put in shape and a successor appointed.

18. A librarian should never enter into a business dealing on behalf of the library which will result in personal profit.

19. A librarian should never turn the library's resources to personal use, to the detriment of services which the library renders to its patrons.

IV. RELATION OF THE LIBRARIAN TO HIS PROFESSION

20. Librarians should recognize librarianship as an educational profession and realize that the growing effectiveness of their service is dependent upon their own development.

21. In view of the importance of ability and personality traits in library work, a librarian should encourage only those persons with suitable aptitudes to enter the library profession and should discourage the continuance in service of the unfit.

218   COLLEGE LIBRARY ADMINISTRATION

22. Recommendations should be confidential and should be fair to the candidate and the prospective employer by presenting an unbiased statement of strong and weak points.

23. Librarians should have a sincere belief and a critical interest in the library profession. They should endeavor to achieve and maintain adequate salaries and proper working conditions.

24. Formal appraisal of the policies or practices of another library should be given only upon the invitation of that library's governing authority or chief librarian.

25. Librarians, in recognizing the essential unity of their profession, should have membership in library organizations and should be ready to attend and participate in library meetings and conferences.

V. RELATION OF THE LIBRARIAN TO SOCIETY

26. Librarians should encourage a general realization of the value of library service and be informed concerning movements, organizations, and institutions whose aims are compatible with those of the library.

27. Librarians should participate in public and community affairs and so represent the library that it will take its place among educational, social, and cultural agencies.

28. A librarian's conduct should be such as to maintain public esteem for the library and for library work.

XI

Student Assistants

In practically all college libraries considerable use is made of student assistants. They perform routine tasks such as desk duty in the library and in departmental reading rooms, and shelving, filing, and typing. When they are carefully selected and well trained and when they are not so numerous as to overwhelm the library staff with supervisory duties, student assistants can render useful service to the library while helping themselves financially and educationally. They are also potential recruits for librarianship since work experience is a factor influencing students to turn to the field of librarianship. Librarians should cultivate this opportunity by working closely with students, offering a variety of assignments, and explaining opportunities in the library field.

PROBLEMS INVOLVED IN STUDENT EMPLOYMENT

There have been, traditionally, two contrasting points of view regarding the employment of students in the library. On the one hand, librarians have exaggerated the influence of student employment in developing initiative and character. This point of view sees only virtue in student help, and attributes only favorable and beneficial results to such activity. On the other hand, there are librarians who feel that student employment interferes with the work for which the students principally come to college and that it has decidedly adverse effects on the service of the library. However one feels about this, the fact remains that librarians can hardly escape the necessity of employing and training student assistants.

One of the chief problems presented by the employment of students relates to the number of part-time student assistants the library is obliged to employ in order to cover its work schedule. Student help is notoriously inefficient without proper training and careful supervision. The proportion of full-time staff members to part-time student assistants is, therefore, a matter of importance in operating a library efficiently. There are at present no standards to determine what this ratio should be; if there were they would probably be of little use. In the last analysis the amount of student help in proportion to full-time staff is a question for each college to answer for itself. College instruction could probably be carried on if the library staff were reduced to two or three librarians for ordering and cataloging books and a student staff for policing and handing out books over the loan desks. But if the college expects its library to familiarize students with the use of books and to provide the kind of educational service that is advocated throughout this book, then the professional staff must be large enough and sufficiently free from routines and supervisory duties to give proper attention to readers' needs. The prevailing ratio between full-time staff and student help for a selected group of college libraries is shown in Table VI. If these data are typical of college libraries generally, there is no apparent relationship between the size of a college and the ratio between full-time staff and student hours of help, although libraries with small staffs have a higher ratio of student assistants than those with large full-time staffs. The median ratio between full-time staff and the hours per week of student part-time assistants is one to nineteen.

Another problem is the frequency with which student assistants shift hours, stop work the week before quarter or semester examinations, and change positions. But something should be said on the other side also. As a group, student assistants have a far wider acquaintance with the library than other students and they help to explain to their classmates some of the mysteries as well as the irksome details which are necessary in the operation of a busy library. Most students add a note of geniality to the staff. They learn to appreciate the library and librarians. When they win honors either academically or athletically, the staff is proud to bask for a moment in their reflected glory. At unusual and slack times in the schedule, such as a lunch or dinner period, students usually can be found to take care of the desk duties. When a staff member becomes suddenly ill, there will always be student volunteers to help out. Working with stu-

Table VI

RATIO OF FULL-TIME STAFF TO STUDENT HELP *

Library	Full-Time Staff	Hours of Student Help per Week	Ratio of Full-Time Staff to Student Hours per Week
Vassar	28 ¼	130	1: 4.60
Amherst	20	105	1: 5.25
Randolph-Macon	7 ½	48	1: 6.40
Carleton	10 5/12	75	1: 7.20
Washington and Lee	6 ½	51 1/2	1: 7.99
Goucher	9	89	1: 9.88
Williams	11 ½	115	1:10.00
Bryn Mawr	16 ½	184	1:11.03
De Pauw	13 ½	150	1:11.11
Reed College	7 ½	90	1:12.00
Beloit	9	120	1:13.33
Wabash	7 ⅛	100	1:14.03
Woman's College of the U. N.C.	19	363	1:19.10
Bowdoin	6	120	1:20.00
Winthrop	7 ½	160	1:21.33
Earlham	6	134	1:22.33
Ripon	3	72	1:24.00
Birmingham-Southern	5	128	1:25.60
Southwestern at Memphis	6	156	1:26.00
Southeastern La. College	9	255	1:28.33
Coe	5	162	1:32.40
Davidson	4	135	1:33.75
Kalamazoo	4	145	1:36.25
Northwestern State College of La.	15 ½	576	1:37.16
Madison	5 ½	240	1:43.63
North Texas State College	24	1068	1:44.50

* Source: Questionnaire, Summer, 1959

dents as individuals in the actual operation of the library is a healthy antidote to the guidance, discipline, and wariness which are necessary in dealing with them in large numbers as users of the library.

Full-time Clerical Assistants vs. Student Assistants

There is a widespread feeling that it is poor economy for any library to have too few full-time staff members to supervise student help properly,[1] whereas, to the outsider, it would appear that student help would be the most economical way to operate the library. Brown and Bousfield explain why this is not the case:

> The time expended on the almost continual training of new student attendants is one factor which should be considered. Another more important consideration is the inability of students to work a sufficient length of time to gain the experience necessary for many library duties which can be performed by clerical assistants of several years' experience.[2]

In a study of student employment practices in six well-known college libraries, Helen Brown observed that it had been found desirable to replace some part of student service by full-time clerical assistants.[3] She further stated that "the employment of a clerical worker to replace several student assistants working an equivalent number of hours is a great saving in the cost of staff time for training and supervision."[4] This statement is true, of course, but the problem of most librarians is to convince their college administrators that the staff time thus saved can be utilized for services which are vital to the development of the student and to his advancement along the road toward real education.

The one type of work in which students are almost universally used in college libraries is circulation work. There are two principal reasons why this is so. In the first place there are a good many routines in connection with circulation work such as charging, carding, calling in books, and shelving. Students can perform these duties satisfactorily provided they are carefully supervised. At least one staff member is generally available at the loan desk to give this supervision. In the second place, circulation work varies in volume from hour to hour, from day to day, and from week to week. This variation requires great flexibility in scheduling if service is to be given efficiently and economically. It is easier to provide this flexibility with a large number of part-time student assistants than it is with a full-time clerical assistant. It is also possible to schedule student assistants more easily at irregular hours. All libraries in the Brown survey "emphasized the greater leeway of irregular time which an amount of money spent for student service can give over the same amount spent for clerical service." [5]

On the other hand it has been found that clerical assistants produce better results as typists than do student assistants. There is a surprisingly large amount of detailed routine in the acquisition and preparation work of a library which can be done more efficiently by persons giving full-time service. To do the work satisfactorily in the first place requires several weeks and sometimes months of careful training and supervision. If the librarian or department head in charge of this work is obliged to give this training to several student assistants, and perhaps to repeat it frequently because the turnover in student help is high, he will be pushed to complete his own work and will have no time for improving or developing the service. Typical examples of duties for which full-time help is preferable to student help include: the typing of catalog cards, alphabetizing and filing in the card catalog and shelf list, the preparation of book orders after the bibliographical checking has been completed, and the general office work of the librarian.

SELECTION OF STUDENT ASSISTANTS

In many small college libraries, the staff is composed largely of student help. The quality of service depends much upon the ability of this student staff; therefore, a careful and intelligent selection of student assistants is a matter of great importance.

Basis of Selection

Brown and Bousfield regard ability as the sole basis of appointment:

There is one principle which does not seem to be generally recognized in the appointment of student attendants. The all-important function of a college library is to serve its clientele. Students should be selected to work in the library solely because of their ability to do the work better than other candidates. Considerations such as aid to needy students and the value of preparing students to enter the library profession, are entirely subordinate. The employment of students with these objects in view may result in deterioration of service to many for the benefit of a few.[6]

Although in theory students should be selected solely on the basis of their personal fitness, in practice it is often necessary to give consideration to factors other than ability. The very existence of student employment on the campus is evidence of the necessity of providing needy students with some form of remunerative work. In her study, Miss Brown found that the factor of need was a first consideration in several situations in the appointment of students to library positions. And all librarians, in the colleges she studied, reported giving special consideration to students interested in library work as a career. The consideration of a student's financial need as one factor in selection is not necessarily a handicap to wise selection. It should be remembered that the needy students are often more actively motivated in their studies and work than the average student. On the other hand, inability to pay full tuition or college expenses is no guarantee that the student will render good service.

The ability to do the work assigned is a rather vague and indefinite criterion of selection. It must be interpreted in terms of definite qualifications. The opinions of a number of librarians and staff members in charge of student assistants on the first ten qualities desired in a good student assistant are tabulated in Table VII. Other qualities mentioned less frequently included: subject knowledge, ability to get along with people, familiarity with the collection, and contact with student life. Accuracy is no doubt stressed because a large amount of student time is spent in such tasks as shelving, charging, and discharging books—duties in which repeated errors would cause great inconvenience to readers and a considerable waste of time. Courtesy is not mentioned in the first ten qualities but it cannot be emphasized too strongly in the selection and training of student assistants. For most of the regular routine tasks librarians prefer to start with freshmen and sophomores since there is the possibility they may be retained for a three- or four-year period.

TABLE VII

QUALIFICATIONS REQUIRED FOR STUDENT ASSISTANT
WORK IN ORDER OF FREQUENCY OF MENTION

Qualification	Frequency of Mention
Accuracy	68
Availability	54
Good health and eyesight	35
Need	28
Ability to type	26
Ability to use card catalog	21
Neatness	21
Ability to take responsibility	20
Experience	15
Quickness	10

Source: Brown, *op. cit.*, p. 48

Methods of Selection

Student employment is made possible in college libraries from two principal sources: (1) scholarships or grants-in-aid, and (2) special funds allocated to the library for student service. In a few exceptional instances, student service may be paid for from general college funds without a direct assessment against the library budget.

Although there is insufficient evidence in print on which to base an opinion regarding the respective merits of each of the plans mentioned above, there seems to be little doubt that the direct employment of student assistants from library funds provides a degree of flexibility in the management of student help which is not always possible under a scholarship plan. The underlying purpose of scholarships is to provide financial help for students of high scholastic promise. It has already been

pointed out that scholarship is not regarded as a first requirement by librarians in the selection of student help. In line with
the basic assumption upon which scholarships are awarded, it is
also true that there are sometimes special requirements regarding
the training and work given to students. More serious, however,
is the situation reported in certain colleges where the librarian
does not have the final authority in the selection, appointment,
and dismissal of students employed on a scholarship basis.[7] If
the librarian is held responsible for the operation and service
of the library, there should be no interference with his authority
to select assistants qualified to do the work required of them.

In practically all colleges where student assistants are paid
from library funds, the selection of help is made from an
"eligible" list by the librarian or the staff member in charge of
student help. The "eligible" list is composed of all those students who have shown need of part-time employment in order to
remain in college. In a few colleges the selection of student
assistants is made by the librarian without reference to an
"eligible" list or to any outside authority; and in others, the
selection and assignment of student help to all college departments is made by the personnel officer. In the last instance there
is the danger that the real qualifications for the job will be
subordinated to the student's need for a job.

The Selection Process

The selection of student assistants is usually based on information obtained from high school and college records, application
blanks, and personal interviews. Some colleges have used psychological tests to predict the performance of student assistants
in library work.

A study of the high school and college records of students
who have applied for work will increase the chances for choosing
successful assistants. At the University of North Carolina it has
been found that freshmen who rank fairly high in their high
school classes (usually in the top fourth) make better student
assistants. Although grades should not be the determining factor,
they are one of the best indicators of general intelligence and
ability.[8] In evaluating ability, character, and attitude, the extra-
curricular activities of students in high school and the recom-

mendations of teachers should also be considered. Usually these records are available from the central records office or registrar of the college. The group selected on the basis of their past records should be asked to come in to the library to fill out an application blank and be interviewed.

Another important tool of selection is the application blank. Many libraries have realized that the application blank for student assistants must be different from that for regular full-time employees. For instance, it is important to know the student's local address, class in school, his major, special skills, extracurricular activities in college, the number of hours per week he can work, the hours he will be available for work, and whether or not he will be available next session. Answers to these questions can best be obtained from a standard application form. Of course, the application blank for students should also include some of the same information obtained from applicants for regular, full-time positions: marital status, educational qualifications, language ability, previous library experience, and other work experience.

Possibly the most important step in the selection process is the interview. The interview should be relaxed and informal. The student's personality traits, personal appearance, attitude, and responsiveness can best be appraised from the interview. These are sometimes the determining factors in the employment of students.

One library has successfully used psychological tests in the selection of student assistants.[9] Tests which evaluate specific skills such as typing and shorthand may be particularly valuable in selecting students for jobs requiring these skills. General intelligence tests may be useful in screening out those people who have a minimum level of ability desired for the jobs. However, tests must be used with caution and with professional advice. Many colleges have central testing agencies which may help in advising or administering an employment testing program.

TRAINING AND SUPERVISION

The employment of student assistants is not completed until they have been properly introduced to the general policies of the library regarding such matters as method of payment and personal conduct, and have been trained in their particular positions. The best training comes from actually doing the work under careful supervision, but it is necessary to give new students a general orientation and specific instruction in their particular work at the outset. The responsibility of the supervisor is heavy in this regard. I. T. Littleton, who deserves special praise for his thorough outline of methods of training circulation assistants, recommends a general orientation to explain the purpose of the department, the relationship of the job to other jobs in the department and to other departments, and general library and circulation department policies.[10] It is necessary to follow up the orientation with individual instruction and guidance by the supervisor. This can be done by means of a tour, personal explanation, and simple tests. Such instruction is supplemented by manuals and instruction sheets, close supervision of the actual tasks during a preliminary period, and group meetings held at times when they will interfere least with work schedules.[11] The major responsibility falls upon the supervisor to develop the skills and potentialities of the students chosen. Littleton cautions that "this training must be systematic and complete, based on sound principles and methods; otherwise new assistants will not do their jobs well." [12]

One of the perennial problems of student help is keeping students long enough to repay a systematic program of instruction. On this subject, one writer with first-hand experience in supervising student help suggests seven principles to observe: (1) keep the student interested, (2) give him adequate explanations, (3) encourage him to express his opinions, (4) do not overestimate or underestimate his capabilities, (5) cultivate his sense of responsibility, (6) adapt his duties to his talents and background, and (7) commend him occasionally for work that is well done.[13] To illustrate but one of these principles, she reminds the librarian that he cannot put a student on a steady diet of shelving books. "Two hours at a time will satiate anyone's appetite for the task. Wherever possible, assign only reasonable lengths of time to be spent in routine duties." If the work is adapted to their talents and interests, students will not only prove more reliable and diligent in their tasks but they may also be encouraged to consider librarianship as a career.

Records of Service

As an additional aid to supervision and instruction, most libraries attempt, by one means or another, to measure the accomplishment of student assistants in service. This is done largely on the basis of personal opinion and comparison, but a few libraries use special rating forms to evaluate student services. Such a form is best kept as simple as possible, perhaps rating each student from "Very Good" to "Unsatisfactory" on such points as attitude, attendance, interest in job, quality of work, quantity of work, ability to work with others, and initiative.

A rating form is more valuable if discussed with the student so that he is aware of his weaknesses as well as his strengths. Some libraries require supervisors to fill out rating forms for student assistants at regular intervals or each time assistants are considered for raises in pay. Libraries receive many requests for information about former student assistants from companies, government agencies, or other libraries and individuals many years after both students and their immediate supervisors are no longer employed. For this reason it is wise to maintain a record of the student's work experience for several years after he terminates his employment.

Hours and Wages

Most librarians feel that the number of consecutive hours and the total number of hours per week a student assistant can work have a great deal to do with the value of his services to the library. Brown and Bousfield are of the opinion that "better results will be obtained if no student is employed for less than fifteen hours per week." [14] More attention should be given to discovering, by experimentation, the real facts regarding the minimum number of hours a student can work each week and still render effective service. It may possibly develop that the number of hours is not as significant as differences in the ability of students and in the types of work to be done.

In regard to the wages of student assistants, it is considered best to pay students on a graduated wage scale rather than at a fixed rate. A base wage should be established with provision for increments for superior work on a quarterly or semester basis. Some libraries will base this scale solely on class standing and work experience. Others will pay a higher beginning salary for different kinds of work. Thus the regular beginning wage paid for shelving may be increased by five to twenty-five cents an hour for special skills involving typing or art work. One library reports a graduated pay scale to recognize and reward attendance for undergraduate study in library science, the hope being that this will prove an added inducement to students to consider librarianship as a career. All these provisions have merit in that they reward the student for experience, interest, and superior work, but it must be remembered that the differential in a graduated scale of student wages is relatively small and that too elaborate a system may not be worth the time and effort necessary to administer it. Most libraries will find it satisfactory to have a base wage on a par with other student positions on the campus and to provide a small increase for good work experience each quarter or semester.

NOTES

1. Camp, Mildred. "Student assistants and the college library." *Lib. jour.* 59:925, December 1, 1934; Randall, William M. *The college library.* Chicago, A.L.A. and the University of Chicago press, 1932, p. 65. For a further discussion of the relative merits of full-time versus part-time workers, *see* Jesse, William. *Shelfwork in libraries.* Chicago, A.L.A., 1952, p. 61-2

2. Brown, Charles H. and Bousfield, H. B. *Circulation work in college and university libraries.* Chicago, A.L.A., 1933, p. 55

3. Brown, Helen M. "Conditions contributing to the efficient service of student assistants in a selected group of college libraries." *Col. and research lib.* 5:51, December, 1943

4. *Loc. cit.*

5. *Loc. cit.*

6. Brown and Bousfield, *op. cit.,* p. 56

7. Brown, *op. cit.,* p. 45, 47

8. The writer is indebted to I. T. Littleton for this section on *The Selection Process.* Mr. Littleton is Head of Technical Services, D. H. Hill Library, North Carolina State College, Raleigh.

9. Oberheim, Grace M. "The prediction of success of student assistance in college library work." *Educational and psychological measurement* 2:379-85, October, 1942

10. Littleton, I. T. "Training circulation assistants." *Southeastern librarian* 6:82-5, Summer, 1956

11. For example, Midland college, Fremont, Nebraska. Library. *Manual for student assistants; general information, circulation desk and shelving.* Fremont, Nebraska, The Library, 1957

12. Littleton, *op. cit.*, p. 85

13. Wannarka, Marjorie. "How to keep your student help." *Catholic lib. world* 27:170, January, 1956

14. Brown and Bousfield, *op. cit.*, p. 58

XII

Book Selection and Acquisition

To provide a plentiful supply of good and useful books is the college library's *raison d'être*. Library materials are the core around which sound teaching and other educational activities of the college take place. For these reasons, if for no other, book selection and acquisition demand attention and study.

FACTORS AFFECTING BOOK SELECTION AND ACQUISITION POLICY

Several important factors bearing on the selection and acquisition of books in college libraries are summarized in the following pages. They are significant for the college librarian for purposes of budgeting, book buying, and formulating a policy of book acquisition.

The Size of the College

There is apparently a very definite correlation between the size of the college and the number of volumes added annually to its library. Data on this point are provided in Table VIII.

While the average number of books added annually per student is practically constant in colleges of all sizes, it is evident that the colleges with larger enrolments are adding many more books than those with small enrolments. The number of new books published in any given year is constant and therefore the small college library presumably should be adding as many of these titles as the larger college. Two additional factors must be taken into consideration, however.

In the first place, the college with larger enrolments will need many more duplicates of books both for assigned reading purposes and for general reading. The trend is away from teaching by the textbook, and in many of the newer fields of the social

TABLE VIII

AVERAGE NUMBER OF VOLUMES ADDED 1958-59 BY
LIBRARIES OF SELECTED COLLEGES OF
VARIOUS ENROLMENTS

Enrolment for Year Ending Fall Quarter, 1958-59	Number of Colleges	Average Number of Volumes Added for Year	Average Number of Volumes Added per Student
1000 and over	28	5,227	2.6
500 to 1000	32	2,020	3.0
under 500	45	1,625*	5.6*

* The imbalance in these figures results from the inclusion in the statistical sample of institutions having small student bodies and acquisitions far in excess of the average (e.g., Northwestern Lutheran Theological Seminary). Omitting these "exceptional" colleges one arrives at a figure for this group that closely approximates those given for the other two categories. The above table was derived from figures given for the first institution in each group of five in Groups IV, V, and VI as reported in "College and University Library Statistics, 1958-59," *Col. and Research Lib.* 21:25-87. January, 1960.

sciences, where library materials are used most heavily, it is not possible to use a single text even were this desirable. The result is that students are referred to parts of many books—far more than they could be asked to own, or even to cooperate in buying, though this is done in some institutions. If the college library does exist to serve the undergraduate and to implement the primary business of teaching within a specified curriculum, it seems inescapably obvious that the library must provide an adequate number of class and stack duplicates as a first duty.

In the second place the larger colleges usually offer a greater range of courses than the smaller colleges. The size of the book acquisitions necessary for supporting these courses will be affected considerably by the variety of course offerings. Colleges with an extensive program of courses will need many more of the books currently published if satisfactory service is to be given. Perhaps the combination of these two factors—the variety of course offerings and the provision of class duplicates—is sufficient to account in large part for the differences in annual book acquisitions among colleges of varying enrolments.

The Nature of the College Program

The nature of the educational program of a college has a direct bearing on its selection and acquisition of books. As has already been suggested, colleges vary greatly in the nature and extent of their course offerings and this in turn affects the requirements of book acquisition and service.

The particular slant or educational theory underlying the college program also affects the book collection. The educational theory adopted by St. John's College, Annapolis, for example, presupposes a different type of library collection from that usually found in colleges. Students at St. John's are required to do intensive reading in 100 great books which they are encouraged to own themselves. Their library need for current material in the social sciences would presumably be much less than that of a college which attempts to provide for survey courses in the lower division of a four-year liberal arts program. In such a college, currency of publication and extensive duplication are stressed.

There are other colleges which offer graduate work and emphasize research and where the results of research are more in evidence than in some universities. It hardly needs to be made clear that the demands upon the library for research materials in these institutions will be greater than in colleges where the sole aim is teaching.

Any variation in a particular college from the traditional liberal arts program will also affect selection and acquisition. If there are business, engineering, or home economics courses, there may well be a need for specialized technical and vocational material quite outside the range of what is usually required for the physical and biological sciences, the social sciences, and the humanities.

The Nature of the Curriculum

For the great majority of liberal arts colleges, the most important influence upon the book stock of the college library will be the nature of the curriculum. Within the confines of the liberal arts program the opportunity for variation is considerable, and among small colleges, which are seldom able to develop all departments equally, variations from the norm are to be expected.

Any development of one department or group of departments over others will be reflected in book holdings. Are the departments of the physical and life sciences among the stronger within your college? Then that fact is likely to be reflected in a relatively larger total periodical list and a relatively smaller total book collection. Are the social sciences dominant? The effect, then, on the total book stock may well be a larger percentage of currently published books, periodicals, and ephemeral material like pamphlets. If the humanities are strong, the result will be a larger demand for books which are felt to have stood the test of time, for these are the primary materials upon which serious work in that area depends.

Even more important at any given moment in a library's history, however, is the rate of change within the curriculum. If the college administration or its curriculum committee is attempting to correct imbalance within the curriculum or to follow new leads in modern college education, the library may face drastic revision of its customary plans for book acquisition. The addition of one or more faculty members in a particular area with a consequent increase in the number and types of courses offered can change considerably the aspect of a book collection.

But it is not only the addition of traditional types of courses that affects the acquisitions program. Newer methods of teaching and of organizing and using materials are also important tools of change. Although it seems impossible to weigh qualitatively or statistically the effect of survey courses upon the average college library,[1] it is impossible to doubt that the introduction of such courses has an influence upon the purchase of books. And a study of honors work in colleges has revealed that it leads to considerable use of bibliographical and specialized materials which are not commonly found in college libraries. Although much of this material was secured through inter-library loan and photographic reproduction, substantial purchases of more scholarly and technical materials were found necessary in a number of cases.[2]

The Size of the Book Collection

The gross size of the book collection of a college is not a matter of real significance in measuring the adequacy of the library or in determining its book selection and acquisition policy. Nevertheless it remains a live question in our professional writings; it is emphasized in the published statistics of libraries; and it is sometimes used as a rough yardstick in evaluating the resources of college libraries. For these reasons it cannot be ignored in any discussion of book stock.

There was a time when the most specific item among the requirements of the several accrediting associations was the total number of volumes in the college library. The figure was set at 8,000 volumes. More recently these associations have recognized the absurdity of setting a minimum number of volumes as a standard of excellence and have emphasized instead the desirability of a careful selection of books and journals for appropriate courses in a given curriculum. The initial estimates of experienced librarians were considerably higher than the minimum recommendations of the pioneer standards of accrediting associations. Some of these have been summarized by Blanche P. McCrum, from whom the following estimates are quoted:

Bishop, W. W., University of Michigan—100,000 to 150,000 volumes.

Gilchrist, D. G., University of Rochester, stated that a considerable number of librarians would consider 100,000 conservative.

Kerr, W. H., Claremont Colleges—50,000 for 200 to 500 students; 75,000 for 800 or 1,000 students.

Works, G. A., University of Chicago—75,000 to 100,000 volumes for a college library with a student body of not more than 2,500.[3]

In its recently published "Standards for College Libraries," the Association of College and Research Libraries says regarding the size of library collections:

An analysis of small college library statistics suggests that no library can be expected to give effective support to the instructional program if it contains fewer than 50,000 carefully selected volumes. . . . Since there appears to be a correlation between the growth of the student body and the growth of the collection, there is a convenient measure based upon observation of the development of college libraries, which may serve as a guide: up to 600 students, 50,000 volumes; for every additional 200 students, 10,000 volumes.[4]

While most college librarians share the view that the under-graduate book collection should be a live and compact library, they would hardly fix upon any top figure beyond which the library collection should not grow. However, as a book collection increases in size above a certain point, which may vary from library to library, little-used books clutter up the shelves and make the handling and use of active books more difficult. In this connection, one should remember that book selection is a two-phase process embracing not only the selection of books to be added to the collection but also the selection of books to be retained. Thus book selection does not stop when a volume is placed on the shelves. Indeed, in this sense, each book in the library's active collections must be selected not once but many times. If the college library is to provide its users with easy access to a viable stock of functional materials, it is essential that the book stacks be kept clear of dead wood. Systematic, discriminating weeding of the collections is the primary way in which useless materials can be kept from accumulating. As Dr. Charles Gosnell remarks, "A librarian who buys and never weeds will have a library full of weeds." [5] To justify its retention in the regular college library collection, a book should be able to meet the criteria applied to currently selected materials.

The Adequacy of the Book Collection

The service rendered by a college library depends in no small measure upon the adequacy of its book collection, and this in turn is dependent upon the policy of selection and acquisition. No single evaluative procedure available is entirely satisfactory, but a combination of several may be expected to produce a picture of the adequacy of the collection which is useful and consistent.

These procedures, which are discussed fully in the final chapter of this book, include the checking of the library's holdings against standard lists such as the *Catalogue of the Lamont Library* and Bertalan's *Books for Junior Colleges,* and against selective lists of reference books and current periodicals. A positive correlation was shown by Waples [6] to exist between the adequacy of the college library's reference collection and the periodicals it currently receives and the general quality of the entire book collection. The use of standard lists and selective reference and current periodical lists is contraindicated when these lists have been used as buying guides by the library.[7] In any evaluation in which a standard checklist is used, "the evaluator must spend a good deal of time and care on the proper evaluation of findings."[8] A third method defines book collection values in terms of library use,[9] and a fourth uses as a measure of adequacy the ratio of success to failure in efforts to secure books.[10] In order to assess the adequacy of a specific library, the character and nature of the general education program of the institution it serves must be taken into account. Standard lists supplemented by subject bibliographies in the field of instruction offered by a given college are generally used in an evaluative survey of resources. The procedure followed by the Mount Holyoke College Library is helpful and suggestive to colleges contemplating a self-evaluation.[11] In selecting subject bibliographies to supplement the standard lists for checking purposes, three criteria should be kept in mind: (1) the bibliographies should contain books of a level in scholarship suited to the intellectual and linguistic attainments of undergraduate students, (2) they should be selective and should provide critical notes, and (3) they should be so arranged that the checking of their titles against the card catalog is a possible and practical task. Still another evaluative method, a quantitative one involving measurement and analysis of expenditures for library materials over a given period of time, the comparison of results with data from other institutions, and the relation of expenditures to various aspects of the book collection and the total institutional budget, is cogently discussed by Rudolph Hirsch.[12]

The Amount of Funds Available

Other factors affecting book selection and acquisition are the physical nature of the library building, the nature and activity of faculty interests, the specific condition and the precedents existing in each institution, and the amount of funds available. All of these vary according to the individual college, but the last seems worthy of special comment.

Discussions of college library book collections frequently mention insufficient funds for purchase. Certainly a book collection for any purpose whatever cannot be built up without a regular, yearly expenditure of money. It is difficult and perhaps impractical to set up a definite minimum sum without which no college library book collection worthy of the name can be acquired, though there is strong evidence to support the establishment of minimum standards below which it is not possible to fall and yet build or maintain a sound book collection. The program of library service described in the Association of College and Research Libraries' recently issued *Standards for College Libraries* would "normally require a minimum of 5 per cent of the total educational and general budget." [13]

The problem of funds may be approached in another way. One may assume that a college administration will appropriate a certain yearly sum for the buying of library books. If the amount is deemed too small relative to the size and reputation of the college, in comparison with other college libraries, or for any other reason, the librarian should speak his mind on the point to the administration. But this does not absolve him from administering the sum at his disposal to the college's best advantage.

First demands on all college library book funds come from courses taught in the curriculum and from general reference. If the total sum for books is relatively small, all the money must be spent for these two purposes since the teaching of courses and the general information necessary to back it up are the core of any college educational program.

In any growing or changing college worth its salt, there will, of course, be other demands. There will be demands to fill in the gaps in the collection. There will be demands for research, however small in comparison with the research requirements of universities. There will be demands for recreational or extra-curricular reading, for special collections, or even for rare books. But none of these should be filled until the first two, for teaching and general reference, are met. It is not impossible that if the librarian understands this order of precedence, it could become a potent weapon in his hands for better financial support.

If the college general appropriation for books remains small, it may be possible to satisfy in other ways demands which, strictly interpreted, do not pertain directly to teaching or reference. There are frequently small special funds which accrue to the library; and there are others which might be used for the library if the librarian clearly stated its special needs.

Participants in the Book Selection Process

Broadly speaking, no member of the college community should be excluded from the process of book selection. Presumably even the college electrician may have his book requests honored by the college library if he knows a good book when he sees one (don't be too sure that he doesn't) and if there are funds for purchase. As noted in Chapter VI above, many college libraries serve the book-reading members of the general population of the villages or towns where they are located, and some also serve certain of the book needs of their alumni—a stretching of the concept "college community" beyond geographical limitations. Wherever there are any tendencies toward broadening the community served by the college, participation in book selection will increase accordingly, although the new relationships resulting from it may remain wholly informal. Such participation may be considered feasible and good when it enriches or at least does not interfere with the college's more formal program.

But such manifestations can take place, of course, only on the periphery of book selection. The core of the process must always be concerned directly with the college educational program, where the pattern of participation is fairly regular and consistent. Substantial participation in selection should be anticipated from five groups: the administration, the faculty, the librarian and the library staff, the faculty library committee, and the students.

The Administration

The part of the college administrator in book selection is an important one and does not permit of much difference of opinion or of prolonged discussion. Randall and Goodrich describe his duties as three. First, he must see that enough funds are provided to permit purchase of an adequate number of good and useful books for library shelves. Second, he will ask cooperation of the faculty in the book selection process and "will make sure that the individual members are capable of furnishing this co-operation." Third, he will select a capable librarian.[14] These are large demands but they are primary, and if they can be satisfied, some of the most pressing problems in book selection can be readily solved.

In certain practical, day-to-day contacts, one should not forget, furthermore, that the college president and the college dean stand in a relationship to the library not very different from that of teaching members of the faculty. The librarian should be aware that they, too, ought to suggest books for purchase. If the president has come to his present position from a field of learning, he may still be interested in material in that field. Certainly the library should be at pains to call to his attention and provide, upon his suggestion, books dealing with the newer developments in higher education and in personnel administration. Likewise, the dean may be interested in the most recently available work on the curriculum or on student counseling.

The Faculty

There is need for close cooperation between the librarian and the members of the faculty in book selection. This truism is substantiated by several studies, of which J. Periam Danton's "The Selection of Books for College Libraries" [15] is particularly valuable. As Dr. Danton points out in another article, summarizing this phase of book selection:

The librarian's relationship to each of the principal elements of the college community—faculty, students and administration—has been expounded frequently and at length, but his relationship to the members of the faculty as selectors of books has been only casually noted. This seems strange when one considers that both the librarian and the faculty member are, today, working primarily through the medium of printed materials, when one considers that such materials constitute their commonest meeting ground and when one remembers, further, that each has or should have much to contribute to the bibliographical activities of the other. Lack of knowledge of the factors which are of importance with respect to the building up of college library book collections has no doubt resulted in the *laissez-faire* philosophy which says that, since faculty members know and teach certain subjects, the selection of all curricular (and perhaps most other) books should be left strictly in their hands. The universality of the practice derived from this philosophy is common knowledge. At first glance it appears to be sound reasoning. The fallacy lies in the facts, first, that faculty members are not equally conscientious and industrious in reading reviews of books and publishers' notices; second, that they are not equally well trained bibliographically; third, that they frequently neglect to carry out the actual mechanical process of submitting titles for purchase; and fourth, that they do not have such inevitable and constant contact with bibliographical tools, announcements of publications and the like as to assure their knowledge of every important new publication. In a number of ways . . . the librarian can decrease the effect of these factors; by so doing, he will improve materially the collection which he administers and he will win the confidence and thanks of his colleagues on the faculty.[16]

Beyond this there is need for more specific information that will reveal more exactly the extent to which faculty members should be expected to make selection, and need for a determination of the types of material which they are best qualified to choose. In the absence of such studies it is possible only to offer suggestions of the type of materials faculty members use in making their selections and to point out the opportunities that are afforded for library-faculty cooperation:

1. Abstracting and scholarly or technical journals containing reviews are usually regarded by faculty as reliable sources of information about books. The number of these journals to which faculty refer in the course of a year's teaching is considerable. The library must provide the most important of these journals and make them available to faculty in a way that will encourage their use as book selection tools.

2. Bibliographies in books and journals and even footnote bibliographical citations are commonly used as sources of information about books to be ordered by the faculty. A listing of the more important journals in subject fields which contain frequent bibliographies and book summaries would prove useful. The library has the means for finding such information through the *Bibliographic Index* and through first-hand knowledge of the subject coverage of individual journals.

3. Most faculty members use subject bibliographies at least occasionally in selecting books for purchase. More use of these important tools could be made. Dr. Danton suggests that the

appearance of a new bibliography may even "be made the occasion of a systematic check of the library's resources in the field or fields concerned." [17]

4. Publishers' announcements are of varying importance and interest to faculty members in the choice of books for library purchase. Some publishers issue cards with descriptive notes, contents listing, and bibliographical information. These are useful in calling new books to faculty attention. However, they should not be used as substitutes for evaluative, informative reviews when selecting books.

5. Faculty members who are extensive book and library users regard catalogs as a valuable source of information, especially the catalogs distributed by English dealers in second-hand books and those issued by the larger American book dealers.

Good book selection involves not only a carefully formulated policy of book selection and faculty cooperation, but some definite organization within each teaching department. The following suggestions seem appropriate:

1. The head of a teaching department should make it clear to his staff that book selection is important, that recommendations are welcome, and that all should participate.

2. A department may properly order material which is immediately useful to it even though this material may be intended primarily as a contribution to some allied field. It may eventually prove to be of even greater value to some other department, but these things balance out.

3. In some departments the head appoints a member of the staff to be responsible for receiving all recommendations for purchase by the department. Others feel that no active teacher can give the time necessary for this additional responsibility. But those who use the plan say that recommendations flow more easily and with less reticence to a younger man in the department.

The faculty library committee also has an important stake in book selection, and influences it directly through its advice on allocation of the book fund. It must not, however, be allowed to take over any of the administrative functions which legitimately belong to the librarian. Dr. Danton's study laid bare the fact,

if indeed it had not already been accepted, that one of the
frequent contributing causes of weakness in a college library
collection is a library committee which functions as a book
selection agency.[18] This is not to say, however, that the library
committee is not important in the job of selection. It can be
particularly useful in maintaining liaison between the librarian
and the faculty as a whole. And as individuals who recommend
books in their own fields, its members, with their knowledge and
background, can contribute greatly to the building of a sound
book collection. Moreover, as Flora B. Ludington has noted, the
faculty library committee can help to maintain not only a highly
desirable faculty interest in the library but also "an appreciative
understanding of its educational function." [19]

The Librarian and the Library Staff

In order to administer the selection of books effectively, the
librarian must have a thorough knowledge of the purposes of the
college, of the curriculum, and of the integration of the library
with instruction. He must be a person of broad knowledge,
trained in the methods of evaluating books, and must be willing
to spend the necessary time and effort to keep informed on the
current output. He must be able to see the library collection as
a whole and to assess its strengths and weaknesses. He must be
able to secure faculty cooperation and interest in book selection,
for without it the program will lack effectiveness.[20] Studies have
shown that where the librarian and faculty cooperate in a sustained program of thorough and careful book selection, the resulting book stocks have proved themselves educationally effective—
which is, after all, the primary objective of college library
service.

Some of the principal duties of the librarian in book selection
are to:

1. Direct the total process of book selection along sound
lines. He should plan a long-range program for the development
of the collection with reference to what to buy and where and how
to buy most economically and efficiently.

2. Afford the administrative officers a clear understanding of the significance of this program in attaining college objectives and of the funds needed to support it.

3. Call upon the library committee for help in allocating book funds in such a way as to inspire interest and confidence.

4. Administer the book fund in such a way as not only to secure faculty cooperation but at the same time to provide an adequate general fund to develop the reference collections, the periodical files, and the books for general reading; and to take care of expensive sets which no one department can afford to purchase from its allocation, and of the acquisition of books and journals overlapping departmental interests.

5. Work increasingly for the interest and cooperation of faculty members since their enthusiastic participation determines in large measure the excellence of book selection. In addition to methods previously mentioned, the librarian may order books on approval for advance examination, send pertinent announcements and catalogs to instructors, call their attention to reviews and notices which they might otherwise overlook, and send regular statements of book fund balances to departments so that they may plan their book purchases from month to month if need be.

6. Study regularly bibliographies, book-reviewing media, catalogs, and other book selection aids which may suggest desirable purchases or information which should be called to the attention of the faculty.

7. Make it a point to spend time each week in book selection.

8. Enlist the interest of the student body in making suggestions for purchase.

9. Enlist the full cooperation of the staff in developing the collections. This point is further developed by Miss Ludington who says:

In regard to the assistance which the chief librarian can expect from his staff, he will find that the reference librarian is in the peculiarly strategic position of being the most intensive single user of the entire book collection and in close contact with the faculty and students. . . . In libraries where the staff is numerous enough to permit some degree of specialization, expert book selection service assistance can be given by the staff members. . . . Even with a small staff, some specialization is possible.[21]

Several academic libraries have formed committees consisting of library staff members whose function is to suggest and recommend purchases, from the library's general book fund, of materials in broad support of the curriculum which do not fall within the purview of any of the instructional departments or which cross disciplinary lines. These library staff committees, pooling staff knowledge, have managed to fill in many gaps and to round out collections. Frequently the valuable subject knowledge of the young professionally trained librarian remains unused and his potential undeveloped. It should be one of the duties of the resourceful chief librarian to tap, energize, and help develop the junior staff member's book knowledge.

To return to the chief librarian, then, his responsibility for the book selection process is both an administrative and an educational responsibility. In addition to handling the purchase of books, he exercises control over the selection program. This responsibility is in line with the general administrative principle that in any organization there must be a central controlling authority to guide and coordinate activities. The librarian must select many books himself, but the ability to secure the full cooperation of everyone on the campus who is competent to aid in selection is equally important.

The Students

Although students can hardly play as important a part in the selection of books as the faculty, the librarian will ignore their suggestions and their assistance, where it can be rendered, only at his peril. Many a student knows a good book choice when he sees one, and student opinion on the readability of particular volumes can sometimes be the chief verdict on their usefulness. In extra-curricular reading matter, suggestions from undergraduates are a matter of first importance; and if they cannot be expected to choose the books within courses, it should not be forgotten that even there they are the ultimate consumer.

Librarians can cultivate student interest in book selection by placing a box for suggested purchases in a convenient spot and by displaying new and interesting books on a special shelf or rack. Greater attention to and regularity of student recommendations may possibly come from a student library committee—inaugurated, of course, on student initiative.

Buying Policies of the College Library

There is a good deal of haphazardness in the building up of most college library book collections. The faculty initiate most of the orders in the special fields of their several departments of instruction. The librarian and library staff order as a matter of course many books of obvious importance which are not definitely in departmental fields, and in a good many more purchases they merely follow a hunch based on their knowledge of what is likely to be used, what is readable or in demand, and on an experienced awareness of many minor straws of evidence. The method has its advantages in leaving "money free to be applied in bringing personal enthusiasms to a tangible fruition, [and] in satisfying existing desires before those surmised for the future. There is zest in this, both for instructors and the library staff, while working up a field in which no one is interested can get rather mechanical." [22]

Where there is plenty of money and bibliographical enthusiasm, selection may not need to be carefully planned. But in colleges where every dollar in the book budget must count and where faculty interest in book selection is only routine, then the absence of a systematic plan of acquisition is likely to encourage a passive attitude on the part of most toward their responsibilities for book selection. A few, the most aggressive, will be rewarded for their aggressiveness, but the collection as a whole will suffer. Personal enthusiasms have a way of going beyond actual college instructional needs. If the book collection is to serve the educational purpose of the college, the need for a continuous organized effort to study and develop the collection cannot be overemphasized. This means at the outset that the college must decide in advance what it wants to accomplish in developing its library.

What to Buy

The college library wants first, of course, to get the books needed for instruction and for direct faculty study and investigation. The standards published by the Advisory Group on College Libraries for the Carnegie Corporation itemize the college library book needs as follows:

Book Collections

  I. The book collection should contain the standard books of general reference.

 II. The book collection should contain the standard reference books useful in the specific fields covered by the curriculum of the college.

III. The book collection should further contain:

    a. an adequate stock of important general books—that is books not specific to any one curricular field;

    b. an adequate stock, for each curricular field, of books concerning:

      1. the field as a whole;

      2. those divisions of the field in which courses are offered and members of the teaching staff are interested;

      3. other significant divisions of the field;

    c. an adequate stock of books concerning such important specific fields of interest as may not be treated in the curriculum; and

    d. an adequate stock of books appropriate for leisure reading.

 IV. The college library should receive, bind, and preserve accessibly a selected number of general periodicals, and the standard scholarly periodicals in the fields covered by the curriculum. The continuity and completeness of the sets should be maintained.[23]

Just to say, however, that the college library needs reference works, curricular material, books for general reading, and scholarly journals for investigation and study is not to settle the entire question of what the college library should buy. Among the more specific questions that must be answered are the following:

Should the library use its funds largely for current purchases or should it attempt to round out its collection and fill in gaps where they exist? If most of the funds are allocated to departments for book purchases as they probably should be, there will not be money for both purposes. Randall has suggested a method of providing funds for filling in gaps in the library's collection which calls for the establishment of a rotating fund. A portion of the book fund each year would be set aside for the purchase of materials in one of the basic fields of instruction, the reserved portion of the book fund being used one year by the humanities, the next year by the physical sciences, and so on.[24]

Another workable arrangement would be for a certain part of the book budget to be set aside in a special fund administered by the librarian, with the advice of the library committee, from which faculty members and members of the library staff could recommend purchases. The person recommending such a purchase would be expected to justify his recommendation in terms of actual use and value to the college, and requests for purchase should be subject to careful review by the librarian and library committee before final approval is given.

However, before devoting any considerable amount of the book fund to retrospective purchases, the library should investigate the possibilities of consolidated holdings, central control and storage, and acquisition of little-used materials in cooperation with other libraries in the region. The Hampshire Inter-Library Center has been an outstandingly successful operation of this type, and a survey of its literature, especially its annual reports, furnishes details of many of the financial and organizational aspects of this kind of cooperative venture. At the time this book went to press, Keyes D. Metcalf was conducting a survey to determine the possible bases of such cooperation among a group of libraries in Maine.[25]

Should the college library purchase textbooks? The librarian's task here would seem to be that of acting as a brake on the all too frequent tendency on the part of many faculties to order textbooks singly and in multiple copies. Dr. Branscomb says the librarian "must convince first his committee and, with their aid, the faculty and administration that in buying books of this sort the college will get less for its money than for most other purchases." [26] One method might be to make a list of fairly recent but already outdated textbooks held by the library. It should be said, of course, that this dictum does not hold for the teachers college library and some of the larger college libraries, where special collections of textbooks are built up for educational and historical purposes.

Should the college library buy rare books? This is a ticklish problem and one in which there appears to be no unanimity of opinion among librarians. If the term "rare books" is interpreted broadly to include old and contemporary examples of fine printing, binding, and illustration, then it would be a mistake to adopt a rigorous policy of exclusion. Such books have an aesthetic and historical value which cannot be denied and thus have a valid place in the library. But so long as funds are needed for the more practical necessities of the library, the purchase of rare books should be discouraged.

Most books of this type will probably reach the library through gifts. Such gifts can be encouraged by maintaining contacts with friends and alumni. While the college library should not attempt to emulate the university library in this respect, one of the aims of the liberal arts college is to create some scholars and bibliophiles whose later career in universities may be aided by an early acquaintance with finely printed and rare book material.

Should the college library purchase popular non-fiction and fiction not related to any particular course of instruction? A middle ground on this question is taken by many college libraries, probably the majority, which apportion a definite, limited amount of money each year for the purchase of such material. Usually one or two copies of the best titles will be purchased, more if necessary, depending on the size of the student body and the demand for the books. In some cases a rental collection in the library or in the bookstore will meet the needs of those wanting light recreational reading. In general, the policy of buying multiple copies of what seem to be the best of these books rather than attempting to extend the range of such holdings would appear to be sound. A frequent and careful discarding of unneeded duplicates after the demand for the title no longer exists is necessary in order to keep the stack shelves from being cluttered with dead wood.

Should the college library purchase research materials? It is exceedingly difficult to draw the line which hypothetically divides materials for undergraduates from materials for advanced research. Certain cases are obvious. The standard editions of Chaucer, even though infrequently consulted by undergraduates who have their text, would seem to belong to the former. The Chaucer Society publications, on the other hand, would seem to belong quite clearly in the second. Between such definite examples lie innumerable gradations.

The purchase of research materials solely for individual faculty use should be subordinated to the adequate fulfillment of the primary book needs of students. If such material is needed for a class project, however, or if the material will be used by more than one department, then the justification for purchase seems more evident. For the occasional request from individual faculty members for highly specialized materials in a field, the service of inter-library loan and microfilm should suffice. Such a service has been strengthened by library cooperation, by liberalized loan policies, and by the development of the bibliographical resources of the college library in such manner as has already been pointed out in Chapter VII.

Library Cooperation as a Means of Expanding Collections

Cooperation is a word that is appearing with increasing frequency in library literature, and so many cooperative enterprises are being undertaken that the question is rapidly becoming not whether one should cooperate, but with whom—a question that must be answered by each institution in terms of its own needs and situation. Experience has shown that library cooperation is not a way to save money. It is rather an avenue through which local, regional, and national library resources can be broadened, strengthened, and controlled. Inter-library loans, union catalogs and lists, cooperative storage ventures, cooperative acquisitions agreements (though here the college library probably can do little except in special cases),[27] exchange of materials, centralized processing, and filming programs, are some of the methods through which cooperation can be instrumental in accomplishing the aims mentioned, but these methods cost money. This fact is one which librarians and college administrators must face squarely in considering cooperative enterprises and in assessing the worth of their projected results. One should be chary of the cooperative venture as a possible economy measure, but should approach it as a possible way to make more effective use of available funds and to improve resources.

Where and How to Buy

College libraries buy most of their materials through several, if not all, of the following sources: publishers, book jobbers and dealers, local booksellers, secondhand booksellers, subscription agents. For the individual library, one or two of these agents will seem more important than the others, but each one has special advantages for certain kinds of purchases.

Publishers. It is frequently true that a publisher will give greater discounts on book purchases than other agents, but any supposed advantage in such discounts will quickly be set down as a financial illusion when an examination is made of the increased paper work entailed by dealing regularly with numerous individual publishers. Particularly in small libraries, whose minimum staffs continually struggle for time to do the more important educational jobs demanded of them, the ordering of books from many agencies is an uneconomic use of time, effort, and money.

The case against dealing directly with publishers in foreign countries is doubly strong. Experience has shown that such arrangements bog down in time lost, in high transportation costs, annoying formalities, and in the uncertainty of remittances.

Nevertheless for certain types of purchases, ordering from domestic publishers may sometimes prove most satisfactory. Advantages of such buying may occur for:

1. "On approval" orders because of the liberal examination period offered by many publishers.

2. Rush orders when the publisher's regional offices are not far from the library (although regional offices usually carry small stocks) or when the publisher is located within the same state or nearby.

3. Pre-publication offers (usually for expensive purchases which after publication offer little or no discount).

4. Orders obtainable only from the publisher.

5. Books issued in small editions by local or specialized publishers.

These opportunities, even if used to the full, will make up but a small percentage of the total purchases of the library.

Book Jobbers and Dealers. The best source of books available to the college library is the book jobber or dealer. He is able to give a substantial discount on bulk orders. He is familiar with library procedures and with library needs. If he handles the major portion of the library's orders, he may also be prepared to handle smaller items on which he makes no profit, and special purchases like continuations and even out-of-print books. He can simplify adjustments, which are frequent in all order work.

Naturally book jobbers and dealers are influenced in their relations with librarians by the amount of business they get. This is a strong argument for placing as many orders as feasible with a single book jobber whose discounts and service are known to be good. If much of the regularly advertised book stock is ordered from local sources or directly from the publishers, the librarian cannot expect the jobber simply to handle continuations, specialized works, and the more ephemeral type of material, all of which involve much work and little profit.

A good metropolitan jobber can handle satisfactorily all domestic and foreign publications needed in the average college library. If foreign purchases are extensive, then the practice of selecting foreign agents has much to commend it.

The selection of a good jobber involves these considerations, among others:

1. Personal acquaintance with his organization or knowledge of his service from libraries acquainted with it.

2. Discounts. These will depend on (a) the volume of library business; (b) type of materials bought; (c) the ability of the dealer to supply some books in good secondhand condition; (d) the efficiency with which library orders are prepared and sent to the dealer. The good bargainer will check his discounts from time to time on the basis of a year's orders. But he

will remember that to change dealers frequently is costly and detrimental to good library service.

3. Service. The book jobber's service to a library can be measured by the size of his stock, promptness and care in delivery, transportation arrangements, and method and ease of adjustments. One very important point to consider also is the "follow-up"—the accuracy and the promptness with which a dealer reports back on "shorts," i.e., on out-of-print and out-of-stock items.

4. Supplying of secondhand copies in good condition. Most book jobbers do not include this element in their service, but where they can supply occasional secondhand copies of books in print (always at a greater discount than for new copies), their service to libraries is greatly enhanced.

Local Booksellers. Purchasing from a local bookseller has usually proved unsatisfactory for the college library. His experience and the size of his stock seldom allow him to meet library needs, and the greater part of the library's requirements he will not have on hand. Furthermore, his discounts generally do not equal those available through a metropolitan dealer, and his service is likely to involve delay and inconvenience.

There is no reason, of course, to discriminate arbitrarily against a local book shop, and at least one metropolitan college librarian has found local dealers to be an eminently satisfactory source of book material.[28] If the bookman's discounts equal those obtainable elsewhere, it is logical to give him some share of library business in more popular books. And in any case, it is worth the librarian's time to know something of the local bookseller's stock, particularly if it includes some secondhand or out-of-print books, for the rare moment when the library may require quickly and without regard to cost something that he may have.

Dealers in Remainders. Remainders make up a very special and deceptive class of books—living as they do in a twilight between in-print and out-of-print. Discounts are large, but the library which buys remainders simply because of such discounts will be deceiving itself. Too often the "bargain" turns out to be a book which for college library use is not worth its shelf space.

Out-of-Print Dealers. Most out-of-print books are secondhand. Those not secondhand will usually be noted as "mint condition," "dust wrappers," or "as new"—notations which indicate top physical condition but which will not greatly mark them off from sound secondhand copies unless the books are rare.

For the college library, the out-of-print dealer usually comes next in importance after the book jobber. The librarian has been advised to work regularly through one to two dealers as a sound practice. If more than two dealers are used, it involves excessive office and clerical work to be fair with the dealers by keeping them posted on items supplied. It may also create an artificial rise in prices for particular books and discourage some of the dealers in their efforts.[29] Advantages of this system will be the stimulus of competition and greater speed in securing out-of-print items. Having a single dealer should not prevent the library from occasionally (say, twice a year) sending out complete want lists to many firms with request for a report of items in stock within a month.

With the appearance of *The AB Bookman's Yearbook* (issued annually since 1954) it has become much easier both to locate the out-of-print dealers and to ascertain their specialties. If the temptation to employ a half dozen dealers at once in finding the same list of books ought to be resisted by the librarian, it should nevertheless be feasible now for the library seeking a considerable number of books in one field to go direct to a dealer who specializes in that field, even though the contact is entirely new.

In any event, the library must have a want list, keep the list up-to-date, and notify its dealer or dealers of revisions. Quotations of prices should be requested, and those that exceed the list price by any considerable margin should not be accepted without careful scrutiny by the librarian and the faculty member concerned. Time and effort will also be called for to scan dealer catalogs, visit out-of-print book stores whenever possible, enlist the aid of faculty members or other scholars, and keep bibliographical details tucked away in the mind for future use. To the true scholar or book hunter, no other kind of book buying seems so rewarding.

Importations. In acquiring materials issued abroad, the majority of college libraries utilize the services of American dealers specializing in imports. The fewer risks, lessened paper work, and generally greater speed and economy afforded by such an arrangement certainly seem to indicate the wisdom of this method of purchase. When a college library contemplates an extensive program of foreign book purchases, it should study this phase of the acquisition process of the nearest good university library and carefully investigate the relevant literature [30] before embarking on its program.

Subscription Agents. Subscription agents are representatives who take orders for material and sometimes ask for payment in advance of delivery. These representatives visit libraries for the purpose of selling in advance expensive reference sets not ordinarily sold through the regular trade channels. If the agent directly represents a reputable publisher, the chances are that his product is a good one and worthy of careful consideration. If he represents a company which has acquired the right to the sale of job lots of subscription books, his product may be worthless. Subscription agents' offers should be: (1) checked with the *Subscription Books Bulletin*; (2) ordered, if possible, on approval for inspection; and (3) purchased only when they fill a particular need.

ESSENTIALS IN ACQUISITIONS WORK

After books are selected, they have to be secured by the library through a process commonly termed acquisitions or order work. The former term is sometimes used to include book selection as well. In the small college library the librarian will handle the order work in addition to his administrative and book selection duties. In the medium-sized college library he may have an order librarian or at least a clerical assistant to help him. In the large college library there will probably be an order librarian with several assistants. For the sake of convenience the term "order department" is used throughout the present chapter and is to be interpreted to mean those individuals concerned with the actual acquisition of material in the small, medium, or large college library whether by purchase, exchange, or gift.

Certain relationships are important in acquisitions work.

Relationship to Book Selection

The order department receives a great deal of information about books in announcements, reviews, catalogs, and in other forms frequently useful to the selector. A judicious selection of this material or notes based on the information contained in it should be routed to the book selection people. This point has already been mentioned in the discussion of participants in book selection.

After funds are allocated to the college teaching departments, the order department has in part the responsibility to see that books are ordered. If a department lags in sending in its orders, the cause may be plain faculty inertia, faulty ordering routine on the part of the library, or both. The order department should see that the channels for sending book orders are definite and satisfactory to the various departments. Proper forms or cards should be available for this purpose. Periodic statements of book balances should be sent to departments.

The order department has also the responsibility to see that book funds are not overdrawn, or, if a particular department has not sufficient funds to meet essential needs, that funds are transferred from the general library fund or the material purchased from the general library fund.

The order department must determine whether material recommended for ordering is already in the college library in some form or other. If a duplication is not discovered before the order is sent out, it often will not become evident until after the library marks of ownership have been placed in the book. Sometimes a book suggested for purchase is actually published as one of a numbered series, such as the transactions of a learned society, or the studies of some university. If, as too often happens, the department recommending the book does not mention this, only searching on the part of the order department will prevent a duplication.

From experience in searching and in ordering, the order department is made aware of strengths and weaknesses in the collections. It is therefore incumbent upon the department to be continuously on the watch for bargain opportunities to fill the lacunae, and to call the attention of the proper departments to such opportunities when they occur.

There are phases of order work which require careful cooperation with other departments of the library. There are "rush
orders" for the reserve department which must receive special
treatment if a teaching course is not to suffer; there are replacements recommended by the circulation department, and the consideration of special editions to meet particular course needs;
and there are decisions to make with the reference department
concerning documents and other material.

Relationship to the Business Office

In practically all colleges the relationship between the library
and business office is a close and important one. At the very
least this relationship will involve:

1. Presenting library bills approved for payment to the business office.

2. Checking ledger sheets from the business office so that the
library may keep an accurate running record of its accounts.
Differences and adjustments should be attended to promptly.

Because their contents are unique, not interchangeable like
shoes, ships, and sealing wax, books do not lend themselves to
the substitution of something "different, but of comparable quality." For this reason the library should be autonomous in the
selection of its book suppliers. Further, because expedition is
frequently the deciding factor in securing materials from secondhand dealers, and because course requirements sometimes dictate
speed in ordering, processing, and making specific books available for study, the library should be authorized to place orders
directly with its suppliers. This may be done through the appointment of the librarian as deputy to the purchasing agent. Where
such an arrangement can be effected, the library must assume
the obligation of maintaining such financial records as may be
necessary to furnish the business office with periodic statements
of total expenditures and encumbrances from the book fund, and
must maintain them accurately and in such a manner that the
fiscal officers of the institution will feel confident that the library
is in complete control of the funds allocated to it. Such an
arrangement would not preclude the maintenance of encumbrance
records in the business office if the latter feels this is essential.

The need for close working relation with the business office is apparent in college libraries where central control is exercised over the expenditure of funds and where orders are sent on requisitions to the purchasing department of the college. The necessity for friendly relations and a clear understanding of each other's problems is fairly obvious here, and there are certain conditions which are important in insuring the best cooperation:

1. The procedure for preparing requisitions and, later, the required number of bills for payment must be clearly worked out and understood by the library.

2. Regular statements of the library account should be secured from the business office.

3. Both the librarian and the business office should be diligent in attempting to insure speed in ordering and delivery of materials, and in approving invoices for payment.

Organization

Almost all acquisitions are made in one of three ways: by purchase; by exchange, of which there are two kinds; or by gift.

Purchase is, of course, the most important method, but the librarian who concentrates upon it to the exclusion of other types of acquisition will make a sad mistake. The problem of gifts, for example, is not something which can be left to take care of itself. If the librarian is indifferent or cool toward gifts, he may, in the long run, discourage a certain amount of legitimate interest in the library. Such an attitude can have a harmful effect on public relations. However, the librarian should be particular about what gifts he accepts, exercising over gifts added to the library collections the same discretion and applying the same criteria as pertain to materials acquired by other means, and making it clear to donors that acceptance of gift materials does not necessarily imply their permanent addition to the library's collections. The faculty, the college administration, and the librarian should work together in developing a policy defining the types of gifts that are desirable for the college, and the librarian should be free to decide whether all or a part of a gift is to be added to the collection, exchanged, sold, or discarded. The library should also be extremely careful not to accept gifts upon which the donor imposes restrictions that tend to interfere with sound library administrative practices.

As regards exchange, when the college library has at its disposal one or more college-sponsored serial publications, it may use these effectively as exchange media. Although in general college libraries are not so fortunate, most of them have from time to time duplicate materials which may be exchanged.

Exchange of duplicates is a common college library practice, but the low esteem in which it is sometimes held can be seen in the fugitives from a pulp mill and bait for the ash can which, on exchange lists in the past, have all too frequently obscured the whole and useful book. According to Elsa M. Loacker, the participating library should prepare its lists according to an improved and standardized scheme,[31] of which the following are the principal features:

1. Elimination of worthless and damaged books.

2. Elimination of old textbooks; of handbooks and encyclopedias roughly between five years (more if there is no new edition) and fifty years old; most fiction; all reprints of magazine articles.

3. If the stock of books is large, division into broad classifications like English literature, economics, history, natural science (with subdivisions), and so on.

4. Standardization of entries by following those on Library of Congress cards with some simplification.

Exchange of books and other materials was facilitated for some libraries by the inauguration of the United States Book Exchange in 1949.

Growing out of the American Book Center for War Devastated Libraries and emphasizing in its early days the rehabilitation of libraries abroad, the USBE collects, lists, and distributes research materials from and to libraries all over the world. At present, the USBE, a private, nonprofit corporation, acts as a "reservoir into which a library can channel materials it does not need and from which it can obtain, for the cost of handling, periodicals and books it wants." [32] While it is unique in the service it offers, the USBE has not proved to be of equal value to all libraries, and it is only one of several exchange systems, organized to a greater or lesser degree, available to the college librarian. Details concerning the USBE and a number of other exchange systems may be found in Edwin E. Williams' recent survey of the USBE.[33]

Except for the "selection" of certain kinds of gifts, organization for acquisitions work is essentially the same for gifts, exchanges, and purchases. The process should be straight and undeviating, from selection through checking and ordering, till the book and all the pertinent information about its arrival are safely in the hands of the cataloger. Wherever possible, the process should be streamlined and simplified.

The person or personnel responsible for acquisitions work must combine business skill with a thorough knowledge of trade bibliography. The major duties involved are:

1. Personally examining all requests for orders to determine whether the library already has them, and where and how to order them.

2. Supervising and handling of all orders whether for purchase, gift, or exchange.

3. Calling to the attention of the librarian and faculty desirable purchases based on firsthand acquaintance with the strength and weakness of the collection. This calls for a systematic plan of continuous cooperation among the various departments of the library. It means also that the order department should maintain "want" lists of desired items and should keep an alert eye for possible bargains in catalogs and announcements.

4. Keeping accurate records of book fund accounts in order to avoid purchases in excess of departmental allocations, to show where departments are lagging in book orders and need to be stimulated, and to provide flexibility in book funds so that estimated needs may be adjusted when occasion demands.

The principles to be kept in mind in organizing acquisitions work are:

1. All acquisitions functions should be centralized and cleared through one person or order department.

2. Records should be kept to essentials and as far as possible should be designed to serve the needs of the staff and readers in

using the material as well as those of the person or department doing the actual order work. As a general rule, they should not duplicate approximately similar types of records kept elsewhere for the same material.

3. In the treatment and handling of orders there seems to be a valid reason for distinguishing between books and serials. Distinctions may be made in types of serials or in methods of acquisition, but to all of these there are too many exceptions. As one writer has aptly put it: "A broad line of demarcation, that between serial and nonserial material, offers the least possible source of difficulty." [34]

Order Routine

A good order routine makes a pattern of check and double-check. It will be designed for two purposes which may seem diametrically opposed—to bring a desired book to the library as speedily and as efficiently as possible; and to check carefully all along the way against the possibility that the original desire has been misguided, and in that event to stop the process instantly. A sound routine is one that keeps the two purposes in a fine equilibrium.

One college library has developed a "two-card" order system, in which one card is finally used in the shelf-list.[35] Another system that has much to be said for it is that of multiple order slips. With a single typing of the order form, a number of carbon copies are made.[36] Five such copies might be distributed this way: (1) the first copy to the dealer as the order; (2) the second copy to Library of Congress as the Library of Congress card order; (3) the third and fourth copies to the outstanding order file; and (4) the fifth (a stiff card) to the main catalog as a temporary author or main entry card. When books are received and checked, the third copy of the card may be forwarded to the catalog department to be used as a work-slip and the fifth copy sent to the faculty member ordering the book as notification of its receipt and cataloging.

While the details may differ according to predilections and size of staff and building, the essentials of a good order routine are the same for all types of libraries. An adequate routine will proceed something like this:

1. A request or order card arrives with as many of the bibliographical details on it as the person asking for the book can be persuaded to supply, together with his name, the name of the department, and perhaps the initials of the responsible member of the department who approves the order.

2. The card goes to the chief librarian who approves the order or indicates why he thinks the book or books should not be ordered.

3. When necessary the card is checked with appropriate bibliographies and the bibliographical facts corrected or supplemented if need be.

4. The card is checked with the library catalog, the books-on-order file, and the books-in-process file to make certain that the book wanted is not already present, about to arrive, or in process of being cataloged and made ready for the shelves.

5. The bibliographical facts are set down in an order letter along with the facts about other books to be ordered. The date of order and name of the book dealer are entered on the card, and the card is filed alphabetically by author in a file of books-on-order.

6. Library of Congress cards may be ordered at this time or after the book is received. For this purpose, a copy of the order card may be used or a special order made up. It is advisable to order Library of Congress cards in advance for current American books, but not to order cards for out-of-prints, books offered in sales catalogs, and the like until the publications have been received.

7. The book arrives and is checked with the bill. Date and net price are entered on the order card. The price is charged against the appropriate book fund or department allotment.

8. The book is sent forward for preparation for the shelves.

SOURCES OF INFORMATION ABOUT BOOK DEALERS IN THE UNITED STATES

No attempt is made at comprehensiveness in the listings below, and the more obvious sources of information (e.g., advertisements in library journals and reviewing media, and materials distributed by book jobbers) have been omitted.

American Book Trade Directory. Issued triennially by the R. R. Bowker Company, this work contains information about dealers in foreign books, importers and exporters, export representatives, wholesalers to libraries, and general information about the book trade in America.

The AB Bookman's Yearbook. This annual publication of the *Antiquarian Bookman* is devoted primarily to the specialist book trade. It lists dealers in out-of-print materials by their specialties, carries information about specialist publishers, and offers a wealth of information about the o.p. trade in general.

Library Journal. The April 1 number of the *Library Journal* each year carries a buyer's guide to suppliers of library materials, including wholesalers of books.

Book Dealers in North America, 1956-57. This is the second edition, revised and enlarged, of a work originally issued by Sheppard Press, London, in 1954. It contains a list of book dealers in the United States and Canada, arranged geographically. In addition there are lists of dealers arranged alphabetically and according to specialty. Although intended primarily for use abroad, it is nevertheless a useful directory for the American librarian. Succeeding editions will probably be forthcoming.

Notes

1. Walling, Ruth. "Book requirements of survey courses." *Lib. quar.* 12:75-93, January, 1942

2. Stanford, E. B. "Honors work and the college library." *Lib. quar.* 12:221-45, April, 1942

3. McCrum, Blanche P. *Estimate of standards for a college library.* rev. ed. Lexington, Va., Journalism Laboratory, Washington and Lee University, 1937, p. 23-4

4. "Standards for college libraries." *Col. and research lib.* 20:278, July, 1959

5. Gosnell, Charles F. "Systematic weeding." *Col. and research lib.* 11:138, April, 1950

6. Waples, Douglas and others. *Evaluation of higher institutions.* IV. The library. Chicago, University of Chicago press, 1936, p. 16-17

7. Burns, Norman. "Accrediting procedures with special reference to libraries." *Col. and research lib.* 10:157, April, 1949; Pattillo, Manning M. "The appraisal of junior college and college libraries." *Col. and research lib.* 17:399, September, 1956

8. Hirsch, Rudolph. "Evaluation of book collections." *In*: Yenawine, Wayne S. ed. *Library evaluation.* Syracuse, N.Y., Syracuse University press, 1959, p. 15

9. Stieg, Lewis. "Technique for evaluating the college library book collection." *Lib. quar.* 13:34-44, January, 1943

10. Coney, Donald and others. *Report of a survey of the Indiana University library.* Chicago, A.L.A., 1940, p. 50, 52

11. Ludington, Flora B. "Evaluating the adequacy of the book collection." *Col. and research lib.* 1:305-13, September, 1940

12. Hirsch, *op. cit.,* p. 16-17

13. "Standards for college libraries," *op. cit.,* p. 275

14. Randall, William M. and Goodrich, Francis L. D. *Principles of college library administration.* 2d ed. Chicago, A.L.A. and the University of Chicago press, 1941, p. 88

15. Danton, J. Periam. "The selection of books for college libraries." *Lib. quar.* 5:419-56, October, 1935

16. Danton, J. Periam. "The faculty, the librarian and book selection." *Lib. jour.* 61:715-16, October 1, 1936

17. *Ibid.,* p. 717

18. Danton, J. Periam, *op. cit.,* p. 425-6

19. Ludington, Flora B. "College library book selection." *Lib. jour.* 60:8-12, January 1, 1935

20. Arragon, R. F. "The relationship between the library and collegiate objectives." *In*: Fussler, H. H. *The function of the library in the modern college.* Chicago, University of Chicago Graduate library school, 1954, p. 19

21. Ludington, *op. cit.,* p. 11

22. Goodrich, Nathaniel L. "Pleasures of selection." Dartmouth College *Library bull.* 2:160, December, 1937

23. Carnegie Corporation of New York. Advisory group on college libraries. *College library standards.* New York [Corporation] 1932, p. 10-11

24. Randall, William M. *College library.* Chicago, A.L.A. and the University of Chicago press, 1932, p. 104

25. Council on library resources, inc., Washington. *Recent developments,* no. 41, July 23, 1960, p. 2

26. Branscomb, Harvie. *Teaching with books.* Chicago, Association of American colleges and A.L.A., 1940, p. 186

27. Downs, Robert B. "Cooperative planning in acquisitions." *Southeastern librarian* 6:110, Fall, 1956

28. Pickett, A. S. "An experiment in book buying." *Lib. jour.* 84: 371-2, February 1, 1959

29. Allen, William H. "Second-hand book buying for libraries." *Lib. jour.* 59:378, May 1, 1934

30. Fall, John. "Problems of American libraries in acquiring foreign publications." *Lib. jour.* 24:101-13, April, 1954

31. Loacker, Elsa M. "Streamlining the exchange of duplicates." *Lib. jour.* 66:381, May 1, 1941

32. Williams, Edwin E. *A serviceable reservoir; report of a survey of the United States book exchange.* Washington, The exchange, 1959, p. 7

33. Williams, *op. cit.*

34. Rothman, Fred B. and Ditzion, Sidney. "Prevailing practice in handling serials." *Col. and research lib.* 1:167, March, 1940

35. Allez, George C. "Order routine for the small college library." *Wilson lib. bull.* 17:642, 645, April, 1943

36. Matthews, Sidney E. "Multiple order form slips." *Lib. jour.* 82: 635-8, March 1, 1957

ADDITIONAL REFERENCES

Bach, Harry. "Acquisition policy in the American academic library." *Col. and research lib.* 18:441-51, November, 1957

Bixler, Paul. "Censorship and selection: the librarian as a trustee of the public's right to know." *In*: Illinois. University. Library school. *The nature and development of the library collection.* Champaign, Ill., distributed by Illini Union Bookstore [1957], p. 117-33

Busse, David. "The role of the wholesaler." *In*: Illinois. University. Library school. *The nature and development of the library collection.* Champaign, Ill., distributed by Illini Union Bookstore [1957], p. 104-16

Carter, Mary Duncan and Bonk, Wallace John. *Building library collections.* New York, Scarecrow Press, Inc., 1959

McCrum, Blanche Prichard. "Book selection in relation to the optimum size of a college library." *Col. and research lib.* 11:138-42, April, 1950

McKeon, Newton F. "The nature of the college-library book collection." *Lib. quar.* 24:322-35, October, 1954. *Also in*: Fussler, H. H., ed. *The function of the library in the modern college.* Chicago, University of Chicago Graduate library school, 1954, p. 48-61

Merritt, L. C. and others. *Reviews in library book selection.* Detroit, Wayne State University press, 1958

Metcalf, Keyes D. "The essentials of an acquisition program." *In*: Randall, W. M. ed. *The acquisition and cataloging of books.* Chicago, University of Chicago press, 1940, p. 76-94

Skipper, James E. "The continuing program of book selection and acquisition." *Lib. resources and tech. serv.*, 2:265-71, Fall, 1958

Stanford, Edward B. "Increasing library resources through cooperation." *Lib. trends* 6:296-308, January, 1958

Sweet, Arthur P. "Forms in acquisitions work." *Col. and research lib.* 14:396-401, 452, October, 1953

Tauber, M. F., and associates. *Technical services in libraries.* N.Y., Columbia University press, 1954

Thornton, Eileen. "Cooperation among colleges." *Lib. trends* 6:309-25, January, 1958

Vosper, Robert, ed. "Current acquisitions trends in American libraries." *Lib. trends* 3:333-470, April, 1955

XIII

Selection and Acquisition of Special Types of Materials

A shorthand definition of "special types of material" conveniently includes any material not a book which contributes to the learning process. Here it includes older materials like serials and newspapers as well as audio-visual aids like the phonograph record and the motion picture.

SERIALS

A serial has been defined as any publication, whether issued at regular or irregular intervals, with some scheme for consecutive numbering, and intended to be continued indefinitely. By definition, then, serials include annuals, monographs, and government publications in series; periodicals; and continuations such as almanacs, yearbooks, proceedings, and transactions.[1] In the college library the most important body of serials are the journals and government publications. Because of the special problems involved in handling government publications, they are treated separately in this chapter, but the primary serial record may well serve for such publications in series as well as for the other types of materials mentioned above.

Importance in the College Library

Serials are particularly important for the advanced student preparing term papers and the graduate student who may need thesis source materials. Their value to the science faculty in teaching and research has been pointed out too frequently to necessitate further comment. The use of scholarly journals in the humanities and social sciences is equally important to the faculty. The reading of the results of recent scholarship in these fields is as necessary for instruction and research as is familiarity with recent advances in chemistry or physics. A teacher in the social sciences has put the case emphatically. Most of his colleagues, he states, have the intellectual humility to admit that their "sciences" are still seeking to establish first principles. They cannot honestly use any single text as truly authoritative. They are dependent on the results of new investigations into theory and evidence which are available only through the journals. Journals are also used extensively in general reading. They help to strengthen the library's cultural reading collection and perform an educational service in this respect by making students cognizant of the contributions and developments in fields other than those in which they are majoring.

Selection

The periodical collection in a college library is built up largely on the advice of the faculty. The librarian's contribution is necessarily limited to a selection of the more general journals for recreational and cultural reading, and even here the advice of faculty members should be requested and considered. It is evident that the chief objection to faculty selection arises from the sharp disagreements among scholars as to which journals are indispensable. The appointment of a new department head frequently brings upon the library the reproach that fundamental sets are lacking in his field. While it is difficult to eliminate the personal prejudices of individual selectors, it is possible to modify the limitations of this method of selection by determining whether or not periodicals requested are indexed in one or more of the general and special periodical indexes and by checking requests against existing periodical selection tools. New titles present an additional problem, since they are not yet indexed or listed in any guides, nor has their permanent value been proven. They should be selected with great care and watched carefully to see if they should be continued.[2]

In an effort to attain objectivity in the selection of periodicals, at least three statistical methods have been used. In one of these, the opinions of a varied group of experts were statistically summarized for an extensive list of periodicals.[3] In another, circulation in a particular library was used as a criterion.[4] But the method perhaps most widely applied was a third, first tried by Professors P. L. K. Gross and E. M. Gross of Pomona in the field of chemistry.[5] Their method was a deductive one. The relative importance of journals in a particular field was determined through the tabulation and summation of bibliographical references culled from key journals during a specified period. Since one or another of these methods has been applied to a number of other fields, the statistical plan of evaluation has obviously merited a certain amount of approval from experts. However, there is one serious objection to the statistical method as applied to the selection of journals in the college library. The tabulations of foreign and scholarly journals in most of the studies show an emphasis on foreign journals out of all proportion to the needs of the undergraduate and to the funds available for periodical purchases. While an average of six foreign journals in the periodical holdings of 205 college libraries reported on in Dr. Randall's study [6] appears very inadequate, it seems more absurd to expect a college library to supply undergraduate students with eighteen foreign journals in the field of mathematics alone.[7] The statistical method will prove most valuable as a selection device for the large college and university library, and as an aid in determining the necessity for completing back files of journals for certain years, primarily for journals in the natural and physical sciences.[8]

In the selection of journals, it should always be kept in mind that the original cost of subscription is only the first expense and that the subscription will probably be maintained over the years, with the compounded costs of processing, binding, and storage. Because of these costs and the limited funds most college libraries have available for the purchase and care of journals, consideration must be given in selection to the availability of rarely used journals in neighboring libraries. The college library's first obligation is to meet the primary needs of the many rather than the unusual needs of a few. Even large libraries find it difficult to secure and maintain files for all their needs. In consequence the idea of cooperation has received more and more favorable attention in determining the acquisition of journals in college libraries. Cooperation on the undergraduate level is practicable only for those highly specialized journals which will be infrequently consulted in any one library. Thus, as regards the unusual needs of the scholar and research worker in the college, it is in the interest of college libraries to make selections with a view to rendering as many such items as possible available in a given region. For this purpose finding lists of journals received by several libraries in a region have been prepared quite widely.

Administrative Organization

A considerable diversity of procedure in the handling of serials from the point of selection to the point of use is noticeable in college library practice. Rothman and Ditzion point out these distinctions in the following statement:

> Some libraries have a periodical division, a document division, a continuation division, a serial division, and a gift and exchange division. In these libraries the department chosen to handle the material is determined not only by form but by source as well. Part of a set is ordered and handled in one department, at least as far as its early processes are concerned; another part of the same set is received by gift or exchange and passes through another department for the early stages of preparation.[9]

The authors of this quotation arrive at very much the same conclusion as J. Harris Gable, whose pioneer work in the treatment of serials recommended the complete centralization of all types of serials work—acquisition, cataloging, binding, circulation, and reference—in one department.[10] The advantages of complete centralization are:

1. Improvement of service to the reader.

2. Ease and economy in administration. Duplication of records is eliminated. The serials catalog becomes a record of acquisition, a record of location, a record of gaps—in short, a complete record of all the information necessary for the acquisition, treatment, and use of material.

3. The same persons handle all the necessary records, thus eliminating possibility of error or duplication of material.[11] As a result of a survey of the methods of handling serials in 126 college, university, and public libraries, Rothman and Ditzion found that complete centralization of functions relating to serials offers the best solution to this problem. Osborn [12] has pointed out,

however, that "complete" centralization is impossible. He prefers the term "self-contained serials department" and even then questions the advisability of placing the cataloging function within it. Opposed to this conclusion, however, are a number of hard facts, of which the most important is probably expense.

The case for the self-contained serials department in which all work relating to serials is carried on would seem to be strong where the staff is sufficiently large and where the physical conditions are right. But in colleges with libraries of rather limited budgets, it would not seem that the separate serials department could be fully recommended when by that is meant the placing of all work with serials under a separately organized part of the library staff. Many libraries would prefer to keep reference service under the direction of the reference department. It is not possible to classify readers. When a reader comes to the library no one on earth can tell in advance whether the information he wants is to be found in serials, books, or in other types of materials. It is likely, moreover, that the concentration of financial accounts in one department is more efficient and desirable. And it is certainly true that for many libraries, the cost for additional staff would be prohibitive. The most practicable working arrangement would seem to be a combination of methods within the framework of the regularly established departments of college libraries. Under such a plan the organization of work might be laid out in this manner:

1. The acquisition of all serial matter would be handled in a separate division of the order department. If there are no divisions in the department, the records and routines for handling serials would still be kept separate and distinct by the person responsible for ordering.

2. The serials record in the order department would be a complete file of all information necessary for the acquisition, treatment, and use of serials. This record would be for the use of the library staff, and essentially for the serials division. Its detail might make it unintelligible to readers, and it might be inconveniently placed for their inspection.[13]

3. There would also be a "visible reference index" of periodicals currently received for convenience in handling reference

questions. This listing, contained in standard visible index equipment or even in mimeographed form,[14] and complete neither in listing types of serials nor in fullness of information, might be sufficient to answer most reference questions.

4. Because of the experience gained in handling serial records in acquisitions, the person in charge of this work might also be responsible for the binding record kept in the same place.

The organization suggested above requires a capable and strong person as serials assistant. He should be a good administrator and have a knowledge of foreign languages. The organization provides for the maximum of integration of technical processes and retains most of the advantages claimed for complete serial decentralization.

Purchase of Serials

There are a number of good magazine subscription agencies, and far better service will be secured if orders for journals are placed with one of them rather than with publishers or with a local agency. The advantages of the national magazine agency are several:

1. Billing is done at one time, annually.

2. A reliable agency will notify a library of changes in a magazine's status and follow up missing numbers or errors in mailing.

3. Continuity in receipt of issues is better assured.

4. Cost adjustments are more easily made.

5. Discounts will be greater since the local agent will himself be dealing through a national agent.

6. Routine work of the library is greatly reduced.

An agency may also handle continuations. Such an arrangement should secure prompt delivery of annuals, eliminate a number of routines, and save time in selection.

Exceptions to the above method of placing subscription orders are usually of three kinds:

1. Some serial publishers will not allow subscriptions to be placed through agents, and libraries must order direct.

2. Foreign subscriptions can best be handled through an American jobber specializing in foreign publications and imports.

If a considerable number of journals come from any one foreign country, it may be advantageous to deal with an agent in that country.

3. Some advantage can be gained through direct library membership in certain societies. Most societies issue books and monographs in addition to journals, bulletins, proceedings, or transactions. These materials are available to members at a discount in excess of normal library discounts.[15] In many instances membership *must* be held by, and all transactions must take place directly with, the library.

There are a number of other general rules to follow in placing subscriptions. For one thing, the library should avoid the immediate closing or beginning of the calendar year in placing its subscriptions, since the dealer is swamped at that time with gift and other individual orders. For another, it is well to remember that some publications offer special discounts for two- or three-year renewals through subscription agencies, and that for well-established journals the library should take advantage of such offers.

A library should not change its agency often, but it is well to check serial discounts every few years and to ask for several bids. Reasons for changing to another agency lie in the size of discount, in the quality of service (following up missing numbers and errors in mailing and billing, for example), and in the completeness or spread of service. For some institutions, of course, state laws may determine or limit the frequency with which bids may be taken.

Exchange

The value of exchange of periodical files has always been recognized more widely than that of other material. For years libraries had operated more or less independently, issuing "want" and "exchange" lists on the basis of first come, first served. Though some still issue such lists, the exchange function is now generally sustained through cooperative ventures, two of which should be familiar to college librarians. In 1940 the Duplicates Exchange Union was established. Originally confined to periodicals, it extended its scope to books in 1944, and now has about

150 members. At least twice a year each member library mails lists of its duplicates to other members, from which items may be obtained for the cost of postage. The other venture, the United States Book Exchange, was established in 1949. It had been widely hoped that it would become a national center for surplus materials but it has not yet proven its value for all libraries, although many do make good use of it.[16] These means of exchange should be investigated by the librarian in terms of cost, time, and convenience.

Binding

Periodicals are the backbone of the college library's reference materials. Those which are indexed in the general indexes and whose back files are frequently called for should be bound, since a good quality of binding gives them durability and maximizes the chances of keeping them intact. They represent a substantial and continuing investment which must be safeguarded by an additional investment in binding and rebinding. Such binding should be done regularly, but should interfere as little as possible with the reference needs of the collection.[17] To postpone binding from year to year, to risk the possible loss of unbound numbers of journals, and to allow expensive books and journals to depreciate through neglect of binding or a poor quality of binding is unsound library administration and false economy. College library materials, as Pelham Barr has pointed out, demand the very best of binding materials and treatment—buckram or heavy cloth and boards, strong and careful sewing, powerful protection at the hinges, and, for some types of papers, hand sewing for ease of opening.[18] There are, however, some materials which may be bound in a less expensive binding without sacrificing the investment of the library and with considerable benefit to users of the library. Examples are journals that have an intensive initial use but are referred to only occasionally thereafter, and documents that appear in near-print forms. Specifications for less expensive binding vary among binding firms. In one type, for example, the journals are sewed and bound in lightweight buckram or cloth. The only collation done by the binder is for maps, plates, and narrow margins. Lettering is omitted and must be done by the library.

In another type, plain board covers are used, the bindery does no collating, and no special treatment for inserts, narrow margins, etc. is given. These economies permit a lower charge for binding. The amount of material which can be bound in this manner is definitely limited and should be carefully scrutinized by the librarian before it is sent to the binder. Also, binders are not usually eager to furnish this type of binding, and claim that the savings are not great enough to compensate for the inferior quality.[19]

A close working relationship between the library and the bindery will pay dividends in good binding. Well before the expected date of binding, the file of a volume of a magazine should be examined for missing numbers. These should be ordered from the publisher or magazine agent, and title pages and indexes for such magazines as furnish them should also be asked for if not automatically supplied.[20] The primary responsibility for complete periodical files being delivered to the bindery rests with the librarian in charge, but responsibility for collation belongs to the binder. Shipments to the binder must be accompanied by specific instructions for placing supplements and supplementary pages, for binding in or leaving out separately paged advertisements as well as covers,[21] and for the style of binding wanted.[22]

Most binding firms doing work for libraries will furnish binding slips and color samples. These are to indicate style, material to be used, lettering, and any other special directions to be given the binder. Binders keep records (called "rub-offs") of such facts about individual journals previously bound for the library, and the library will keep its own records of the particular rub-offs which the binder has. Since maintenance of style and quality in a set of journals or within particular files is desirable, librarians are not likely to shift their work from one bindery to another except for compelling reasons.

When journals or other serials have a very limited usefulness which does not seem to warrant any binding expense, several alternatives are possible. They can be kept in some unbound storage form such as cardboard file boxes, or Magafiles, or merely tied. Another possibility is to bind them into volumes by a drilling-and-stitching method or by using liquid plastic and case binders.[23]

The problems of library binding have been much discussed by librarians and binders in recent years, and practical steps have been taken to facilitate the solution of problems of common interest to both groups. In 1934, the American Library Association and the Library Binding Institute established a joint committee to work together in maintaining the highest possible standards in binding. This committee has established standards of quality for binding and a guide to fair prices, and has given valuable assistance on binding matters to individual librarians.

GOVERNMENT PUBLICATIONS

College instructors, particularly those in the social sciences, recognize that government publications provide primary sources for student projects and term papers as well as for their own research; good examples are the hearings before congressional committees, since their subjects are always among the most important agitating the public mind and since the testimony is usually drawn directly from American life. Librarians have frequently noted the importance of documents for reference work; useful types, for example, are census material and the reports of government investigation and research, and of course, those publications giving facts about the personnel and structure of the government itself. There can be no doubt of the general usefulness of government publications or of the variety of purposes which they can serve.

The handling of these publications, however, is complicated by at least two important factors. One difficulty is inherent in the mass and variety of the government's output. Estimates of federal publication in recent years would put the figure of annual production at anywhere from 20,000 to 30,000 titles, depending on methods of bibliographical apparatus designed to unlock this material for general use; but such has been the expansion of "ephemeral" material (some of it very important) in near-print form that there has been no available index both inclusive and up to date. The librarian who would have a thorough grasp of the field of federal government publication can give little of his professional time to anything else.

Another difficulty is the method of distribution of government publications. The number of such publications held by a college library is not dependent so much on the size of the college, the quality of the library's collection, or the original demand for governmental material as it is upon whether the library is a depository or non-depository. College libraries which have received designation by law as depositories for publications of the federal government make up but a small minority of all college libraries.[24] Non-depository libraries must select and order separately most of the government publications they desire, in many cases receiving them only through purchase from the Superintendent of Documents.

So important is the difference between depository and non-depository that much discussion must hinge upon it. The problems of the depository library, regardless of the size of its other collections, are of one kind, and library literature is liberally sprinkled with references to them. But although at least 80 per cent of all college libraries are non-depository, their problems have not received great attention.[25]

Much of what has been said of publications of the federal government applies also to state publications, but certain problems are even greater in this field. There is no one bibliographical listing of available state publications. The nearest thing to it is the *Monthly Checklist of State Publications* issued by the Library of Congress, but it is not complete. Many states issue checklists of their publications through a state agency, but there is usually no distributing center—a condition that increases tremendously the paper work necessary to obtain state publications.

Publications of local governments will mean much or little to a college library according to whether or not it has assumed full or shared responsibility for such acquisition and housing. Frequently the chief responsibility for such acquisition lies with the public library in the area. But if the public library is small or for other reasons cannot assume the job of caring for local government publications, the college library should not shirk that responsibility.

Documents issued by the United Nations and its specialized agencies have become increasingly important to the college library. Though they are published in great number, most libraries will want only a relatively small number of titles. Fortunately, the bibliographic control over them is centralized, and their identification and acquisition presents no real problem.

Selection

Nearly all college depository libraries are "partial" depositories. By prearrangement they already receive certain publications, and for them selection cannot be said to be the continuing problem which it is for the non-depository.

The librarian in the non-depository college library will have no question about the need for such standard reference works as the *Statistical Abstract of the United States*, the *Official Congressional Directory*, the *United States Code*, and the *United States Government Organization Manual*, or for such periodicals as the *Congressional Record* and the *Monthly Labor Review*. It is impossible to make out a list of government publications required in every college library, but it can be said that identification of indispensables for a particular library is much simpler than the problem of selection, which begins where the indispensables leave off.

Primary tools of selection will be the file of the *Monthly Catalog* for older publications, and for current material the latest issue of the *Monthly Catalog*; *Selected U.S. Government Publications*, now published biweekly; selected listings in *Publishers' Weekly*, and "U.S. government publications" in the *Booklist and Subscription Books Bulletin*. Advantages of the *Monthly Catalog* for the non-depository library are its relative comprehensiveness and the fact that it is now published with very little lag behind the date of publications indexed. It has been recognized that government publications have particular relevance for teaching departments of economics, education, home economics, health, political science, sociology, and history, and the librarian can frequently obtain the assistance he must have in selection if he will route the *Selected U.S. Government Publications* to interested faculty members of these departments for checking. Other leads to current publications may be the announcements of government reports in newspapers and the selected lists published frequently in journals in special fields, as, for example, the

American Political Science Review in the field of government. Teachers in the physical and life sciences have their needs also; in some cases special government lists should be routed to them.[26]

Only occasionally will the college library need state publications other than those of its own state. The *Monthly Checklist of State Publications* can serve as a primary tool, as well as the checklist of publications issued for the state by its designated agency. Publications of the United Nations and the specialized agencies are listed in the *United Nations Documents Index*. The Public Affairs Information Service *Bulletin* (PAIS) can serve as a useful bibliography of important documentary publications from all levels of government—local, state, national, and international. Scholarly journals in the various fields also note important documentary publications.

Ordering

One of the chief advantages of the depository library is that most, if not all, of its ordering is taken care of automatically. For the non-depository library ordering can be something of a chore.

Federal publications can be acquired by request from the representative of the congressional district in which the library is located or from either one of the senators elected from the state, by purchase from the Superintendent of Documents, by request from the government bureau or department issuing the publication, by purchase from dealers, by exchange with other libraries, or by gift from individuals. Congressmen and federal administrative officials can usually supply current material available for free distribution if requests reach them without too much delay. But often there is no clear distinction between what may be given to the library and what must be purchased. On this point it may be noted that two or three begging letters will prove more expensive to the library than the dime or quarter for which many a publication can be purchased. In any case some of the library's most substantial reference works and continuations must be purchased. Furthermore, perhaps because sales prices are at cost and congressional distribution has sometimes been wasteful, the trend in government opinion has been toward placing more and more material under restrictions of purchase.

Usually, acquisition will be by purchase from the Superintendent of Documents. Prices of documents are held to a minimum and their cost for the average library will be only a small portion of the budget. The alternative methods of purchase, by legal tender, coupons, or on account, are described in the *Monthly Catalog* and make the ordering of federal documents relatively simple.

State and local publications are more difficult to obtain, if only because of the number of sources and diversity of regulations. The issuing agency is the usual source, though some states have provided for a central distribution point and at least two, Louisiana and California, have provided for the organization of state depository libraries for their publications.[27]

While many documents are important for research, they are for the most part seldom used. If the college library intends to buy large blocks or runs of documents, the acquisition of these in microreproduction should certainly be considered.[28]

Organization for Use

The depository library will usually shelve its government publications as a collection by themselves, and instead of cataloging them with other library material and incorporating entries in the library catalog, will organize them by the Superintendent of Documents classification. Close by the collection will be shelved the catalogs, indexes, and checklists necessary for use of the collection. Such an arrangement has the advantage of bypassing the enormous amount of cataloging which would be required otherwise,[29] and although it will take the principal time of one or more librarians for checking and for reference work, there is the additional advantage that students and other users can quickly gain a knowledge of the remarkable size and variety of government publications.

In contrast, the non-depository library will do best to incorporate government publications in its general collection along with other material: bound or substantial paper-bound volumes, if important, will be cataloged and shelved with other books; pamphlets in important series will be bound in volumes or put in pamphlet boxes and cataloged; pamphlets not in series can be put in vertical files—for the large college probably in separate files with arrangement by issuing bureau, but for the smaller library in the general vertical file along with other pamphlet material; and periodicals will be treated like other periodicals.[30]

It was formerly said by some librarians of experience that copious entries for government publications in the library catalog made a simpler and more understandable key to discovery than government catalogs, but it is doubtful today whether the complexities of author and other entries can be easily fathomed by the amateur or infrequent user of government materials. In any case, the library which incorporates government publications in its general collection must "bring out" government holdings with frequent displays on bulletin boards and on display tables and perhaps by means of special lectures to students on the variety and use of government publications.[31] The whole problem of use, in fact, stands in need of further thought and study.

For the college library, depository or non-depository, there are three minimum essentials for ensuring the use of government publications:

1. They must be given adequate shelving and orderly arrangement.
2. Printed catalogs and indexes should be provided.
3. Provision should be made for informed reference assistance and supplementary publicity.

NEWSPAPERS

Newspapers have not only current importance; properly cared for and indexed, they form a primary historical record that is unsurpassed.

Selection

What and how many newspapers should the college library receive? In J. H. Gable's study, the average number taken by small and medium college libraries was 11 and 12 respectively, and for large college libraries, 30.[32] But more important than numbers is the quality of the papers. The only currently published major newspaper index in America is that of the *New York Times*, and the importance of an adequate key to the news as well as this newspaper's soberness and broad coverage should make the *Times* the first choice in almost any college library. One or two other metropolitan newspapers will be needed, preferably from cities near enough so that immediacy will be served. One of the most useful newspapers with national and international coverage is the *Christian Science Monitor*; other excellent newspapers of national significance are the *St. Louis Post-Dispatch* and the *Washington Post and Times-Herald*.

The small or medium-sized college library will want to take one or more purely local newspapers, whether these are country weeklies or city dailies. The newspaper collection of the large college library should be expanded well beyond such a minimum. It is likely to include a greater variety of regional domestic newspapers and a few outstanding foreign newspapers to give breadth and as much national and international representativeness as possible.

Organization for Use

A newspaper reading room is usually beyond the needs of the college library. Current issues may be kept with current periodicals, either on shelves or fastened to sticks arranged on a rack.

A college library will wish to maintain a file of the *New York Times*, and frequently it will have the responsibility of maintaining a file of one or more local newspapers. The maintenance of newspaper files was once a major headache for librarians, but the tremendous growth of runs of newspapers on microfilm [33] and the general acceptance of this form because of the savings in binding and storage have made this a real problem only for files of old newspapers, and even then microfilm may permit their discard.[34] It is safe to say that almost every major newspaper in the world is now available on microfilm. The logical practice for college libraries is to subscribe to newspapers in the original; then, if a permanent file is desired, the microfilm edition should be subscribed to as well, and the original discarded when the microfilm is received. Back files of foreign newspapers, even on microfilm, need not be maintained, except perhaps for the London *Times,* since they are useful only for specialized research and can be acquired on microfilm when needed.

Several librarians have called attention to the need for the indexing of local newspapers by libraries. Paul Foster has pointed out that a relatively quick and simple method is to index under specific headings, entering as many as fifty items on a single large card.[35] Personnel and budget will usually not permit this "extra," either in a form so simplified or in one more complete, but if they do, and no public library in the vicinity can do the job, the college library may very well assume the responsibility for it.

RARE BOOKS

One of the subjects upon which librarians have expressed remarkably diverse opinions is the importance of rare books for a college library. For example, the late Dr. Randolph G. Adams felt that the college library is the natural repository for rare books. He assumed that the library should befriend the private collector, and should seek to attract gifts from him by offering his books a safe and guarded resting place.[36] On the other hand, Warren L. Perry is somewhat skeptical of the ability of the small college library to care for more than a minimum collection; he differentiates between the library's and the collector's notion of the subject; and he suggests that the library will do better to purchase its rare books slowly and carefully, with an eye to their use, rather than to accept every proffered gift.[37] One can conclude that the librarian who wishes to face the problem of rare books must not only examine the controversial library literature on the subject but take into consideration his own and his library's circumstances. If properly done, the establishment of a rare book collection is an expensive proposition, and this expense will have to be justified.[38]

It has been said that rare books stimulate the student's intellectual curiosity.[39] But it would be a mistake to consider this true of the majority of students, and even for the minority rare books will act as a stimulant only if an effective method of introduction is devised. At Williams College the curator of the

Chapin Library was able to relate the importance of the books in her collection to students who took her course in "The History of the Printed Book." Presented thus, the rare book can have cultural, aesthetic, and historical meaning for the undergraduate. But a collection is unlikely to have much meaning if it is allowed to lie fallow or if it is made up of rarities, curiosa, first editions, association copies, and manuscripts acquired solely because they are unique or unusual, and it should certainly not be set up merely to segregate books whose use is discouraged.

What is a rare book? Roughly, it is any book printed before 1550, any English book printed before 1720, any American book printed before 1800 or, for states west of the Appalachian Mountains, somewhat later (following the schedule of printing dates given on the endpapers of McMurtrie's *History of Printing in the United States*, Vol. II); or an association or autographed book, a fine binding, a book printed in an edition of 750 copies or less, or last, a book which costs more than $25.[40]

The college library which is able to build collections of all these types will be more rare than its own books but nearly all college libraries will have the opportunity to build collections in at least one or two of these fields. For example, the college library which makes no effort to discover and build a collection of local imprints or of local historical material, when no public or other library in the vicinity is making such an effort, is dull or impoverished indeed.

In spite of hesitations and difficulties, a number of college libraries have acquired rare book collections of note. In 1933 the late T. W. McGregor established a fund by which college libraries were offered $500 annually for an approximate period of ten years provided an equal amount was set aside by the college, the total of $1,000 to be spent for the purchase of "rare source books in history." In the fifteen libraries that took advantage of the offer, some notable collections have developed.[41] Other collections established are the Hardy collection at Colby, the Horace Mann collection at Antioch, the Finley collection on the Northwest Territory at Knox, the Browning collection at Baylor, the Robinson Jeffers collection at Occidental, and the Robert Frost collection at Agnes Scott.[42]

While there are some separate buildings housing extensive rare book collections, only the largest and wealthiest institutions can afford such a luxury, and even a separate room in the library with a full- or part-time attendant is beyond the means of most colleges. The most practical substitute is a section of the stacks that has been screened off, or even a bookcase with a glass or wire screen door that locks. In any case, air conditioning of the area in which the collection is stored is essential. There should be provision, of course, for qualified readers to work with such a collection, and cases should be available for the exhibition of such material in the building.

Upon the closeness of supervision or protection of the rare book collection depends the amount of marking necessary for the books. Book collectors are disturbed over markings of any kind and at least one or two libraries have eliminated all markings. Rare books are certainly not to be treated in this respect like other library books. Adequate supervision should make unnecessary the usual book "preparation." A bookplate may well be used, but other necessary information can be penciled in, and the shelf location can be indicated by a "typed strip of paper which is slotted so that it may be slipped over the top edge of a back fly-leaf, and projects only slightly above the binding." [43]

Because of their unique character and fragile quality, a collection of manuscripts, particularly if sizable, can present a real problem. College librarians should be chary about accepting collections which may be lavished upon them. Most colleges cannot afford the time or personnel demanded by the special nature of manuscripts. Nevertheless, the library may want to acquire some manuscript materials—the letters and papers of a noted alumnus, perhaps, or archives relating to the institution itself or to an important local event—and will have to give them some basic treatment. This entails, above all, conservation. Each piece should be carefully inspected, treated if necessary, and stored in sturdy containers, either firmly upright or on shelves. Manuscripts are usually classed in groups according to their subject, and the containers might be identified in a general way by subject. [44]

PAMPHLETS AND CLIPPINGS

New pamphlets are among the liveliest materials dealing with current affairs, and when they have grown old they can become the most curious, entertaining, and sometimes the most useful source material for historical research. Let those who doubt the value of pamphlets read Lester Condit's persuasive *A Pamphlet About Pamphlets*,[45] a most illuminating introduction to the subject. But of course librarians have seldom doubted the usefulness of pamphlets. They have only doubted at times their own ability to care for them adequately.

Offhand, the pamphlet material may not seem as important for the college library as for the public library. Nevertheless, the college librarian should encourage members of the faculty to select pamphlets for purchase and should promote their use through publicity and displays. In some areas pamphlets are a leading form of material—in the labor field, for example, where much source material never appears in full in book form, and in vocational guidance where the conditions and interests may rapidly change. Especially in the small college library can pamphlets have an important place. An authoritative number from the *Headline Series* or *Public Affairs Pamphlets* will be read when a longer, more heavily documented work on the same subject will not; and in some cases when the subject is not represented in the curriculum and when the budget is small, a soundly written pamphlet will serve as a substitute for more expensive material. Students may even be advised to acquire pamphlets for themselves. The college library could profitably offer free certain brief bibliographies or reading lists, or it may sell selected pamphlets.

Some fear or distaste has been shown for the tone of propaganda which marks certain pamphlets. But this is nothing to cause fundamental difficulty. If disturbance over propaganda rises again as it did in the years immediately after World War II, the librarian might set up a "propaganda table" in the library and place there the most extreme examples with accompanying explanations and directions to consult the pamphlet file where more sober material is kept.

Sources

Historically noteworthy pamphlets will be found in the catalogs of secondhand book dealers, usually specialists. Current
pamphlets are listed in the *Vertical File Index, Publishers'
Weekly, Booklist and Subscription Books Bulletin, Wilson Library
Bulletin,* and many other sources. Ireland's *Pamphlet File in
School, College and Public Libraries* contains an extensive list of
bibliographical sources.[46]

Pamphlets may spring up anywhere but the majority of the
most important have established sponsors.[47] Excellent pamphlet
materials are to be found in series published by associations and
commercial and university presses. Because of the paper work
and other detail necessary in ordering pamphlets, it is preferable
to subscribe directly to the entire series or to order individual
pamphlets through the library's book dealer.

Organization for Use

A number of librarians have favored treating pamphlets like
books and giving them full cataloging. It is unlikely, however,
that the library will be able to cope with the flood of current
material in this way except at the expense of other services, and
the time spent in cataloging might be better applied to arranging
the file in such a way that users can consult the material without
assistance. Nor is cataloging really necessary with most pamphlets, since what is important about them is the subject rather
than the author or title, and the subject can be approached through
the vertical file. In practice, most libraries will probably follow
a mixed formula: cataloging those pamphlets which belong to an
important series (like the pamphlets of the National Planning
Association, which are useful if kept together) and those needed
for classroom work or useful because the library has little else on
the subject; and reserving the pamphlet file for all others which
are worth keeping for any length of time.

It should be noted that many of even the most timely pamphlets coming into the library may be described as ephemeral at
best. A good method for handling such pamphlets will be simply
to stamp them with library marks, place them on racks or shelves
where they may be easily seen, and allow them to be borrowed.

When their current use has passed, the library may catalog some and send others to vertical files, but many will be discarded.

Miscellaneous cataloged pamphlets are sometimes bound together for better preservation, but the value of this practice is doubtful, since particular pamphlets thus lose their identity, and when one pamphlet in the volume is being consulted, the rest are unavailable to other readers. A more frequent modern practice is the use of pamphlet boxes; pamphlets which are cataloged but have been left unbound can then be shelved advantageously alongside books on similar subjects without fear of physical damage. Another alternative is to bind the cataloged pamphlet individually in pamphlet boards—an expensive practice if too generally indulged in. If the pamphlet is thin enough, stapling it into a folder or binder made especially for the purpose will save time and money, and will be neat and permanent. An ordinary desk stapler is not suitable for this; a more powerful stapler, which can be purchased from one of the library supply firms or a local office supply company, should be used.

Uncataloged pamphlets will usually be placed in a vertical file under subject headings. The *Readers' Guide* is a good authority for subject headings,[48] but in any case an authority list should be kept so that it can be checked for headings for incoming pamphlets.

Clippings have traditionally been included with pamphlets in a vertical file. For a college library which receives the *New York Times* and its *Index* plus much other currently indexed material, clippings may not be so necessary as in public libraries. They will be useful, however, for items of state and local interest which are usually not indexed. Clippings that have permanent value or that will be used frequently should be mounted on a good grade of paper; those of temporary or unproved value may be kept in envelopes.

One of the chief problems of maintaining a vital pamphlet is weeding. Both subject headings and the pamphlets themselves must be examined at frequent intervals on the basis of current interest. Headings will be expanded and contracted, not drastically, but, especially in the college library with a restricted curriculum, slowly in accordance with changing needs. Pamphlets whose usefulness has vanished will be discarded, but only after careful consideration has been given to other material available in the library on the same subject.

MAPS AND ATLASES

Maps are a specialized kind of library material. There are perplexities in their selection, and it is both difficult and expensive to organize and house them. These are obstacles which are not easily overcome. Nevertheless, because of the growing importance of maps, they demand more than cursory treatment.

A map is defined as a graphic presentation of a portion of the surface of the earth on which we live, or even of the whole globe, on a plane surface, usually with a high degree of generalization and with the addition of data and some descriptive matter. An atlas is a collection of maps which are often on various scales and of various types. Principally because they represent a curved surface on a plane surface, maps are only approximations. Two maps representing exactly the same area and similar data may differ markedly according to the kind of projection. Hence for the cataloger and the user of maps, the projection becomes one of the most important facts to be noted.

The values of a good map collection are several. For one thing, maps supplement the book in the teaching function of the library; they make graphic certain large physical and statistical facts which even the most brilliant verbalization does not easily make clear or comprehensible. They are used most frequently by geography and geology departments, but they are seeing increased use also in the social sciences and in other departments. Other important uses of maps are in research, in drawing or preparing other maps on which various data are to be plotted, and in general reference work.

Selection and Acquisition

The selection of maps involves four factors: area to be covered, scale of map, type of map, and date.[49] For the gathering of a general collection, the first is the most important consideration. Areas can best be organized by countries, since these are the units with which we are most familiar.

Scale or intensity of coverage is a second factor. For convenience, maps may be divided into three groups: large, medium, and small scale. Since it requires many sheets to cover an area on a large scale, the library is unlikely to be able to acquire this type of map except for the area immediately surrounding its geographical location. Most topographical maps fall in the medium-scale group, as do most basic national maps which are drawn on the scale of one inch to one mile or close to it. Small-scale maps are the kind usually found in atlases, aiming at representing on a single sheet an entire country or a continent. Their weakness is abstraction and the necessary obliteration or omission of many important details.

Maps may further be divided into two types—general and specialized. The first includes only such features as are shown in most maps of the area. The second includes maps emphasizing a particular feature or made to fit a special use.

Date is the fourth factor. This will help to indicate changes in the basic information presented, and will be important also where an effort is made to acquire maps of an historical nature. In the latter instance, the librarian is urged to select his date carefully and abide by it, since unplanned acquisition can be very expensive and inefficient.

Maps may be purchased from commercial dealers like Rand McNally, or from scientific societies and institutes like the National Geographic Society. But by far the great majority of maps will come from government sources.[50]

Organization for Use

Except for the library that possesses an exceptionally large number of maps, in which case a separate room is desirable, the map collection should be kept in the reference room, where it will be of most use. For storing maps there are horizontal and vertical type files which are available from various library equipment firms. The horizontal type are more generally used, but the different makes should be carefully compared in terms of durability, capacity, convenience, and cost. Counter-height cases have the advantages of accessibility and of providing additional work and consulting space. A sufficient amount of table space for consulting is essential, as is good lighting. Depending on the type of material on which they are printed, old and rare maps, and sometimes others, should be mounted on muslin or even laminated.[51]

For the atlases a roller shelf unit, similar in general outline to the horizontal map case, will be the best accommodation. But for the few atlases in the usual reference room a smaller atlas case with sliding shelves will be sufficient.

Cataloging of maps is one of the more difficult of processes. Account must be taken of projection, because of the distortion resulting from the representation of a curved surface on a plane surface; of the process of reproduction; of the authorship, frequently lost in anonymity; of the title, sometimes given in two or more languages. Some classification scheme is important for maps, and no one has improved upon the objectives or general principles set down by S. W. Boggs.[52] They are summarized as follows:

1. To provide for each map a definite position in the map files in relation to every other map.

2. To bring together in the files those maps which will most frequently be used together.

3. To record on the catalog card pertinent information, including that which is peculiar to maps.

4. To make cards approximately uniform with Library of Congress cards.

5. To develop an adequate system or body of headings relating both to subject matter and areas covered by maps.

6. To make headings similar to those used in books and periodicals.

The manual for cataloging maps prepared by Boggs and Lewis [53] has been influential in many smaller libraries. Since then, the availability of printed Library of Congress cards has made the task of cataloging maps much simpler.

MICROREPRODUCTION

Perhaps no other technical development in recent years has been discussed so much in library writings as the reproduction of materials on microfilm and microcards, and in Microprint;

and nothing since the turn of the century is likely in the long run to have as much influence on library service.

There are a number of forms of microreproduction, with different characteristics and uses. They may be divided into two major subdivisions: transparent (read by transmitted light) and opaque (read by reflected light). Within these subdivisions are several types,[54] but for the purposes of most college libraries it is necessary to be familiar with only three: microfilm, microcards, and Microprint.

Microfilm usually comes in 35mm. width, in pieces or on rolls up to 100 feet long, and requires a special machine for reading. It has proved most useful as a substitute for bound files of newspapers since it saves much space and binding expense and is easy to handle, more permanent, and more easily replaceable. The question of substituting microfilm for back files of journals has received some attention. The suggested procedure [55] is as follows: (1) the library subscribes to the journal currently; (2) it places a subscription for the microfilm edition which is received at the end of the volume year; (3) the original copies of the journal are kept, unbound, until the demand for them has subsided or until they are worn out, when they are discarded. The arguments for this procedure are based on the binding and cumulative storage costs for periodicals, the danger of deterioration and mutilation, and the fact that the use of periodical issues is greatest immediately after they appear, falling off sharply after one year. The librarian considering this should weigh carefully the disadvantages of microfilm—for example, the inconvenience to users, the poor reproduction of some illustrations—and exercise caution in the selection of titles.[56]

Microfilm can be used for inter-library loan. Where articles from periodicals or chapters from books are asked for, a microfilm of the original can frequently be obtained for little or no more than the expense of transporting the heavier materials, and the borrowing library or the individual for whom it borrows will have the additional advantage of owning the film copy permanently. In addition, when a requested item is unavailable for loan because of its rare nature, poor condition, or some other restrictive characteristic, a microfilm reproduction may be feasible.

It should be noted that many microfilming agencies require assurance that the film is to be used for research and that all of them place the responsibility for any possible infringement of copyright on the borrowing library.

The other major uses of microfilm are for the reproduction or preservation of rare books and archival or ephemeral material, for the economical acquisition of scarce materials, and for the publication of lengthy works of highly specialized interest, such as dissertations. Thus, accepted originally by librarians for its space-saving quality (displacing as little as 2 per cent of the original in the case of newspapers), microfilm has grown in importance as a means of acquisition, and librarians should keep informed of the materials published in this form.[57]

The second type of microreproduction is the microcard, which is an opaque process. Microcards are approximately 3 x 5 inches in size. On these cards the microtext has been photographically transferred, but the classification and cataloging information is reproduced in full-size print. Its primary advantage over microfilm is ease of use even though a reading machine is necessary. The microcards are simpler to file and handle than microfilm and they may be consulted more rapidly because there is no need to look through an entire reel of microfilm to locate the chapter or page desired. More and more titles are becoming available in this form. Microprint is still another opaque process, published on 6 x 9 inch cards. It also has the advantage of enabling the user to locate information quickly because of the individual cards, and because the inclusive contents are printed in full-size type at the top of each card. In addition, because Microprint is produced by offset printing, it needs no special care. Because these opaque processes are on individual cards which do not lend themselves to self-service, they are not as satisfactory for serials and newspapers as microfilm.[58]

Equipment and Its Care

Many different machines for the viewing of microfilm are available, and new makes and models are constantly appearing. Great care should be taken in the purchase of a machine, not only because of the initial expense but because of the cost of maintenance and the inconvenience to users when the machine is out of order. No machine is equally good for all situations, and the librarian who is considering the purchase of a machine should examine the models available and talk to other librarians about their experiences with machines.[59]

Microfilm can be easily torn or broken unless care is taken in placing the film on the reader and in winding and unwinding. The lens flats require frequent cleaning with soft tissue paper to prevent the surface of the film from becoming scratched. It is advisable that one member of the staff give close supervision to the use of the reading machine and other microfilm materials, that loading and unloading of film be restricted to those familiar with it, and that directions accompanying the machine, particularly for cleaning, be followed closely.

A library handling a considerable amount of film should own, in addition to a reading machine, a re-winder, which is useful for cleaning film, and a good splicer for mending breaks. Microfilm that is processed expertly can be preserved almost indefinitely as long as it is protected against excessive moisture, dryness, dust, temperature extremes, and careless usage. Storage facilities for collections of all sizes have been marketed, from small boxes to large cabinets.

Sources of Microreproduction

Microfilm can be obtained from most large university and research libraries and a number of commercial firms.[60] Microcards and Microprint are available primarily through commercial firms.[61]

Organization for Use

Microfilm can be shelved with books but it seems most advantageous to shelve it by itself. The latter method is mandatory where a humidifying cabinet is used; it simplifies classifying and takes full advantage of the opportunity to save space.

Rolls of film are kept in small cardboard cartons, and the cartons can be filed consecutively in cases large enough, if regular book shelving is used, to utilize the full depth of space originally intended for more bulky material. If film is shelved by itself, strips which are individually too short for a full reel can be spliced together, but in that case the sequence of items should be given on the carton. The very shortest strips, of no more than a few inches, may be something of a nuisance to the library; they can be mounted on or inserted in plastic or heavy paper holders, but these may need a special reader.[62]

Classification can be simply a film symbol followed by serial numbers given successively to the reels of microfilm as they are received, or, where a serial run like a newspaper is currently being received, a variation of the scheme can be adopted. Cataloging should be no more complicated than necessary but should follow that for books with reasonable closeness.[63] The author, title, date, and publisher should certainly be included, and specific reference to length and to the fact that the film is a copy should be incorporated. Microcards can also be classified by serial numbers. With cataloging information and, frequently, Library of Congress numbers already supplied, they present no cataloging problem. They are also simple to store—each group of cards can be inserted in an envelope, marked with the classification, and kept in a separate tray. Microprint is received in boxes which can be shelved directly.

The college librarian who embarks on a program of acquisitions of microreproductions should be conscious of the dangers of overenthusiasm. An overwhelming number of titles are available and the temptation may be great to purchase large blocks or sets of important research material. Selection must be exercised carefully, and the more frequently used current works must not be ignored for little-used materials. Mechanical equipment, suitable for reading each type of microreproduction, must be purchased and serviced. Material that has been transferred to a more permanent form still has to be cared for, and this also may require special facilities and the training of personnel. Finally, it should be remembered that originals are almost always preferred by users. There is no denying or underestimating the savings afforded by microreproduction, but satisfactory service cannot be measured in terms of cost.[64]

MUSIC AND RECORDINGS

The conception of what should make up a music collection has changed rapidly in the last few years. Particularly has it changed within the college library, which is interested in music chiefly for purposes of general education. Whereas the music collection was once either nonexistent or composed of a group of books and scores designed mainly for reference or for music specialists, today the number of collections has greatly increased and their purpose has become more popular.

The causes of the change are several. For one thing, there has been a general recognition that the position of music has been one of the weakest within the curriculum of the liberal arts college; clearly this was the chief reason why the Carnegie Corporation organized the College Music Set some years ago and distributed it so widely. For another, following the introduction of the long-playing record in 1948 and its immediate popular acceptance, classical music has become more widely known and appreciated. The college student today is frequently a musical sophisticate, and will not be content with equipment and collections that would have seemed adequate a generation ago. Another cause is the diversity of types of material that now appears on recordings. Not only music, recordings of which run the gamut from primitive chants to contemporary jazz, but every form of written and aural art—plays, poetry, readings of classics —is now represented on records which permit listeners to hear some of the world's great actors, poets, and writers.

Indeed, so important has the recording become that its frequent designation as one of the "audio-visual aids" is something of a misnomer. For the general student, whose musical role must be largely limited to appreciation, it has become, at least so far as the library is concerned, the primary material—with books and scores serving as aids. The musical illiterate will not read music books or pursue scores as a first step, but he may be induced to tackle them after he has profited from a rich introductory experience with recorded music.

To what extent do college librarians administer music scores and recordings? Such information is not readily at hand. In his summary of "The Place of Newer Media in the Undergraduate Program," C. Walter Stone writes:

Referring back to arguments for and against separate agency versus library administration of audio-visual services, I might add at this point that separate agencies have tended to develop audio-visual services mainly in terms of films, filmstrips, tape recordings, and recording and projection equipment, whereas libraries generally offer more diversified service with materials but have, to an appreciable extent, ignored campus needs for motion pictures, filmstrips, and audio-visual equipment.[65]

Most libraries are in the business of handling music scores and records whether they like it or not, but for those that are considering the possibility for the first time there are articles outlining the pros and cons of centralized audio-visual service which may be read with profit.

The materials in a music collection—books, scores, sheet music, records, recordings, and special equipment—are important for teaching purposes in music, language, literature, speech, psychology, and other courses. Records can also be used in organized extra-curricular activities—for dances, for sound effects in college plays, and as background in showing silent motion pictures. But their greatest importance can be for individual or group cultural purposes.

Acquisition of Records and Scores

Members of music and other departments may be depended upon to assist in the selection of much music material. But where records are widely circulated, the librarian may depend upon an evaluation of college community desires and upon the many sources of reviews in professional and popular journals such as the *Saturday Review,* the *Library Journal,* and *Notes,* the quarterly journal of the Music Library Association. The monthly *Schwann Long Playing Record Catalog* provides a complete listing of long-playing records.[66]

A record library may logically be built up around a core of the best-known musical masterpieces—the works of Brahms, Beethoven, Tchaikovsky, Wagner, and so on. But for making certain that the development of the library is an even one, the following outline might be followed:

I. Music by great orchestras
    a. Symphonies
    b. Concertos
    c. Ballet music
    d. Overtures
    e. Suites and tone poems
II. Instrumental music
    a. Piano
    b. Violin
    c. Other instruments
III. Music for voice
    a. Opera
    b. Choral music
    c. Song
IV. Miscellaneous
    a. Popular music
    b. Folk music
    c. Diction records

Some purchases might be made in each of these areas from the very beginning since each has its particular appeal and its contribution to make to cultural breadth.

A similar though more modest plan may be followed in buying scores. Certainly the first purchases of scores should be for cultural rather than professional purposes, and as Jerrold Orne has pointed out, it is best to proceed "from the best known to the least known, from the most needed to the least needed." [67] Scores are expensive, however, and any considerable purchase of them will involve for the library additional binding costs. Since scores are used by musicians, they must be bound so that they can lie flat on the music stand. This requires a special type of binding.[68] Before the college library embarks on any extensive program of acquisition of scores, it should take these difficulties into serious consideration.

Organization for Use

If the music collection is small, and there are few or no phonograph records or no phonograph, music can very well be shelved with other library materials in the main collection. Since this is now rarely the case in college libraries, the tendency is to have a separate music room or library. Such a music room should be large enough to permit group listening. Since individual listening is equally important, library tables should be equipped with turntables and earphones, and, if possible, listening booths should be available.[69] Duckles lists four requirements for listening equipment:

(1) It must be sturdy, particularly as to motors and turntables; (2) it must be simple to operate with a minimum of controls and speed adjustments; (3) it must have good tone quality, within the practical limitations enforced by its location; and (4) it must be economical in the matter of record wear and ease of maintenance.[70]

The music room will house not only music but other materials, particularly special or non-musical records, which naturally belong there; and it may forestall other demands for decentralization. Such a collection would probably include all music materials—reference and circulating books on music and music periodicals, as well as scores and records.

Because of the care and the expense of maintaining record collections in good condition, many libraries are unwilling to lend them except for class use. Records are expensive and delicate, and must be handled carefully. A few basic suggestions for their care are worth mentioning: moisture content of the storage room should be kept to a minimum, and the temperature should be kept low also; all records should be stored vertically, in smooth packaging materials; records should be cleaned before playing and before storing.[71] Standard record shelving is 12 inches deep, with partitions 6 or 8 inches apart to hold the records upright, and is available from most library furniture suppliers. Other suggested means for taking care of records are storage bins built to the width of the records, with slanted front and back, or vertical files. If the records are to be loaned for outside use, protective carrying cases should be provided and full directions for care and use printed in each album.

About the classifying and cataloging of records there has been much difference of opinion. A number of classification schemes have been suggested: (1) by form; (2) by company number; (3) by performing medium; (4) by composer; and (5) by accession number.[72] If there is an adequate catalog, this last method, which is the simplest, is also practical. It is especially recommended for collections in closed stacks.

No matter how small the collection, a shelf list will usually be necessary, and the catalog will frequently be called into use. The catalog will be particularly useful for the location of a single number which may be contained in a group of selections. The large music library will have its own catalog, and except for books on music no duplicate entries would seem necessary for the main library catalog.

Music cataloging has become more and more complex, but two developments in recent years have eased the librarian's task. The first of these is the expanded coverage of Library of Congress printed cards. Cards for a limited number of music scores had been issued for years. In 1943 cards were made available for all types of music and in 1953 for sound recordings. Today cards are available for almost any record, domestic or foreign. The second development was the appearance in 1958 of the *Code for Cataloging Music and Phonorecords*.[73] The section on simplified rules will be adequate for all libraries except those containing the most extensive research collections.

VISUAL AIDS

Many of the materials for learning, other than books, are considered today under the general term "audio-visual aids," and a few colleges have recently grouped all these aids together in a special department within the library. Such departmentalizing within the library has certain advantages: the materials and their organization can develop proportionately along with other materials and methods for learning; the library can more easily afford and accommodate the necessary technical direction; the servicing of materials and equipment can be coordinated more easily; and the audio-visual budget is more likely to be adequate and less likely to cut into other financial needs.[74]

Departmental organization of audio-visual materials within the college library has not, however, been the traditional practice. Even though in 1946 the College and University Postwar Planning Committee recommended the library as "the logical agency to handle these teaching aids," [75] a later survey made by the ACRL Committee on Audio-Visual Work showed that only 15 per cent of the 575 institutions responding had a centralized audio-visual service in the library. However, more than half the respondents endorsed a statement that the library should administer and service all materials of communication, including audio-visual materials.[76] Though libraries may not have deliberately refused the handling of these materials, neither colleges nor libraries have, for the most part, either promoted their full use or encouraged their growth in any orderly fashion. It is certainly true that while discussion of audio-visual aids in the library frequently groups the various types together, in actual practice they have more often been separated. The present-day college library may have an excellent collection of one type of audio-visual material and little or nothing of other types.

Should a library plan to accept a central role in the college's audio-visual program, it might note the principles declared by C. W. Stone. (1) The responsibility for materials selection should be decentralized; (2) the preview and study of materials should be held near the reading areas related to the subject; (3) the purchase, distribution, and maintenance of facilities should be centralized; (4) acquisition and processing should be centralized and there should be a unified catalog; and (5) the library should not be responsible for the production of new materials.[77]

Because of the variety of the materials and the equipment necessary to use them, and because some of the materials and equipment are unfamiliar and have only recently been standardized, any new steps in acquiring visual aids should be carefully taken. Standards of selection and purchase must be set up and maintained. H. C. McKown and A. B. Roberts put the standards in the form of questions.[78] For the college librarian the most important would seem to be the educational purpose of the material and the extent to which it will accomplish that purpose; authenticity; ease of operation or use; cost; and ease of repairs and replacements.

Maps, microfilms, and recordings, as related forms, have already been discussed. Motion pictures, which are sometimes mistakenly considered the only visual aid, will be examined in a later section. There are many other forms. Some are:

1. Photographs and reproductions
2. Post cards
3. Stereographs—three-dimensional pictures, most useful in elementary learning
4. Lantern slides (of several kinds)
5. Filmstrips (sometimes called slide films)
6. Sound filmstrips or filmslides
7. Diagrams, charts, and graphs
8. Radio and television

Educators would probably include also the college field trip, which lies entirely outside the library province, and the bulletin board.

It is this variety of forms that causes some librarians to hesitate to accept the responsibility for audio-visual materials, but not all are of equal importance for the college library. Of the visual forms listed above, pictures, slides, and filmstrips may at the present time be considered the most important for college libraries. Within the limits of this chapter, however, there is not space to devote full treatment to each of these types. There will be some discussion of pictures, as an example of the problems that are encountered, and references will be given in the notes at the end of the chapter to some of the many guides treating the other forms.

The primary use of these materials is likely to be for instruction in various classes. This may be especially true for anything that demands projection on a screen. Pictures, however, can also be accurate and reliable reference tools, and a good collection will make a large pool from which to draw materials for displays. In a number of colleges, furthermore, photographs, reproductions of oil paintings, water colors, and etchings have been framed and organized for lending to students and other members of the college community for long periods. On this level pictures have great cultural value.[79]

Organization for Use

Pictures. Picture collections may be acquired in many ways. It is possible to build a large useful collection from discarded books and magazines, from advertising material, rotogravure sections of newspapers, travel circulars, pamphlets and other sources.[80] If the collection is to be of greatest usefulness in a college library, however, it is likely that some material will have to be purchased from reputable dealers and museums, American and foreign.[81] It will be best to have as well-rounded a collection as possible within the limits of available resources, and the librarian is advised to think of pictures as something more than an adjunct to the art department.

The pictures in a small collection may be unmounted if filing space is limited. Most college libraries, however, prefer to mount their pictures.[82] In large college libraries where the picture collection is to be extensive, material may be housed in boxes, but where the collection is to be examined by the borrower or user, it is preferable to use legal size steel or wooden filing drawers or, even better, filing cabinets made up of many compartments with a drop front for each tier.

Classification and cataloging practices vary widely. As to whether a catalog is necessary or not, no one has presented the alternatives and the conditions surrounding them better than Eleanor Mitchell:

> The question of a card index to the collection should be decided only after considering the cost of preparation in time, labor, and materials in relation to the projected use to which such a catalog would be put. In the small college or university with a limited art enrolment and few or no graduate students, there is scarcely a need for a catalog of the collection. But in the larger university, with emphasis on graduate study or in the museum dealing with a varied public, a catalog is highly desirable and insures the tracing of every iconographic detail. Whether or not a catalog is planned every collection should have an authority file of place and personal names. Other special indexes may prove valuable in lieu of a catalog: an index of colored reproductions, an index of architects when architecture is filed under period or country and city, or an index of portraits where painting and sculpture are filed by artist. The presence of a catalog reduces in one sense the worries of the classifier. If a photograph of an object may logically be filed in any one of three places, the classifier may decide upon one and make subject cards for all three to prevent the photograph's being "lost" to the public. [83]

There is no standardization in classification schemes, but most frequently the primary division of the collection is by subject such as architecture, sculpture, painting, and the various minor arts; [84] under the subject arrangement, subdivisions are by period, country, and then alphabetically by city or artist. Another method is to divide material first into large culture cycles. Still other college libraries have grouped photographs by courses. The last is inadvisable. A more general organization is preferable; if considered useful, a list of photographs for a course might be kept separately.

Framed Pictures. If pictures are to be loaned for hanging and for extended use in student rooms or faculty homes, they will demand additional or separate preparation. Glass as a form of protection is too heavy and too expensive; an effective substitute is to coat the surface with the lightest shellac. Pictures should be attractively but not too heavily framed, and screw eyes and wire should be attached to them. The unit cost of buying large reproductions, many in color, and of preparing them in this manner is high, but the number of pictures in an effective loaning collection can be relatively small and the cultural value considerable. [85]

Postcards. Excellent postcards, at much lower cost than photographs and other reproductions, are obtainable from many art dealers and museums. Since their subjects are frequently the same as or closely similar to those represented in the picture collection, advantage should be taken of any opportunity to relate the two collections. If pictures are unmounted and kept in folders or envelopes, postcards might be included along with them. If pictures are mounted, postcards, of course, will have to have their own separate, smaller files. If, on the other hand, the picture collection is large enough to need a catalog, cards for postcards might well be interfiled in it.

VISUAL AIDS: MOTION PICTURES

In spite of some preliminary difficulties in using it, one must agree today with partisans of the educational motion picture that it is a powerful aid to learning and that it will be used more and more in the future. Whereas some non-book materials have made their way into the college library only gradually, motion picture films have been welcomed much more readily.

Does the motion picture demand markedly different treatment from other library materials, or is it essentially just one more item to be absorbed into the library's circulation system with a minimum of strain and stress? To date, the answer seems to be something of a compromise. The handling of films requires special technical skill and added staff. A particular film costs considerably more than an individual book, and it can be ruined far more easily. Owing to these factors the small college library is inhibited from adding any substantial number of motion picture films to its library stock.

Nevertheless it is not too difficult for the college library, whatever its size and resources, to provide its community adequately with educational films. This is made possible through the established and widespread practice of rental and loan. Among the distributors are universities as well as government agencies and commercial dealers.[86] Better than most other library materials, the educational film has seemed to lend itself to a form of inter-library loan, to the building of regional library collections, and to cooperative buying and ownership in association with other libraries.[87] By these means, without setting up a film laboratory or establishing a film center of its own, the college library can usually provide adequate exhibiting service.

Selection and Ordering of Films

One of the most difficult processes in the handling of films is selection.[88] Films should be selected carefully, primary attention being given to their use in a particular instructional or learning situation. If a film is being considered for purchase, it should be exhibited first before those teachers who are likely to use it. If a film is to be obtained by loan or rental, it should be ordered well in advance and the time of its arrival should be long enough before its scheduled showing so that the teacher may preview it and make notes upon it. Standards for selection may be similar to those set up for other visual aids. Films may be obtained by purchase, by rental or lease, free, or through cooperative film libraries.[89]

Organization for Use

Educational films are 16mm. and noninflammable. The problem of storing and preserving such materials has sometimes been exaggerated; the Society of Motion Picture and Television Engineers has determined that best conditions of temperature and humidity for books are also best for films.[90] If no cabinets are available, film containers or cartons may be shelved upright on regular library shelves; a strip of wood running lengthwise on the shelf will prevent cartons from rolling forward. Cartons may be tagged with a strip of adhesive tape on which has been put the title and the classification. Films should be kept free from grease and dirt and should occasionally be cleaned by being run through plush moistened with carbon tetrachloride. A splicer for repairs and a rewinder for inspection will also be needed by the library handling its own films.[91]

Films should be cataloged as nearly like books as possible, and cards may be filed either separately or in the main catalog. Since the *Educational Film Guide* provides descriptive notes and a subject index, and Library of Congress printed cards are available for films and filmstrips, classification and cataloging problems are relatively simple.

Arrangement for storage, mending, inspection, classification, and cataloging can be avoided, of course, if the college library obtains all its films by borrowing or rental. In fact, most distributors of educational motion pictures explicitly ask all borrowers to refrain from rewinding film before returning it or from doing any mending beyond what may be necessary in an emergency to complete a showing. But whether a library borrows or stores films or does both, it must keep careful booking and exhibition records. There should be a schedule book for the use of projectors, and a schedule sheet for each film to be exhibited. Request slips for films may be filed at the library desk under the date that they are due to arrive, and the file checked daily or regularly by the assistant in charge. It may also be necessary for the library to keep a list of available projector operators. Whether the library purchases or borrows film, however, it will be a better arrangement for operation of projectors and other needs of administering motion picture film if part or all the time of one or more library assistants is devoted to these tasks.

Purchase and Care of Equipment

Collections of pictures, slides, and filmstrips are unlikely to be given maximum use unless the library also owns and circulates a projector. In selecting equipment for still projection, the different makes should be compared side by side for their ease of operation, sturdiness, picture quality, and amount of heat reaching the film or slide. The machine should handle more than one type of material, and the ease of shifting from one type to another is a factor to be considered.

Considerations in the selection of a motion-picture projector are ease of operation, accessibility to controls, quality of sound reproduction, weight, sturdiness, and the simplicity of the rewind process.[92] These machines represent a substantial investment for the library, and care should be taken in their selection and maintenance and in the purchase of accessory equipment.[93]

Dealers and Equipment

To avoid the danger of slighting some reliable manufacturers and dealers, a selective list is not offered. Instead, the reader is referred to the notes giving sources which list firms. He should also consult the "Buying Guide" in the April 1st issue of the *Library Journal,* the regular "Goods and Gadgets" column and the annual "Guide to Library Equipment and Supplies" in the A.L.A. *Bulletin,* and news items in other professional journals. Where service is a paramount factor, perhaps the best method to follow in deciding on a reliable supplier is to consult with other librarians and take advantage of their experience.

Notes

1. Gable, J. Harris. *Manual of serials work.* Chicago, A.L.A., 1939, p. 28; Osborn, Andrew D. *Serial publications; their place and treatment in libraries.* Chicago, A.L.A., 1955, p. 12-17

2. Trumper, Virginia M. "Problems concerning periodicals in the small college library." *Southeastern librarian* 9:119-21, Fall, 1959. Two general guides for the selection of periodicals are: Farber, Evan I. *Classified list of periodicals for the college library.* 4th ed., rev. and enl. Boston, F. W. Faxon, 1957; Southern association of colleges and secondary schools.

Commission on colleges and universities. *Classified list of reference books and periodicals for college libraries.* 3rd ed. Atlanta, [The association], 1955. Titles of new periodicals are contained in a number of sources. The monthly *New serial titles,* published by the Library of Congress, is of course the most inclusive, but it gives no information about the price or contents. Twice a year "New periodicals of 19—" appears in *Col. and research lib.* This feature summarizes the nature of each periodical selected for listing and gives bibliographical and price information. The *Lib. jour.* frequently contains reviews of new periodicals, particularly those of a more general interest. "Births, deaths, and magazine notes," appearing in the *Bull. of bibliography,* notes new titles.

3. Waples, Douglas. "Periodicals for the college library; prepared from a list by Dr. Eugene Hilton." *North central association quar.* 8:425-43, April, 1934

4. Hunt, Judith W. "Periodicals for the small bio-medical and clinical library." *Lib. quar.* 7:121-40, January, 1937

5. Gross, P. L. K. and Gross, E. M. "College libraries and chemical education." *Science* n.s. 66:385-9, October 28, 1927

6. Randall, William M. *The college library.* Chicago, A.L.A. and the University of Chicago press, 1932, p. 81-2

7. Allen, Edward S. "Periodicals for mathematicians." *Science* n.s. 70:592-4, December 20, 1929

8. Stevens, Rolland. "Characteristics of subject literatures." Chicago, ACRL, 1953 (ACRL monographs, no. 6) ; Osborn, *op. cit.* p. 39-40. The most extensive use of the statistical method appears in Charles H. Brown's *Scientific serials; characteristics and lists of most cited publications in mathematics, physics, chemistry, geology, physiology, botany, zoology, and entomology.* Chicago, ACRL, 1956 (ACRL monographs, no. 16)

9. Rothman, Fred B. and Ditzion, Sidney. "Prevailing practices in handling serials." *Col. and research lib.* 1:166-7, March, 1940

10. Gable, *op. cit.,* p. 38

11. Rothman and Ditzion, *op. cit.,* p. 168-9

12. Osborn, *op. cit.,* p. 25-6

13. For various forms the serials record may take, *see:* Osborn, *op. cit.,* p. 84-119

14. Osborn, *op. cit.,* p. 85-6; Trumper, *op. cit.,* p. 122-3

15. Orne, Jerrold. "Serials information clearing house." *Serial slants* 1:10-17, April, 1951

16. Welch, Helen M. "Publications exchange." *Lib. trends* 3:423-31, April, 1955; Thom, I. W. "Duplicates exchange: a cost analysis." *Lib. resources and technical services* 1:81-4, Spring, 1957; Williams, Edwin E. *A serviceable reservoir; report of a survey of the United States book exchange.* Washington, The exchange, 1959

17. Hughes, M. H. "Periodical binding schedules for improved reader service in university and college libraries." *Col. and research lib.* 13:223-6, 231, July, 1952; Feipel, Louis N. and Browning, Earl W. *Library binding manual.* Chicago, A.L.A., 1951, p. 12-14

18. Barr, Pelham. "Binding requirements of college libraries." *Lib. jour.* 61:245-6, March 15, 1936

19. Ditzion, Sidney and Norman, L. M. "Problems of periodical and serial binding." *Lib. trends* 4:253, January, 1956

20. The *Faxon librarian's guide,* published annually by the F. W. Faxon co., lists frequency and dates of publication; records of index, title page, and volume; and appearance in the general periodical indexes for more than 3,000 American and foreign periodicals. For a discussion of problems in obtaining back periodicals, *see:* Abrahams, Jack. "A forward look at back periodicals." *Serial slants* 4:7-11, January, 1953

21. Osborn, *op. cit.,* p. 234-6, discusses the pros and cons of omitting advertising and covers.

22. Feipel and Browning, *op. cit.,* p. 21-30. This work, prepared by the Joint committee of the A.L.A. and the Library binding institute, provides an excellent introduction to the entire process of binding. It should be remembered, however, that it was prepared by commercial binders and disparages anything less than standard-type binding. The Library binding institute also publishes a periodical, the *Library binder,* which appears twice yearly and is available to librarians from the institute.

23. These methods are described in pamphlets issued by at least two of the library supply firms: Gaylord bros., inc. and Demco library supplies.

24. Many more public libraries have been designated as depositories than college libraries. Depositories have been selected on a geographical basis, one depository being allowed for each congressional district plus one for each senator within the state he represents plus a number of others like land-grant colleges. Depositories may either receive all government publications or they may select in advance what they shall receive. *See:* Jackson, *op. cit.,* p. 4-7

25. A notable exception in the field is: Miller, Kathryn N. *The selection of United States serial documents for liberal arts colleges.* New York, H. W. Wilson co., 1937. Its usefulness, however, is very much limited by its age.

26. Additional titles of value in the selection of federal documents are: Hirshberg, Herbert S. and Melinat, Carl H. *Subject guide to United States government publications.* Chicago, A.L.A., 1947; Leidy, W. Philip. *A popular guide to government publications.* New York, Columbia University press, 1953

27. Tilger, Ellen R. "Louisiana documents; they're free—and easy." *Louisiana library association bull.* 20:123-6, Summer, 1957; Thomas, Martin E. "California state documents distribution." *Calif. librarian* 12:101-3, 119-20, December, 1950

28. Jackson, Ellen P. *Manual for the administration of the federal document collection of libraries.* Chicago, A.L.A., 1955, p. 15-19

29. Boyd, Anne M. *United States government publications.* 3rd ed., rev. by Rae E. Rips. New York, H. W. Wilson co., 1949, Appendix B; Moll, Wilhelm. "A fresh look at the treatment of documents." *Lib. resources and technical services* 4:43-4, Winter, 1960

30. Helpful in determining the most desirable system are the following: Jackson, *op. cit.*, p. 22-32; Markley, Anne E. *Library records for government publications.* Berkeley, Calif., University of California press, 1951, p. 16-22

31. One program is described *in*: Estes, David E. "Government publications in the classroom." *Col. and research lib.* 20:78-80, January, 1959

32. Gable, *op. cit.*, p. 176-7

33. For example, *see*: U.S. Library of Congress. Union catalog division. *Newspapers on microfilm.* 3rd ed. comp. under the direction of George Schwegmann. Washington, D.C., The library, 1957. It lists approximately 8,000 titles, of which about 1,650 are foreign.

34. Osborn, *op. cit.*, p. 246-7

35. Foster, Paul P. "Neglected sources of history." *Wilson lib. bull.* 9:351-7, March, 1935

36. Adams, Randolph G. "Place of rare books in a college or university library." *Col. and research lib.* 2:27-32, December, 1940; "Librarians as enemies of books." *Lib. quar.* 7:317-31, July, 1937

37. Perry, Warren L. "Can the small college library afford rare books?" *Col. and research lib.* 1:105-7, December, 1939

38. Baughman, Roland O. "Conservation of old and rare books." *Lib. trends* 4:240-1, January, 1956. This is a useful article and it raises a number of caveats that should be considered.

39. Powell, Lawrence C. "Functions of rare books." *Col. and research lib.* 1:101, December, 1939; Bevis, Dorothy. "Rare books in the college library." *A.L.A. bull.* 53:149-52, February, 1959. For a similarly optimistic view regarding manuscript materials, *see*: Gotlieb, Howard B., "The undergraduate and historical manuscripts." *American archivist* 23: 27-32, January, 1960

40. Individual libraries will want to set their own criteria. These should not be too liberal, else materials will come into the collection whose presence cannot be justified, and the entire concept will be jeopardized. On the other hand, there may be some books which do not fit any of the criteria, but only need the protection of a supervised collection. Some considerations—rather specialized, perhaps, for college libraries—in establishing criteria are discussed *in*: Howes, Wright. "A rare book: its essential qualifications." *Lib. trends* 5:489-94, April, 1957. An actual set of

criteria, the University of California's Rare book code, is found *in*: Tauber, M. F. and others. *Technical services in libraries.* New York, Columbia University press, 1954, p. 305-6

41. Powell, *op. cit.,* p. 99-100

42. For other examples, *see*: Ash, Lee. *Subject collections; a guide to special book collections and subject emphases as reported by university, college, public and special libraries in the United States, the Territories, and Canada.* New York, R. R. Bowker, 1958

43. Powell, Lawrence C. "Problems of rare books in the college and university library." *Lib. jour.* 64:272, April 1, 1939. A survey of the practices of a number of major libraries in marking and cataloging rare books may be found *in*: Weidle, Catherine. "The cataloging and conservation of rare books." *Missouri lib. association quar.* 19:14-18, March, 1958

44. Bond, W. H. "Manuscripts and the library." *Lib. trends* 7: 511-16, April, 1959; *see also*: the entire issue of *Lib. trends* 5:no. 3, January, 1957, which is devoted to "Manuscripts and archives."

45. Condit, Lester D. *A pamphlet about pamphlets.* Chicago, University of Chicago press, 1939

46. Ireland, Norma O. *The pamphlet file in school, college, and public libraries.* rev. and enl. ed. Boston, F. W. Faxon, 1954. This work should prove generally helpful in the organization of a pamphlet collection.

47. *Ibid.,* p. 163-204, "Partial list of organizations, etc., that issue pamphlets."

48. Fritts, Mary H. "Streamlining the pamphlet collection." *Wilson lib. bull.* 15:408-9, January, 1941; other sources for subject headings are listed *in*: Ireland, *op. cit.,* p. 29-33

49. Espenshade, Edward B. "Maps for the college library." *Col. and research lib.* 8:133-5, April, 1947

50. There is no single complete list of sources for the acquisition of maps. Following are some that are useful for the college library: Thiele, Walter. *Official map publications.* Chicago, A.L.A., 1938; *Current geographical publications,* the monthly periodical published by the American geographical society; Bowman, Nellie M. "Publications, maps and charts sold by the U.S. government agencies other than the Superintendent of documents." *Special lib.* 44:53-65, February, 1953; *Price list 53, maps,* available from the Superintendent of documents. *See also*: Felland, Nordis. "Periodical aids to map acquisition." *Lib. jour.* 75:438, 488, March 15, 1950; Espenshade, Edward B., Jr. "A guide to map sources for use in building a college map library." *Col. and research lib.* 9:45-53, January, 1948. The Map information office, United States geological survey, Washington, D.C., acts as the center for information about maps and will answer requests for advice and data. For a thorough discussion of types of maps available from governmental sources and their usefulness in college libraries, as well as for comments on general problems of a map collection, *see*: Mueller, Anna. "Use and handling of government maps in libraries." *Calif. librarian* 21:56-62, 78, January, 1960

51. Le Gear, Clara E. *Maps: their care, repair and preservation in libraries.* rev. ed. Washington, D.C., Library of Congress, Reference department, Map division, 1956. Globes and atlases are also discussed in this invaluable work. It is brief, but describes clearly every aspect of the care of maps, from unwrapping them upon arrival to filing them for use. Useful suggestions for the filing of maps may also be found *in*: White, R. C. "Ideal arrangement for maps in a library." *Special lib.* 50:159-61, April, 1959

52. Boggs, Samuel W. "Problems of classifying and cataloging maps." *In*: A.L.A. Committee of public documents. *Public documents, 1936.* Chicago, A.L.A., 1936, p. 114-15

53. Boggs, Samuel W. and Lewis, Dorothy C. *The classification and cataloging of maps and atlases.* New York, Special libraries association, 1945. A summary of the Boggs-Lewis classification as well as of other schemes is provided *in*: White, *op. cit.*, p. 154-9

54. Tate, Vernon D. "Microreproduction and the acquisitions program." *Lib. trends* 3:432-3, April, 1955

55. "Use of microfilm for periodical storage." *UNESCO bull. for lib.* 11:53-6, February-March, 1957

56. Trumper, *op. cit.*, p. 121-2; Meals, Frances L. and Johnson, Walter T. "We chose microfilm." *Col. and research lib.* 21:223-6, 228, May, 1960. The latter article presents some useful data based on the experiences of two junior college librarians who report the successful substitution of microfilm for back files. *See also*: Harkins, W. G. and others. "Microfilm in university libraries: a report." *Col. and research lib.* 14: 307-16, July, 1953

57. Catalogs from commercial firms; *Newspapers on microfilm, op. cit.*; Phila. bibliographical center. . . . *Union list of microfilms.* rev. & enl. Ann Arbor, Mich., J. W. Edwards, 1951 (Supplements, 1953-57) ; *Microfilm clearing house bull.*, appears irregularly as an appendix to the Library of Congress *Information bull.*

58. Osborn, *op. cit.*, p. 250-3

59. For the various types, *see*: Ballou, Hubbard W., ed. *Guide to microreproduction equipment.* Annapolis, Md., National microfilm association, 1959. Almost every type of machine is described along with illustrations. Information is given about price, uses, dimensions, technical specifications, and equipment for filing and storing microtext. The *Guide* does not recommend any particular machine. The National microfilm association plans to keep information in this *Guide* up-to-date with items in its *National micronews.*

60. There is no one directory of microfilm suppliers. Most sources are listed in the following: A.L.A. Resources and technical services division. Copying methods section. *Directory of institutional photoduplication services in the United States.* comp. by Cosby Brinkley. Chicago, The sec-

tion, 1959; Special libraries association. Committee on microfilming and documentation. *Directory of microfilm services in the United States and Canada.* New York, Special libraries association, 1946

61. Tilton, Eve M., comp. *A union list of publications in opaque microforms.* New York, Scarecrow press, 1959, contains almost all titles in this form available, as well as the names and addresses of publishers. Entries were compiled through 1958, and supplementary volumes are planned.

62. Scott, Peter. "Advances and goals in microphotography." *Lib. trends* 8:477, January, 1960; Ballou, *op. cit.*, p. 415-19; Ballou, H. W. and Rather, J. C. "Microfilm and microfacsimile publications." *Lib. trends* 4:184, 189, October, 1955

63. Fussler, H. H. *Photographic reproduction for libraries; a study of administrative problems.* Chicago, University of Chicago press, 1942, p. 82

64. Downs, Robert B. "Libraries in minuscule." *Col. and research lib.* 18:11-18, January, 1957

65. Stone, C. Walter. "The place of newer media in the undergraduate program." *In:* Fussler, H. H., ed. *Function of the library in the modern college.* Chicago, University of Chicago Graduate library school, 1954, p. 87. Favoring centralized library service, *see:* Swank, R. C. "Sight and sound in the world of books." *Lib. jour.* 78:1459-64, September 15, 1953; for an opposite viewpoint, *see:* Shepard, B. "Problems of music library administration in the college or university." Music lib. association *notes* 11:359-65, June, 1954. For information about the present status of the administration of records, *see:* Bennett, Fleming. "Audio-visual services in colleges and universities in the United States. . . ." *Col. and research lib.* 16:11-19, January, 1955

66. Published by W. Schwann, inc., 137 Newbury Street, Boston 16, Mass. Basic selection tools that can be used as a guide in building a music collection and in purchasing either scores or records include: Darrell, R. D. comp. *Schirmer's guide to books on music and musicians.* New York, Schirmer, 1951; "One hundred basic works for the record library," *in:* Cross, Milton J. and Ewen, David. *Encyclopedia of the great composers and their music.* Garden City, N.Y., Doubleday, 1953, v. 2, p. 919-26; Kaho, Elizabeth E. *Analysis of the study of music literature in selected American colleges.* New York, Bureau of publications, Teachers college, Columbia University, 1950 (Teachers college contributions to education, no. 971), p. 69-72, listing 134 compositions studied in college music courses. Important guides to records include: *Records in review.* Great Barrington, Mass., Wyeth press, 1955-   ; Clough, F. F. and Cuming, G. J. *World's encyclopedia of recorded music* and supplements. London, Sidgwick and Jackson, 1952-   ; Myers, K., comp. *Record ratings; the music library association's index of record reviews.* New York, Crown, 1956; Sackville-West, E. and Shawe-Taylor, D. *Record guide.* rev. ed. London, Collins, 1955; *Guide to long-playing records.* New York, Knopf, 1955

67. Orne, Jerrold. "The music library in the college of the future." *In*: Music lib. association. *Music and libraries.* Washington: Music lib. assoc., 1942, p. 41

68. Smith, E. E. and Watanabe, R. T. "The music library in its physical aspects." *Lib. trends* 8:610-12, April, 1960

69. Davies, David W. "Audio-visual materials." *In*: Fussler, H. H. *Library buildings for library service.* Chicago, A.L.A., 1947, p. 91. It may be noted at this point that a discussion of tape recordings has been omitted. This is not because their importance is not recognized; on the contrary, it is felt that, considering their convenience, permanence, and fidelity, they will eventually replace phonorecords. But within the past year many technical changes and advances have occurred in the field, so that any discussion of tape would be tentative at best, and possibly misleading. However, librarians should certainly be aware of their existence, and keep abreast of their development and applications. Also, many of the general remarks made herein regarding phonorecords will apply to tape recordings as well.

70. Duckles, Vincent H. "Musical scores and recordings." *Lib. trends* 4:171, October, 1955; "Problems of music library equipment." Music lib. association *notes* 11:222, March, 1954

71. Pickett, A. G. and Lemcoe, M. M. *Preservation and storage of sound recordings; a study supported by a grant from the Rockefeller foundation.* Washington, Library of Congress, 1959. The study is necessarily technical, but the authors have realized this and present the practical findings in their "Conclusions."

72. Miller, Philip L. "Cataloging and filing of phonograph records." *Lib. jour.* 62:544-5, July, 1937; Marco, G. A. and Roziewski, W. M. "Shelving plans for long-playing records." *Lib. jour.* 84:1568-9, May 15, 1959; Haskell, Inez. "The cataloging of records, musical and non-musical, for a general library." PNLA *quar.* 9:150-5, July, 1945

73. Joint committee on music cataloging. *Code for cataloging music and phonorecords.* Chicago, A.L.A., 1958

74. Swank, Raymond E. "University of Oregon's audio-visual service." *Col. and research lib.* 9:304-5, October, 1948; Stickney, E. P. and Scherer, H. "Developing an a-v program in a small college library." *Lib. jour.* 84:2458-9, September 1, 1959

75. College and university postwar planning committee of the A.L.A. and the ACRL. *College and university libraries and librarianship; an examination of their present status and some proposals for their future development.* Chicago, A.L.A., 1946, p. 47

76. Stone, *op. cit.*, p. 86

77. *Ibid.*, p. 95-7

78. McKown, H. C. and Roberts, A. B. *Audio-visual aids to instruction.* New York, McGraw-Hill, 1940, p. 41

79. Johnson, B. Lamar. *Vitalizing a college library.* Chicago, A.L.A., 1939, p. 87-8

80. Ireland, Norma O. *The picture file in school, college and public libraries.* rev. and enl. ed. Boston, F. W. Faxon, 1952, p. 1-5. This can be used as a general manual, though its approach is a most basic one. *See also*: Underhill, Charles S. "Sketch for a picture collection." *Wilson lib. bull.* 30:539-40, March, 1956

81. There are many sources of pictures. Ireland, *op. cit.*, p. 6-9 lists some; Special libraries association. Picture division. *Picture sources: an introductory list.* ed. by Helen Faye. New York, Special libraries association, 1959 is a comprehensive guide and also provides a good bibliography. The standard guide to filmstrips is the *Filmstrip guide.* New York, H. W. Wilson, 1948- . Also useful is *Educator's guide to free slidefilms.* Randolph, Wis., Educator's progress service, 1949- ; Falconer, Vera M. *Filmstrips—a descriptive index and user's guide.* New York, McGraw-Hill, 1948. Periodicals in the audio-visual field list and review filmstrips, as do many other journals for their subject fields. For color prints, *see*: UNESCO. *Catalogue of colour reproductions of paintings prior to 1860.* 4th ed. Paris: UNESCO, 1957; UNESCO. *Catalogue of colour reproductions of paintings, 1860-1957.* 4th ed. Paris, UNESCO, 1957; Brooke, Milton and Dubester, H. J. *Guide to color prints.* New York, Scarecrow press, 1953

82. *See*: Ireland, *op. cit.*, p. 13-14, 25-7 for suggestions on mounting and filing; *also*: Underhill, *op. cit.*, p. 540. The catalogs of library supplies firms also will be useful here.

83. Mitchell, Eleanor. "The photograph collection and its problems." *Col. and research lib.* 3:177, March, 1942

84. Ireland, *op. cit.*, p. 50-132 contains a list of picture subject headings; *see also*: Underhill, *op. cit.*, p. 540-2

85. Johnson, *op. cit.*, p. 83-8

86. Reid, Seerley and others. *Directory of 3,660 16mm film libraries.* Washington, Government printing office, 1959 (Office of education, bull. 1959, no. 4)

87. Dale, Edgar and Ramseyer, L. L. *Teaching with motion pictures; a handbook of administrative practice.* Washington, American council on education, 1937, p. 20

88. The standard source is the *Educational film guide.* New York, H. W. Wilson, 1936- . It is now kept up-to-date by annual supplements, and contains an alphabetical title list of 16mm films with descriptive notes, followed by a subject index; also useful is the annual *Educator's guide to free films.* Randolph, Wis., Educator's progress service, 1941- . Brown, James W., Lewis, R. B. and Harcleroad, F. F. *A-V instruction: materials and methods.* New York, McGraw-Hill, 1959 contains a "Classified directory of sources" on p. 532-44, as do other textbooks on audio-visual instruction. Recent films are reviewed in a number of audio-visual journals, such as *Educational screen and audio-visual guide* and *Film world and a-v world.* Many professional journals review films relating to the particular fields.

89. Reid, *op. cit.*

90. Davies, *op. cit.*, p. 92

91. McDonald, Gerald D. *Educational motion pictures and libraries.* Chicago, A.L.A., 1942, p. 109-15

92. Quinly, William J. "Audio-visual materials in the library." *Lib. trends* 5:296, October, 1956; Fayen, Philip. "Criteria for AV equipment." *Educational screen and audio-visual guide.* 38:476-8, September, 1959

93. McDonald, *op. cit.*, p. 123-9 discusses these matters at length. There are any number of sources for information on types of projectors and equipment. The standard one is the *Audio-visual equipment directory.* 6th ed. Fairfax, Va., National audio-visual association, 1960. It is up-to-date and comprehensive, containing descriptions of almost every type and make of equipment, illustrated, with technical data and prices. It also contains a list of manufacturers of accessories. The information in it can be kept current through the periodicals in the audio-visual and library fields. Other lists of suppliers and manufacturers can be found in the Buying guide issue of the *Library jour.*, the annual "Guide to library equipment and supplies" in the A.L.A. *bull.* and *in:* Brown, Lewis, and Harcleroad, *loc. cit.* and other audio-visual texts.

ADDITIONAL REFERENCES

Serials

Cabeen, Violet A. and Cook, C. D. "Organization of serials and documents." *Lib. trends* 2:199-216, October, 1953

Clough, Eric A. *Bookbinding for librarians.* London, Association of assistant librarians, 1957

Davis, Albert H. "The subscription agency and the library—responsibilities and problems from the dealer's viewpoint." *Serial slants* 1:14-19, October, 1950

"Exchange of duplicate periodicals." *Serial slants* 2:11-13, October, 1951

Lessing, Ralph. "Subscription problems as seen by an agent." *Serial slants* 4:5-7, January, 1953

Orr, R. W. "Few aspects of acquiring serials." *Lib. trends* 3:393-402, April, 1955

Stratton, John B. "Libraries and commercial binderies." *Lib. trends* 4:301-11, January, 1956

Government Publications

Ahn, Herbert K. "Increasing international understanding: an introduction to the publications of international organizations." *Calif. librarian* 21:29-36, January, 1960

Cabeen, Violet A. and Cook, C. D. "Organization of serials and documents." *Lib. trends* 2:199-216, October, 1953

Moor, Carol C. and Chamberlin, Waldo. *How to use United Nations documents*. New York, New York University press, 1952

Ryan, Mary. "United Nations publications." *Calif. librarian* 20:167-71, 194, July, 1959

Newspapers

Iben, I. "Place of the newspaper." *Lib. trends* 4:140-55, October, 1955

Muller, Robert H. "The selection of daily newspapers for a college library." *Col. and research lib.* 10:27-31, January, 1949

Rare Books

Adams, F. B. "Long live the bibliophile!" *Col. and research lib.* 16:344-6, October, 1955

Peckham, Howard H. "Rare book libraries and collections: introduction." *Lib. trends* 5:417-21, April, 1957

Shaw, Charles B. "Special collections in the college library." *Col. and research lib.* 18:479-84, 517, November, 1957

Wing, Donald G. and Vosper, Robert. "Antiquarian bookmarket and the acquisition of rare books." *Lib. trends* 3:385-92, April, 1955

Pamphlets and Clippings

Brady, M. E. "Care of fugitive materials." *Wilson lib. bull.* 26:258-9, 261, November, 1951

Ferguson, E. "Pamphlets are worth the trouble." *Wilson lib. bull.* 33:45-7, September, 1958

Wyllie, J. C. "Pamphlets, broadsides, clippings, and posters." *Lib. trends* 4:195-202, October, 1955

Maps and Atlases

Espenshade, E. B. "No one source for acquiring maps." *Lib. jour.* 75:431-2, March 15, 1950

Ristow, W. W. "Maps in libraries; a bibliographical summary." *Lib. jour.* 71:1101-7, 1121-4, September 1, 1946

Ristow, W. W. "What about maps?" *Lib. trends* 4:123-39, October, 1955

Whitmarsh, Agnes. "Maps and photographs." *In*: Fussler, H. H., ed. *Library buildings for library service*. Chicago, A.L.A., 1947, p. 78-80

Woods, B. M. "Map cataloging: inventory and prospect." *Lib. resources and technical services* 3:257-73, Fall, 1959

Yonge, Ena L. "These maps are essential." *Lib. jour.* 75:440, 442, March 15, 1950

Microreproduction

Ballou, H. W. "Photography and the library." *Lib. trends* 5:265-93, October, 1956

Bechanan, H. G. "The organization of microforms in the library." *Lib. trends* 8:391-406, January, 1960

Born, L. S. "History of microform activity." *Lib. trends* 8:348-58, January, 1960

Power, E. B. "Microfilm as a substitute for binding." *American documentation* 2:33-9, January, 1951

Thompson, L. S. "Microforms as library resources." *Lib. trends* 8:359-71, January, 1960

Music and Recordings

Bixler, Paul H. and Mills, Julia. "We shall have music." *Lib. jour.* 66:16-19, January 1, 1941

Curry, D. "Building a record collection." *Ontario lib. review* 38:252-5, August, 1954

Quinly, W. J. and Farrell, E. J. *On record; a manual on starting a record collection.* Jefferson City, Mo., Missouri state library, 1951 (mimeographed)

Visual Aids

"Check list on the organization of picture collections." *Special libraries* 50:252-4, July, 1959

Hill, M. D. "Prints, pictures and photographs." *Lib. trends* 4:156-63, October, 1955

Horn, A. H. "Special materials and services." *Lib. trends* 4:119-22, October, 1955

Johnston, A. M. "College libraries need a-v materials." *Lib. jour.* 81:1957-9, September 15, 1956

Keen, Eunice, comp. "Aids for use in cataloging and classifying audiovisual materials." *Lib. resources and technical services* 1:189-97, Fall, 1957

Parker, J. A. "Brief history of the picture collection." *Wilson lib. bull.* 30:257-8, 264, November, 1955

Reinhardt, P. A. "Photograph and slide collections in art libraries." *Special libraries* 50:97-102, March, 1959

Shores, Louis. "Audio-visual dimensions for an academic library." *Col. and research lib.* 15:393-7, October, 1954

XIV

Business and Financial Affairs

The business and financial administration of the college is entrusted to a number of individuals, each of whom is directly or indirectly responsible to the president. Aside from the management of the endowment fund which is handled by the treasurer and the finance committee of the board of trustees, the business and financial affairs of the college are commonly delegated to a business manager whose activities include accounting, making out financial reports, cooperating in the preparation of the budget, employing non-academic personnel, supervising the physical plant, managing auxiliary enterprises, purchasing, and collecting student charges. The bursar and superintendent of buildings and grounds under these circumstances are responsible to the business manager, but in colleges where there is no central business officer, these officials report directly to the president. The bursar and the business manager together with the dean generally make up the core of the president's advisory committee on the budget. In effect it is this committee which approves or disapproves the library budget.

The librarian's relations with the business manager include the placement of purchase orders, the payment of bills, the checking of the business manager's monthly accounts against the library's financial records to insure that the library budget is not being exceeded, the determination of insurance inventories and coverage, the inventory of equipment, the employment of non-professional help (unless there is a separate personnel officer), the approval of major repair and renovation of the library building and equipment, the transfer of funds from one budget category to another, and sometimes the collection of library fines when the library has been unsuccessful in its efforts. A satisfactory relationship with the business manager is based on the application of common sense and good business management to the handling of the activities outlined above. The business manager will expect the library to keep within its budget, to route all its orders through the business office unless the library is authorized to order books and other library materials directly from dealers and publishers, and to forward its bills promptly for payment. He will probably be sympathetic to the library's budget requests if they are prepared in a practical and level-headed way and are properly explained, but he will expect the librarian to accept gracefully the judgment of the budget committee if it cannot accomplish all he desires in any one budget year. Likewise, he will expect the librarian to use his appropriation wisely and to give an exact accounting of the fund he administers. On the other hand, the librarian has a right to expect full cooperation from the business manager in delegating authority to the library to purchase books and journals directly from dealers instead of through the business office if this seems desirable in the local situation, in maintaining up-to-date monthly reports on library expenditures and fund balances, in safeguarding library interests where endowment and gift funds are concerned, in taking a broad view and not a penny-pinching attitude toward the library's development, and in assisting the library to meet unusual and unexpected financial obligations should they arise after the budget is approved.

The physical plant is under the immediate direction of the superintendent of buildings and grounds. His confidence and good will are most important to the welfare of the library. Janitors and maids are employed and supervised by him. All major utilities such as air conditioning, heating, and lighting are maintained and serviced by his staff. Major repairs, cleaning, and painting are decided upon and scheduled by him. If a library is poorly served in these essential maintenance matters, it will be severely handicapped in its program. If the relations are good, the buildings and grounds staff can be one of the most helpful friends the library has on the campus.

SOURCES OF INCOME

There are three main sources of library funds. The principal source is the allocation from the current operating funds of the college. Whether the college is publicly or privately controlled matters less in this connection than the amount of additional money the library may need during any one budgetary year. The factors which count most in securing an adequate allocation are the availability of funds—the president has only a relatively small amount of *free* money to allocate each year—and the persuasiveness of the librarian in presenting the budget.

In privately controlled colleges, especially, libraries receive funds from endowment sources. Some of the older established Eastern college libraries have substantial endowments, but for most colleges the share of income received from this source is comparatively small. Most typically, endowment funds are given for books in special subject fields. They may come as a memorial to a distinguished faculty member or college officer, alumnus, student, or friend of the college; as a class gift; or as a gift from a local foundation or organization. If the librarian is given an opportunity to suggest the nature of a book endowment, it is best to leave the field unspecified since a particular subject may not be nearly so important in the years ahead as it is today. Salaries of librarians and funds for building maintenance have also been secured through endowment although this is quite unusual.[1] One of the major drawbacks to endowments is the decline in purchasing power caused by inflation. A general endowment for library purposes which yielded fifty thousand dollars in 1942 has lost more than 50 per cent of its purchasing power today because of the spiral of inflation during the past eighteen years. "Yet the fact that the library is endowed appears to act as an excuse for the college administration to fail to provide additional funds from other sources. It thus happens that the endowed libraries are often less adequately supported than those which depend upon appropriations from current income."[2]

A third source of income for college libraries is grants and individual gifts. The largest of these are from foundations and include gifts for book endowment, acquisition of materials, buildings, bibliographic activities, and general library support.[3] The Carnegie Corporation, Rockefeller, and General Education Board grants of the nineteen-thirties have already been mentioned. In recent years, small private and junior college libraries have benefited from the Association of College and Research Libraries grants sponsored by the United States Steel Corporation, Remington Rand, National Biscuit Company, Lilly Endowment, and others. These grants have been awarded for book additions, personnel, microfilm files of newspapers, equipment, and support of special programs.[4] Practically all colleges receive gifts of personal libraries, books, and money for book purchases from members of the faculty, alumni, and friends of the college. Many libraries have Friends of the library groups, with or without a formal organization, which assist the library directly by making donations or indirectly by influencing others to make gifts. For all their interest and generosity, library donors can be something of a problem. Not infrequently they attach great value to gifts which have very little value or which are not appropriate to the library's needs, and they frequently feel that their benefactions deserve separate and distinctive treatment. The price of cultivating library donors is devoting many hours of additional work to directing their efforts toward desirable goals, securing their understanding of the library's policy on gifts, and frequently saying *no* when a proposed gift is obviously misdirected or of no value to the library. The need for an established policy on gifts is rooted in the fact that the library's best friends, not excluding the president and the faculty, can sometimes be its worst enemies in the handling of gifts. As spokesman for the college, the president is frequently consulted first about a possible library gift, whether it is an offer of last year's file of *Fortune* or something more substantial. Alumni sometimes approach their former professors with offers of old copies of the college yearbook or catalogue. If the college president and faculty accept such gifts or indicate that they believe the library would be delighted to have them before consulting the librarian, they place him in a very embarrassing position, particularly if the gift is valueless or if the conditions of acceptance make it expensive and difficult for the library to administer the gift. In this regard the principles formulated by the Bowdoin College Library are noteworthy because they (1) stress the point that keeping gifts intact does not best serve the purpose of either students or faculty, (2) make clear the library's position with regard to the disposal of duplicates and unneeded volumes in a gift collection, and (3) represent what has been established college practice since the policy was initiated by the president's action and formulated by the librarian and library committee.[5] Although prepared with the particular needs of the public library in mind, the policy statement of the American Library Association on gifts also contains useful suggestions for the college librarian.[6]

Some libraries may regard fines as a fourth source of income although it is doubtful whether the monies collected are sufficient to pay the salary-hours and postage spent in recording and trying to collect them. As a matter of good business practice, all money from fines, sale of duplicates, or other sources should be turned over to the college bursar who usually credits it to a restricted fund account. If the library is permitted to use this money for current operation, the money will be transferred later to whatever fund account is necessary to make it available for library use.

THE BUDGET

The most important element in the financial picture of the college library is the budget. The budget is an estimate of what sums the library will need in the coming year or biennium for carrying out its program. If the budget is made up several years in advance of disbursement, as is necessary in some state colleges, it is difficult to estimate accurately the financial needs of specific known objectives. It should be emphasized, therefore, that the budget is only an estimate which separates all proposed expenditures into categories such as salaries, books, supplies, travel, and equipment. No two budgets could be expected to be exactly alike in content, form, or presentation because each library has its own peculiar problems. Such variables as the size and type of college served, the methods of teaching, the concept of what services the library should provide and what may properly be left to other library resources, the organization of the library, and the physical plant—all these affect budgetary practice and amounts. Nevertheless, the essential elements of the college library budget are the same. They may be reduced to fundamental principles and applied to the preparation of any college library budget.

Principles of Budget-Making

The first principle is that the librarian should be invited by the president or chief budgetary officer to submit the library budget. He has the knowledge and experience to estimate detailed needs and to plan for both immediate operations and long-term requirements. He may consult the library committee and department heads about book funds and the library staff about personnel and other administrative costs, but the final choice of what goes into the budget and how much to ask for should rest with him.

The second principle is that the budget should be submitted and approved in time for the selection and recruitment of new personnel before the next academic year begins. Normally this means that the budget should be approved several months before the end of the regular academic year. The absence of responsibility and fixed schedules in budgetary matters makes for a weak college and a weak library.

The third principle is that the librarian should request sufficient funds in each category of the budget to support a sound program of library development. As an extremely conscientious administrative officer, the librarian may budget too little. When a faculty member comes to see him shortly after the new budget goes into effect and is told that his request must be turned down because of lack of funds, this may be an indication of faulty or timid budgeting on the part of the librarian. It may point to the fact that the librarian has not consulted as widely or as thoroughly as he should have in preparing the budget. If a college is to flourish, its library collections must grow. If the library grows, its services expand and the cost of maintaining these services mounts accordingly. To attract and hold qualified men and women librarians, colleges are going to have to pay higher salaries than formerly, and the annual increase in the budget for personnel should reflect this need. A rate of salary increases of at least 8 to 10 per cent will be needed annually for at least another decade based on the experience of the past five years (Table IX). Money for capital outlay—buildings, remodeling, and equipment —is as insufficient as operating funds. The fact that most college

TABLE IX

ANNUAL PERCENTAGE INCREASE IN LIBRARY SALARIES AND WAGES, 1955-59 *

College Library	1955	1956	1957	1958	1959	Average Annual Percentage Increase
Antioch	2.8%	26.4%	-6.3%	16.3%	6.2%	8.5%
Beloit	8.8	2.3	3.8	4.1	10.0	5.7
Dartmouth	1.8	13.5	7.8	17.1	9.7	9.8
Davidson	7.7	4.7	14.7	- .7	7.7	6.7
Lawrence	8.8	1.8	20.7	21.4	11.5	12.6
Mount Holyoke	1.2	10.4	3.9	11.3	16.6	8.5
Randolph-Macon	1.8	3.4	8.3	7.9	22.0	8.4
Smith	2.8	2.5	2.5	13.3	7.3	5.1
Vassar	6.6	-4.1	14.6	4.2	11.1	6.3
Washington and Lee	4.3	6.9	2.5	11.0	6.8	6.2
Wellesley	7.9	3.5	1.8	1.0	21.4	6.9
Williams	2.5	- .7	13.6	35.7	5.4	10.6

* Source: "College and university library statistics." January issues of *Col. and research lib.* 1955-60

libraries in the country have not sufficient space indicates that building budgets have not kept pace with growing needs.[7]

A fourth principle is that the budget should represent library planning in terms of educational goals and not be simply a "crisis" operation in which urgent current needs are hastily converted in dollar estimates to meet a budget deadline. Planning to meet educational goals implies that the library will take into account proposed new curricular changes, the impact of new courses and instructors on library book and personnel funds, the possible use and expenditure for microfilm in order to slow down the consumption of rapidly dwindling shelf space, the cost of a new graduated pay scale for student help, the effect of price increases in binding, and the like. A corollary of this principle is that the library should be efficiently and effectively using every dollar in its proposed new budget. A look at the traditional processes of charging books, lettering books, copying cards, and similar time-consuming and costly operations should reveal many ways in which machines can simplify, expedite, and speed up routine work. The result may be an immediate increase in the budget for equipment but in the long run the library must incorporate these mechanical aids into its processes in order to operate efficiently.

A fifth principle is that the budget should be reasonably flexible in its execution. If a staff member is ill or if a typist resigns in the middle of the year, it may be necessary to employ extra student assistants to help out for weeks or even months. If an emergency need should arise requiring the purchase of an additional typewriter after the library budget is approved, the library should be permitted to substitute this need for one or more of the equipment items specified in the budget. Changes such as these require that the librarian have some discretionary authority in spending from the budget. Unless the college is required by law to follow a rigid budgeting pattern, the librarian should seek authority from the president to make alternative choices where they are in the best interests of good library service.

A final principle of budgeting is that the classification of the budget categories should enable the library to check its financial records easily against the periodic balance statements sent out by the bursar as well as determine the financial information that is regularly called for in self-surveys, and by accrediting associations and other organizations.

Preparation of the Budget Statement

When the information needed for making the estimates for the library budget has been assembled, the next step is the preparation of the budget itself. Where good practice is followed, the business office sends out forms to the library and other departments with the budget of the current year set forth in the first column of the form. The form also provides a second column for the librarian's request, a third column for the dean's recommendations, and a fourth column for the president's final decision. In the sample reproduced (Form 1) the staff is listed separately on sheets attached to Form 1 and the equipment items are listed on the back of the form.

In addition to completing the budget forms, the librarian may properly accompany his budget submission with a brief statement justifying and supporting the request for specific sums set forth in the budget. No set rules can be given for preparing this statement, but the librarian should bear in mind the impact of inflation on the cost of books, periodicals, binding, and supplies; the increase in enrolment, particularly in publicly controlled colleges; the probable need for annual salary increases at least comparable to those of the past five years; and the possible impact of new technological developments on library economy and efficiency. The far-reaching investigations now under way by the Library Technology Project of the American Library Association and by other groups sponsored by the Council on Library Resources hold great promise. Libraries can expect machines and equipment specifically designed for library use to appear in increasingly large numbers in the near future. Finally, as a check on the entire budget the librarian may find it worthwhile to compare the budget totals with the present standards of college library support (Chapter XVII) and with the expenditure patterns of similar colleges. Comparative data should be used cautiously when other libraries are involved. Unless the libraries serve colleges having the same type of program, are

BUDGET REQUEST

CHELSEA COLLEGE

BUDGET REQUEST, FISCAL YEAR ENDING ___June 30, 1960___

DEPARTMENT ___Library___   BUDGET ACCOUNT ___528___

Budget Categories	Budget Current Year	Requested by Department	Recommended by Dean President	
Personal Services (Detail Attached)				
Prof. Salaries				
Cler. Salaries				
Student Wages				
Annuities				
Total Personnel Budget				
Travel				
Equipment				
Supplies				
Other Categories				
Books, Periodicals, and Binding				
Endowment (Books)				
TOTALS				

similar in size, and are situated in approximately the same geographical area, the comparison may be invalid. In general, a careful study of the library's own activities and needs provides the soundest basis for justifying budget estimates.

Distribution of the Budget

Administrators and librarians have shown considerable interest in a guide or formula for distributing the budget total to the several categories or items in the budget. Since there is no reliable formula, the librarian checks the distribution of his budget with comparable data compiled from the latest statistics of library expenditures which through 1960 have appeared annually in the January issues of *College and Research Libraries*. By way of illustration, current distribution of funds is shown below for one group of publicly controlled colleges and another of privately controlled colleges. Table X shows the percentage of the total expenditures spent for books (books, periodicals, and binding), salaries and wages, and other items (supplies, travel, etc.). Table XI affords a further breakdown of the expenditure pattern to show the relative amounts spent for full-time staff and student assistants, as well as for books and binding. If the library discovers a marked difference in its own budget ratios from the average of the current expenditure pattern in colleges of similar size and program, there is probably a need for further investigation and a possible redistribution of funds.[8]

ADMINISTRATION OF THE BOOK BUDGET

The book fund is one of the largest and most important items in the library budget. The policy of administering this fund follows two general patterns. The first places the entire book fund in the hands of the librarian, to whom applications are made by faculty members when they order their books. The second distributes all unrestricted book money into fixed portions which are carefully proportioned to the needs of each of the teaching departments. Of the 48 colleges and university libraries studied in the Land-Grant Survey, 35 stated that they made a formal division of the book fund.[9] In almost all of the 35 de-

TABLE X

PERCENTAGE DISTRIBUTION OF EXPENDITURES
IN COLLEGE LIBRARIES, 1958-59 *

Type and Enrolment	No. of Libraries	Salaries and Wages %	Books, Periodicals, and Binding %	Other %
Publicly Controlled College Libraries With Enrolments Under 1400	73	62.3	31.0	6.7
Privately Controlled College Libraries With Enrolments Between 500 and 1000 (Selected List)	36	58.7	34.7	6.6

* Source: *Col. and research lib.* 21:[25-88], January, 1960

TABLE XI

PERCENTAGE DISTRIBUTION OF PERSONNEL AND BOOK FUND
EXPENDITURES IN COLLEGE LIBRARIES, 1958-59 *

Type and Enrolment	No. of Libraries	Salaries and Wages		Book Fund	
		Staff %	Student %	Books and Periodicals %	Binding %
Publicly Controlled College Libraries With Enrolments Under 1400	73	84.3	15.7	87.2	12.8
Privately Controlled College Libraries With Enrolments Between 500 and 1000 (Selected List)	36	88.6	11.4	85.3	14.7

* Source: *Col. and research lib.* 21:[25-88], January, 1960

nominational colleges surveyed by Reeves and Russell, the funds for new books were similarly apportioned among the departments of instruction.[10] Among 105 colleges surveyed by Hans Muller, 77 operated under formal apportionments.[11] A check of 27 leading colleges in the summer of 1960 by the writer revealed that 19 of the total allocated book funds to departments. Such evidence as the foregoing points to the fact that most college libraries allocate book funds to the teaching departments even though in some colleges the spending of the entire book fund is placed in the hands of the librarian. The advantages of apportionment are summarized by Muller as follows:

1. Apportionment ensures the obtaining of an evenly distributed and well-rounded book collection.

2. It provides a safeguard against unreasonable demands from a few faculty members.

3. It stimulates the faculty to participate more actively in book selection, since it enables departments to feel that there is some money available which they can call their own.

4. It guards the librarian against the possible charge that the expenditure of book funds has been unjust to some departments.

5. It prevents the clash of personalities among the faculty.

6. It curbs the exercise of an excessive degree of discretionary power and arbitrariness on the part of librarians.[12]

While the apportionment plan has proved practical and useful in a large number of colleges, it is not entirely free from disadvantages. The chief objections to apportionment appearing in the professional writings are summarized by Muller in the article previously mentioned:

1. Several writers have pointed out that apportionment leads to a waste of money. Some departments are allotted much less money than they need, whereas others have too much money to spend. Thus apportionment has the effect of hampering the departments that could really use the money.

2. The apportionment plan is said to prevent any systematic building up of the library book collection.

3. Complaints are occasionally voiced about the excessive amount of red tape and bookkeeping involved in the apportionment plan.

4. Librarians have also frequently complained about the tendency for apportionments to remain fixed for too long a period —in disregard of the changes in the curriculum. The reason for this lack of flexibility is that changes are difficult to make, since no department is willing to consent to a reduction of its own allotment.[13]

The advantages of keeping all book funds in one lump sum are that it permits shifting funds to meet special needs or to buy expensive items, eliminates considerable bookkeeping, and encourages faculty members to order good books beyond their departmental fields. Under this system it is more difficult, of course, to curb excessive buying by a few department heads. On the other hand, it is often true that the heavy book-buying departments are the ones that make the most use of the library. Theoretically, at least, the plan of centralizing funds in the hands of the librarian is sound if (1) funds are so ample that it will seldom be necessary to deny a faculty request, or (2) funds are so small that formal apportionment is hardly worthwhile and may even discourage faculty buying. Since there is seldom enough money to say "yes" to all requests, this places the entire responsibility for deciding when to say *no* upon the librarian. Unfortunately few librarians have the omniscience to make such judgments.

Assuming that book funds are to be apportioned, the next step is to determine the method. This problem is not quite so weighty as the voluminous literature on the subject would seem to indicate. In actual practice, the library has only a very small amount of *free* money to allocate each year. A considerable portion of the book fund is firmly committed long before the actual allocation to departments is made. The first step in apportionment is to make three broad allocations to (1) fixed charges, (2) general fund, and (3) departmental fund. Even this process can be simplified by making the decision on each of the three allocations in the order named. In that event the total of the third category is arrived at by adding the first two categories and subtracting the result from the total book fund.

Fixed Charges

Although, strictly speaking, there are no "fixed charges," this term is applied to expenditures which recur annually and whose amounts can be readily determined in advance. It is good practice, therefore, to remove a sum from the total book budget to cover the following: (1) renewal of journal subscriptions, (2) binding, (3) purchase of Library of Congress cards if these are not charged to the Supplies fund, (4) postage, express, and freight charges on book orders which are not normally billed on the book invoices, and (5) sales tax if the library has to pay this tax. These items can be estimated with reasonable accuracy on the basis of the previous year's expenditures where the total amount of the budget to be allocated is known. Since new subscriptions in the coming year cannot be anticipated, these are usually charged to the departmental allocation during the first year.

General Fund

After the "fixed charges" have been set aside, the next withdrawal from the total budget should be a sum for the general fund which normally takes care of reference books, books of wide general interest, books which cut across the lines of academic disciplines, books which, though not peculiar to a particular curriculum, are significant in their own right, and recreational reading. Sometimes the general fund includes a small reserve fund for very expensive items which no one department could afford to purchase from its own fund. It may include money for duplicates and replacements if these charges are not assessed to the departmental allocations. The proportionate size of the general fund will naturally depend on what types of material are included in it, but Muller's findings may be regarded as typical of the pattern today. In a group of sixty-four liberal arts colleges, he found that the average percentage of the general book fund "was 28 per cent; the range extended all the way from zero to 70 per cent. Two distinctive modes were noted at 25 and 33.3 per cent. . . ." [14] Replies from fourteen midwestern colleges queried about their book budgets by C. Stanley Urban, Department of History, Park College, support Muller's findings. "Several well-known colleges have a policy of withholding a large reserve fund, approximately from 30 to 45 per cent of the total funds available for books . . . and placing this at the disposal of the librarian to be used in the purchase of such materials as he feels would benefit the college as a whole." [15]

Departmental Allocations

As was suggested earlier, a majority of college libraries allocate the departmental portion of the book fund. Some libraries which do not apportion funds eliminate all bookkeeping records; others maintain records of one sort or another in order to plan the acquisition program and to control departments which, if unrestrained, would spend the entire book budget on their own specialities. These records usually consist of one or a combination of the following: a file of book orders arranged by department with net prices on each card, the number of books ordered by each department, or the percentage of the total expenditure by department. One library which does not allocate funds maintains a record of purchases by subject instead of by department. The retail price of books is added to catalog records after the classification numbers are assigned.

There is almost universal interest in an objective method of allocation, particularly on the part of college administrators and faculty members, but most librarians are disinclined to believe that a scientific formula is really possible or practical. Even with a so-called objective method of allocating funds, certain subjective judgments are used in arriving at the percentage indices and almost all librarians agree that the final percentage must be adjusted by the librarian and library committee to take into account certain intangible factors which cannot be reduced to a formula. Moreover, the collection and preparation of data are time-consuming. Where an objective formula is used, the factors most commonly reduced to numerical weightings before they are combined into one percentage index are: enrolment (enrolment times credit hours weighted for class level), courses (semester hours at course level), faculty (number by rank), and book cost. More difficult to reduce to a formula but sometimes included are two additional factors: the extent of publication in the several subject fields and the use made of the library by courses in the different departments. Factors which normally are not or cannot be measured by the formula but which are taken into account by the librarian and library committee in adjusting the final percentage index are: the status of the collections in the different fields, the need for new material in a course, the introduction of new courses, and the addition of new faculty members during the coming year. The best accounts of the construction of formulae are cited in the chapter bibliography together with a summary of the methods used by several libraries.[16]

While there are some librarians who do not allocate to departments and others who apply an objective formula to the distribution of the funds, the great majority make such allocations on a personal or pooled judgment basis with assistance from the library committee. The procedure may vary in detail but is essentially as follows:

1. The estimated amount needed for "fixed charges," previously discussed, is withdrawn from the total appropriation after the sum is approved by the library committee. Each member has before him a breakdown of the estimated cost of current serial subscriptions for the year for which the allocation is to be made.

2. The general fund, amounting to about 25 per cent of the appropriation, is then withdrawn from the balance.

3. The remainder is allotted to departments according to the pooled judgment of the librarian and the library committee, taking into account the expenditures of the previous years, the amount each department is already receiving in the lump sum allocation for "fixed charges" which includes periodical subscriptions and binding, the success of departments in building adequate collections, the amount of unspent balances at the end of last year, departmental cooperation in spending their funds throughout the year instead of in a crash operation the last month of the year, the present status of collections, the addition of new faculty members and courses in the departments, and the relative need of different departments for library materials. Judgment is necessary, and unfortunately departmental pressures may sometimes influence the results. Nevertheless, a group of conscientious faculty members and the librarian can develop sufficient

experience to arrive at a pretty shrewd guess at what is fair to each department in relation to the total amount to be allocated. Experience is not an infallible guide and mistakes can be made, but the pooled judgment method enables each member of the committee to express his opinions and to test what he thinks against the opinion of others. The results are more frequently good than bad.

INSURANCE

For insurance purposes, the library needs both an inventory of equipment, mentioned later in this chapter, and, even more important, an inventory and evaluation of the library's materials resources and catalog card records. One of the types of insurance maintained by most colleges is fire and extended coverage, which is carried on all buildings and contents on a blanket form of 90 per cent co-insurance basis. Most librarians with experience in insurance matters have expressed the opinion that this type of insurance coverage is inadequate for the library. They point to the fact that it does not properly take into account the value of the contents of the library.

Different methods of making an estimate of the insurance needed on the library's contents have been worked out.[17] They combine three elements: (1) insurance (blanket) covering the bulk of the collections based on an average per volume cost, (2) specific coverage insurance, which applies to one kind of property such as notable rarities, and (3) insurance covering adequately the replacement value of the several card catalogs, including the cost of cards plus the processing costs reduced to a unit card basis. The determination of the value of resources covered by the blanket policy makes allowance for some variation from the average insurable rate for bound journals, government documents, and microtexts, and also for depreciation (e.g., fiction) and appreciation (e.g., fine arts books) for varying types of material. These various estimates are totaled to give the library's evaluation of the cost of its materials. If the insurance is written on a co-insurance basis, it is important to review the insurable values of the various types of material every three or four years. The spiral of inflation at present more than counter-balances depreciation.

LIBRARY BOOKKEEPING

There would appear to be almost as many methods of keeping financial records in college libraries as there are libraries.[18] This fact alone makes it impractical to attempt a detailed and technical treatment of financial records in this chapter. On the other hand, even though different situations require different forms of records, the underlying principles are the same. It is of first importance, therefore, to know the reason why records are kept and their uses. This much is attempted in the following discussion, together with a suggestion of the minimum essential records without which a library cannot reasonably determine its financial condition.

Purposes and Uses of Records

The fundamental purpose of library bookkeeping is to keep expenditures within the budget. Some other important uses of these records are to: (1) aid in the preparation of the annual report and the following year's budget, (2) provide the factual monetary basis for making decisions on book and personnel expenditures, (3) assist departments in making a wise and systematic use of their book fund allocations, and (4) furnish information for library reports, studies, and surveys.

How Library Financial Records Differ From Accounting Records

Most college libraries keep their financial records according to a single-entry system and do not attempt to record receipts, the expenditure record being the primary transaction in which they are interested. When the budget is approved and set up in the librarian's office, the income of the library remains relatively stationary except for small sums which are received from fines, replacements, and the sale of publications. The single-entry system for recording expenditures is, therefore, obviously an incomplete record of the library's financial condition and would not be considered sufficient where great importance was attached to sound principles of accounting. It is true, moreover, that the financial records of the library ordinarily make no provision for determining the depreciation on equipment and that certain items of expense such as books and binding are regarded as "operating expenses," whereas in accounting procedure they would be regarded as capital investment.

To point out these shortcomings of library records is not to suggest that the financial records of college libraries are hopelessly inadequate or inefficient. As viewed by an accountant they might be considered quite incomplete and unsystematic; but for all practical purposes and for the uses for which they are intended, the conventional library records serve reasonably well. If for any reason it is necessary to show the unit cost of operations in the library, then a much more elaborate and exact method of bookkeeping is necessary.[19]

The Financial Records

There is great diversity in methods of keeping accounts. The essential points to keep in mind are that the records should be the simplest possible consistent with efficiency, should enable the librarian to keep expenditures within the limits of the budget, and should permit rapid and convenient checking against the business office ledgers. To get right down to bedrock, it would be possible to manage with a library record reduced to (1) a second card file of orders out, arranged by department or fund, to serve as a record of encumbrances, (2) a card file of orders received, similarly arranged by department or fund, together with a tape record of the total expenditures to date clipped to the front of the file to serve as a control on expenditures, and (3) a file of approved invoices which carry such information as the invoice number, date forwarded for payment to the business office, and possibly purchase order number. The difficulty with such a simple set of records is the problem of checking the business office ledger sheets without consulting three separate records. If this checking had to be done in the business office, it would be exceedingly cumbersome for the library to transport its several card records.

The principal records most libraries keep in one form or another include (1) the monthly financial report, (2) a current record of encumbrances and expenditures, and (3) a record of approved accounts payable.

1. *The Monthly Financial Report.* A monthly financial report, which indicates in summary form for the librarian the expenses and balances in the various categories of the budget

at the end of each month, is extremely useful in the management
of the library. It is essential with respect to book funds, where
there are departmental allocations, and with respect to all other
categories except salaries. The latter do not vary from month to
month under normal circumstances, and the librarian can readily
determine exceptions at any time by keeping a record of absences
without pay, late appointments, and similar divergences from the
regular payroll, or simply by checking the balance with the
business office.

In the *Monthly Financial Report,* disbursements are shown
for each of the major items in the budget, and book funds are
broken down to show the expenditures and balances of each
department. This record may consist of a single sheet (Form 2)
for each month, arranged in vertical columns. The various categories of the budget are entered in the first column to the left,
the amount of each budget category in the second column, the
encumbrances for the month in the third column, the expenditures or bills paid in the fourth column, the total encumbrances
and expenditures in the fifth column, and the free balance in
the sixth column. Perhaps an additional word is necessary about
the encumbrance column which actually shows the outstanding
contracts or orders for each budget category, except Salaries and
Student Wages, at the end of the month. For example, there are
outstanding book orders for Art (Form 2) amounting to $72.01,
for Reference books amounting to $161.61, and for Supplies
amounting to $124.90. The librarian determines the amount of
the encumbrance in each category by maintaining on cards a fund
file of orders out or keeping a subsidiary ledger for each object
in the budget classification.

2. *Current Record of Encumbrances and Expenditures.* The
simplest method for this purpose is the use of multiple order
slips or cards arranged so that one card may be filed by fund
while the duplicate is arranged by author in an alphabetical file
of outstanding orders. This first file serves as a record of encumbrances. It may be totaled at any time to determine how much
money is encumbered for outstanding orders against a particular
fund. When a book is received, the card may be withdrawn from
the fund file and transferred to another fund file of expenditures

MONTHLY FINANCIAL REPORT

Budget Categories	Budget	Encumbered	Expended	Month Ending July 31, 1960	
				Total	Free Balance
PERSONAL SERVICES					
I Staff	$30,000		$2,500.00	$2,500.00	$27,500.00
II Student	5,000		154.00	154.00	4,846.00
TRAVEL	200				200.00
EQUIPMENT	500				500.00
SUPPLIES	800	124.90	20.92	145.82	654.18
BOOKS					
I Fixed Charges					
Periodicals	2,600	495.00	320.22	815.22	1,784.78
Binding	1,600				1,600.00
Transportation	200		112.86	112.86	87.14
Sales tax	300		15.00	15.00	285.00
L.C. cards	1,000				1,000.00
II General Fund					
General books	800	161.23	112.07	273.30	526.70
Reference books	500	161.61	90.84	252.45	247.55
Replacements	200	54.77	12.19	66.96	133.04
Recreational books	200	99.22	25.46	124.68	75.32
III Departmental Fund					
Art	600	72.01	61.70	133.71	466.29
Biological Sciences	2,000	34.20	6.00	40.20	1,959.80
Education	500	4.90		4.90	495.10
History	1,200	115.85		115.85	1,084.15
Physical Sciences	2,000	151.15	7.00	158.15	1,841.85
Romance Languages	800	35.70	28.00	63.70	736.30
Social Sciences	500	263.10	182.64	445.74	54.26
TOTAL	$51,500	$1,773.64	$3,648.90	$5,422.54	$46,077.46

approved. If a running tape record of the total of the expenditures is kept at the front of each fund, it is possible to add this total to the encumbrance file for the same fund and to determine the exact balance in the fund.

In place of these simple card records, some libraries prefer to maintain a subsidiary or fund ledger for each object or fund in the budget classification (Form 3). Each transaction is entered under date, vendor, order number, encumbrances, and expenditures. It is to be noted that there are three columns under encumbrances and under expenditures. The last figure in the balance column under encumbrances gives the total outstanding in orders for books, supplies, etc. At any time, therefore, it is possible to determine if the orders to be placed against any specific fund will exceed the amount budgeted to the fund. The order numbers, vendors' names, and expenditures provide a method for maintaining balances and checking on bills about which there is some question.

The method of posting entries in the subsidiary fund ledger may be illustrated from the example reproduced in Form 3 for the library allocation to Art. On July 8, funds amounting to $56.70 were encumbered on order number 5362Q with Wittenborn and Co. The total outstanding orders on that day stood at $61.70 including the Schucman order of $5.00 for July 2. On July 28, books were received from Wittenborn and Co. on order number 5362Q. The amount was entered in the paid column under encumbrances and deducted from the balance of outstanding orders to reduce the total encumbrance to $72.01. At the same time the bills were approved and posted in the expenditure column reducing the balance of the budget for Art to $538.30. Since this transaction represented the last entry for the month, the total of encumbrances and expenditures for July 28 was then posted on the *Monthly Financial Report* and the sum of both deducted from the original budget to obtain the free balance as in Form 2.

3. *Record of Approved Accounts Payable.* When bills are approved and forwarded to the business office for payment—usually once a month—the library may maintain some record of these bills for checking purposes. This record brings together all library bills approved for payment during the month, in-

FORM 3

SUBSIDIARY FUND LEDGER

ART

BUDGET $600

Date 1960		Vendor	Order Number	ENCUMBRANCES			EXPENDITURES		Free Balance
				Paid or Cancelled	Issued	Balance	Amount	Total	
1 July	2	Louis Schucman	5626Q		5.00	5.00			600.00
2	8	Wittenborn & Co.	5362Q		56.70	61.70			
3	8	E. Weyhe	5363Q		77.86	139.56			
4	12	E. Weyhe (cancelled)	5363Q	6.75		132.81			
5	26	Jenkins Bookstore	5457Q		2.25	135.06			
6	26	E. Weyhe (cancelled)	5363Q	1.35		133.71			
7	28	Louis Schucman	5262Q	5.00		128.71	5.00	5.00	595.00
8	28	Wittenborn & Co.	5362Q	56.70		72.01	56.70	61.70	538.30
9									
10									

cluding such information as the date the bill was forwarded for payment, source of purchase, brief author and title, order number, invoice number, and cost. It provides on one or two sheets a convenient record for checking the ledger sheets of the business office, second and third bills from a dealer, a publisher's statement, and other details. A file of duplicate bills in the librarian's office, arranged first by month and second by dealer and stamped individually with the date of approval and such other information as is necessary, would serve for reference and verification. It would not, however, be so convenient for quick reference as a page-listing. Moreover, most libraries file their duplicate bills alphabetically by dealer for the entire fiscal period.

4. *Student Payroll Summary.* The wages of most student assistants are paid on an hourly basis once a week and the payrolls are ordinarily made up by the librarian and sent to the business office. A simple payroll form (Form 4) gives the total number of hours for the week in the first column, then the rate, name of employee, and gross earnings. One copy of the payroll is sent to the business office weekly and a duplicate copy is maintained by the library for totaling its student payroll costs monthly and entering on the monthly ledger report. In a library of some size, each department will submit a card for each student employee, confirming his working hours for the week, which will then be converted into gross earnings and entered on the student payroll summary by the librarian's secretary.

5. *Record of Petty Cash.* In general, petty cash accounts are handled in two principal ways: (1) in some libraries, fines and replacement monies are turned into petty cash directly by the library; and (2) in other libraries, the petty cash fund is established by a cash payment from the treasurer's office, it being assumed that fines and other collectable income are turned over to the college and are not credited to the library. This is regarded as the best practice by most finance officers.

If the first method is used, a special account book should be kept of all income and expenditures. If the second method is followed, whereby fines revert to the college or state funds, it is necessary for the library to establish a petty cash fund for small items of expenditure by drawing a certain amount of

DEPARTMENTAL PAYROLL SUMMARY

CHELSEA COLLEGE
DEPARTMENTAL PAYROLL SUMMARY

DEPARTMENT _____   EXPENSE ACCOUNT NO. _____

Period from _____ to _____ 19 _____

Hours or Days	Rates per Hour or Day	Name of Employee	Gross Earnings

Totals _____   _____

Approved _____

Department Head _____

money from the treasurer's office. This sum, amounting to whatever is thought necessary to take care of petty cash expenditures for a month or more, is charged against the library's "supply" fund, and a record is kept by the librarian so that he may include the amount in the monthly record of expenditures (Form 2, page 341) for the particular month when it is withdrawn. The money is placed in a petty cash box and vouchers are secured supporting every payment from the fund. When the petty cash money is exhausted, a statement of all payments made from the fund, together with supporting vouchers, is turned over to the treasurer who pays the library an amount equal to the total disbursements as shown by the statement. In this plan the fund remains intact after it is created. The only record the librarian has to make is the statement of payments with supporting vouchers and the deduction from the "supplies" fund of the library each time a withdrawal is made to replenish the fund.

6. *Other Records.* Most libraries keep a record of book costs. This can be done by keeping the original order card, after the book is received and the cost entered on the card, in a permanent "orders received" file. Such a record becomes bulky and libraries sometimes microfilm it annually or maintain the permanent book order cost record on the shelf list. The purpose of keeping the record is to determine readily the original cost of a book and to have some record of book costs for insurance purposes.

Another useful record for the library is a card file of major equipment. This should be made in duplicate, one copy to be kept in the business office and the other in the library's files. It should indicate the name of the item, the date purchased, the cost, and such information as serial numbers for typewriters. This record facilitates equipment purchasing and replacement, makes possible a more considered judgment in placing replacement orders or in deciding on repair versus replacement, and also provides an accurate inventory for insurance purposes.

NOTES

1. Lester, Robert. "Carnegie corporation aid to college libraries." *Col. and research lib.* 1:75-6, December, 1939; endowment for directorship of Harvard University library, *see: American library and book trade annual, 1960,* ed. by Wyllis E. Wright. N.Y., Bowker, 1959, p. 139

2. Randall, William M. and Goodrich, F. L. D. *Principles of college library administration.* 2nd ed. Chicago, A.L.A. and University of Chicago press, 1941, p. 43-4

3. "Grants to libraries, 1958"—an annual summary appearing in: *American library and book trade annual, 1960, op. cit.,* p. 133-40

4. See January issues of *Col. and research lib.* for annual announcement of ACRL committee awards; Jackson, W. V. "The ACRL grants program: a report of its first four years." *Col. and research lib.* 20:401-11, September, 1959

5. *Report of the Faculty Committee on the Library, 1958-59.* Bowdoin College, p. 4

6. "Gifts and bequests." A.L.A. *bull.* 33:59-60, October 15, 1939

7. Moran, Virginia L. and Tolman, Mason. "College library study." *Lib. jour.* 76:1907, November 15, 1951

8. Harrer, G. A. "Library expenditures: an examination of their distribution." *Col. and research lib.* 18:210-12, May, 1957; Littleton, I. T. "Distribution and cost of library service." *Col. and research lib.* 17:474-82, November, 1956

9. U.S. Office of education. "Survey of land-grant colleges and universities." *Bull.* 1930, no. 9, Vol. I, pt. VIII. Washington, Government printing office, 1930, p. 652

10. Reeves, Floyd W. and Russell, John D. "The administration of the library budget." *Lib. quar.* 2:269, July, 1932

11. Muller, Hans. "The management of college library book budgets." *Col. and research lib.* 2:321, September, 1941

12. *Ibid.,* p. 332

13. *Ibid.,* p. 332-3

14. *Ibid.,* p. 324

15. Urban, C. Stanley. "Certain aspects of the division of the library book budget among departments at several mid-western colleges." *Missouri lib. association quar.* 13:3, March, 1952

16. Randall, William M. "The college-library book budget." *Lib. quar.* 1:421-35, October, 1931; Reeves and Russell, *op. cit.,* p. 268-78; Hekhuis, Lambertus. "Formula for distribution of library funds among departments." *Lib. jour.* 61:574-5, August, 1936; Falley, Eleanor W. "Impersonal division of the college book fund." *Lib. jour.* 64:933-5, December 1, 1939; Ellsworth, Ralph E. "Some aspects of the problem of allocating book funds among departments in universities." *Lib. quar.* 12:486-94, July, 1942; Coney, Donald. "An experimental index for apportioning departmental book funds for a university library." *Lib. quar.* 14:422-8, July, 1942; Vosper, Robert. "Allocation of the book budget; experience at U.C.L.A." *Col. and research lib.* 10:215-18, July, 1949, Pt. 1.

Some other college library methods are briefly summarized below. It should be borne in mind that all libraries using a formula adjust the results to take into account factors such as the present state of the collections which are not measurable.

Carleton: Allocation is based on the cost factor, enrolment, and "course usage" determined by credit hours at course level. The cost factor is arrived at by a study of the net purchase price paid for departmental books during the preceding year. "Course usage" is determined by rating one student credit hour as 1 in courses numbered in the 100's, 2 for each student credit hour in 200 courses, and so forth. Thus a course Botany 215 (a three-hour course) with an enrolment of twelve students would be counted as 72 units (12 x 3 x 2). All units so ascribed to Botany would then be divided by the total number of units for all departments to establish a percentage or index figure.—Richards, J. H. "Allocation of book funds in college libraries." *Col. and research lib.* 14:379-80, October, 1953

Bowdoin: The departmental allocation is determined by assigning a number of units to each department. The librarian initiated the plan by studying departmental expenditures for books during the past ten years and assigning twenty units to history which had spent the most for a number of years. Other departmental allowances were scaled in relation to history. After the deduction of serials, binding, and general books from the total book appropriation, the balance is then divided by the number of units operating during the allocation year to get the value of the base unit.— *Report of the faculty library committee on the library, 1958-1959*, p. 6-9

Wellesley: A Book Index formula is constructed by determining: (A) the number of faculty in each department, (B) the number of courses, excluding sections, and (C) the units of instruction offered by each department. The formula is based on a four-year average of allocation.
  Faculty Index. Data requested from Recorder's Office. Includes: Number of faculty of the rank of Instructor or above. Based on actual teaching load. (Nine hours per week is accepted load. If only one three-hour course taught [semester], counted as 1/3 Faculty). Percentage is derived by dividing number of faculty or teaching load of each department by total number of faculty or total teaching load for a given year.
  Courses Index. Data requested from Recorder's Office. Percentage derived by dividing number of courses offered or course load of each department by total number of courses offered or total course load for a given year. Number of divisions of a course not included. This data was used later in reviewing the allocation schedule for the need of duplicate buying.
  Units of Instruction Index. Figures taken from data prepared annually by the Dean's Office. "A unit of instruction equals the instruction of one student one hour a week for a semester. Conference periods (for example, the fourth hour of certain language courses) and laboratory periods are not counted." Percentage derived by dividing the units of

instruction for the year of each department by the total units of instruction. The unit of instruction data is considered the most important factor in the formula and is given double weight.

After computing a departmental percentage average of the last four years for each of the factors above, an index percentage (X) is derived for each department by the use of the formula $X = \dfrac{A+B+2C}{4}$

When the allocation schedule was derived by the book index it was reviewed to take into account such factors as:

1. duplicate buying
2. average amount actually spent by each department during the past four years.
3. high cost of books in certain subject fields
4. library use
5. extent of a department's collection
6. current book production in the subject field

—Letter from Helen M. Brown, Librarian, Wellesley College, to author, July, 1960

Goucher: This plan is based on the Falley article referred to above. It takes into account (1) the average cost of books, (2) the number of books published that are suitable for purchase by a department of any good college without particular reference to the Goucher program, (3) the number of students in each department, and (4) the "library use of course" in each department. The second factor is determined by checking the *Publishers' Weekly* for the month of November and counting the number of books in each department judged suitable for a good college library whether purchased by Goucher or not. The "library use of course" is a subjective rating of course use made by the assistant librarian in charge of public services.

---

17. Singer, Dorothea M. *Insurance of libraries.* Chicago, A.L.A., 1946; Deale, H. Vail. "Insurance re-evaluation." *Lib. jour.* 80:2814-18, December 15, 1955; Mixer, Charles W. "Insurance evaluation of a university library's collection." *Col. and research lib.* 13:18-23, January, 1952

18. Trent, R. M. *Financial records for college libraries* (Unpublished Master's thesis, School of Library Service, Columbia University, 1939), p. 3

19. Rider, Fremont. "Library cost accounting." *Lib. quar.* 6:335-6, October, 1936

ADDITIONAL REFERENCES

American council on education. National committee on the preparation of a manual. . . . *College and university business administration.* Washington, D.C., American council on education, 1952, 2 vols.

Wight, Edward A. *Public library finance and accounting.* Chicago, A.L.A., 1943

XV

Interpretation of College Library Service

The terms publicity, public relations, and interpretation are sometimes used synonymously. They are not the same thing. The choice of *interpretation* in this chapter was made, however, for reasons less of logic than of sensibility. As a term, interpretation is a little more sober than publicity, a little less pretentious than public relations. Applied to the field of college librarianship it may be defined as the act or process of bringing information about the college to bear on library functions and policies, and the interpretation of library functions, policies, and procedures to the public served by the college library.

The question is sometimes raised whether interpretation is really a separate activity or merely a by-product of good service. Public relations experts have tended, perhaps not unnaturally, to magnify their importance to the point where some of them, at least, claim credit for every activity that builds good will. Those librarians who are suspicious of or fed up with the glib patter of the publicist tend to belittle the importance of interpretation and to maintain that no amount of striving after good will can compensate for inability to give good library service to students and faculty.

In order to answer the question raised above, it is necessary to examine the aims of interpretation and to inquire why this activity is important to college libraries. It is generally agreed that the functions of the college library are not fully understood either by those who are responsible for its welfare at the top level or by those who use its services. Even less well understood are the essential staff activities required for the attainment of college library aims and the carrying out of its functions. Ask any student what a librarian does and his generally unfurrowed brow immediately clouds up. The professor will parry the question with a witticism or else state frankly that the librarian hands out the books at the loan desk. Yet no one should leap too quickly to the wrong conclusion. Students, faculty, and administrators know the importance of books in education, and they associate libraries and librarians with books. If they do not know what librarians do to make these books available or if they do not fully appreciate the work of reference staffs, it is largely because they have not heard enough about such matters. The more they use the library, the more they are likely to accept its services as a matter of course. It seems reasonable to conclude, therefore, that efforts to improve public relations directly, rather than as a mere by-product of good service, are worth while. A good interpretation program will not only explain what libraries are for, what they need, and what librarians do, but will also call attention to educational needs on the campus to which librarians can make a real contribution.

Most libraries are either so understaffed or so busy that there isn't much time for the kind of program implied in the foregoing. Consequently library interpretation is often a haphazard affair, whereas the more systematic and definitely pointed it is, the more effective it will be. In the small college library the librarian will have to work out the interpretation plan, using student help to arrange exhibits, to make signs, and to keep the library looking attractive. In the larger college library, the planning and over-all direction of library interpretation may well be delegated to a staff member who has a special flair for it. There may be a committee on exhibits, a clerical assistant or one or more talented student assistants for art and sign work, but it is still important to have one person coordinate these activities.

Consciously or unconsciously everyone connected with the library performs an interpretation function of some sort. Where there is direction to the program, the approach is twofold: (1) through personal contact between the librarians and the individuals or groups using the library, and (2) through the planned distribution of information about the library. The persons with whom the library must work are (1) college administrative officers, boards and committees, faculty, and students, and (2) off-campus groups such as the local community, alumni, Friends of the library, and professional associations. Information about the library will be disseminated principally through the annual report, handbook, college catalogue, book bulletins and booklists, local and student newspapers, bulletin boards, posters, exhibits, and displays.

LIBRARY RELATIONS ON THE CAMPUS

The relationship of the library to the faculty and to committees has already been discussed so frequently in several chapters of this book that it is unnecessary to say anything further at this point. For the faculty, the common denominator of library interpretation lies in getting the books they want and getting them as fast as possible. But since the librarian's relationship with the president is said to leave something to be desired [1]—perhaps a great deal—it may not be out of place to point briefly to its significance, even at the risk of repetition. Also the librarian's relationship to students deserves mention even though it has been referred to briefly under personnel and even though the real impact of the library upon the student is often made through the professor. Finally under this heading it is pertinent to emphasize the important role of the staff in its direct contact with students.

College presidents are busy people. They seldom have time to use the library and consequently must rely upon the librarian to keep them informed about its needs. If the library is either brilliantly or poorly managed, the president will learn about it from the faculty, students, and even alumni. But if the library needs new equipment or additional staff, he will hear nothing about it except from the librarian—at least to begin with. As a consequence, the librarian must make every effort to keep the president informed about library progress and problems. He should be careful to present all sides of his recommendations and problems because the president cannot give whole-hearted support without fully understanding the nature of the need. If he uses memoranda—and they should be used sparingly—they are more likely to influence the final decision if they are brief and clear. The fact that the president has little time to use the library is a drawback to his understanding of its problems and usage. He should be encouraged to use it, and the librarian should have both the grace and the courage to tell him that his occasional presence there will have a good deal of influence on the students' attitudes toward the library and reading. If he is told that he may call the library at any time for information about specific questions in his work and that he may use a carrel or private study in the library whenever he has an opportunity to pursue his personal studies, his working relations with the library will have got off to a good start.

In this day of rising enrolments and multiple calls upon the budget, any one of which may at times drive a president to desperation, he is much more likely to be sympathetic to the library's budget requests if he understands clearly how they relate to the general pattern of college objectives. The reputation of the college depends in large part on its success in carrying out its declared objectives, and, whatever they are, the library has a challenging part in their realization. The choice of information and the method of presenting it are important. Studies of the use of the library by students, or of some particular faculty-library cooperative effort to promote independent reading, will help to explain what the library is doing and will encourage the president to bring the librarian into the councils of his advisory committees. He will help to build a better library service if he clearly understands its hopes and expectations in terms of instructional ends. This is not to say that the library is unimportant in its own right or that it must always nestle under the umbrella of the faculty in seeking assistance from the administration; but it does recognize that the first demands upon the college's funds are for instructional purposes and that the president is more likely to be influenced in his final decision if he sees the library need as a sound educational investment.

Whereas the librarian is chiefly responsible for maintaining good working relations with the president, the members of the library staff, including student assistants, are "the library" to students and must be answerable in large measure for the impression which students have of the library. First impressions are said to be lasting ones, so clearly the staff must give a new student a friendly and warm welcome to dispel his preconceived notions of the coldness and dullness of libraries.

The critical points in dealing with the majority of the library's constituency will, of course, be the reference and circulation services. Courtesy, conscientiousness, and adaptability are required at reference

and loan desks under circumstances which may often be strained. . . .
The library staff must continuously refrain from treating them [students]
with condescension—an attitude which all too often makes them feel that
their library is no more than a petty bureaucracy designed to frustrate
them. An important part of an academic library's public relations program must be a deliberate sensitivity to the requests and complaints of
undergraduates.[2]

Students meet the library as they would a person and what they
find there will determine their impressions. If the building is dull
and poorly lighted, it will confirm the image of the library stereo-
type. If it is bright, nicely furnished, clean, and comfortable,
students will be attracted by it and will boast of it to others. In
the friendly atmosphere of a college campus, there can be less
formality, less rigidity, and fewer rules than might be possible or
desirable in a university. "Even when enforcing rules and collecting fines—factors which sometimes strain relationships between students and staff—judgment should be exercised by the
staff. Of course rules, fines, and penalties are necessary but the
staff can, upon occasion, take into account human frailties, and
soften the application and even make exceptions in certain cases." [3]
The everyday association of the staff with students is more important than any other type of library interpretation. This contact
may be something as simple as the exchange of greetings across
a loan desk or it may be the more serious meeting of student and
reference librarian in discussing a term paper assignment. Or
it may even lie in the post-card wording of an overdue notice or
a request to a faculty member to return a book wanted by another.
The handling of these minutiae are none the less important because they are simple and routine.

Library Relations Off Campus

The off-campus groups with which the library is concerned
include the college community, alumni, Friends of the library,
professional associations, and accrediting associations.

Relations With the College Community

In both service and interpretation, it is important that the
college librarian take into account the community in which the

college is located. A few libraries, such as Oberlin, maintain public library service for residents of the community. In most colleges, provision is made for people in the community to use the library or to take out books of a scholarly nature which are not needed at the time by the faculty or students.[4] Every college library has a great many volumes which it can well afford to share with the people of the community, although it is admittedly difficult to know when a book will be needed by members of the college faculty or student body. If the college is located in a large city, it may feel obligated to require local residents to borrow through the public library on an inter-library loan basis, or it may even be necessary, in order to safeguard the interests of the students, to limit the hours of service available to the community or to restrict use to special groups such as school teachers, ministers, and scholars in the community.[5] In most college communities the demands are so few that restrictions are unnecessary and the resulting good will helps the reputation of the college and the library.

Relations With Alumni and Friends of the Library Groups

The opportunity to be helpful to alumni has already been mentioned in connection with the circulation and reference services of the library. Alumni who live in the college community will use the library directly; others may seek the loan of books by mail. Still others will want information which draws upon special or unique materials in the collections of the library and which requires extensive reference searching. Occasionally the library will have the opportunity to supply a reading list on a specific subject, in which case the librarian functions like a readers' adviser in a public library. In the case of highly specialized requests, the library may have to draw upon the special knowledge of the faculty.

Alumni can be particularly helpful to the library in forming a Friends' group, in donating gifts for book purchases, and in enlisting the support of persons in a position to be of genuine assistance to the library. In order to develop friendly relations, the librarian arranges exhibits for Alumni Day and tries to meet as many alumni as possible, works closely with the alumni secretary in order to keep him informed about library services and library needs, and furnishes the alumni magazine with notes about outstanding acquisitions, memorial book gifts, special services, and news likely to be of interest to the alumni. Not infrequently the best picture coverage in connection with a library story will be found in the alumni publication.

Some colleges have found that an organization of Friends has added much to the strength and usefulness of the library. The latest survey shows that thirty-seven out of sixty-nine respondents have a Friends of the library group actively functioning.[6] The purposes of such organizations, listed in order of their importance by a librarian with long and successful experience in a Friends' organization, are: "(1) to educate members to the needs of the library by helping them to understand what the library is trying to do and what it must have to accomplish its objectives; (2) to develop friends who will assist the library in its search for materials; and (3) to raise money for library materials and library operations."[7] All three purposes subserve the major aim of strengthening of the book, journal, and manuscript resources of the library. Not all the organizations are successful, but there have been notable accomplishments. During their first decade of activity Friends of the Dartmouth College Library bought scarce individual works, rare books, and contributed money estimated in all to amount to "well over $50,000 and . . . not far from $100,000."[8]

Friends' organizations do not require elaborate machinery to be successful. Some have a constitution, by-laws, dues, regular meetings, and officers; others dispense with all formality. The local conditions seem to govern the situation, but the one essential is a professor, alumnus, or layman who is sufficiently dedicated to turn the crank and keep the wheels moving. Benjamin Powell describes this individual as "a sparkplug, a behind-the-scene director, close to the library, who must keep the wheels oiled and occasionally must pull the whole business back on its course."[9] Unless there is some one person among the alumni, faculty or college friends who has the interest and energy to create and maintain enthusiasm in the organization, it is likely to degenerate quickly into a group of well-wishers. Although the librarian remains in the background, he has an important contribution to make in furnishing information about the library's present status and plans for the future and in preparing lists of desiderata. Sometimes the college or the library provides office space, supplies, and the clerical labor necessary to putting out a bulletin. Probably half or more of the college and university libraries with a Friends' organization issue some sort of publication varying in size from a single sheet to a substantial magazine.[19]

Participation in Professional Associations

The librarian's participation in professional associations has a twofold value in library interpretation. In the first place, the local newspapers are quite likely to carry notices about the library and staff members who are attending national and state meetings, particularly if they are participating in an official capacity, contributing a paper, or taking part in committee work. If the college distributes a weekly or monthly faculty information bulletin, the librarian and staff members will also be mentioned here as representatives of the college at their meetings. In the second place, library meetings are stimulating and refreshing and the librarian returns from his discussions with fellow librarians ready to try out new methods and ideas. By keeping the local librarian in close touch with the most important developments in the library field, the professional meetings serve as a constant vitalizing force in his everyday work and contacts with faculty and students. Confident and enthusiastic staff members, alert to new ideas and new ways of making libraries useful, win the confidence and respect of their teaching colleagues.

THE MEDIA OF INTERPRETATION

Up to this point an attempt has been made to show the importance of close and cordial relations between the library and certain groups and organizations which use its services or contribute to its growth and development. The remainder of this chapter will be devoted to a description of the media which are commonly used to interpret the services of the library to these groups.

These media were mentioned at the beginning of the chapter but be listed here again for the sake of clarity and emphasis:

Annual reports
Handbooks
College catalogue
The newspaper
Bulletin boards and posters
Booklists and book bulletins
Exhibits and book displays

Practically all these media will be used by the library or in the interests of the library, large or small, at one time or another. As the library grows larger, it devotes more time and attention to its own publications and to the presentation of the library through other college publications. Regardless of its size, however, the library, as expositor of the good things to be had from the printed page, should take special pains with its own publications whether these consist of form notices or a monthly list of acquisitions.

Annual Report

The annual report to the president is both an accounting and a record of accomplishment. The main topics to be covered in the report are the state and growth of the collections, services to readers, preparation of materials, personnel, and perhaps a brief summary taking stock of the present and outlining the problems of the immediate future. Statistical material should be standardized in form and presented in an appendix with such interpretation as is necessary in the text. Russell has listed in the form of a table all the topics covered by twenty-five reports which he considered outstanding among the several hundred investigated in his study.[11]

The report should not be too archival. An effort should be made to avoid technical terminology and to express the pertinent ideas so that they will be readily grasped by one unfamiliar with library procedures. The report should be mimeographed so that copies may be sent not only to the president but to faculty members, Friends of the library, donors listed in the report, and other librarians. Highlights from the report may be submitted to the alumni magazine, local newspapers, and Friends' publications. Excerpts from the report are sometimes featured in the library's book bulletin or on the cover sheets of the monthly list of current acquisitions.

Handbooks

These handy booklets are a veritable mine of current facts about the library to help the student and faculty member use its services. Sometimes a separate handbook is prepared for the faculty.

The student library handbook is intended primarily as an instructional leaflet. No amount of window dressing will make it a useful handbook if it is poorly arranged and poorly written for this purpose. The important thing is to introduce the student to the library in the way he would normally use it in connection with his studies. To illustrate with one specific example: under the heading "How to Find Books Easily," the library introduces the card catalog as the logical starting point in the student's investigation, interprets its use by means of sample cards and brief notes, tells what a call slip is and how it should be filled out, directs the student to the book shelves and the particular section indicated by the call number, tells how the book may be charged out, and repeats briefly the rules and period of loan. This same approach is used throughout the handbook. An effort is made to link specific library aids with the student's class work. The description of periodical indexes offers the opportunity to associate these tools with the preparation of source themes. The index may also serve as a device to make the association of library aids with class problems more vivid and understandable. Kraus' study of the library handbook as a simple, inexpensive instructional tool suggests the topics to be included and the method of presentation.[12]

Cartoons, pictures, line drawings, and card reproductions add to the attractiveness and usefulness of the handbook. The style of writing should be simple and clear; the text should be introduced by a friendly note from the librarian. Most libraries mimeograph their handbooks and some use an 8" x 11" size with holes punched for convenient filing in the student's notebook. A printed handbook is superior, of course, to one that is mimeographed or lithoprinted. If the names of staff members, library hours, and other items of information likely to change frequently are printed on the inside front and back covers of the handbook, it is possible to effect some saving in revisions. A new cover for a new edition is necessary in any event and the suggestion above will make less likely the need for frequent revisions of the text. Copies of the handbook are distributed to new students during orientation week and to others at the loan desk.

A library handbook for the faculty serves to keep the faculty informed of library methods, hours of service, regulations, and special services. It is also a useful device for relating library services to instruction. The nature of its contents is suggested by a brief description of a typical example. This twenty-four page mimeographed handbook opens with a well-worded introduction which describes a special collection within the library intended to serve the general education program, outlines the means by which faculty and the library staff can work together to improve instruction, and explains the restricted but significant way in which the library can aid research. The major resources of the library, from trade bibliographies to the library's special "ana" collection, are described next. Reference service and the joint faculty-library responsibility for instructing the student in using the library form a third section. Book selection and acquisition policies and procedures precede an even longer section on the audio-visual services of the library. Reserve book procedures also come in for detailed explanation, and a final section is devoted to special services such as faculty studies, lounge, seminars, and inter-library loan. The text is followed by floor plans.

Frequent revision is perhaps not as important as in the case of the student handbook. A detailed index will greatly facilitate use.

The College Catalogue

Florence King's 1938 study of the college catalogue showed how distressingly inadequate most accounts of the library were and how difficult it was to find information about the library because of inadequate indexing.[13] The important points to include in the catalogue about the library are a statement of its role in college education and a description of its resources, assistance given to individual students, library hours, special collections, and other libraries on the campus and in the community. The library staff should be listed with the faculty or separately next to the faculty. The mention of special collections has a significance beyond their possible research value. The knowledge to an outside reader that a library has such collections, takes proper care of them, and relates their use to instruction may well prove an incentive to him and to other benefactors to make donations to the library. The catalogue is also an important source of college history. Without detracting from the main purpose of the statement about the library, it should be possible to set forth briefly the important highlights of library history, and to add, from year to year, significant facts which will be of special interest to the future historian.

The Newspaper

The student newspaper carries regular news stories about the library, library hours, letters of complaint from readers, announcements of exhibits, changes in staff, and editorials. Some protective as well as promotional measures are necessary if one is to retain his sanity in dealing with student newspapers. An experienced librarian offers the following advice:

We want and need library representation there but no doubt any of you who have been associated with student reporting know the pitfalls of inaccuracy and poor judgment. A conference between the librarian and each incoming editor might create an atmosphere for the exchange of ideas and the discussion of library objectives and activities. Should this not prove feasible the librarian could encourage the student reporters to come to him for interviews so that they might be provided with material for articles.[14]

If the paper is sometimes a threat, it is also the librarian's opportunity. In every college library there are pamphlet collections, bibliographical tools, government documents, as well as unique and unusual materials which are not used as much as they should be because students do not know about them or do not understand their usefulness. If the librarian can interest a student editor or reporter in writing about these topics imaginatively, he renders a service to the education of students.

Usually the college news editor or news bureau is responsible for any library news in the local newspapers. It is desirable, therefore, that the editor be given an opportunity to visit the library and to learn something about the purposes and procedures of the library as well as to become better acquainted with the staff. If the editor has this understanding, he will be quick to see the news value of such library events as important gifts, exhibits, poetry readings, a musical program, assistance to readers, or an experiment in setting up a dormitory library with paperbacks.[15]

Bulletin Boards and Posters

Bulletin boards and posters offer many possibilities for interpreting library services. They may be used to stimulate interest in selected books on a particular subject; to call attention to special resources and services; to present short, graphic summaries of important national and local news; and to announce programs and lectures. Posters not only guide and instruct but have cultural values also. A striking poster may have an aesthetic appeal comparable to that of a beautiful piece of sculpture or a finely printed book.

In planning bulletin boards, it has been found useful to keep an informal file of ideas for bulletin board use—titles that appeal; slogans; notes on special days, authors, and events; pictures; book jackets; and pictorial or outline maps. An effort should be made to connect national, educational, literary, scientific, and local campus events with the use of library materials. Signs and posters should be used sparingly on bulletin boards and should be designed and lettered tastefully. They are most frequently used to guide the reader—to show the student how to fill out a "call slip," or to announce library hours or a holiday during which the library will be closed.

Bulletin board displays will not command attention unless some care is given to their arrangement and design. These suggestions will help to make them more effective:

1. Neatness, simplicity, and visibility are essential.

2. Few displays should be shown simultaneously in one room or area.

3. Long lists of explanations on the board will not be read.

4. When the subject is changed, the form of the display should be changed, or else the color scheme, or both.

5. Pictures, jackets, captions—all should emphasize one idea.

6. Captions and slogans should be brief and arresting, unhackneyed, confined to a single idea, yet expressed with clearness and force.

7. A few book jackets, neatly trimmed and well displayed, are more effective than a great many shown at one time.

8. Letters and lettering should be neat, simple, carefully spaced, and well proportioned to the size of board or poster.

9. Arrangement of material on the bulletin board may be
   a. bisymmetric, with formal balance—i.e., with a reversed pattern to the right and left of a vertical center line.
   b. informal, with occult balance, using a "beam scale" arrangement in which symmetry is gained through balance by size, weight, and/or color.
   c. dynamically balanced, so that material is arranged to bring about a forceful line movement of the eye, properly stopped at points of interest at beginning or end.[16]

Posters, pictures, book jackets, maps, and current book lists are the staples of any bulletin board display. If they are thoughtfully chosen and tastefully displayed, they will attract attention and encourage some students to further reading. If they are untidy, unattractive, and incompetently done, they are not worth the time and effort spent on them. The library should do just as much in display work as it can do well. Sometimes students and teaching departments will be willing to cooperate. If there is desirable display space near a main line of traffic, the Art Department may be persuaded to arrange a changing monthly display of one or two good pictures.

Booklists and Book Bulletins

The most common form of library publication is the weekly or monthly mimeographed list of recent acquisitions which contains a page or so of introductory notes about the library. In preparing such a booklist, the librarian can either select from or list completely the current titles added to the library. Since the principal demand for this information comes from the faculty who want to know what books are being added in their own and related fields, it would seem desirable to aim at completeness whenever possible. If selection is essential because of the bulk of current accessions, then it is better to eliminate certain classes of material which are less likely to be of use to the larger group than to attempt a haphazard selection of titles from the accessions of each month. One library omits foreign language, fiction, juvenile, and professional library books from its listing.

The format and arrangement of the mimeographed lists of accessions are as varied as their titles. Most libraries use their regular classification scheme, giving suitable captions for each class and arranging titles alphabetically under class. Another plan is to classify the books by subject and to arrange the subjects alphabetically throughout the list. In most cases the information for each title consists of the call number, author, title, and date of publication. For the mimeographed list of accessions, as for the book bulletin, a distinctive title is of considerable importance. Some titles used for the lists include: *Stray Library Leaves, On the Shelf, Library Book List, Library Leaves, Scout, New Books, Recent Accessions*, and *Monthly Record*. Variety is gained and appearance enhanced through the use of a colored cover sheet on which the masthead and title are printed.

While the demand for the mimeographed list of current accessions comes mainly from the faculty, the thing that keeps the publication alive is the librarian's skill in making the cover sheet a regular channel of communication with the faculty. Few librarians overlook the opportunity to use the introductory pages of each number for presenting interesting and informative notes about staff activities, exhibits, gifts, and new services. Some items of a more technical nature, which have appeared in the cover sheets of the current acquisitions list, include the following:

Statement of policy concerning the loan of bound periodicals, stack use, etc.

New periodicals and continuations

Annotated list of important additions to the reference collection

Gifts and acknowledgment of gifts

Faculty publications of the month

Descriptions of important exhibits

Circulation statistics interpreted

Notes on little-known sources of information in the college library

Notes on instruction in the use of the library

The issuance of a mimeographed weekly, biweekly, or monthly list of accessions is the most interesting, and probably the least hazardous, adventure in publishing on which a college library can embark. The factors which insure success are regularity and continuity in issuance, an arrangement of subjects and titles which will facilitate use by the faculty, and a page or two of introductory comment with enough human inspiration, information, and humor to make the list not only a useful tool but interesting and readable. Copies are intended for campus use, but particular issues are sometimes sent to outside friends of the library. Copies are also posted in the dormitories and in departmental libraries and are available for consultation in the main library by students. The faculty mailing list is revised each year to make sure that the current acquisitions list is being sent only to those who really want it and make use of it.

Few college libraries publish a printed bulletin because of the time and expense involved. Unlike the scholarly and bibliographical university journals (*Library Chronicle of University of Texas*, *Harvard Library Bulletin*, Princeton's *Chronicle*, and Yale's *University Library Gazette*), the college library bulletins are characterized by informality of style, simple format, short articles, news notes, and book notes. Although they vary greatly in content, they are intended primarily for campus readers and not for the library profession or the bibliographic world. The bulletin serves several different purposes. Through explanation of the work of various library departments and procedures, it helps to increase the usefulness of the library. By means of brief book reviews and annotated booklists, it encourages the use of books for general and recreational reading. Through descriptions of important collections and special services, it points to ways in which the library may contribute to the educational program. And through frequent listings of donors and brief descriptions of important gifts, it provides a means for appropriately acknowledging gifts and encouraging further donations.

Although it is not widely removed from the current pattern of printed bulletins, Dartmouth's *Library Bulletin* has assets which make it a worthy model for study. It came out first in 1931 and continued to be the inspiration of many other bulletins until it ceased publication in 1953. Its appearance was pleasing and it never failed to make the most commonplace incidents in library work interesting and amusing. Distinction and beauty were contributed through the choice of a high quality of paper and fine typography. In the main, however, its excellence stemmed directly from the variety, interest, and graceful literary style of its contents. This was accomplished in two ways. First, in approaching every aspect of the work of the library—from rare books down to the most mechanical operation in library routine—the editor of the bulletin thought primarily in terms of his readers. Second, the style of writing was direct, pleasant, and witty. There was nothing official or impersonal about it. Some of the types of material qualifying for admission to its pages were the following:

1. Special collections
    Americana
    Italian dialect collection
    Nineteenth- and twentieth-century Spanish plays
    Art library
    Medical library
    Map collection
    Music resources
    Pamphlet collection

2. Explanation of library policies and rules
    Open-stack policy
    Reclassification problems
    Faculty return of books
    Book selection
    Fines

3. Publicity and interpretation
    Notice of exhibits

Excerpts from the librarian's annual reports
Lists of desiderata
Acknowledgment of gifts
Notable purchases indicating lines of interest
Friends of the library

4. The work of departments: Interesting summaries of the functions and procedures in
Catalog department
Order department
Periodicals
Reserves
Bindery
Treasure room
Tower room (recreational reading)

5. Special services
Inter-library loan
Photostats and film
Research services

6. Booklists
Recent accessions—selected and briefly annotated
Occasional articles about books on a special subject
New periodicals

7. Archival material
Reprints of interesting and often humorous letters and documents from the college archives

8. Fillers
Amusing incidents relating to service
Bookish notes

In 1957 the Dartmouth College Library brought out a new series of its bulletin "in response to the Faculty's decision that our new curriculum, toward which the College this year is preparing a transition, shall stress a deeper and more independent use of the Library." [17] The new series is less distinctive than the old in general appearance but has a radar sensitivity to library-instructional relations. If written less light-heartedly than its ancestor, it reports with brilliance and style the Library's concern for bringing books and readers together in a significant and meaningful way. It is the function of the *Bulletin* "to call regularly to notice certain unique or unusual materials that are here available . . . articles on technical library topics, but only when they are a joint concern of teachers and librarians . . . [and] articles on educational policy, in so far as it involves the use of our collections." [18]

Although of a distinctly literary character, Dartmouth's *Library Bulletin* rarely devotes space to booklists and book notes of the conventional type found in public library bulletins. More characteristic of the latter are Colby Junior College's superbly captioned and neatly printed pocket digest, the *Book Pedlar*, which carries several pages of book comment and library news written to meet the needs and tastes of younger students, and *Library Jottings* of St. Vincent College (Pa.), an example of what the small college library can accomplish in a mimeographed bulletin, dressed up with stiff, printed covers. In concise form, *Library Jottings* records the library news, changes in library regulations, noteworthy acquisitions, and anything about the library which may be useful to its patrons.

Book bulletins are distributed on the campus to administrative officers, faculty, and selected groups of students by local mail or from the main library loan desks and the departmental libraries. By outside mail they are sent to trustees, alumni, class secretaries, Friends of the library, editors of library periodicals, library schools, other libraries, and benefactors of the college as a whole.

Book Displays and Exhibits

Through book displays the library calls attention to new books, to materials for special class projects, and to the relationship of library use to campus organizations and activities. Most displays related to instruction are effective only when "they tie in directly with a specific course, a campus event or a campus personality." [19] Color, captions, and a skillful arrangement of the books and jackets or pictures help to make the display attractive.

Exhibits are most commonly prepared to publicize little-known or rare library materials, encourage reading, promote interest in a specific field or group of subject fields, call attention to a particular anniversary or special occasion, acknowledge outstanding gifts, encourage hobbies, relate the library to campus organizations and activities, and publicize faculty research. [20] They take a great deal of time to prepare successfully; it is far better to have a few good exhibits than many of inferior grade during the year even if this means leaving the same exhibit up for longer than a month. In order to attain success, certain steps must be taken and certain points must be borne in mind in the preparation of the exhibit. A committee should be chosen to select and prepare the exhibits. Membership of the committee may come wholly from the staff or it may include faculty and students also, and it should change annually except for perhaps one member to give continuity to the committee's work. An exhibit calendar should be arranged and maintained well in advance of the individual exhibitions. "Planning ahead enables special occasions to be observed, provides time for purchasing needed materials, and serves to discourage people who rush into the library and want an exhibit put up immediately. Of course there is every reason to encourage the help of the faculty and students in the preparation of both the calendar and the exhibits, but at the proper time—not a day or a few days ahead." [21] In the third place, the choice of materials for the exhibit must be made with great care. The underlying purpose is to draw attention to library resources, and the subject of the exhibit should be chosen with this principle in mind. The selection of material often involves considerable research in order to discover what books, articles, manuscripts, maps, or other materials are most appropriate to the theme. Those who have had considerable experience with this process emphasize that the materials must be selected "primarily for their quality, calibre and importance, and never merely for general superficial impressiveness." [22] In fact the documents may seem "rather unprepossessing when lying unexplained in a dimly-lit table case" but when they are imaginatively related to one another and arranged with provocative and adequate captions, they will attract the library patron as a magnet draws iron filings. Of course, the exhibit cases must be well located and well lighted, and there are advantages in having both upright and horizontal exhibit cases. The exhibit committee should have a full supply of exhibit stock and props and a place to prepare and leave materials. In any visual presentation, the use of color and color contrasts is necessary as background to catch the eye of the viewer and to set off the qualities of the materials exhibited. [23]

To an experienced library public relations man, the foregoing will seem like an oversimplified account of the interpretation program of the college library. Let this criticism be admitted at the outset. But to cover in detail all the facets of a sound interpretation program, from the letterhead the librarian uses to the scholarly catalog which a large college library issues in connection with a major exhibit, would burden the mind of the library school student and far exceed anything the average college librarian could undertake. In any case, a reading of some of the excellent references cited in the footnotes will provide stimulation enough for several years' activities.

NOTES

1. "In fact I heard more derogatory language used among the eight presidents who made up the commission on Financing Higher Education about librarians than I heard about any other component part of the university structure."—John D. Millett, quoted in: Association of research libraries. *Minutes,* January 31, 1954, Madison, Wis., Appendix VI; "The college or university librarian today is rarely the object of his master's affection."—Reuben Frodin. *In:* Fussler, H. H. *The function of the library in the modern college.* Chicago, University of Chicago Graduate library school, 1954. p. 100

2. Heron, David W. "The public relations of academic libraries." *Col. and research lib.* 16:144, April, 1955

3. Kellam, William P. "Public relations is a personal matter." Louisiana lib. association *bull.* 19:73, Summer, 1956

4. Shaw, Charles B. "The college library and the individual reader in the community." *In: The college library in a changing world.* Baltimore, Julia Rogers Library, Goucher College, 1953, p. 34-8

5. *The use of the Woman's College library by persons other than Woman's College students and members of the staff.* [Greensboro, N.C., Woman's College library of the University of North Carolina] June, 1952 (1 page)

6. Fox, M. Allyn. "Friends of the library groups in colleges and universities." *Col. and research lib.* 12:353, October, 1951

7. Powell, Benjamin E. "Friends of the library as public relations agents." *Southeastern librarian* 7:89, Fall, 1957

8. "Friends in particular; a financial evaluation." Dartmouth College *Lib. bull.* 4:175, February, 1949

9. Powell, *op. cit.,* p. 92

10. Fox, M. Allyn, *op. cit.*, p. 354. Examples: *Colby Lib. quar.* published by the Colby Library Associates, Colby College, Waterville, Maine. The A.L.A. headquarters library has copies for loan of representative constitutions, publications, publicity pieces, membership cards, etc., in use by existing Friends of the library groups.

11. Russell, John D. and others. "The college library report." A.L.A. *bull.* 30:216-20, April, 1936. The following outline, taken from the article, lists the topics included in typical college library reports and the percentage of reports treating each topic. The percentage is based on the twenty-five best reports.

Topic	Percentage
1. State of book collection	
a. New acquisitions	100
b. Total number of volumes in collection	96
c. Detailed list of gifts and donors' names	76
d. Strength of book collection	36
e. Strength of periodical collection	24
f. Weakness of book collection	32
g. Weakness of periodical collection	24
2. Use	
a. Circulation for home use	100
b. Assigned reading	52
c. Reference	24
d. Attendance	12
e. Special extension services	24
f. Surveys and checks on efficiency of service	24
3. Preparation processes	
a. Cataloging	68
b. Binding	24
4. Personnel	
a. List of staff with positions held	20
b. Training and professional activity	40
c. Need for salary adjustments	0
d. Adequacy or inadequacy of staff	28
e. Turnover	44
5. Finance	
a. General cost of operation	56
b. Unit costs	12
c. Comparative costs	20
d. Needs	8

6. Building and equipment
   a. Improvements made 36
   b. Needs 52

7. Instruction in the use of the library 32

8. Notes of special progress 56

9. Administrative problems
   a. Internal 24
   b. External 16

10. Statement of objectives
    a. Minor 32
    b. Major 36

12. Kraus, J. W. "College library handbooks." *Lib. jour.* 75:716-17, April 15, 1950

13. King, Florence L. "How is the library presented in the college catalog?" *Lib. quar.* 8:92, January, 1938

14. Fritz, Evelyn. "The librarian as middleman." *Southeastern librarian* 7:86-7, Fall, 1957

15. Lansberg, W. R. "How to publicize your purpose." *Lib. jour.* 82:697-701, March 15, 1957

16. Focke, Helen M. *Library bulletin boards.* Cleveland Public Library, n.d., p. 1-2

17. Dartmouth College *Library bull.* 1(ns):1-2, October, 1957

18. *Loc. cit.*

19. Spitz, Edna H. "Integrating library and classroom through effective library exhibits." *Wilson lib. bull.* 32:498, March, 1958

20. Reagan, Agnes. "College library exhibits." *Col. and research lib.* 5:54-5, December, 1943

21. Kellam, *op. cit.,* p. 71

22. Miner, Dorothy. "Another cooperative exhibition for Baltimore." *Maryland libraries* 24:21, Fall, 1957

23. Among many suggestive articles on the specifics of exhibit selection and preparation, see in addition to Dorothy Miner's article: Dalphin, G. R. and English, V. H. "Geographical exhibits." *Lib. jour.* 79:1466-8, September 1, 1954; Sellers, R. G. Z. "Exhibits can be easy." *Wilson lib. bull.* 23:526-7, March, 1949; Urban, A. M. "Displays and exhibits in Maryland college and university libraries." *Maryland libraries*, 24:9-12, Fall, 1957; Miller, Lois. "Now and then exhibit." *Lib. jour.* 80:2058-9, October 1, 1955; and Spitz, E. H., *op. cit.,* p. 498-500

ADDITIONAL REFERENCES

Buchanan, M. B. "Developing a library public relations program." *Lib. trends* 7:253-8, October, 1958

Coplan, Kate. "Some basic policies for exhibits and displays." *Maryland libraries* 24:3-6, Fall, 1957. Carries an excellent bibliography.

Deale, H. V. "Public relations of academic libraries." *Lib. trends* 7:269-77, October, 1958

Harvey, J. F. "Put your library's imprint in print." *Lib. jour.* 81:783-91, April 1, 1956,

Kinder, K. L. "Professional associations' role in public relations." *Lib. trends* 7:312-17, October, 1958

Raper, W. B. "Relationship of the administration and faculty." *North Carolina libraries* 18:42-3, Winter, 1960

Sellers, R. G. Z. "Special services in liberal arts college libraries." *Col. and research lib.* 14:249-54, July, 1953

Thompson, L. S. "Friends of the library." *In: American library and book trade annual, 1960.* N.Y., Bowker, 1959, p. 171-2

XVI

The Library Building and Equipment

The chief characteristic of the college library building is its dynamic aspect, the way in which changes constantly occur. It may well be that a penetrating historical review of college library history during the first half of this century will show that the application of human ingenuity and technological improvements to library buildings has had more to do with the flowering of the American college library than any other single factor. These changes in design, paradoxically enough, have been slowed down by presumably well-educated administrators, architects, and not a few librarians who, even today, think about the library building as if the only considerations were book stacks, seating capacity, collegiate Gothic, and limestone trim. Two other deterrents to change in library design are also worthy of mention. The first is the conservative attitude of architects and college administrators who insist on new campus buildings conforming to the prevailing campus pattern, and the second is the traditional insistence from the same source on some degree of monumentality in library design. Unfortunately monumentality is ill suited to the essential requirements of modern library administration.

How does the college library building of today differ from the conventional building of yesterday? In the first place, it has abandoned completely the distinct demarcation between areas for books and areas for readers. Book stacks are brought into the center of reading rooms and blocks of book stacks are widely distributed throughout the building without barriers of any kind between books and readers. Where a large number of books have to be accommodated, substantial blocks of ranges are segregated, but these are made less formidable by leaving out sections here and there to provide space for tables, easy chairs, and floor lamps to facilitate browsing and examination of materials in the stacks. Reading rooms have become reading areas and there are a minimum of solid supporting interior walls. Where a separation of areas or services is desired, it is made, whenever possible, with movable double-faced book cases, display-type room dividers, screens, planter boxes, and furniture. In this way, as the floor space required for one function in the library increases or decreases, the area can be adjusted accordingly. Control against book losses has been moved from a number of supervisory points throughout the building to a one point exit, leaving the reference and circulation staff free to serve as information centers; in small libraries where economy of operation is a first essential, the circulation and control areas are frequently combined near the exit. Generous provision is made for carrels or individual study desks throughout the building, and there are special rooms designated for typing, smoking, conference, and seminars in addition to the more general reference, reserve, documents, or subject reading areas. The browsing room as such has gone, or, wherever its shadow remains, there is likely to be an inviting alcove or miniature reading area for new books. The design of the building is likely to be based on the modular plan of a series of regular bays with the main floors symmetrical in plan. The modern library is the best lighted of all campus buildings. There is generous use of glass, particularly on the north side, with shading devices such as aluminum screens and louvers to reduce glare and air-conditioning costs. Artificial light, evenly distributed throughout the building from standard troffered fluorescent fixtures or fluorescent tubes mounted behind a plastic louver grid, provides fifty foot-candle power for general reading purposes. Chairs, tables, and occasional furniture break up the regimented appearance of large reading areas and encourage casual reading and browsing as well as study. The noise level is kept low by acoustical treatment of ceilings and walls and by sound-deadening floor coverings. The ventilation has been improved by the installation of air conditioning, although this is a refinement which in actual operation in libraries, at least, still leaves much to be desired. Accommodation has been made for music listening and exciting exhibits, as well as for new reading materials such as microtext. In some libraries provision has also been made for audio-visual aids with preview rooms for showing film and slides for lectures and group programs. Nowhere is the new look more easily recognized in college libraries than in the use of color in the interior—walls, furniture, window draperies, carpets, planters, and pictures. The exterior use of glass, contemporary design, openness of approach and plan, terraces, and covered walks have also helped to give the new buildings a friendly and informal appearance. These changes, it should be emphasized, have not come about overnight. They reflect the dynamic nature of the library building—its state of constant change from closed stacks to open shelves, from barriers to accessibility, from monumental rooms to low ceilings, from dignity to convenience—until it has reached its present form. They reflect also the care, patience, and endless hours of work which many librarians have poured into the shaping of new building programs and plans. No good library building is an accident; the most successful buildings are the result of precision planning.

To Build or Enlarge

Because of the cost of a new building, or because of an attachment to the existing building on the part of older members of the faculty and alumni, the question of enlargement versus building new is frequently raised on the college campus. The solution is one which each institution must discover for itself, but the librarian can demonstrate his leadership by presenting the major points which must be considered in reaching a wise decision. These points include such questions as the following:

Obsolescence

Will remodeling and enlarging the present library merely perpetuate a structure which for library purposes is now obsolete? For example, is there a multi-tier stack breaking the stack and reading areas squarely off from each other? Is the building so badly cut up with small room areas that it is impossible to secure open reading and book space without gutting the insides? If money is invested in remodeling and enlargement, how long will it be before the administration and board of trustees will again be faced with the problem of seeking funds for another addition or a new building?

Inefficiency

Are there fundamental errors in the design of the building which will seriously handicap efficient service in an enlargement? Do access and exit cut across reading areas? Do monumental rotundas and stairways block the use of valuable book and study space? Are the book stack levels and main building floors constructed at different levels so that it is difficult to move freely from one to another or to carry books from one level to another? Are the ceilings so high that it is impossible to provide adequate artificial lighting without installing an expensive false ceiling or using table lamps? Is the present building so cut up that it is impossible to provide a central reference service?

Site

Is the present site the best possible location for library purposes? Is it close to the center of academic activities? Is it as close to classrooms and dormitories as it was when first erected, or has the growth of academic buildings been away from the library? Does the site provide sufficient space for expansion?

Disruption of Service

Remodeling and enlargement will seriously disrupt service in the present structure and will damage books unless temporary quarters can be found during the time of renovation and enlargement—a period likely to exceed one year if the work is extensive. Can temporary quarters be provided or is the college willing to deprive the students of any real opportunity to use the library for one or two years of their college life?

Other Uses of the Present Building

Can the present building be used more efficiently for purposes other than a library? This question should be studied carefully. Perhaps the question should be worded, "Can the present library be remodeled more effectively and economically for other purposes than for library purposes?" One can be certain that there will be strong opposition from the administration and faculty to the use of the present library for any other purpose—

at first. Once the decision is made to build a new library, one can be equally certain that a half dozen different departments will be clamoring for the space in the old library.

Inevitably, the cost of a new building will be raised as one of the issues if not *the* issue in reaching a decision. A new well-planned building will perhaps cost more initially, but in the course of time it will prove an economy. "A good new building, it should be taken for granted, can be far more useful and satis-factory than the old one ever was, for there have been great advances during the recent years in the art and science of library planning. In addition to space for books, therefore, a new build-ing promises better accommodations and service for readers and staff." [1]

PLANNING THE NEW LIBRARY BUILDING

In the planning of a new library building three steps need to be followed: (1) the chief officers of the college should make a tour of new library buildings, (2) the librarian should become thoroughly acquainted with the latest developments in library buildings and equipment, and (3) the librarian and others should prepare a written program.

Planned Tour of Libraries

The first step in planning a new library is to persuade the president to approve, call, and pay for a short tour of recent library buildings by one or two members of the board of trustees, the president or dean and the business manager, the chairman of the library committee or a strong faculty representative, and the librarian. The aim is not to learn how to plan a new library building or to secure a ready-made plan for one's own college. Rather, the sole purpose is to stretch the imagination of trustees and administrators so that they may gain a genuine sense of the spirit of modern college librarianship, see what the library can contribute as a partner in the educational process, and better understand the kind of financial support which will be needed in building an adequate new library. Trustees and administrators are apt to evaluate library needs in terms of the college library on their own campus. They are accustomed to its limitations and are unable to think in larger terms without the challenge of a visit to first-rate colleges with new library buildings. No amount of explanation about the new look in library buildings will make so strong an impression as a few hours visit in a modern college library. It may not be easy to arrange such a trip but if it can be done it will pay rich dividends later. The libraries to be visited should be selected with great care and the arrangements for the visit should be approved and cleared with the head librarians well in advance of the trip. The tour should not be rushed. There should be plenty of time for meeting train and air schedules and ample provision for meals, wholesome entertainment, and leisurely discussions following each visit. The tourists should not be briefed too much by the librarian on what to look for in advance of the trip. The world of books in the fascinating and exciting environment of a new library building should burst upon them as an exciting surprise.

Know What One Wants in a Library Building

It cannot be stressed too strongly that the librarian should be thoroughly informed about library buildings and equipment and should know what his college needs in the way of a new library building. The raw material for his study includes reprints of articles about new buildings, brochures, dedication programs, photographs, written programs, and published plans. Manufacturers' and dealers' catalogs about shelving, mechanical equipment, exhibition cases, lighting, movable partitions, tables, chairs, and the like will all prove useful. The plans and discussions of the institutes sponsored by the Association of College and Research Libraries should be in every planner's file.[2] These contain not only critiques and reproduction of plans but also articles and bibliographies of articles on recent buildings.

The librarian's study of printed materials should be supplemented by visits to successful new library buildings with a view to securing specific information on points which are not thoroughly covered in the professional writings. These visits are important for three reasons: (1) they help to clarify points which are not adequately covered in the writings (e.g., the planning of exhibit equipment); (2) they help to impress upon the librarian the importance of detail (e.g., the location of fountains, the mastering and sub-mastering of the lock system); and (3) they bring out the mistakes as well as the successes of library planning (e.g., the failure to provide any form of convenient entrance to the building for wheel-chair users).

The final purpose of the librarian's study of professional writings, plans, and strengths and weaknesses of other libraries is to enable him to form a distinct idea of what he needs in his own building. It is only when he can define these needs sharply and clearly that he can expect the architect to produce satisfactory results. The essence of good planning is that the librarian should "prepare himself to be an intelligent and effective collaborator with his administrative colleagues and architects, and to be a source of accurate and current information on the subjects which it is his duty to make known to the campus community in this connection." [3]

Probably the most important step the librarian can take in planning the new library is to develop a written program or statement of requirements. Such a statement is intended to insure that the librarian and building committee have thought through the functions of the library as related to their particular institution and the requirements necessary to carry out these functions. The program should explain the use which will be made of each of the facilities needed and the space requirements of each so that the architect will have a clear idea of the problems he is being called upon to solve. [4] It should be inclusive, but compactly written. The librarian must recognize that he cannot include everything in the program and that he may have to accept some compromise when the requirements are translated from words into plans. But there should be no compromise on the parts of the program that establish the nature and character of the services and the relationships of the various spaces.

Before the program can be written there are many matters about educational policy and library administration which have to be settled. Just as the airline pilot cannot proceed without his navigation charts, so the librarian is unable to prepare the program of building without a determination of educational and administrative policies on specific problems which have a direct bearing on the nature of the proposed new library building.

Burchard devotes a most important chapter in his book on the university library building to a consideration of such problems.[5] In terms of college library planning, these are some of the questions which will have to be answered before the written program can be prepared for the architect:

What is to be the size of the institution?

What is to be the essential nature of the college's aim?

What is to be the optimum size of the library collection?

What cooperative agreements are possible with near-by college and public libraries?

What type of library organization will best serve the teaching program?

Is there a likelihood of increased use of the library for individual student work requiring the use of private study carrels?

Shall the college support a system of departmental libraries or are library facilities to be centralized in the new library building?

Is the library to be the center for audio-visual aid services on the campus?

What is to be the site of the new library? Is there a central site available with room for expansion?

In reaching decisions on these and related questions, the librarian must have the advice of the president and a library building committee. The committee should include representatives of the administration and faculty, and it should be authorized to consult any possible source of useful information, including the building and grounds staff, library staff, or student body. At this stage of the planning the librarian needs to identify members of his own profession who are expert in building matters and to secure their assistance both as individuals and as consultants. Some librarians may hesitate to raise questions about consultants and consultant's fees, but in planning one of the most complex and expensive buildings on the college campus, the librarian exposes himself to the sharpest censure if he fails to keep the president and the building committee fully informed of the opportunities to improve both the economy and the efficiency of the new building.

After the written program is completed, it will be turned over to the architect selected to design and construct the library. If the college is committed to an architectural firm without previous library experience, this would be the best time to bring in as a consultant a library architect of proven ability. The architect's first task is to prepare a visualization of the requirements in "preliminary plans," showing a tentative layout of the building in floor plans and elevation. In this stage of the planning it is the function of the architect to provoke discussion, to enable the librarian and building committee to visualize their ideas from many different angles, and to help them arrive at a definite physical expression of the nature and character of the building. These "preliminary plans" will be studied carefully and criticized. The architect may draw one or a dozen sets of them until all parties concerned are certain that they agree on what they want. It may be well at this point to recall the old German proverb that paper is patient. The more one works out one's building problems on paper, the less trouble and annoyance and cost after the structure is erected. In this connection it is of the greatest importance that there be harmony and mutual respect between the architect and the librarian. It is from the skill of one and the imaginative ideas of the other that good library buildings must stem. When the "preliminary plans" are approved the architect prepares the "working drawings" which represent the detailed solution to the requirements set forth in the written program. They are devoid of all frills and stunts. They show the location and scale dimensions of the building on the site; the plan of the different floors; the position of entrances, rooms, corridors, stairways, and other architectural features; and vertical elevations. They indicate the materials used. They are generally accompanied by a detailed statement of the architect's specifications. The working drawings and the specifications constitute a legal contract between the architect and the college. If changes are made after this stage has been reached, the expense to the college will be considerable.

Aids in Preparing the Library Program

College librarians have tried, but not with complete success, to establish formulas or criteria to serve as guideposts in planning the library building. They have established these criteria not, as some have wished, on the basis of sound scientific testing, but instead have been willing to work on a lower, purely empirical plane. They have accepted the judgments of successful practitioners in the field. Whether this makes library science an art or only an humble craft this writer is unable to say, but admittedly it puts the librarian more in the class of the gardener than the engineer, and this is where most college librarians would prefer to be anyway. If there is a blight on the azalea bushes one calls in an experienced gardener and follows his advice. When there is need to estimate the shelving requirements for "Chelsea College" for the next ten years, one calls in an experienced librarian. In the pages which follow, the writer calls on several experienced librarians to offer a few rules of thumb to those who are facing a building program for the first time. The recommendations are neither scientifically demonstrable nor exhaustive, but they may prove helpful.

Reader Capacity

The reader capacity will be affected by the estimated upper limit of enrolment, the availability of efficient study space on the campus and in the dormitories, the existence of departmental libraries, the number of students who commute to the campus, and the character of the instructional program. Estimates of reader capacity range all the way from 25 to 50 per cent of the student body. Keyes D. Metcalf estimates three seats for every ten undergraduates in a completely centralized college library.[6]

Book Capacity

Studies of growth in the book collections of college libraries show that on an average these libraries have doubled themselves every thirteen to twenty-seven years,[7] but no one can tell whether a particular library will follow the general pattern in the future. Probably the best the librarian can do is to study the average annual acquisitions for the past ten years, deduct withdrawals, and arrive at a net annual rate of acquisitions. If this figure is projected for the next twenty-five years, using as a base the anticipated library holdings at the time the new building is scheduled to be occupied and adding 10 per cent for additional gifts which a new building is likely to draw, the resulting total should not be far off. In translating this total into sections of shelving (a section of shelving is 7 feet, 6 inches high and approximately 3 feet wide), Gerould estimates 15 volumes per square foot exclusive of carrels in a multi-tier stack; [8] Henderson estimates 100 cubooks (volumes) to a section—a sound, conservative estimate taking into account adjustments for various sizes of books and for unused space at the end of shelves; [9] and Metcalf suggests 6 books to the running foot of shelving, or 126 volumes to the section.[10] In place of a criterion based on projected volume growth, Metcalf prefers to calculate book capacity in terms of shelving. He would determine the number of sections required to house the present collection, assuming that every inch of shelf space was used, and add 50 per cent to that number to obtain the requirements of the present collection. Future growth would also be figured in terms of sections of shelving, and this figure would then be added to the base number of sections occupied by the present collection. Metcalf cautions that future growth had best be figured at a geometric rate.[11]

Working Quarters

Each library will have to estimate its own growth in staff size, but it should be emphasized that staff working quarters are one of the first areas to become crowded after a new building is occupied. A bottleneck in the efficiency of staff operations in technical services slows down services to students and faculty. Therefore, the provision of ample space for working quarters is just as important as preparing adequately for readers and books. Not less than one hundred square feet should be allotted to each staff member, present and future, all the way from cataloger to student lettering clerk.[12] The main working quarters of the order and catalog librarians should meet this minimum space requirement over and above elevator, closet, toilet, and other utility accommodations. The estimate of staff size should be based on the peak load use of this area. In addition to the order and cataloging quarters, consideration must be given to:

1. Ample space behind the loan desk and a circulation office
2. Quarters for preparing periodicals for binding, and for repairing and mending books

3. Space for receiving and shipping books and sorting large gift collections
4. Central supplies walk-in closet
5. Room for new equipment and for equipment awaiting pickup and repair
6. Space for the preparation of exhibits
7. Offices for each public service department
8. Staff room

Public Catalog

Catalog cases should be free-standing and not built in. The space requirements are best calculated on a per title count of the library's collection, 4 catalog cards per title, and 800 cards per standard sixteen-inch tray. On this basis it is estimated that a library of 50,000 titles would provide a catalog for 200,000 cards which in turn would require 250 trays. For adequate space on all sides of the catalog for users and for consulting tables, an area equal to five to seven times that which is required for the card catalog cases is recommended.[13] The latter is readily determined after the library has decided upon the type of unit catalog it wishes to purchase.

Space Allowance per Reader

Exact spatial requirements for readers can be determined accurately only by scale drawings of the shelving and furniture to be placed in a particular room or area. A rule of thumb guide is 25 square feet per reader, but this will vary all the way from 19 square feet to 36 square feet, depending upon the length of table space allowed per reader, the size of the tables, and the nature of the arrangements of tables of varying sizes. Another factor influencing the square floor area per reader will be the necessary allowance for walls and partitions.[14] Normally each reader will be allowed from 2 feet 6 inches to 2 feet 8 inches of seating space along tables. Aisles between tables on the reader side are 5 feet, and aisles between table ends should not be less than 4 feet.

Fifteen to 20 square feet has been recommended for individual stack carrels, open or closed, and approximately 30 square feet for larger carrels equipped with individual ceiling light, reading lamp, desk shelf, bookshelves, chair, typewriter stand, and a lockable door. Eighty-eight square feet (8′ x 11′) has been found satisfactory for faculty studies.[15]

Lighting

Lower ceilings and air conditioning have made it easier to provide satisfactory general illumination. Many libraries now use recessed fluorescent fixtures, placed end to end in strips running the width or length of the building and spaced three feet apart from center to center. The minimum illumination recommended in reading rooms is fifty foot-candles.[16] However, there are other important considerations in lighting besides the intensity of light. Among these are the reflecting values of ceilings (80 per cent is recommended), walls (60 per cent), table tops (30-57 per cent), and floors (60 per cent).[17] Improper distribution of light, glare, and excessive contrast may be more tiring than insufficient illumination.

Cost

From data based on a forecast of college and university library construction and estimated costs for the ten-year period 1950 to 1960, Keyes D. Metcalf found that "on the average about $1,250 is required to house each thousand volumes and another $1,250 to provide space for each reader."[18] These figures are low because construction costs have advanced considerably since the estimates in the forecast were compiled.

SOME ESSENTIALS IN PLANNING FURNISHINGS AND EQUIPMENT

Librarians need a distinct and well-founded idea of what they want in furnishing a library, and this cannot result from hasty, last-minute discussions with the representatives of library supply houses and manufacturers. It is unwise for the librarian and the architect to spend all their time on building plans, as if they assumed that the furniture and equipment problem would somehow take care of itself. Furniture and equipment representatives can be helpful, but first the librarian should do his own research on these matters. He will find much sound advice in the professional writings of the past ten years, in the latest books on furniture design, and in such illustrated magazines as *Interiors* and *Design Quarterly*. Reading should not be confined to library writings alone but should also include articles on the furnishings of schools, office buildings, and other institutions with similar needs. As in preparing to draft the building program, the librarian should visit other libraries to compare various choices and opinions on furniture and equipment. If the architectural services do not provide for consultants, the librarian should try to persuade the college officials to employ an interior decorator who has experience in or knowledge of the library field. As one experienced library planner has expressed it:

> Twenty years of casually glancing through *House Beautiful*, two or three weeks intensive study of design theories, carefully scanning issues of *Interiors* and the books on commercial buildings, do not qualify anyone to decorate a building costing from a hundred thousand to several million dollars. You may know what you want and the general effect you want to achieve, but you just don't know how to do it—just as an interior decorator does not know how to catalog a book or administer a library.[19]

Careful study of the professional writings on furniture and equipment and conversations with librarians and others suggest the following general observations:

Flexibility

Much of what is gained in flexibility in planning the building can be lost by using fixed, built-in furniture and equipment. Examples are card catalogs, exhibit cases, and supply closets. Experience has shown the advisability of not installing this type of equipment as a fixed part of the building.

Instead of being a liability in preserving flexibility, furniture can be an asset. Double-faced free-standing shelving will serve to partition off one area from another, as, for example, current periodical reading from the reference collection. The free flow of work within the acquisitions and cataloging room can be improved through the use of as few fixed partitions as possible, with counter-height shelving, screens, and planter boxes serving as dividers.

Standardization

Book shelving should be standardized so that all shelving will be interchangeable, section by section, shelf by shelf, throughout the building, except for obvious exceptions where folio, newspaper, or colored shelving is used. Although this principle has been stated many times, libraries continue to be furnished with shelving of all types and varieties built and installed by the building contractor.

A corollary to this is that the librarian should be careful about having individual pieces of equipment designed for special purposes without first investigating whether a standard unit will serve the purpose as well or better. For example, double-faced free-standing cases with sloping consulting shelves will serve in place of an expensive special unit designed to hold the Library of Congress printed catalog volumes. The former has the advantage not only of economy but of expandability. If the atlas collection is likely to outgrow the space of a single standard case, then it is more economical and equally satisfactory to use double-faced counter-height shelving for this purpose by simply adding extra shelves. One librarian writes: "Index tables are a problem. Of the making of magazine indexes there is no end, and they accumulate at an alarming rate." The solution is not index tables. They are bulky, awkward, expensive, and fill up quickly. They are frequently overencumbered with students who take up space studying their own books instead of consulting the indexes. The simple answer is to use double-faced counter-height sections of shelving which provide an ideal surface for consulting heavy volumes, eliminate the problem of non-users of indexes who bar the way to convenient use of the indexes, and permit of expansion limited only by the size of the room.

Comfort, Durability, and Variety

Furniture should be selected for its durability, comfort, and variety. Durability is difficult to determine without a thorough knowledge of standard construction procedures and actual tests; in the last analysis most librarians will have to depend upon the reputation of the manufacturer or library supply house and the experience of libraries which have used their products. Comfort is secured by using good posture chairs and by introducing semi-lounge chairs in areas where no reading tables or only a few reading tables are necessary. Apronless tables permit the use of armchairs and make it possible for the reader to cross his legs under the table. Variety is gained by the use of tables of different sizes, ranging from individual desks to tables which accommodate four or more readers. The modern tendency is to provide small tables for four to six persons because they give a more informal appearance to the room and are less likely to encourage conversation than larger tables. Sofas, semi-lounge chairs, and an occasional round table all help to give a homelike and informal appearance to a reading room. Before chairs are selected, the manufacturers and library supply houses should be asked to submit samples which should be tested for several weeks by staff members and library users. The results of such tests may not be helpful in gauging the quality of construction, but they are a guide to what is comfortable and good-looking.

Economy and Ease of Maintenance

Beauty, comfort, and variety are important in the selection of furniture and equipment, but these need not be divorced from economy of maintenance. A number of illustrations will show the importance of the maintenance factor. Surfaces that receive hard wear require frequent refinishing, which is expensive and which removes the equipment from use for a period of time. Card catalog consulting tables, charging desks, and work tables should have linoleum or plastic top surfaces instead of wood. The light pastel colors used in modern libraries are attractive, but they soil easily. The use of vinyl plastic coverings on columns, walls bordering stairways, corridors, and other places where surfaces are most likely to become dirty will help to keep the building attractive and reduce the repainting bill. It is also possible in most parts of the library to use steel shelving, which is cheaper and mars less easily than wood, without becoming excessively functional. Visible end panels may be covered with wood masks to match the furnishings of the room. Chairs with metal legs require less dusting and maintenance than multi-rung wooden chairs. Vertical venetian blinds are less expensive to maintain than the horizontal type. These are but a few examples of the importance of keeping in mind the cost of maintenance in planning the interior and selecting the furniture and equipment.

Coordination of Colors and Materials

The selection of furniture and finishes should be pleasing and in harmony with the purposes of the room. More formal tables should be used in a reference room than in the current periodical room, and it would be in keeping with the mood and dignity of the former if the backs of chairs had leather upholstery to blend with the rich wood grain of the table tops. The place and importance of color are presented succinctly by a professional interior consultant as follows: "The basic theme to be set throughout the interior should be restful and relaxing. However, this does not mean that somber colors should necessarily predominate. On the contrary, many successful libraries have indulged in bright cheerful colors which . . . give a person an immediate and pronounced uplift. . . . It must be remembered that, although the colors throughout the building should normally become an integral part of the building, they should in effect remain a background for the furnishings and occupants." [20]

NOTES

1. Metcalf, Keyes D. "When bookstacks overflow." *Harvard lib. bull.* 8:205, Spring, 1954

2. A.L.A. Association of college and reference libraries. Buildings committee. *First library building plans institute.* . . . Chicago, ACRL, 1952 (ACRL monographs, no. 4) ; *Proceedings of the 1953 ACRL Building plans institute.* . . . Chicago, ACRL, 1953 (ACRL monographs, no. 10) ; *Third library building plans institute.* . . . Chicago, ACRL, 1954 (ACRL monographs, no. 11) ; *Fifth and sixth library building plans institutes.* . . . Chicago, ACRL, 1956 (ACRL monographs, no. 15)

3. Taylor, Garland. "College and university library buildings." Louisiana lib. association *bull.* 12:41-2, January, 1949

4. Reece, E. J. "Library building programs; how to draft them." *Col. and research lib.* 13:198-211, July, 1952

5. Burchard, John E. and others, eds. *Planning the university library building.* Princeton, N.J., Princeton University press, 1949, p. 14-37

6. A.L.A. Buildings committee. *Planning a library building.* Chicago, A.L.A., 1955, p. 6

7. Rider, Fremont. "The growth of American college and university libraries." *About books* 11:1-11, September, 1940

8. Gerould, J. T. "The college library building . . . ." N.Y., Scribner, 1932, p. 66

9. Henderson, R. W. "The cubook." *Lib. jour.* 59:865-8, November 15, 1934; "Bookstack planning with the cubook." *Lib. jour.* 61:52-4, 122, January 15, 1936

10. A.L.A. Buildings committee, *op. cit.*, p. 5

11. *Loc. cit.*

12. Hanley, Edna R. "Workrooms in college and university libraries." *In: American school and university, 1938.* N.Y., American school publishing corporation, 1938, p. 339-44; Tauber, M. F. "Technical services and the library building." *Southeastern librarian* 10:82-91, Summer, 1960

13. Burchard, *op. cit.*, p. 40

14. Cowgill, C. H. and Pettengill, G. E. *The library building.* N.Y., Journal of the American institute of architects, 1959, p. 3 (reprint)

15. Gerould, *op. cit.*, p. 62; Burchard, *op. cit.*, p. 46-7

16. White, Lucien. "Library lighting standards." *Wilson lib. bull.* 33:301, December, 1958

17. Yenawine, Wayne S. ed. *Contemporary library design.* N.Y., Syracuse University press, 1958, p. 5

18. Metcalf, Keyes D., *op. cit.*, p. 206. This formula was checked against the actual cost of 20 college libraries. In 10 instances the difference between the actual cost and the estimated cost was not more than 25 per cent. In 10 instances the estimated cost varied from the actual cost between 25 per cent and 67 per cent. In almost all cases the estimated cost was higher than the actual cost.

Another rough estimate of cost is based on the total gross square floor area multiplied by the current cost per square foot for public construction in the local area. For example, the area of a proposed new library for 250 readers and 40,000 volumes may be estimated as follows:

	Sq. ft.
Space for 40,000 volumes at 15 volumes per sq. ft.	2,666
Space for 250 readers at 30 sq. ft. per reader	7,500
Add two thirds for service areas and building structure	6,776
2 talking and smoking rooms, each 320 sq. ft.	640
2 small typing rooms, each 150 sq. ft.	300
1 record listening room	400
1 seminar for instruction in the use of the library and of bibliographical materials	340
Margin for unscheduled requirements	1,884
Total gross area to be distributed over the floors	20,506 sq. ft.

19. Koping, James R. "Library furnishings and equipment." *News notes of California lib.* 52:574, July, 1957

20. Van Buren, Martin. "Interior planning of college and university libraries." *Col. and research lib.* 17:235, May, 1956

ADDITIONAL REFERENCES

The ACRL and the Association of Research Libraries have announced co-sponsorship of research leading to the publication of a definitive book on the planning of college and university library buildings by Keyes D. Metcalf, librarian emeritus of Harvard. *Col. and research lib.* 21:136, March, 1960. For an excellent bibliography of college library buildings *see*: Edna R. Hanley's *College and university library buildings.* Chicago, A.L.A., 1939, and the 1953, 1954, and 1955 proceedings of the ACRL buildings institute (footnote 2).

Adams, C. M. "College-library building." *In*: Fussler, H. H. ed. *Function of the library in the modern college.* Chicago, University of Chicago Graduate library school, 1954, p. 62-73

Bean, D. E. and Ellsworth, R. E. *Modular planning for college and small university libraries.* Iowa City, Privately printed, 1948

Byrd, Cecil K. "Site, seats, selectivity; some thoughts on planning the college library building." *Col. and research lib.* 18:127-31, March, 1957

Crosland, D. M. "Use of textile fabrics in a library." *Lib. jour.* 79:2415-16, December 15, 1954

Ellsworth, R. E. "Library architecture and buildings." *Lib. quar.* 25:66-75, January, 1955

Ellsworth, R. E. *Planning the college and university library building.* [Boulder, Col., Pruett Press] 1960

Fussler, H. H. ed. *Library buildings for library service.* Chicago, A.L.A., 1947

Galvin, Hoyt. *Planning a library building. . . .* Chicago, A.L.A., 1955

Hanley, Edna R. *College and university library buildings.* Chicago, A.L.A., 1939

Little, E. A. S. "Remodeling without a straw." *Calif. librarian* 17:110-34, April, 1956

Metcalf, K. D. "Lamont library; function." *Harvard lib. bull.* 3:12-30, Winter, 1949

Muller, R. H. "Critiques of three completed library buildings." *Col. and research lib.* 14:129-30, April, 1953

Quisenberry, S. W. "Color and environment." *Lib. jour.* 75:2104-8, December 15, 1950

Roth, H. "Remodeling and redecorating." *Lib. jour.* 83:3385-6, December 1, 1958

Swearingen, B. C. "Enlarging the small college library building." *Southeastern librarian* 9:129-34, Fall, 1959

Wagman, F. H. "Undergraduate library of the University of Michigan." *Col. and research lib.* 20:179-88, May, 1959

Watson, E. P. "Remodeled library building at Northwestern state college of Louisiana." *Col. and research lib.* 20:210-11, May, 1959

XVII

Evaluation of the College Library

It goes without saying that any good library will find occasion from time to time to measure the effectiveness of its work. This evaluation involves a study of the library's facilities and operations, and a consideration of its success in fulfilling its functions. The preceding chapters in this book provide some of the information necessary for making such an appraisal. This final chapter summarizes the principles and procedures of evaluation.

PURPOSE OF EVALUATION

The purpose of evaluation is to provide a critical analysis of the program and operations of the library, and to make such specific recommendations as seem appropriate. An evaluation can be useful in several ways: (1) it can enable the faculty to discover the complexity of library activities, and in this way show them how intricately related are library and teaching problems; (2) it can provide the necessary information for formulating a program to meet tomorrow's opportunities; and (3) it can provide the college authorities with an account of library problems and the costs of resolving them.

The evaluation may be made by library consultants having no connection with the college community, by the librarian with the cooperation of the faculty and administration, or by a combination of methods. In recent years certain of the accrediting associations have been asking individual colleges to prepare a self-survey which will give as complete a picture as possible of the institution before an accreditation visit. In this situation, the library participates in the self-survey of the college and later in the review and inspection by the visiting team. The appraisal of a library by outside experts independent of any accrediting or professional association is commonly the result of a long-felt need for an inquiry into the condition of a weak library, although the method is of course also useful in bringing to light the achievements of a strong library. The value of the self-survey is intimately tied up with the aims and aspirations of the individual college. The success of the survey lies in the effort which faculty and administrators make to study, understand, and use its recommendations.

BASIC PRINCIPLES IN EVALUATION

Before the work of the library can be evaluated, the librarian must have a clear conception of its purposes in relation to the major objectives of the college. In the final analysis each library must be judged by how well it performs the services required to meet the needs of its particular college. The college's aims and programs constitute a set of educational plans and specifications which should serve as a guide to the library in considering its functions and in examining plans for future development.[1] One might cite as illustrative of library purposes the statement appearing in the *Faculty Handbook* of the Goucher College Library: "The function of the college library is to provide a collection of books and other materials both to support the academic program of the college and to present a well-rounded library in the liberal arts; the collection must be administered not only in support of the work in courses but also as a teaching instrument in itself." As admirable and lucid as the Goucher statement is, it is possible that a more detailed statement would serve better to measure a library's operations in relation to its aims. The standards of the Association of College and Research Libraries emphasize the following points as goals to be sought in college library service:

The college library should be the most important intellectual resource of the academic community.

Its services, given by a competent staff of adequate size, should be geared to implement the purposes of the college's general program and to meet the specific educational objectives of the institution.

Its collections should aim at presenting the heritage of Western and Eastern thought in all its richness, but should stress those particular areas which are central to the curriculum of the institution.

No artificial barriers should separate the library from the classroom or the library staff from the teaching faculty.

Beyond supporting the instructional program to the fullest extent, the library should endeavor to meet the legitimate needs of all its patrons, from the senior professor engaged in advanced research to the freshman just entering upon the threshold of higher learning, to stimulate and encourage the student to develop the lifelong habit of good reading, and to play its proper role in the community and in the wider realm of scholarship beyond the campus.[2]

This is an excellent statement of general purposes, but standards in themselves are not the objectives or goals of a particular library; rather they are "the actual means or conditions which various librarians and college staffs have set for the achievement of the college and library goals."[3] Accordingly, in evaluating the college library, the first principle is to define clearly the specific purposes of the library and their relationship to the educational aims, the central objectives, of the college itself.

The second principle is that the evaluation process should be a college and not just a library process. This may sound difficult at first. Actually in the carrying out of the evaluation, the significance of the principle and the method of implementing it will be readily apparent in measuring the book collections, budgets, and cooperative efforts.

The third general principle is that the evaluation process must be a continuous process of appraisal and improvement, of re-evaluation and re-improvement. A library must again and again take its bearings and reset its course; otherwise it "can automatically drift into the acquiescent traditionalism that marks most such organizations as they mature: regularity of processes and acceptance of limitations."[4] Of real importance, therefore, are the occasional reviews, prepared always in consultation with the administration and faculty, as to what functions the library performs, how well it carries them out, and what it needs to do in order to improve its contribution to the college.

EVALUATION PROCEDURES

Dr. E. W. McDiarmid's *Library Survey* furnishes a practical compendium of evaluative criteria and techniques, based on a study of methods and procedures used in actual surveys. The publication of a number of college library surveys in recent years has provided a useful body of information on current problems of college libraries, techniques for analyzing them, and suggestions for their solution. These surveys have been made at such colleges as Hampton Institute, San Diego State College, Tuskegee Institute, Barnard College, North Carolina State College, Alma, and for the libraries of the Arkansas Foundation of Associated Colleges.[5] For any librarian or college official concerned with judging the adequacy of the college library, the statement issued by the Middle States Association of Colleges and Secondary Schools on *Evaluating the Library* is an admirable and helpful document.[6] Along with an examination of the actual techniques used by accreditation teams in studying the library, the evaluation statement of the Middle States Association has been throughly analyzed by Morris A. Gelfand in a paper presented at the Eastern College Librarians Conference, Columbia University, November 30, 1957.[7] Statistical data useful for making valid comparisons have been collected regularly by the Association of College and Research Libraries, and for a selected number of libraries have been analyzed and interpreted for significant trends each year through 1958-1959 in the January issues of *College and Research Libraries*. The first comprehensive and detailed report on library statistics of the U.S. Office of Education covered the academic year 1939-1940.[8] General standards of college library service have been published by each of the major regional accrediting and professional associations [9] and by the Association of College and Research Libraries.[10] All these materials provide a body of detailed procedures which, if sensibly applied to the facts in the local library situation, will afford a fairly accurate diagnosis of its condition and need.

The procedures for evaluating the service of the college library may be considered under six headings: (1) administration, (2) book collections, (3) staff, (4) finance, (5) physical plant, and (6) library use.

Administration

There is no special technique of evaluation applicable to library administration. Perhaps one would look first for a clear definition of library purpose. The library that has well-defined goals is probably unique, but a statement of purpose is nevertheless important as a guide to policy and practice. Dr. Myron F. Wicke, a leading consultant in college surveys in America, has often affirmed the value of defining aims for the college as a whole and for its separate parts. He has pointed out, among other values, that the process of hammering out a statement of purpose is a wholesome one for staff and faculty, and again, that it is important for teachers and for librarians to stop from time to time to examine both their goals and their methods of achieving them.

One might look next for some indication of the position which the library holds on the campus. Is it one of strength or weakness? Has the librarian been brought into the educational and administrative policy-making bodies of the college? What is the attitude of the faculty toward the library and the librarians? A third guidepost to evaluation of library administration is the general attitude of the library staff to its work. Is the staff alert, imaginative, and scholarly in its approach to library service? Does it think of library service in terms of mechanical daily operations or in terms of the opportunity to help individual students and faculty in forwarding the purposes of instruction?

A fourth approach to evaluating library administration would be to determine whether the library follows the basic principles of good administration. Is there a clearly established, clearly expressed policy of library government? Is the work of the library systematically organized with proper delegation of responsibility and authority to staff members for different phases of the work? Has there been a sincere and genuine effort to assign clerical duties solely to clerical and student staff and to reserve the trained librarians for professional work? Is the library getting the most for its investment in book, binding, and supplies funds?

These are not all the matters which are likely to come under scrutiny in a survey of administration, but they suggest the importance of goals, working rapport, and perspective in the administration of the library.

Book Collections

The adequacy of the college library's book collection cannot be measured in quantitative terms. To judge a collection superior or inferior on the basis of the volume holdings is as absurd as rating a college on the basis of its enrolment. Nor is it really possible to make a fair qualitative appraisal of the book collection without knowing something about the history of the collection, the extent of its use, and the current acquisition and withdrawal policies. For these reasons, the book collection is always one of the most difficult parts of the library to evaluate.

A common method of measuring adequacy is to check the library's holdings against standard bibliographies such as the *Catalogue of the Lamont Library*, Farber's *Classified List of Periodicals for the College Library*, and Bertalan's *Books for Junior Colleges*. The limitation of this method lies in the fact that such lists, particularly in scientific and technical fields, quickly become out-of-date. Then again, book-collection needs differ to some extent from one college to another according to the nature of the curriculum. The standard lists must therefore be supplemented by subject bibliographies in the fields of instruction offered by the particular college.

Studies by Douglas Waples show that a definite correlation exists between the general adequacy of the library's book collection and the adequacy of its reference and current periodical collections.[11] For some years several of the regional accrediting agencies have used selected periodical and reference checklists in measuring the quality of the library book collection. As a result, libraries have adopted the checklists as buying guides and in so doing have depreciated their value for evaluation purposes. It is important therefore to use an up-to-date list of reference books and current periodicals for checking purposes in evaluating a library's collection, and it may be necessary to compile sample checklists instead of using a standard list for this purpose.

Another method of evaluating the collection is the first-hand examination of the shelves of the library. Normally the person or persons doing this checking would be subject specialists (members of the faculty in a self-survey)[12] and the results would be embodied in lists of *desiderata* and withdrawals. When a consultant from the library profession is asked to make such a survey, he will combine the shelf examination with a checking of the library's card catalog against certain standard bibliographies and checklists because it is unlikely that he will have either the time or the competence to appraise collections in a number of subject fields. His examination of the shelves will determine how extensively the collection is overburdened with duplicate titles of old reserve books, textbooks, old editions, multi-volume sets of out-of-date histories, the works of well-known authors in numerous different editions where the one standard edition would suffice, out-of-date scientific works, fragmentary files of journals, materials which have no relation to the curriculum, and gifts of useless material. It is a sound general principle that a college library should be up-to-date and outstanding for curricular related materials rather than for its collection of older materials and curiosities of science and literature. On the other hand, the evaluator should not blindly condemn the library's selection practices because of the first-hand evidence that the collection needs weeding. His findings on this score should be weighed against the results of checking standard lists and supplementary bibliographies. If the material the library has is good and appropriate to curricular needs, the fact that there are too many volumes on the shelves not earning their shelf space by use may be due to lack of faculty stimulation or the librarian's inability to find the time or space to organize a systematic weeding program.

Rudolph Hirsch calls attention to a fourth method of evaluating book collections which "defines values primarily, if not exclusively, in terms of use." [13] This method was utilized by Lewis Stieg in a study of the Hamilton College Library.[14] He kept records of the frequency of the circulation of individual titles, duplication of circulation from year to year, frequency of circulation of books of varying age, and circulation of books listed in the Shaw *List*. The advantages and disadvantages of the method are assessed by Mr. Hirsch—its objectivity as against the fact that popular use is no guarantee of the intrinsic value of the collection. It may be further pointed out that an evaluation based on use would appear to have more value for future selection than for measuring the adequacy of an existing collection.

The evaluation of a collection should also take into account the inability of the library to supply books as evidenced by the records of unfilled requests kept at the loan desk and of inter-library loans of material which the library might reasonably have been expected to have in its collection. A systematic, resourceful, and enlightened program of acquisitions is essential. One has the uncomfortable feeling in examining many college libraries that the collections have just "growed." Here again there are exceptions, but they are the exception and not the rule.

Staff

In evaluating personnel, library surveys take into account the size of the staff, ratio between professional and non-professional employees, academic and professional training, length of service, salaries, supplementary benefits, conditions of work, vacations, promotions, and the professional improvement of librarians in service. Criteria for judging these and other personnel matters are set forth in the college and university library standards of the Association of College and Research Libraries. The personal qualifications expected of college librarians in cataloging, circulation, and reference work have already been discussed in earlier chapters.

In making judgments about the staff, Carnovsky points out that "unless the individual is considered specifically in relation to his job, there is danger that he may be unduly praised or undeservedly condemned because of certain factors which are altogether beyond his control." [15] It is possible to have a good reference librarian who has no ability to prepare a book annotation or annual report. Or, in the larger and broader sense, if the college does not regard the work of the library of sufficient importance to give the staff adequate recognition in the academic community, or if there is no atmosphere of scholarship on the campus, the librarian can hardly be held responsible for a library which functions primarily as a central study hall and for a staff which is chiefly engaged in routine and disciplinary duties. On the other hand, the librarian and the staff have the responsibility to define and understand the purpose of the library in relation to college aims, to become personally acquainted with their faculty colleagues, and to know their teaching methods. They should know what is going on in curriculum matters and have a clear conception of the specific ways in which library support is desirable and possible.

The staff will be expected to have academic and professional training commensurate with the educational standards of the library profession although this does not mean that every cataloger must have a Ph.D. degree. Staff members should show a breadth of knowledge and a critical capacity based on habits of constant and discriminating reading. By their intellectual interests and their skill in human relations, they should help to convey the impression that the librarian is a person whose opinions are important. The library profession suffers from low prestige. Sometimes the manner in which staff members carry out their duties and the conditions under which they work do little to improve this situation.

Library associations help to bring librarians together for professional and personal refreshment. Attendance at professional meetings is desirable when a staff member is vitally interested, particularly when there is opportunity for participation in programs and committee work. On the other hand, the fact that some staff members do not or cannot attend such meetings is not necessarily to their disadvantage. Oftentimes, professional attendance suffers from the fact that many of the younger librarians cannot afford to attend the meetings without a travel allowance.

Finally, a more difficult and intangible factor, but none the less important to consider in evaluating a staff, is staff morale, and this applies to all members of the staff, professional and non-professional. No one should be considered merely as a routine employee. Both the giving of responsibility and the attitude of the librarian and department heads to the staff have a great deal to do with staff morale and its accomplishment.

Finance

There are no absolutes in measuring the adequacy of the library's financial support because the amount of money needed in any one fiscal year is dependent on many different factors. Some of these factors are (1) aims of the college, (2) extent and quality of library service needed to support these aims, (3) present state of the collections, (4) effect of inflationary prices on books and personnel, (5) adequacy of the physical plant, (6) adequacy of the staff, and (7) nature of the organization of the library's services.

Library surveyors use the following criteria in measuring the financial support of the college library: (1) the ratio of library expenditures to the educational and general expenditures of the college, (2) the per student expenditure for library service, and (3) comparison with the expenditures of the libraries of colleges of similar size and program. Based on an analysis of actual expenditures over a number of years, the Association of College and Research Libraries' standards recommend "a minimum of 5 per cent of the total educational and general budget." [16] Where course offerings and enrolments are expanding rapidly and where courses leading to the Master's degree are offered, the Association recommends a higher percentage, and it adds that special budgetary provision should be made for audio-visual materials and services if these are supplied by the library. In calculating this ratio, the educational and general expenditures of the college are defined to include administration, instruction (including the library), research, extension services, plant operation and maintenance, and organized activities related to instructional departments.

In 1951 Moran and Tolman figured that inflation had raised the prewar standard of $25 per student to $50.[17] The spiral of book and salary increases has continued unabated since then. Nevertheless the recommendation of $50 per student is above the median expenditure of college libraries today. In 1958-59 the median per student expenditure for the library among ninety-four publicly controlled colleges with enrolments under fourteen hundred was $39.43. The median expenditure for private college libraries was somewhat less.[18] In measuring both the ratio of library to college expenditures and the per student library expenditure, a more reliable judgment can be made if the comparison is made for a five-year period instead of for just the current year.

In comparing the expenditures of individual libraries it is important to select colleges of approximately the same size, total expenditures, and character and program.

Physical Plant

The physical plant and equipment should be adequate for the effective operation of the library. As obvious as this seems, there are more defects in the physical plant and equipment of college libraries than in almost any other area.

In judging the building and equipment, consideration will be given to the adequacy of such features as the following: (1) site; (2) book and reader space; (3) provision for expansion; (4) the arrangement of readers and materials so as to encourage the greatest use of books; (5) workroom and administrative quarters; (6) space for utilities; (7) lighting, ventilation, and soundproofing; (8) comfort and variety of furnishings; and (9) mechanical equipment. The degree to which college officials will consult and depend upon the librarian in matters relating to the library's physical plant as well as in the planning of an addition or a new building will naturally be a matter of paramount concern in evaluating the library.

Technical Processes

The procedures of ordering, cataloging, classifying, and binding library materials will also be considered in evaluating a library. They will be judged by their efficiency, currency, and acceptance of standard cataloging and classification. Arrearages in all phases of technical processes will be carefully scrutinized because they usually increase the wear and tear on the collection and hinder the effective use of its materials by readers. Unnecessary practices will be discounted, while special efforts to make the collections convenient and easy to use will be commended.

Library Use

The most important evaluative standard and yet the most difficult to apply is the use of the library.[19] It is important to know about use because there is a very real danger that one's general impressions of how much and for what purpose a library is being used may be quite at variance with the actual facts in the case. If the librarian is not careful, he may end up by blunting his own sense of discrimination as to what the library is accomplishing.

Certain factors such as the number of hours the library is open and the program of library instruction have a distinct bearing on library use and may readily be reviewed and appraised in any particular library situation. The Association of College and Research Libraries Standards Committee, while recognizing the limitations of circulation statistics, states that "it is likely, however, that the library service to students is improving if the per capita figures of books on regular loan (two weeks or longer) to students show an upward trend over a considerable period of time." [20] In his volume *Teaching With Books*, Dr. Branscomb describes a number of studies of college library use. The average per capita home circulation recorded in seven studies involving fifty-one institutions varied from 10.28 to 13.86 volumes per student per year. From this evidence he concluded that "the average student draws from the general collection of his college or university library about twelve books per year." [21] On the basis of similar but less extensive evidence he concluded that the average undergraduate borrows, in addition, from fifty to sixty books per year from the reserve collection.

The principal difficulty in using presently recorded and published library statistics as a basis for measuring library use is the fact that they do not tell the whole story. By ignoring the use of books and other materials inside the library building, they leave out what must certainly amount to a substantial part of the use of the college library. Moreover, these statistics were much more meaningful when the stacks were closed and when most of the reserve books were kept behind the reserve or loan desk. For most books except those in the reference and browsing collections, the student was obliged to fill out a slip and present his request at one of the loan desks. This "call slip" became part of the record of library use. When libraries abandoned closed stacks and permitted students to get their own books directly from the shelves, most library use within the building was no longer recorded. To keep continuous detailed records of library use within the building is no longer practicable, even if it were possible, because the results could not possibly justify the staff time and expense involved.

To supplement the record of home use and to get a more realistic picture of the nature and amount of library use, some libraries have been making spot surveys of a type conducted by Dartmouth College in the middle fifties. Samplings were taken at two different times of student reading throughout the campus. Nearly twelve hundred students were involved. The results so far as the library use section of the study was concerned were reported as follows:

In the Library 63 per cent of all respondents were *using their own textbooks exclusively*; 33 per cent were using library-owned books, of which two-thirds were Reserve-Desk books.

In the research areas (Reference Room, Reference Balcony, and Periodical Room) between 60 per cent and 94 per cent of the students were *not* using material shelved in these rooms.

In the Tower Room, at peak loads, the materials being read were almost exclusively assigned textbooks and lecture notes. At times of less pressure the actual *number* of students "browsing" did not vary significantly.[22]

Stimulated by the example of the Dartmouth study, other libraries are now supplementing their regularly recorded statistics of home use by one-day surveys of library use. These may be made each quarter or semester. Each library user entering the library is asked to complete a questionnaire (Form 5)[23] and return it to a student attendant as he leaves. The validity of the results depends a great deal upon the attitude and cooperation of the students filling out the questionnaire. In spite of limitations, however, this type of study has been useful in determining who uses the library, why the user came to the library, and what materials he used when he was there. "If statistics or observation suggest that the library may not be serving as fully as it might or is being used as a study hall with books from outside, look for lecture-textbook or other unimaginative teaching. Since the quality and amount of library use is one of the clearest indices of the kind of teaching the students are getting, experienced evaluators are apt to turn quickly from the library to the classroom. They know that a stimulating instructor creates an inquiring student, who develops resourcefulness because he wants more than routine methods will give him. Thus good teaching and good librarianship unite to produce skilled, self-reliant, habitual library users."[24]

FORM 5
SURVEY OF LIBRARY USE

We need your cooperation and assistance in obtaining as complete an estimate as possible of the daily use made of the Library. Please give thoughtful and careful attention to the questions listed below, and return the questionnaire to the Control Desk attendant before leaving the Library. We ask that you fill out a questionnaire each time you come to the Library today, even though you may have filled out one on previous trips. Your answers will help us to improve library service and to make the Library more useful to you. Do not sign your name.

1. Reasons for coming to the Library this trip (check only those applicable)

   a. To return, charge out, or renew books   _____

   b. To read Reserve books in the Reserve Reading Room   _____

   c. To do assigned reading in library materials other than Reserve books   _____

   d. To look up material for a paper, report, thesis, and so forth   _____

   e. For general reading not assigned in class   _____

   f. To study own books   _____

   g. Other reasons (specify)   _____

2. Materials used in Library this trip (Do not count books you charge out for use outside the Library)

   a. Number of books, journals, newspaper volumes from the main book stacks   _____

   b. Number of books from the Browsing Room collection   _____

   c. Number of government publications from the Documents Center collection   _____

   d. Number of reference books from the Reference Room Collection   _____

   e. Number of books from the Reserve Room collection   _____

   f. Number of books and journals from the Science Library collection   _____

   g. Number of current periodicals in Current Periodical Room   _____

   h. Number of current newspapers in Current Periodical Room   _____

   i. Number of library microfilms, microcards, microprints _____

   j. Number of items in Special Collections Department (manuscripts, maps, rare books, etc.)   _____

   k. Number of phonograph records in Music Listening Room _____

3. Your status (check one)

   a. Freshman _____   e. Graduate student _____

   b. Sophomore _____   f. Faculty _____

   c. Junior _____   g. Staff (other than library) _____

   d. Senior _____   h. Other (specify) _____

- - - - - - - -

Have you turned in another library use questionnaire today? Yes_____ No_____

NOTES

1. See, for example: statements of purpose of the college in Hendrix College and Allegheny College catalogue bulletins.

2. "Standards for college libraries." *Col. and research lib.* 20:274, July, 1959; *also in: American library and book trade annual, 1960.* New York, Bowker, 1959, p. 87-95

3. Russell, John H. "The library self-survey." *Col. and research lib.* 17:130, March, 1956

4. "Towards a five-year plan." Dartmouth College *Lib. bull.* 3:5, December, 1938

5. Tauber, M. F. *Hampton institute library....* Hampton, Va., Institute, 1958; Tauber, M. F. *Barnard college library. ...* New York, Barnard College, 1954; Orr, Robert W. *Tuskegee institute self-study; library consultant's report.* Ames, Iowa, Iowa State College, 1956; Stone, J. P. ed. *Library program for San Diego state college.* rev. ed. San Diego, Calif., The Library, 1958; Kuhlman, A. F. *Libraries of the Arkansas foundation of associated colleges.* Nashville, 1958; Harwell, R. B. and Talmadge, R. L. *Alma college library.* Chicago, A.L.A., 1958; Jesse, W. H. and Ringo, R. C. *Report of a survey of the libraries of the North Carolina state college.* Raleigh, N.C., The College, 1958; Cousins, Paul M., Lyle, Guy R. and Reagan, Agnes L. *Survey report . . . Armstrong college of Savannah library.* Savannah, Ga., The College, 1960; Lyle, Guy R. and Crowder, T. E. *Library survey Georgia state college of business administration.* Atlanta, Ga., The College, 1958

6. Middle states association of colleges and secondary schools. Commission on institutions of higher education. *Evaluating the library; suggestions for the use of faculties and evaluation teams.* The Association, 1957. The statement is reprinted in the New York state library *Bookmark* 17:103-4, January, 1958. A similar guide to preparing the self-survey appears in the Southern association of colleges and secondary schools, Commission on colleges and universities. *Manual for the institutional self-study and periodic visitation program.* [Atlanta, The Association], 1959, p. 18-19

7. Gelfand, M. A. "Techniques of library evaluators in the Middle states association." *Col. and research lib.* 19:305-20, July, 1958

8. U.S. Office of education, Federal security division. *College and university library statistics, 1939-40.* Washington, Government printing office, 1943. This series was discontinued after the third report covering the academic year 1951-52. Some statistical data on libraries appear regularly in the biennial survey of education. The Office of education is also engaged in a series of statistical studies on various aspects of college and university library problems, e.g., "College and university facilities survey . . . 1956-70." Circular no. 603.

9. Oboler, Eli M. and others, comps. *College and university library accreditation standards—1957.* Chicago, ACRL, 1958 (ACRL monographs, no. 20)

10. "Standards for college libraries," *op. cit.*; "Standards for junior college libraries." *Col. and research lib.* 21:200-06, May, 1960

11. Waples, Douglas. *Evaluation of higher institutions.* IV. The library. Chicago, University of Chicago press, 1936, p. 13

12. David, Charles W. "On the survey of a research library by scholars." *Col. and research lib.* 15:290-1, 308, July, 1954

13. Hirsch, Rudolph. "Evaluation of book collections." *In*: Yenawine, Wayne S. ed. *Library evaluation.* N.Y., Syracuse University press, 1959, p. 15-16

14. Stieg, Lewis. "A technique for evaluating the college library book collection." *Lib. quar.* 13:34-44, January, 1943

15. Carnovsky, Leon. "Self-evaluation; or, how good is my library?" *Col. and research lib.* 3:307, September, 1942

16. "Standards for college libraries," *op. cit.*, p. 275

17. Moran, Virginia L. and Tolman, Mason. "College library study." *Lib. jour.* 76:1907, November 15, 1951; Standard nine of the Southern association of colleges and secondary schools recommends a minimum annual expenditure of $30 per student for books, periodicals, binding, supplies and staff salaries. Southern association. . . . *Proceedings of sixty-fourth annual meeting.* Louisville, Ky., December, 1959, p. 198-9

18. "College and university library statistics, 1958/59." *Col. and research lib.* 21:25-87, January, 1960

19. Carnovsky, Leon. "Evaluation of library services." *Unesco bull. for libraries* 13:224, October, 1959

20. "Standards for college libraries," *op. cit.*, p. 277

21. Branscomb, Harvie. *Teaching with books.* Chicago, Association of American Colleges and A.L.A., 1940, p. 27

22. "What is a library?" Dartmouth College *Lib. bull.* 1(ns):46-7, April, 1958

23. When filled out, a tabulation of the results will show (1) the total number of questionnaires turned in, (2) the number of individuals using the library classified by class level and type (student, faculty, or other), (3) the reasons why the reader came to the library (e.g., 400 came to use reserve books, 500 to study their own books, etc.), and (4) what materials were used and the number of each (books in the Reference room, 203; books in the Reserve room, 450; etc.) The interpretation of the results requires great care and thoroughness.

24. Middle states association of colleges and secondary schools. Commission on institutions of higher education. "Evaluating the library suggestions for the use of faculties and evaluation teams." New York state library *Bookmark* 17:104, January, 1958

Index

This index includes citations to authors and titles
only when they are named in the text.

DATE DUE